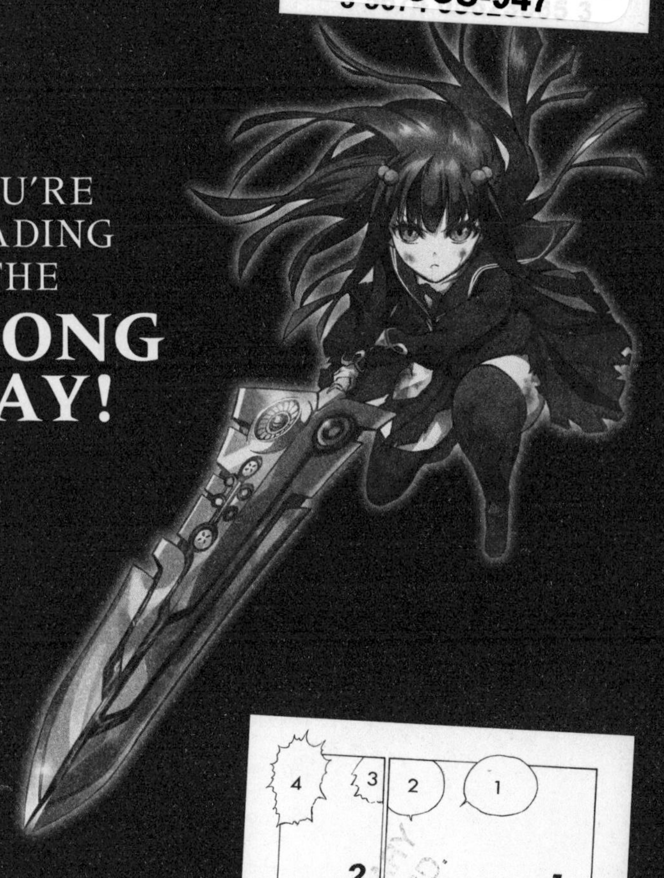

YOU'RE
READING
THE
**WRONG
WAY!**

Twin Star Exorcists reads from right to left, starting in the upper-right corner. Japanese is read from right to left, meaning that action, sound effects and word-balloon order are completely reversed from English order.

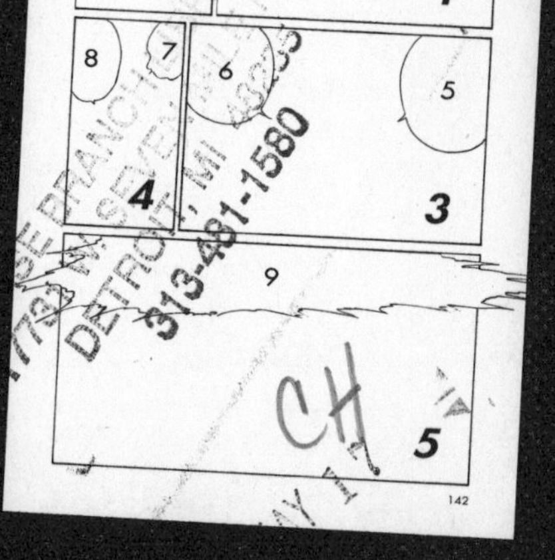
1
2
1
3
4
2
5
6
3
7
8
4
9
5
142

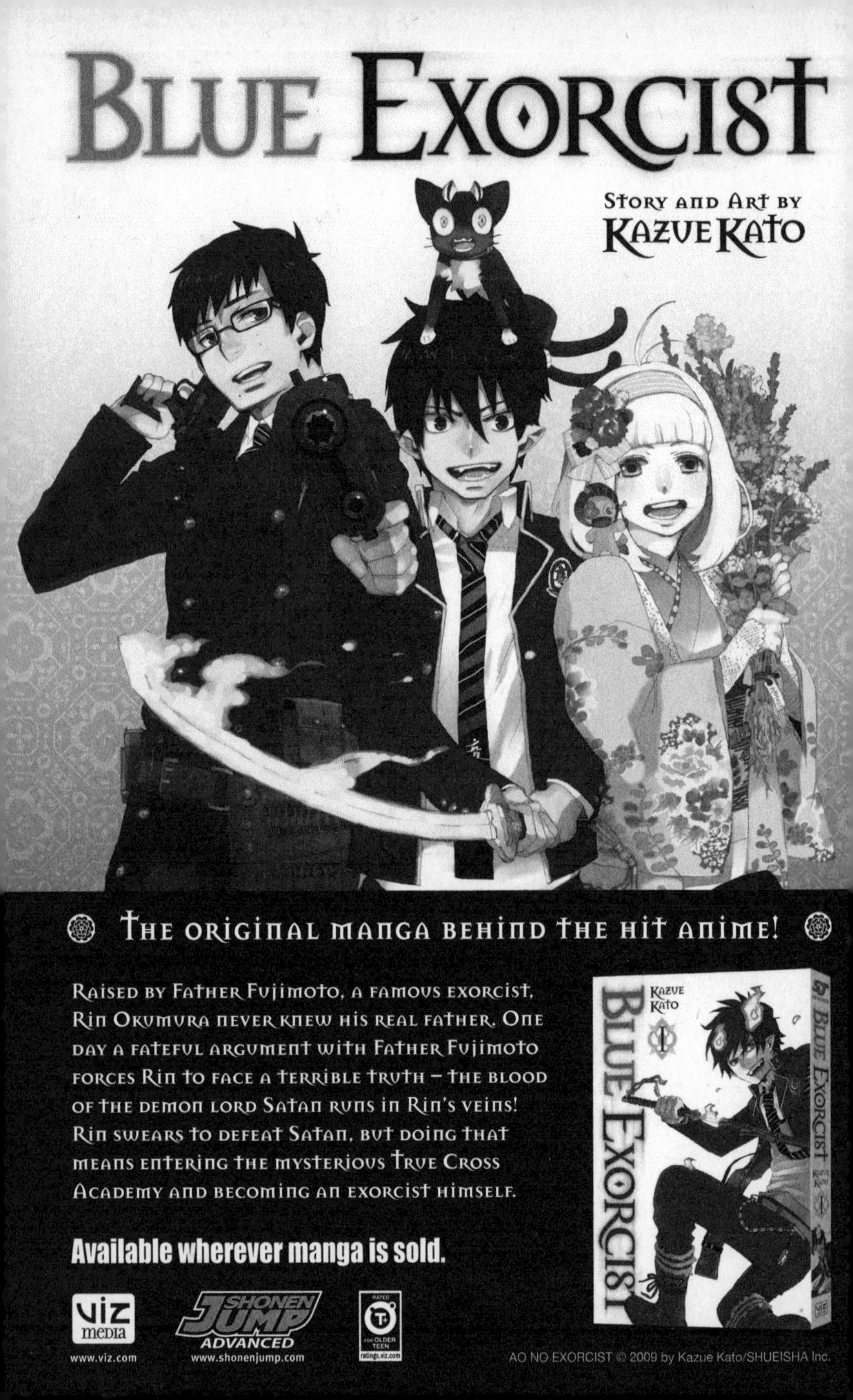
BLUE EXORCIST
STORY AND ART BY
KAZUE KATO
THE ORIGINAL MANGA BEHIND THE HIT ANIME!
Raised by Father Fujimoto, a famous exorcist, Rin Okumura never knew his real father. One day a fateful argument with Father Fujimoto forces Rin to face a terrible truth – the blood of the demon lord Satan runs in Rin's veins! Rin swears to defeat Satan, but doing that means entering the mysterious True Cross Academy and becoming an exorcist himself.
KAZUE KATO
BLUE EXORCIST
1
Available wherever manga is sold.
VIZ media
www.viz.com
SHONEN JUMP ADVANCED
www.shonenjump.com
RATED T+ FOR OLDER TEEN
ratings.viz.com
AO NO EXORCIST © 2009 by Kazue Kato/SHUEISHA Inc.

Twin Star Exorcists

ONMYOJI

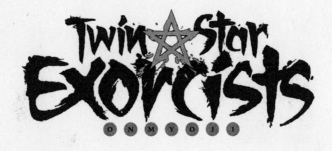

Twin★Star Exorcists

ONMYOJI

7

STORY & ART
YOSHIAKI SUKENO

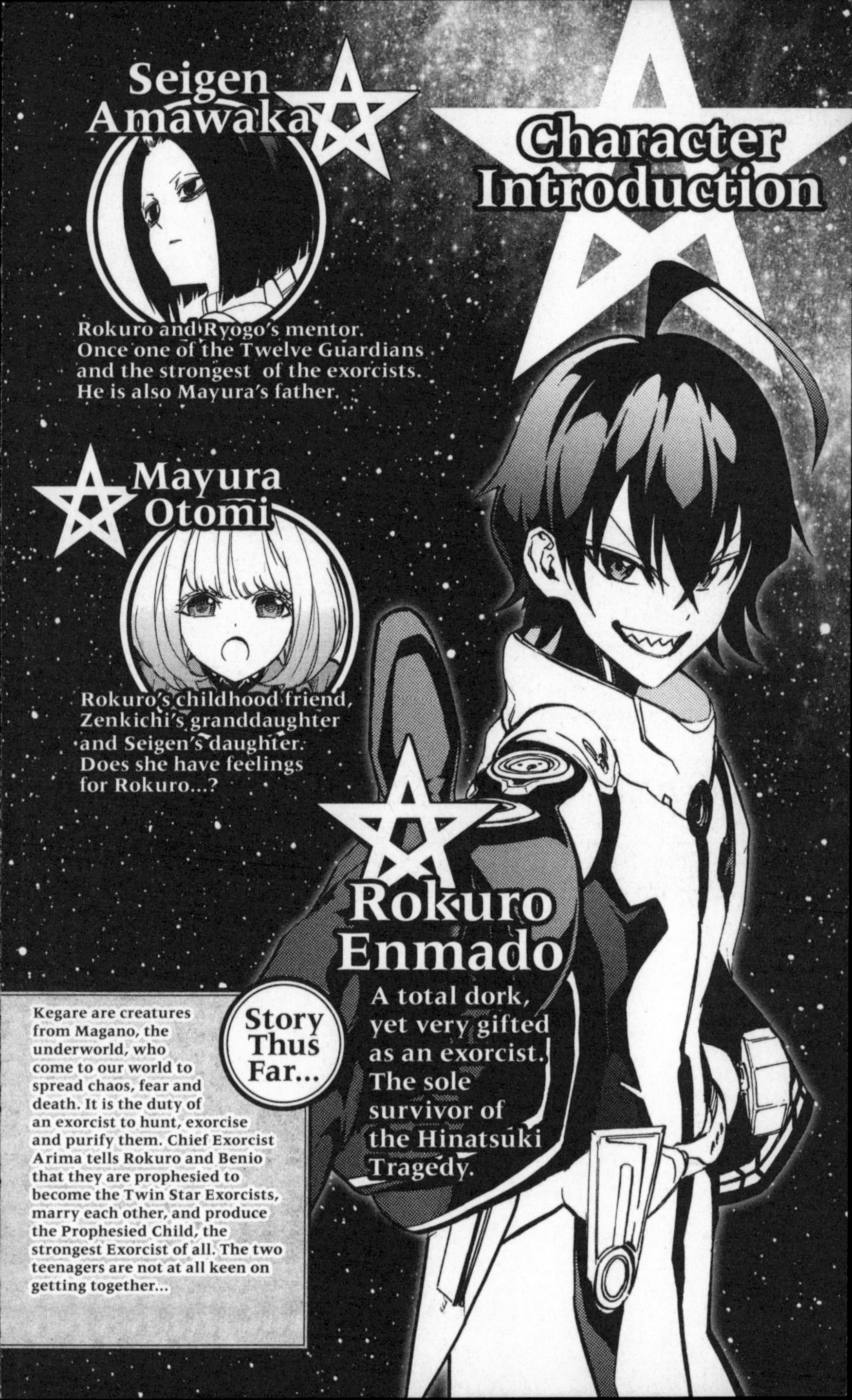

Character Introduction
Seigen Amawaka
Rokuro and Ryogo's mentor. Once one of the Twelve Guardians and the strongest of the exorcists. He is also Mayura's father.
Mayura Otomi
Rokuro's childhood friend, Zenkichi's granddaughter and Seigen's daughter. Does she have feelings for Rokuro...?
Rokuro Enmado
A total dork, yet very gifted as an exorcist. The sole survivor of the Hinatsuki Tragedy.
Story Thus Far...
Kegare are creatures from Magano, the underworld, who come to our world to spread chaos, fear and death. It is the duty of an exorcist to hunt, exorcise and purify them. Chief Exorcist Arima tells Rokuro and Benio that they are prophesied to become the Twin Star Exorcists, marry each other, and produce the Prophesied Child, the strongest Exorcist of all. The two teenagers are not at all keen on getting together...

Ryogo Nagitsuji

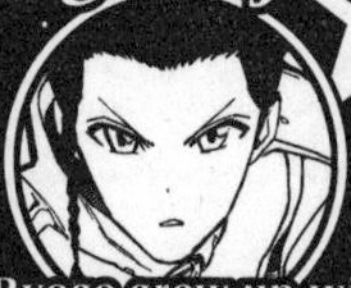

Ryogo grew up with Rokuro and is like a big brother to him. He has great faith in Rokuro's exorcism talent.

Shimon Ikaruga

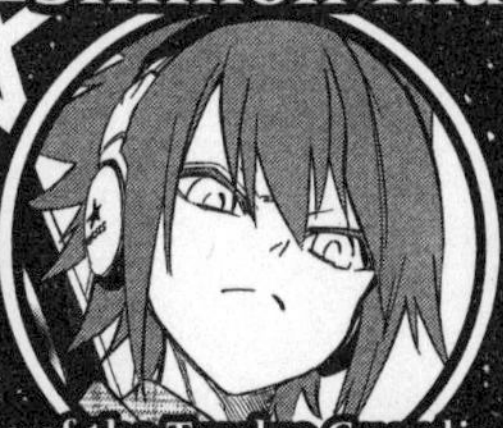

One of the Twelve Guardians with the title "Suzaku, the Vermillion Bird." Easily gets motion sick.

Sayo Ikaruga

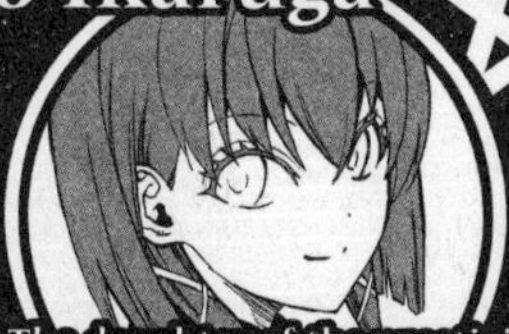

The daughter of the prestigious Tsuchimikado Island Ikaruga family. She grew up with Shimon like siblings. She has a crush on Rokuro.

Arima Tsuchimikado

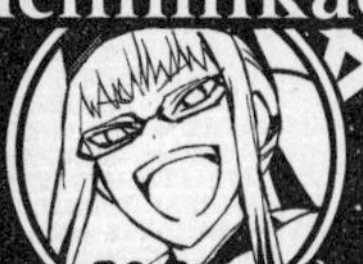

The chief exorcist of the Association of Unified Exorcists, which presides over all exorcists.

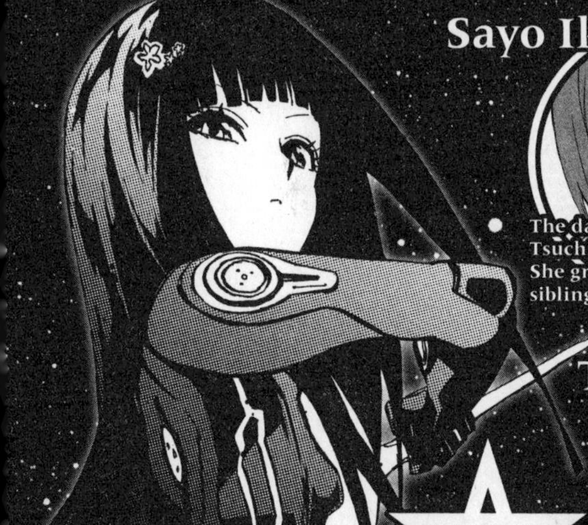

Benio Adashino

The daughter of a prestigious family of skilled exorcists. She is an excellent exorcist, especially excelling in speed. Her favorite food is ohagi dumplings.

Benio's twin brother, Yuto, reappears in Magano, the world of the Kegare, and attempts to kill his sister and Rokuro. After a fierce battle, the two manage to ward him off, but realize they have hit the limits of their power. They desperately want to pursue Yuto to Tsuchimikado Island, the exorcists' front line against the Kegare, but Arima won't allow it until they have grown stronger and can pass the Ascertainment Ritual. Rokuro and Benio have been training hard for two years, and now they are scheduled for their test. To their surprise, their proctor is a young girl named Sayo. Then trouble arises when her Spiritual Protector, Kuzu no Ha, appears before Rokuro...

Twin Star Exorcists

ONMYOJI

EXORCISMS

7

ONMYOJI have worked for the Imperial Court since the Heian era. In addition to exorcising evil spirits, as civil servants they performed a variety of roles, including advising nobles by foretelling the future, creating the calendar, observing the movements of the stars, measuring time…

#22 Curse

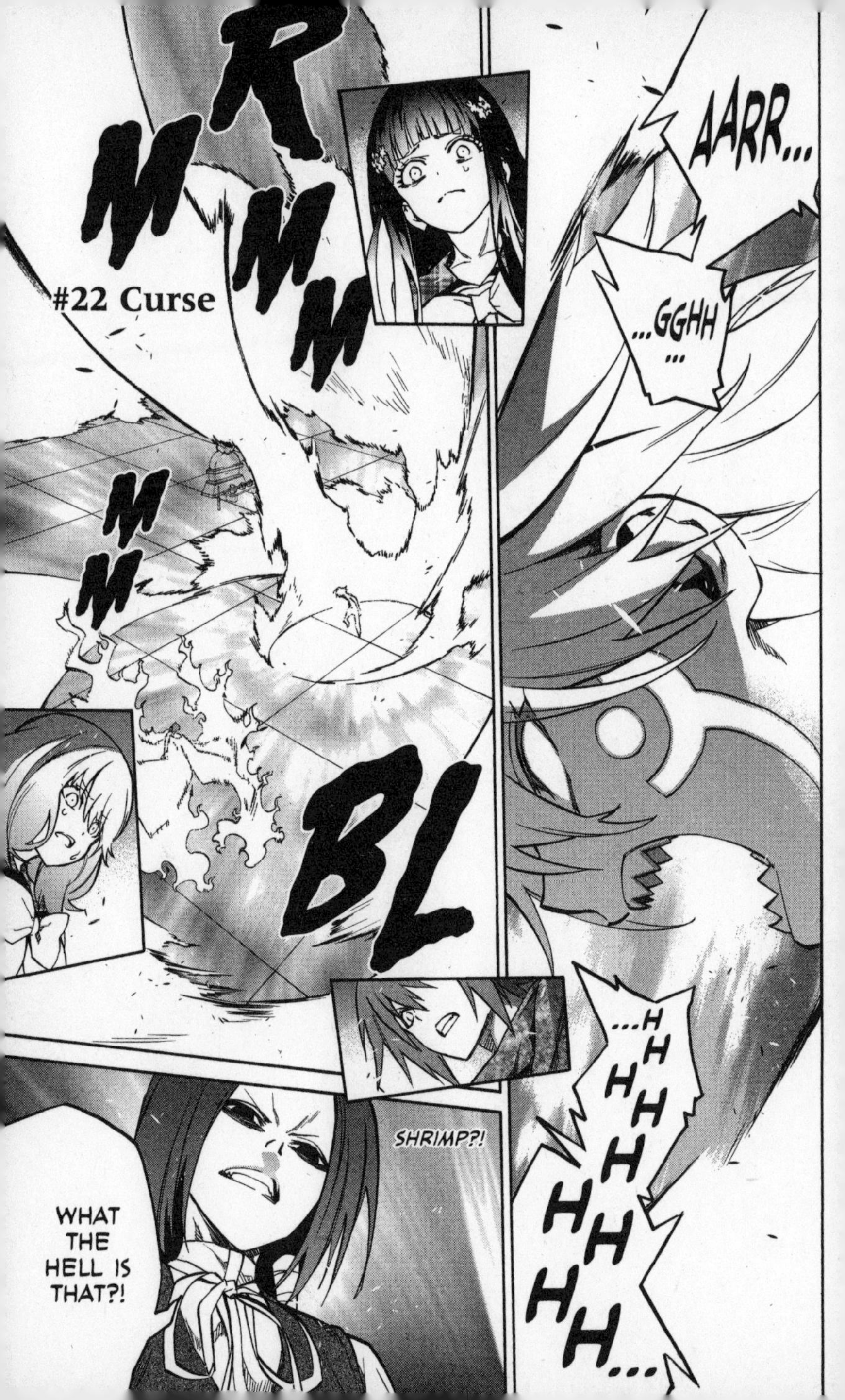
AARR...
...GGHH...
...HHHHHHHHHHH...
RMMMM
MMM
BL
SHRIMP?!
WHAT THE HELL IS THAT?!

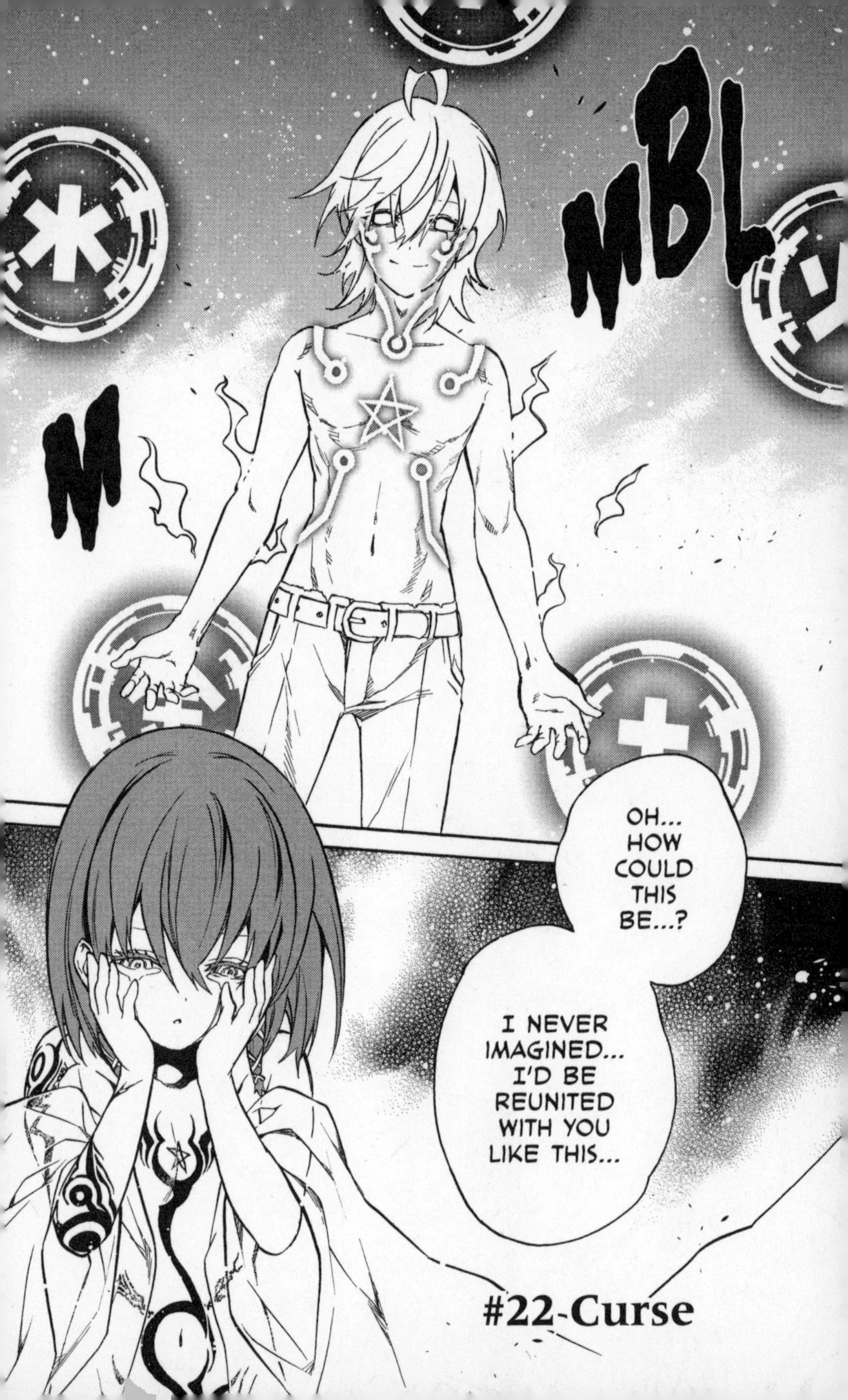
M MBL
OH... HOW COULD THIS BE...?
I NEVER IMAGINED... I'D BE REUNITED WITH YOU LIKE THIS...
#22-Curse

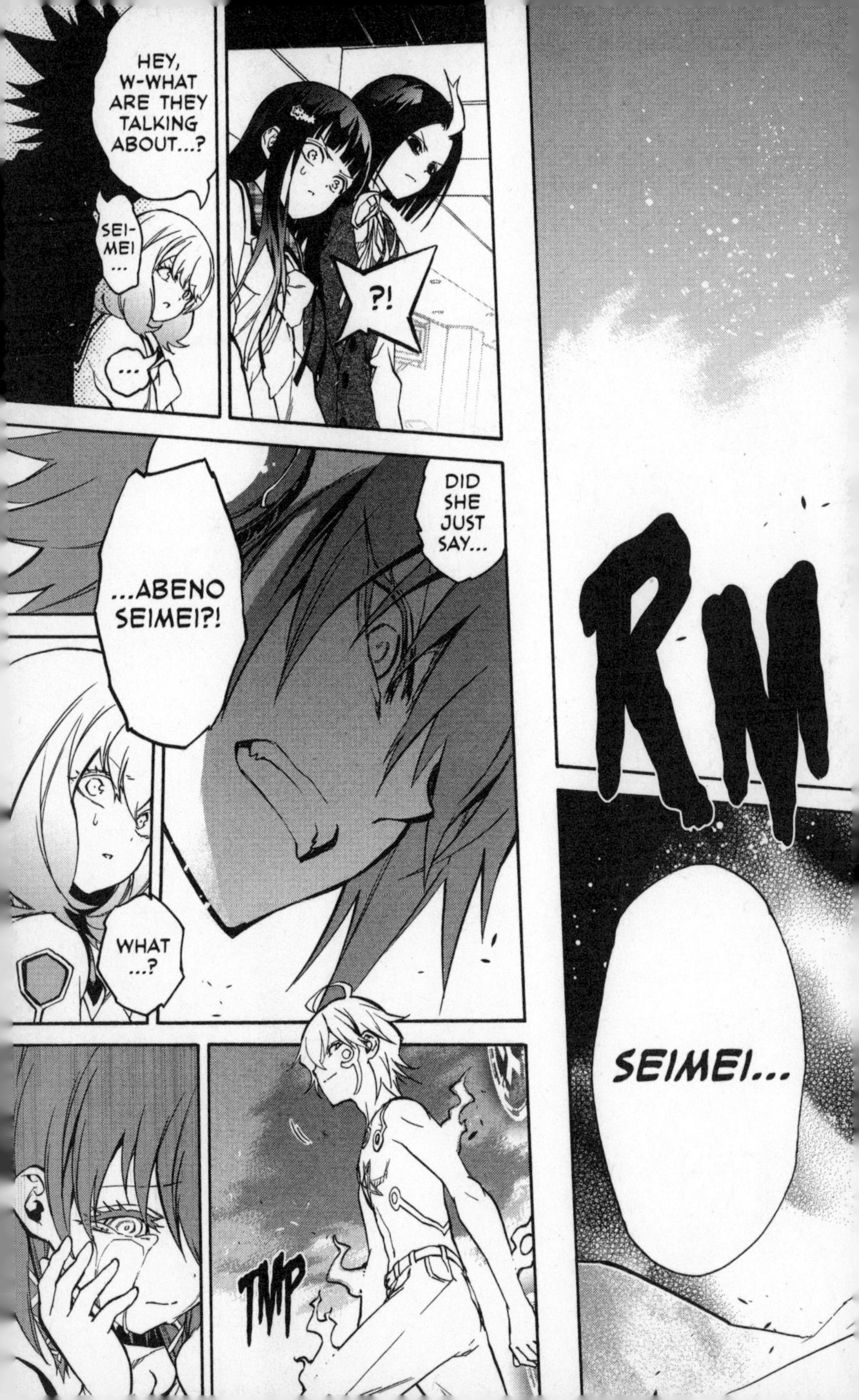
RM
SEIMEI...
?!
HEY, W-WHAT ARE THEY TALKING ABOUT...?
SEI-MEI...
...
DID SHE JUST SAY...
...ABENO SEIMEI?!
WHAT...?
TMP

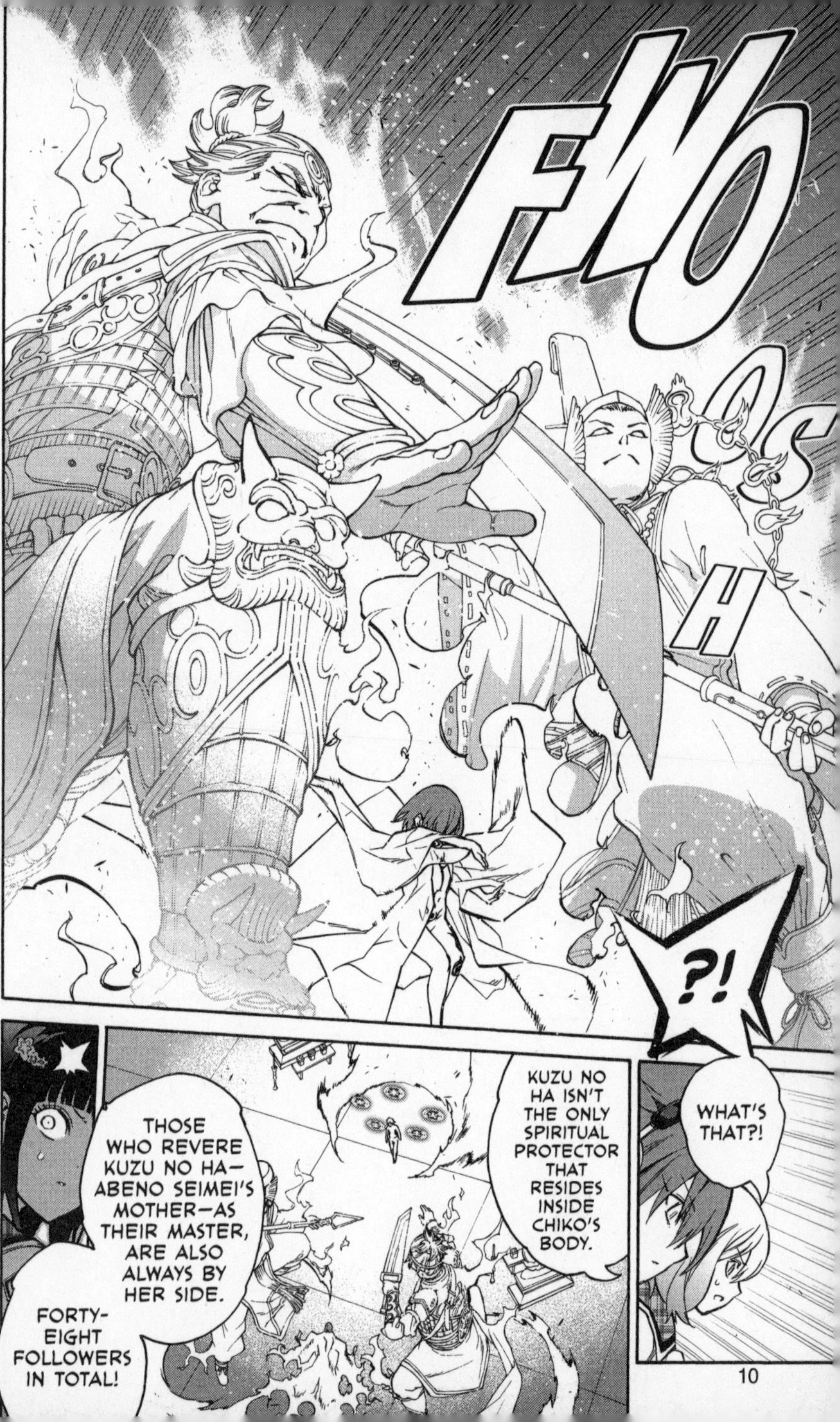
FWOOSH
?!
WHAT'S THAT?!
KUZU NO HA ISN'T THE ONLY SPIRITUAL PROTECTOR THAT RESIDES INSIDE CHIKO'S BODY.
THOSE WHO REVERE KUZU NO HA—ABENO SEIMEI'S MOTHER—AS THEIR MASTER, ARE ALSO ALWAYS BY HER SIDE.
FORTY-EIGHT FOLLOWERS IN TOTAL!

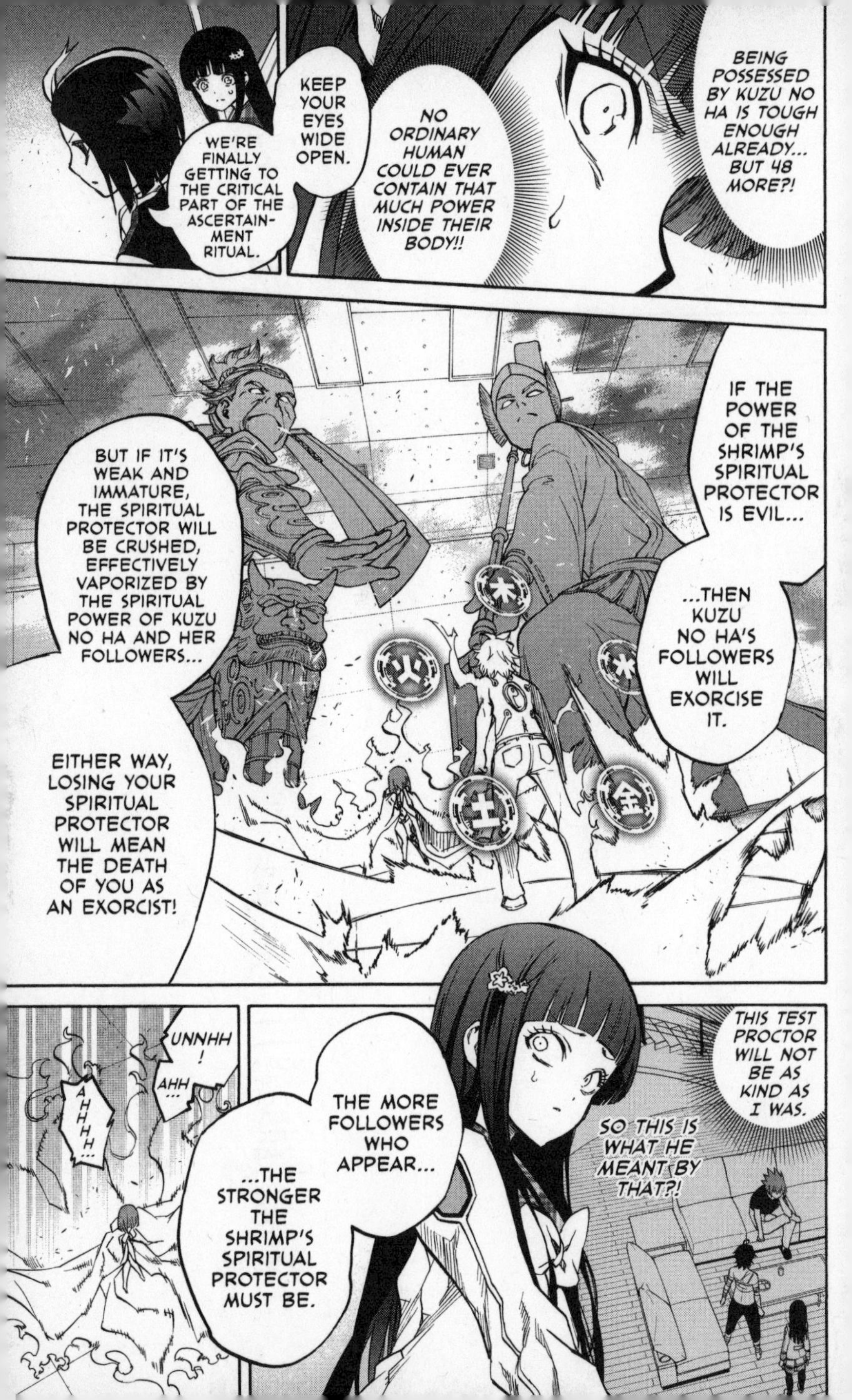
BEING POSSESSED BY KUZU NO HA IS TOUGH ENOUGH ALREADY... BUT 48 MORE?!
NO ORDINARY HUMAN COULD EVER CONTAIN THAT MUCH POWER INSIDE THEIR BODY!!
KEEP YOUR EYES WIDE OPEN.
WE'RE FINALLY GETTING TO THE CRITICAL PART OF THE ASCERTAINMENT RITUAL.
IF THE POWER OF THE SHRIMP'S SPIRITUAL PROTECTOR IS EVIL...
...THEN KUZU NO HA'S FOLLOWERS WILL EXORCISE IT.
BUT IF IT'S WEAK AND IMMATURE, THE SPIRITUAL PROTECTOR WILL BE CRUSHED, EFFECTIVELY VAPORIZED BY THE SPIRITUAL POWER OF KUZU NO HA AND HER FOLLOWERS...
EITHER WAY, LOSING YOUR SPIRITUAL PROTECTOR WILL MEAN THE DEATH OF YOU AS AN EXORCIST!
THIS TEST PROCTOR WILL NOT BE AS KIND AS I WAS.
SO THIS IS WHAT HE MEANT BY THAT?!
THE MORE FOLLOWERS WHO APPEAR...
...THE STRONGER THE SHRIMP'S SPIRITUAL PROTECTOR MUST BE.
UNNHH!
AHH...
AHHHHH...

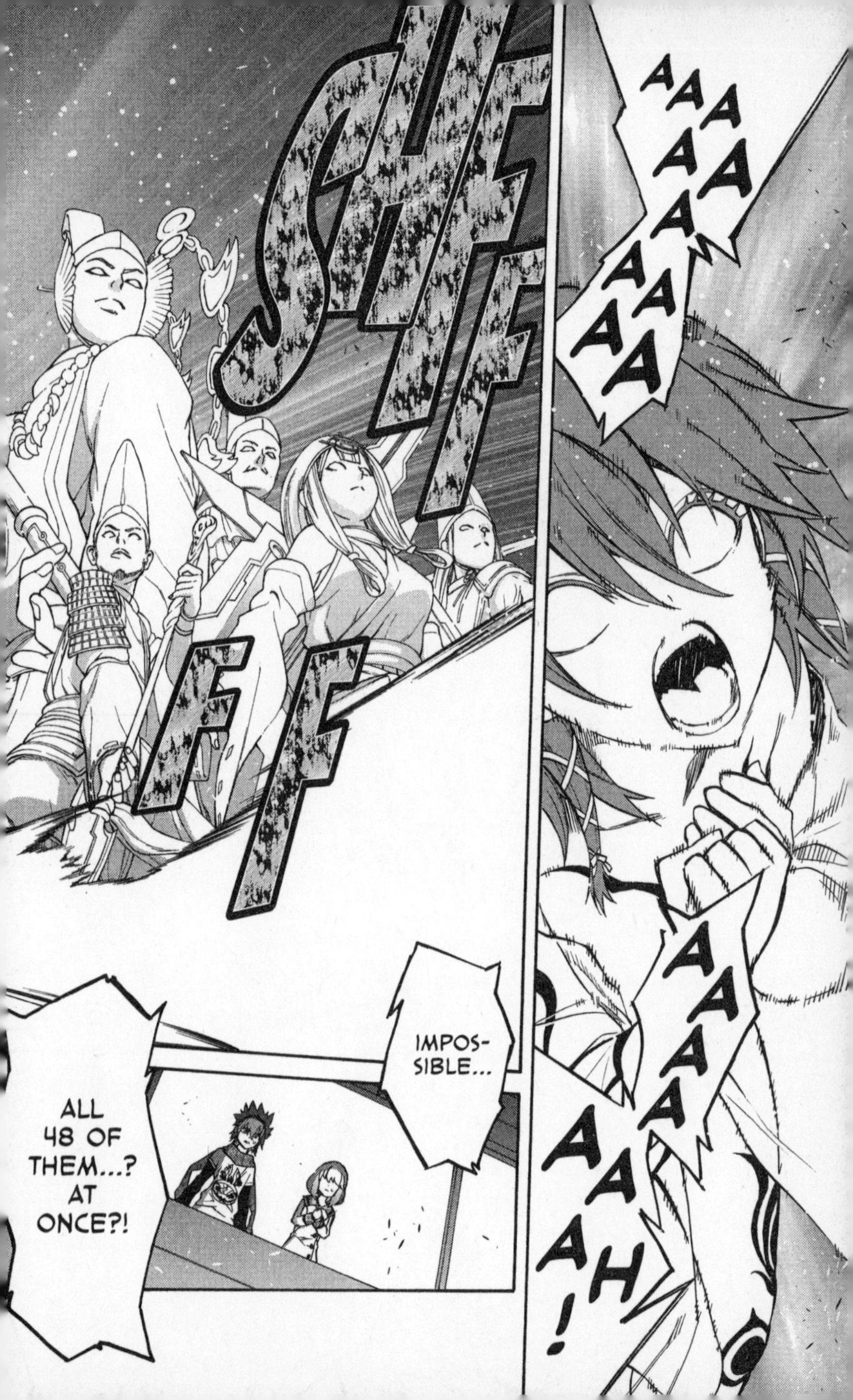

AAAAAAAAA
AAAAAAAAAH!
SHFF
FF
IMPOS-SIBLE...
ALL 48 OF THEM...? AT ONCE?!

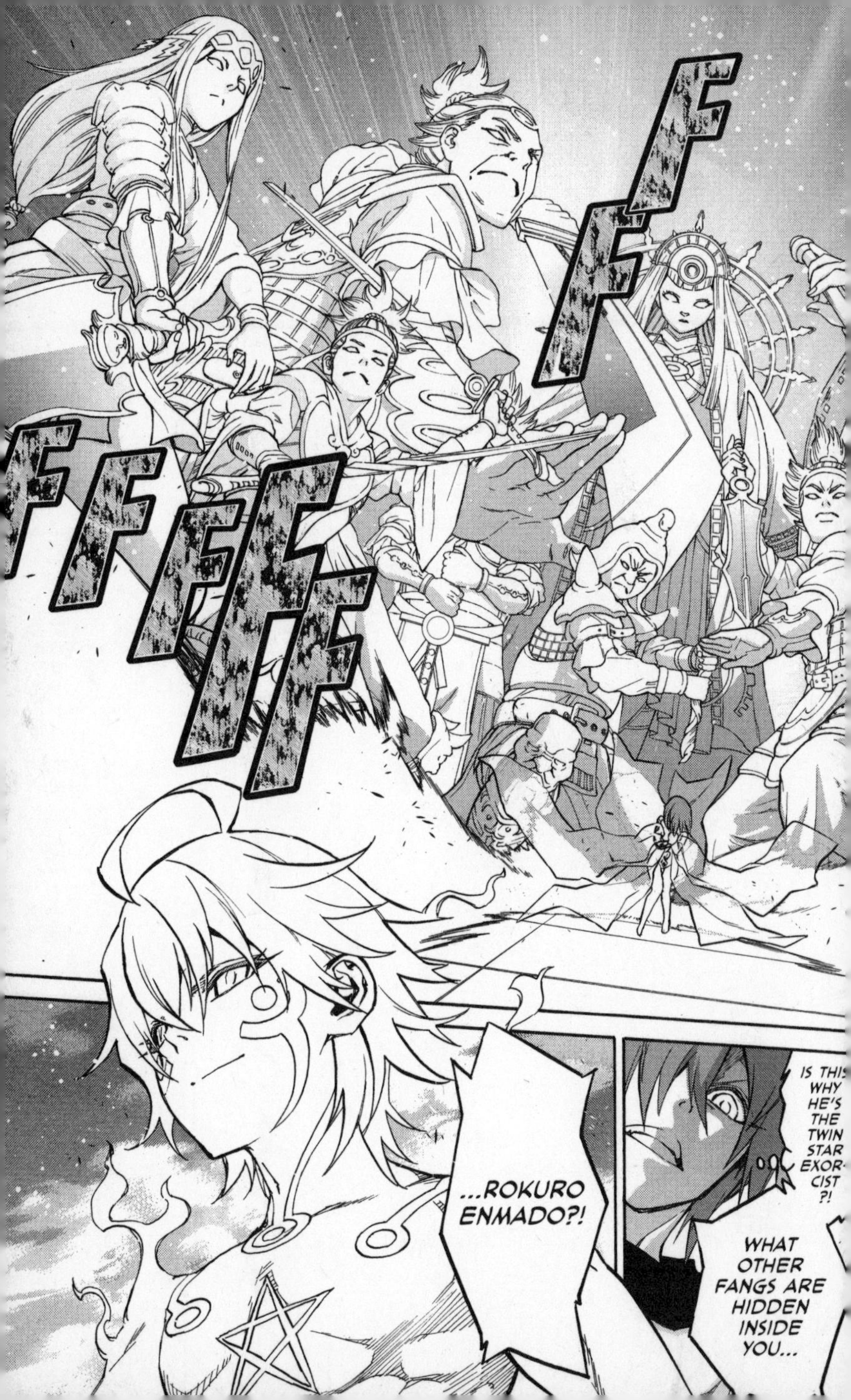
FFF
FFFFFF
IS THIS WHY HE'S THE TWIN STAR EXOR-CIST?!
WHAT OTHER FANGS ARE HIDDEN INSIDE YOU...
...ROKURO ENMADO?!

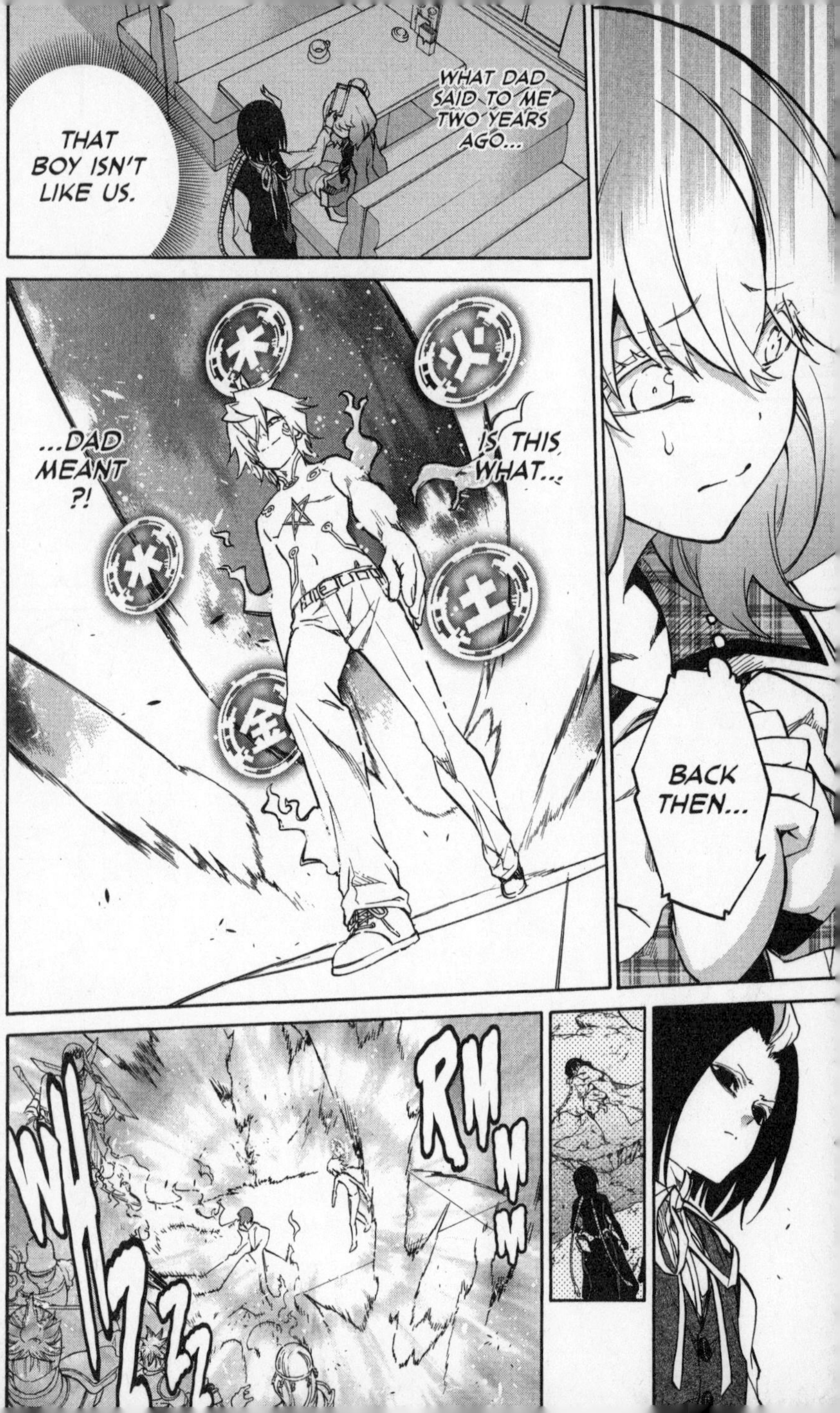
BACK THEN...
WHAT DAD SAID TO ME TWO YEARS AGO...
THAT BOY ISN'T LIKE US.
IS THIS WHAT...
...DAD MEANT?!
RMMMM
WHZZZ

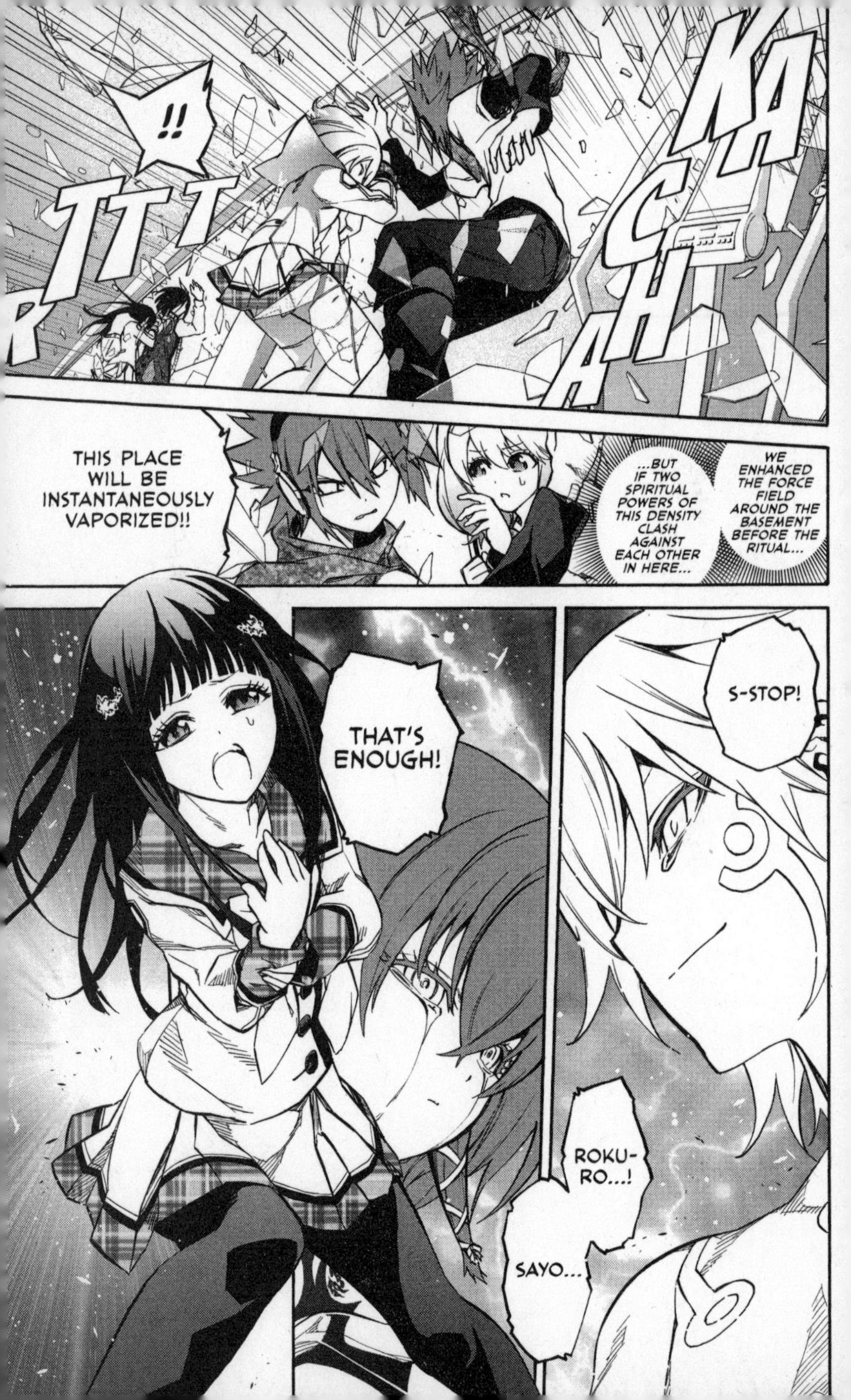
KACHA
!!
RTTT
WE ENHANCED THE FORCE FIELD AROUND THE BASEMENT BEFORE THE RITUAL...
...BUT IF TWO SPIRITUAL POWERS OF THIS DENSITY CLASH AGAINST EACH OTHER IN HERE...
THIS PLACE WILL BE INSTANTANEOUSLY VAPORIZED!!
S-STOP!
ROKU-RO...!
SAYO...
THAT'S ENOUGH!

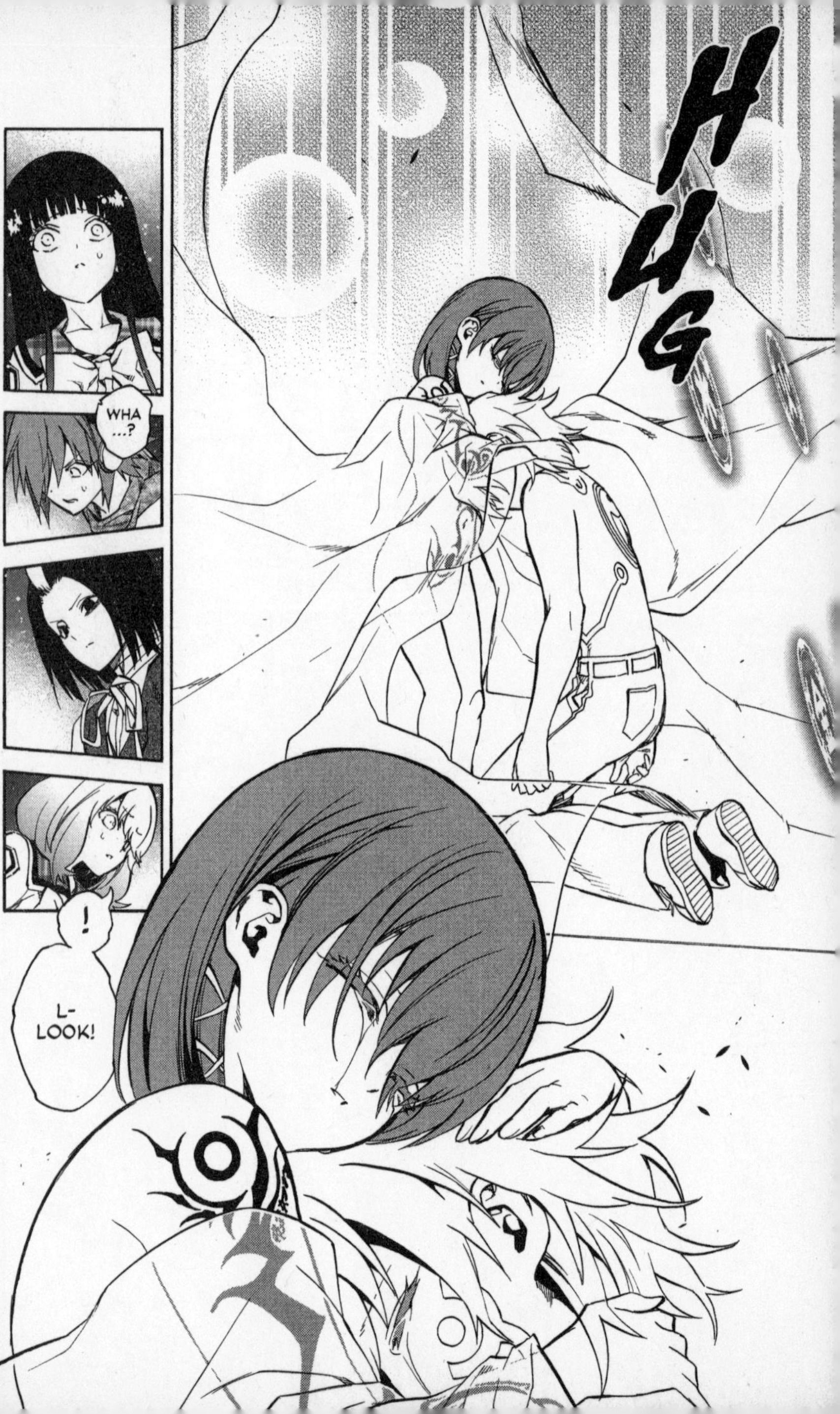
HUG
WHA ...?
!
L-LOOK!

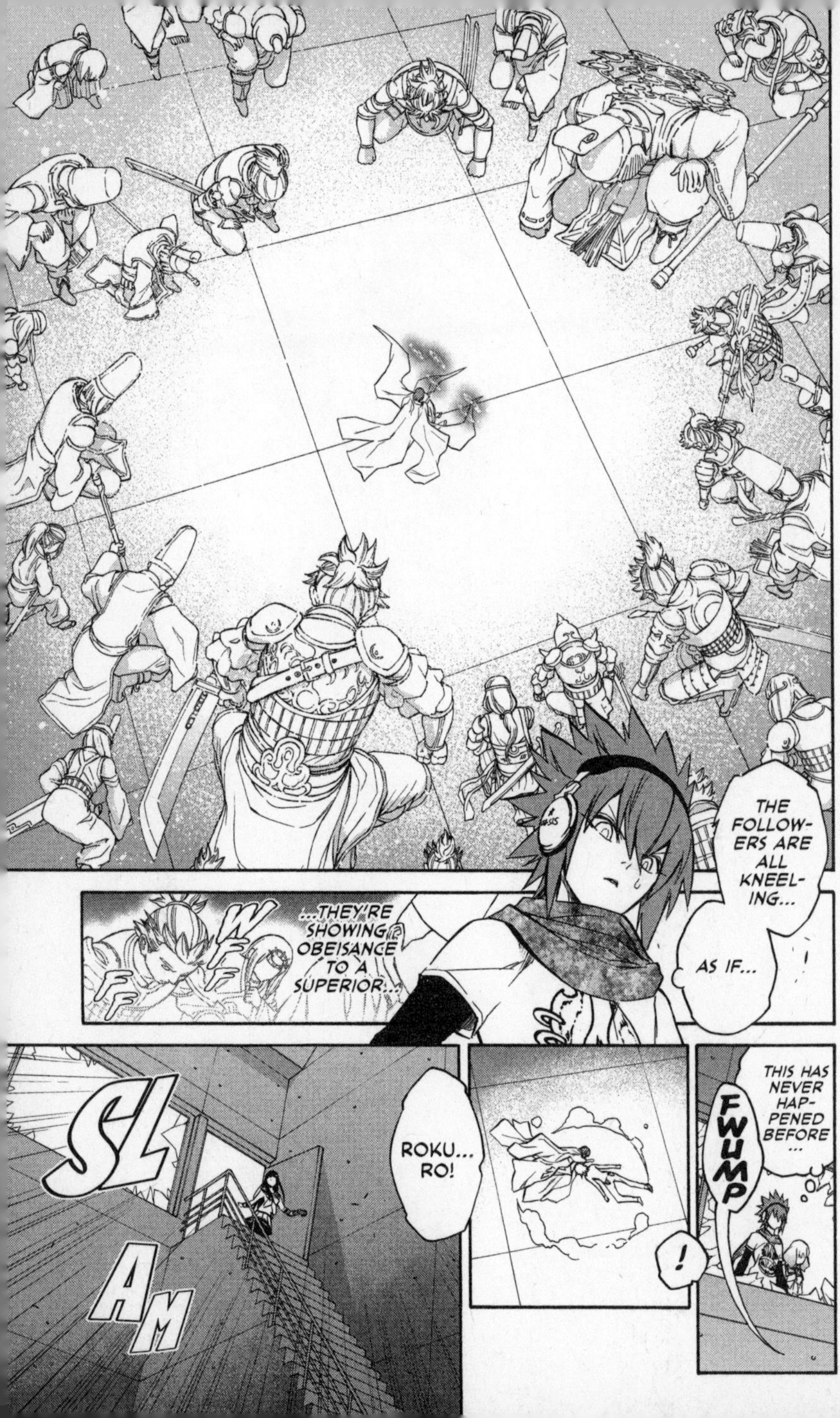
THE FOLLOWERS ARE ALL KNEELING...
AS IF...
!
...THEY'RE SHOWING OBEISANCE TO A SUPERIOR...
WFF
THIS HAS NEVER HAPPENED BEFORE ...
FWUMP
!
ROKU... RO!
SLAM

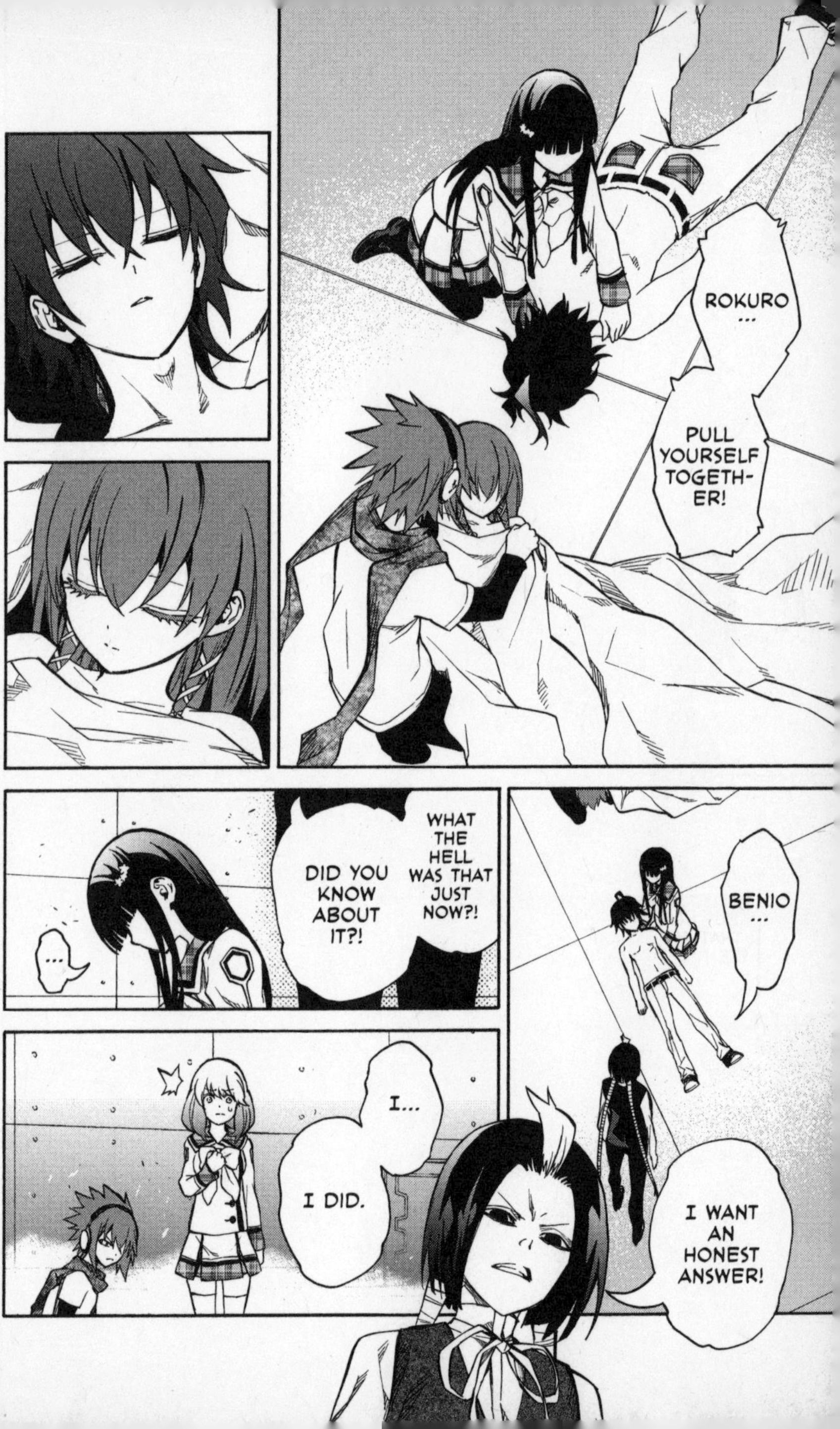
ROKURO...
PULL YOURSELF TOGETH-ER!
BENIO...
I WANT AN HONEST ANSWER!
WHAT THE HELL WAS THAT JUST NOW?!
DID YOU KNOW ABOUT IT?!
...
I...
I DID.

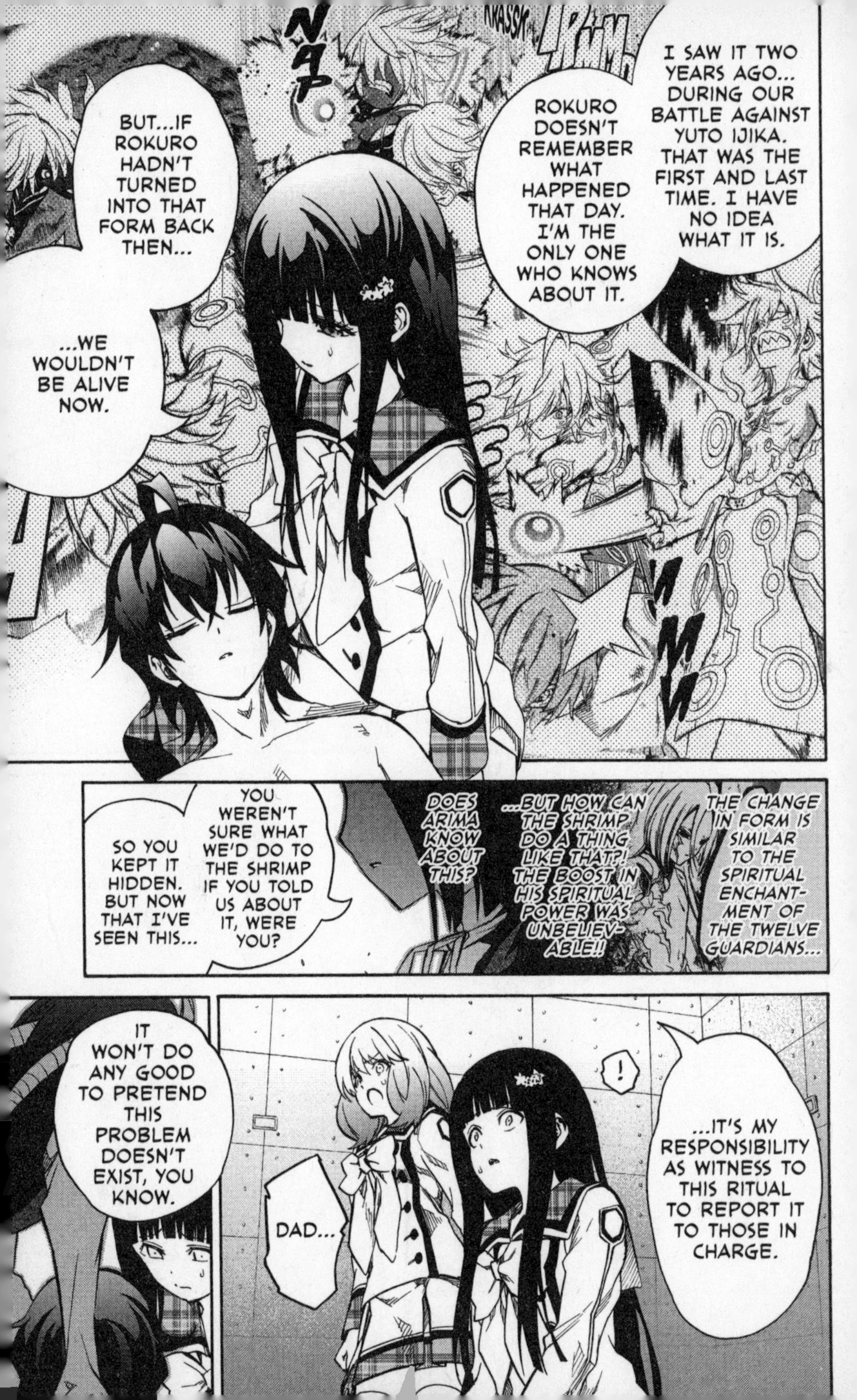
I SAW IT TWO YEARS AGO... DURING OUR BATTLE AGAINST YUTO IJIKA. THAT WAS THE FIRST AND LAST TIME. I HAVE NO IDEA WHAT IT IS.
ROKURO DOESN'T REMEMBER WHAT HAPPENED THAT DAY. I'M THE ONLY ONE WHO KNOWS ABOUT IT.
BUT...IF ROKURO HADN'T TURNED INTO THAT FORM BACK THEN...
...WE WOULDN'T BE ALIVE NOW.
THE CHANGE IN FORM IS SIMILAR TO THE SPIRITUAL ENCHANT-MENT OF THE TWELVE GUARDIANS...
...BUT HOW CAN THE SHRIMP DO A THING LIKE THAT?! THE BOOST IN HIS SPIRITUAL POWER WAS UNBELIEV-ABLE!!
DOES ARIMA KNOW ABOUT THIS?
YOU WEREN'T SURE WHAT WE'D DO TO THE SHRIMP IF YOU TOLD US ABOUT IT, WERE YOU?
SO YOU KEPT IT HIDDEN. BUT NOW THAT I'VE SEEN THIS...
...IT'S MY RESPONSIBILITY AS WITNESS TO THIS RITUAL TO REPORT IT TO THOSE IN CHARGE.
!
DAD...
IT WON'T DO ANY GOOD TO PRETEND THIS PROBLEM DOESN'T EXIST, YOU KNOW.

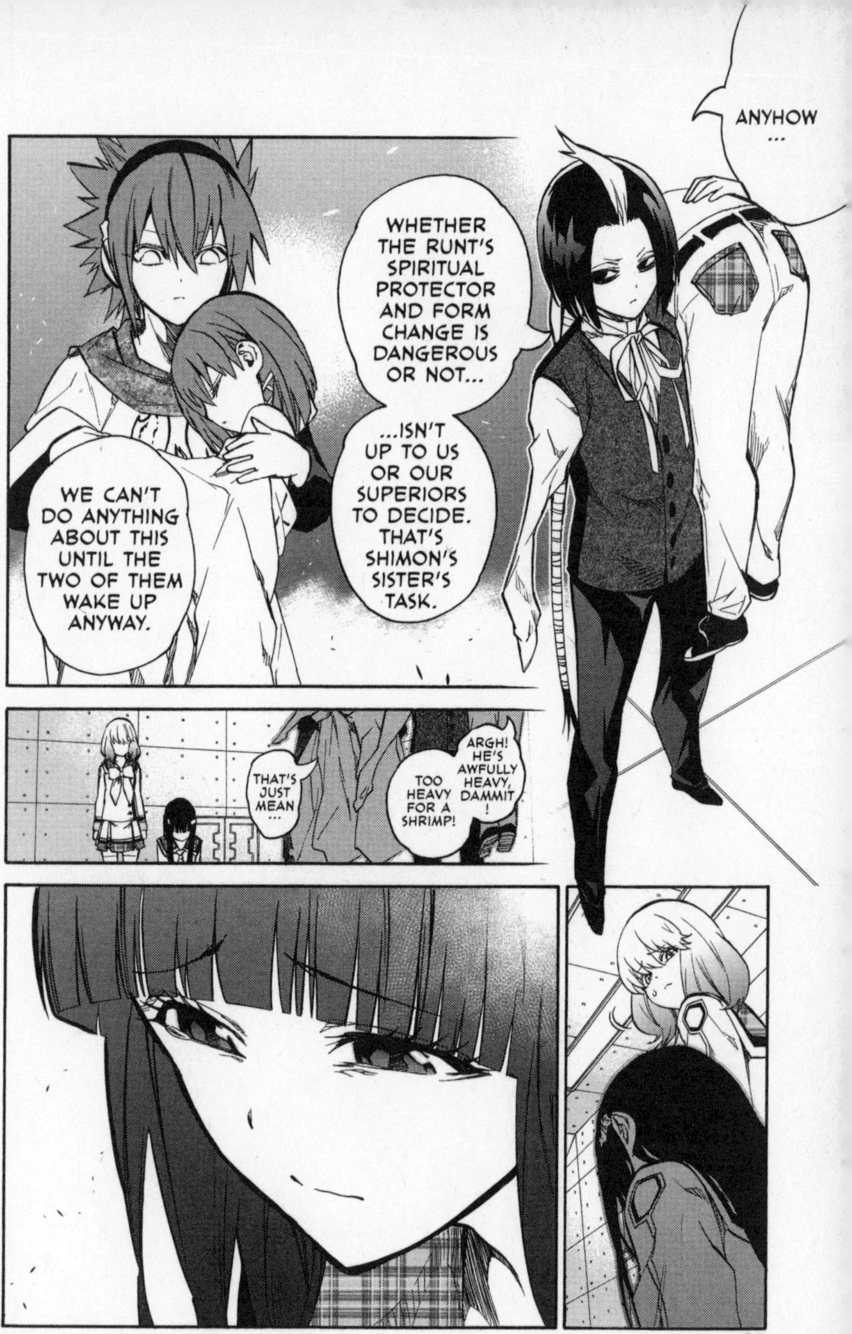
ANYHOW ...
WHETHER THE RUNT'S SPIRITUAL PROTECTOR AND FORM CHANGE IS DANGEROUS OR NOT...
...ISN'T UP TO US OR OUR SUPERIORS TO DECIDE. THAT'S SHIMON'S SISTER'S TASK.
WE CAN'T DO ANYTHING ABOUT THIS UNTIL THE TWO OF THEM WAKE UP ANYWAY.
ARGH! HE'S AWFULLY HEAVY, DAMMIT!
TOO HEAVY FOR A SHRIMP!
THAT'S JUST MEAN ...

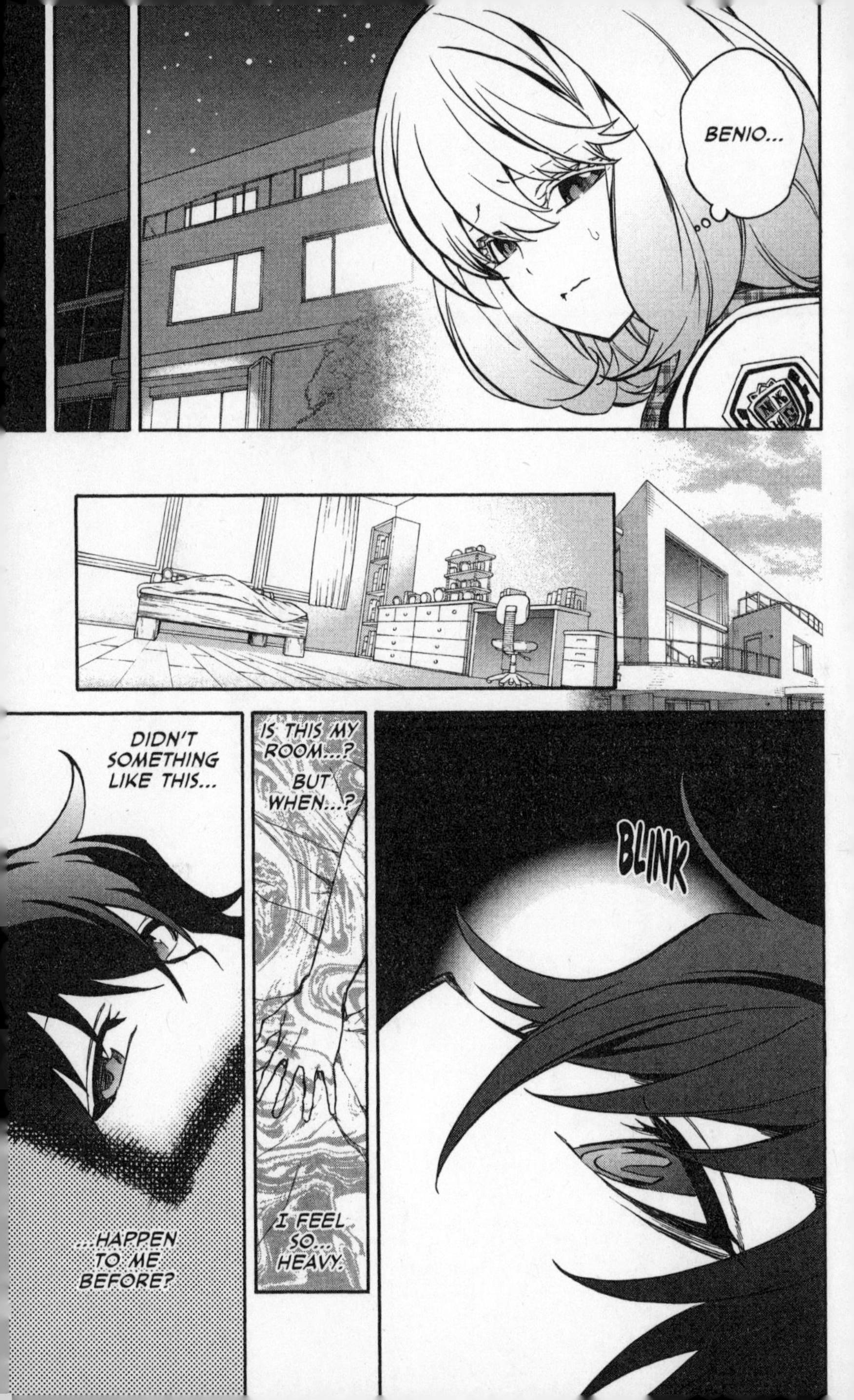
BENIO...
BLINK
IS THIS MY ROOM...?
BUT WHEN...?
I FEEL SO... HEAVY.
DIDN'T SOMETHING LIKE THIS...
...HAPPEN TO ME BEFORE?

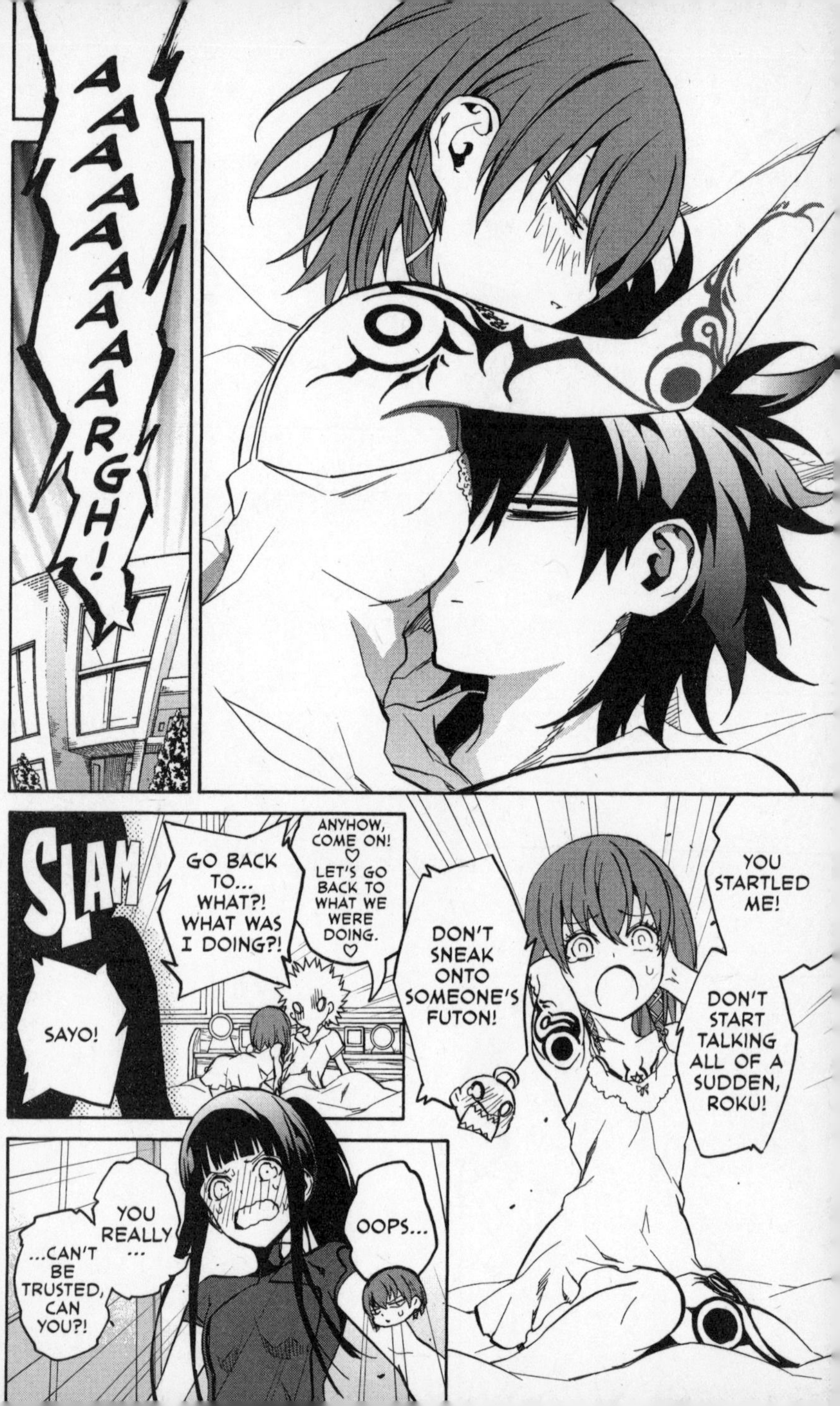
AAAAAAAAARGH!
YOU STARTLED ME!
DON'T START TALKING ALL OF A SUDDEN, ROKU!
DON'T SNEAK ONTO SOMEONE'S FUTON!
ANYHOW, COME ON! ♡ LET'S GO BACK TO WHAT WE WERE DOING. ♡
GO BACK TO... WHAT?! WHAT WAS I DOING?!
SLAM
SAYO!
OOPS...
YOU REALLY...
...CAN'T BE TRUSTED, CAN YOU?!

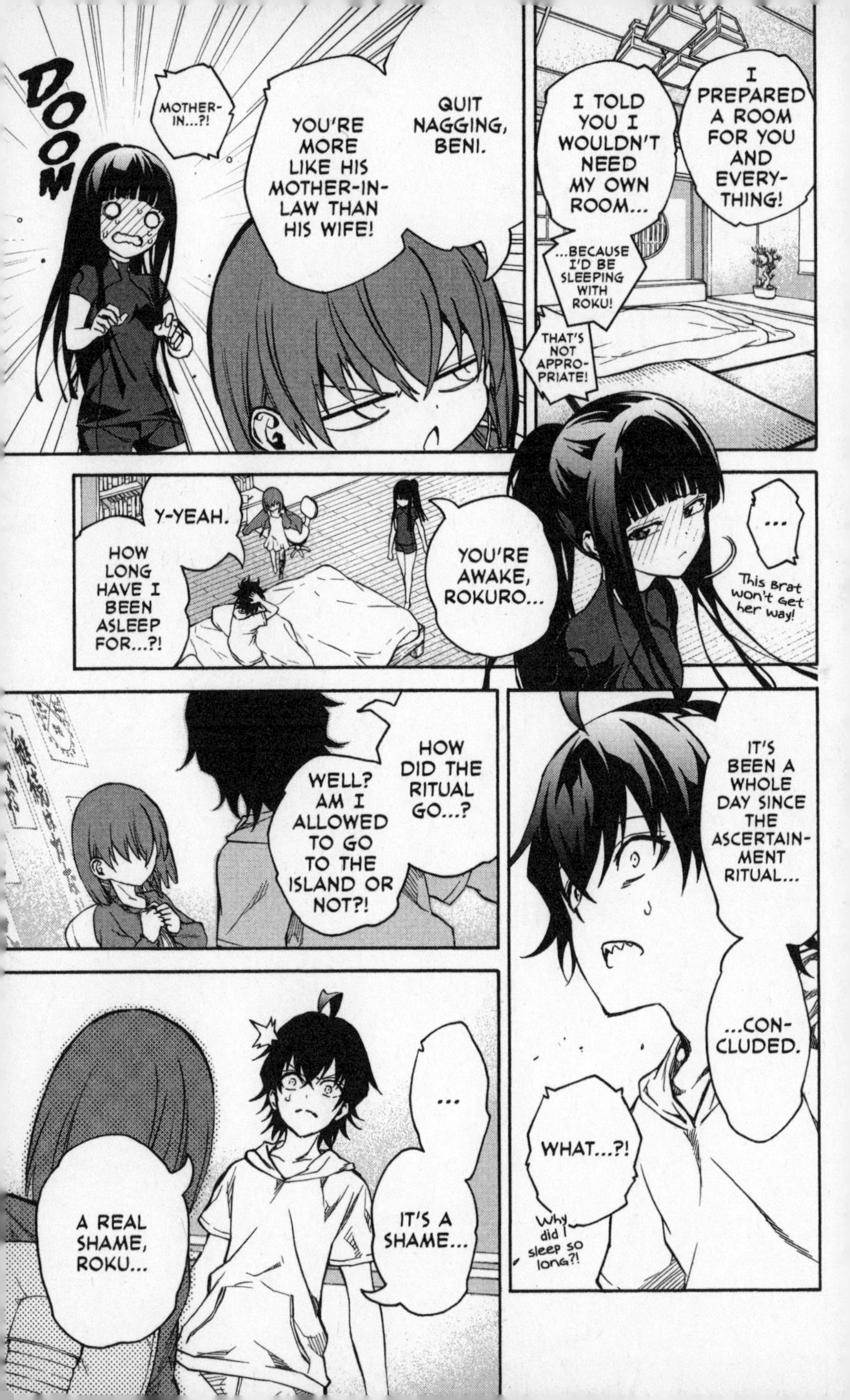
I PREPARED A ROOM FOR YOU AND EVERYTHING!
I TOLD YOU I WOULDN'T NEED MY OWN ROOM...
...BECAUSE I'D BE SLEEPING WITH ROKU!
THAT'S NOT APPROPRIATE!
QUIT NAGGING, BENI.
YOU'RE MORE LIKE HIS MOTHER-IN-LAW THAN HIS WIFE!
DOOM
MOTHER-IN...?!
...
This Brat won't Get her way!
YOU'RE AWAKE, ROKURO...
Y-YEAH.
HOW LONG HAVE I BEEN ASLEEP FOR...?!
IT'S BEEN A WHOLE DAY SINCE THE ASCERTAINMENT RITUAL...
...CONCLUDED.
WHAT...?!
Why did I sleep so long?!
HOW DID THE RITUAL GO...?
WELL? AM I ALLOWED TO GO TO THE ISLAND OR NOT?!
...
IT'S A SHAME...
A REAL SHAME, ROKU...

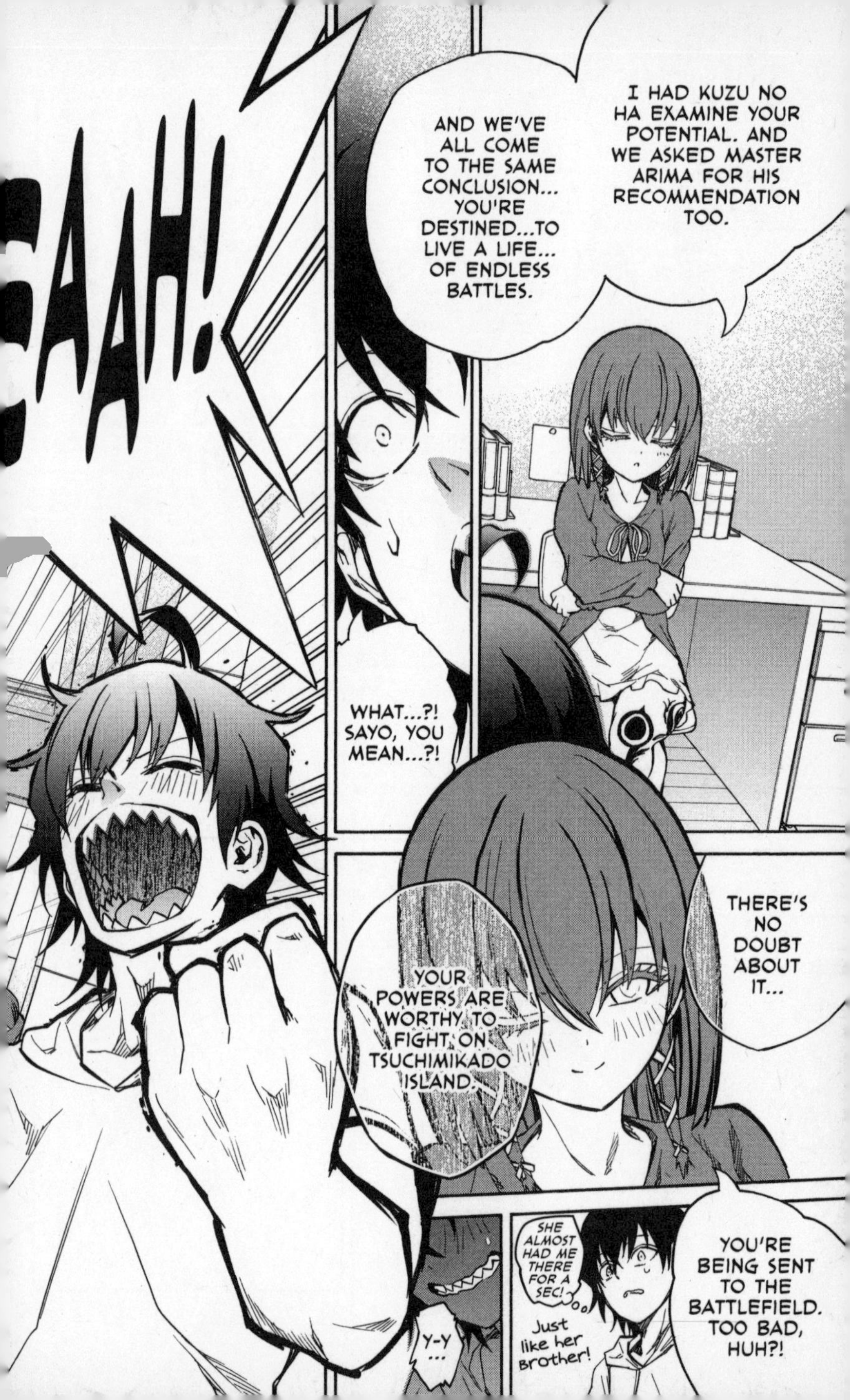
I HAD KUZU NO HA EXAMINE YOUR POTENTIAL. AND WE ASKED MASTER ARIMA FOR HIS RECOMMENDATION TOO.
AND WE'VE ALL COME TO THE SAME CONCLUSION... YOU'RE DESTINED...TO LIVE A LIFE... OF ENDLESS BATTLES.
WHAT...?! SAYO, YOU MEAN...?!
THERE'S NO DOUBT ABOUT IT...
YOUR POWERS ARE WORTHY TO FIGHT ON TSUCHIMIKADO ISLAND.
YOU'RE BEING SENT TO THE BATTLEFIELD. TOO BAD, HUH?!
SHE ALMOST HAD ME THERE FOR A SEC!
Just like her brother!
Y-Y...
AAH!

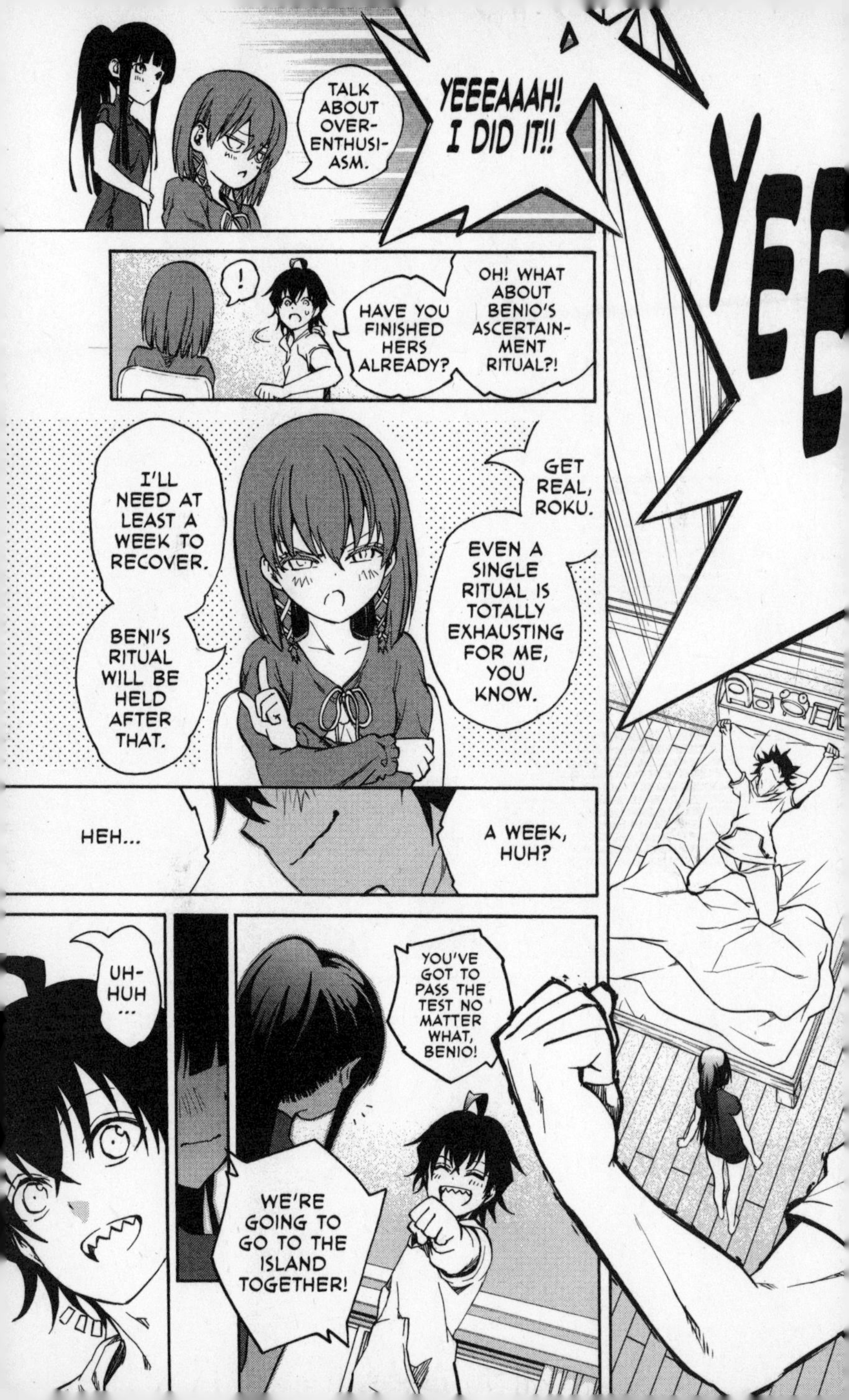
YEEEAAAH! I DID IT!!
YEE
TALK ABOUT OVER-ENTHUSIASM.
!
OH! WHAT ABOUT BENIO'S ASCERTAINMENT RITUAL?!
HAVE YOU FINISHED HERS ALREADY?
GET REAL, ROKU.
EVEN A SINGLE RITUAL IS TOTALLY EXHAUSTING FOR ME, YOU KNOW.
I'LL NEED AT LEAST A WEEK TO RECOVER.
BENI'S RITUAL WILL BE HELD AFTER THAT.
A WEEK, HUH?
HEH...
YOU'VE GOT TO PASS THE TEST NO MATTER WHAT, BENIO!
WE'RE GOING TO GO TO THE ISLAND TOGETHER!
UH-HUH...

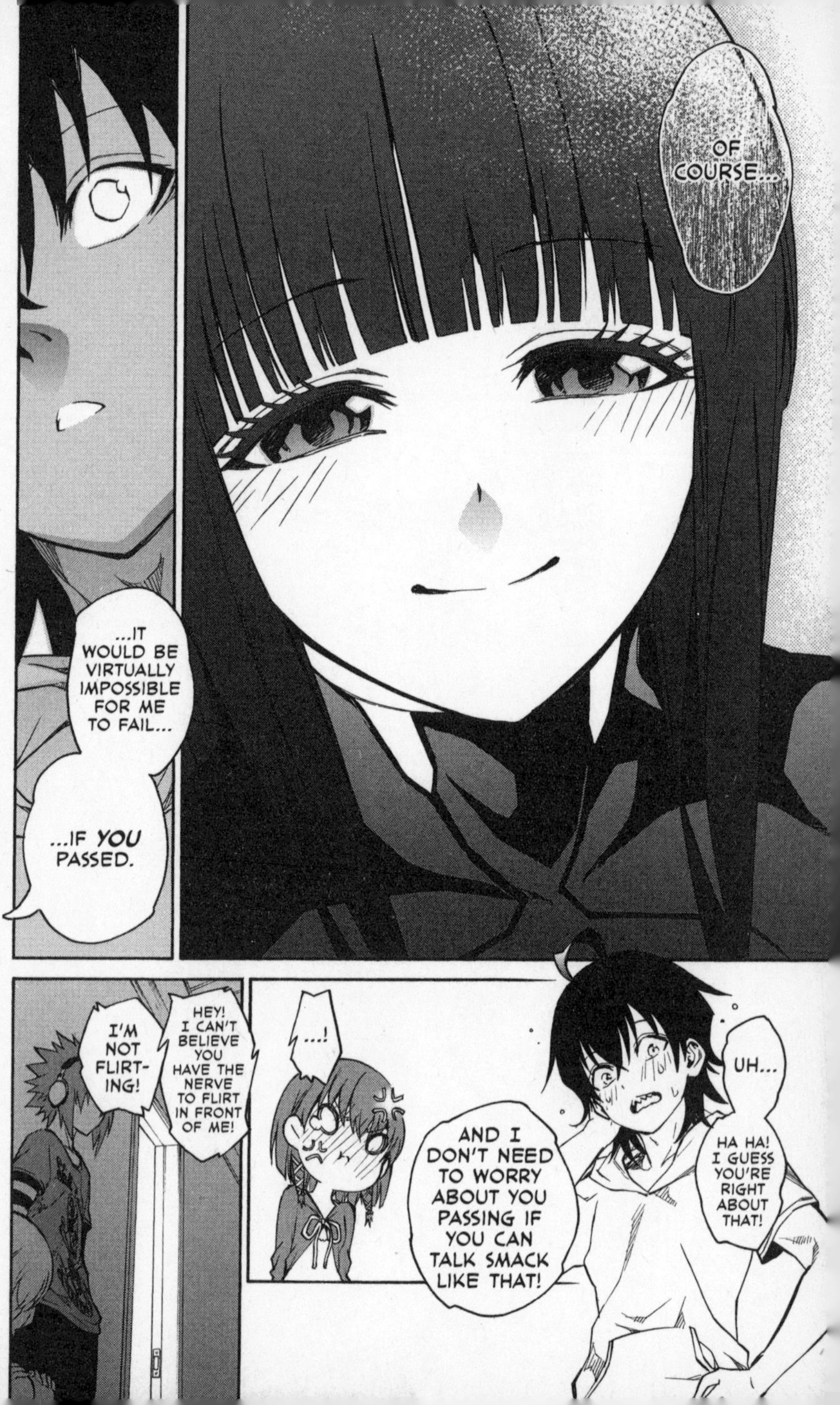
OF COURSE...
...IT WOULD BE VIRTUALLY IMPOSSIBLE FOR ME TO FAIL...
...IF *YOU* PASSED.
UH...
HA HA! I GUESS YOU'RE RIGHT ABOUT THAT!
AND I DON'T NEED TO WORRY ABOUT YOU PASSING IF YOU CAN TALK SMACK LIKE THAT!
...!
HEY! I CAN'T BELIEVE YOU HAVE THE NERVE TO FLIRT IN FRONT OF ME!
I'M NOT FLIRT-ING!

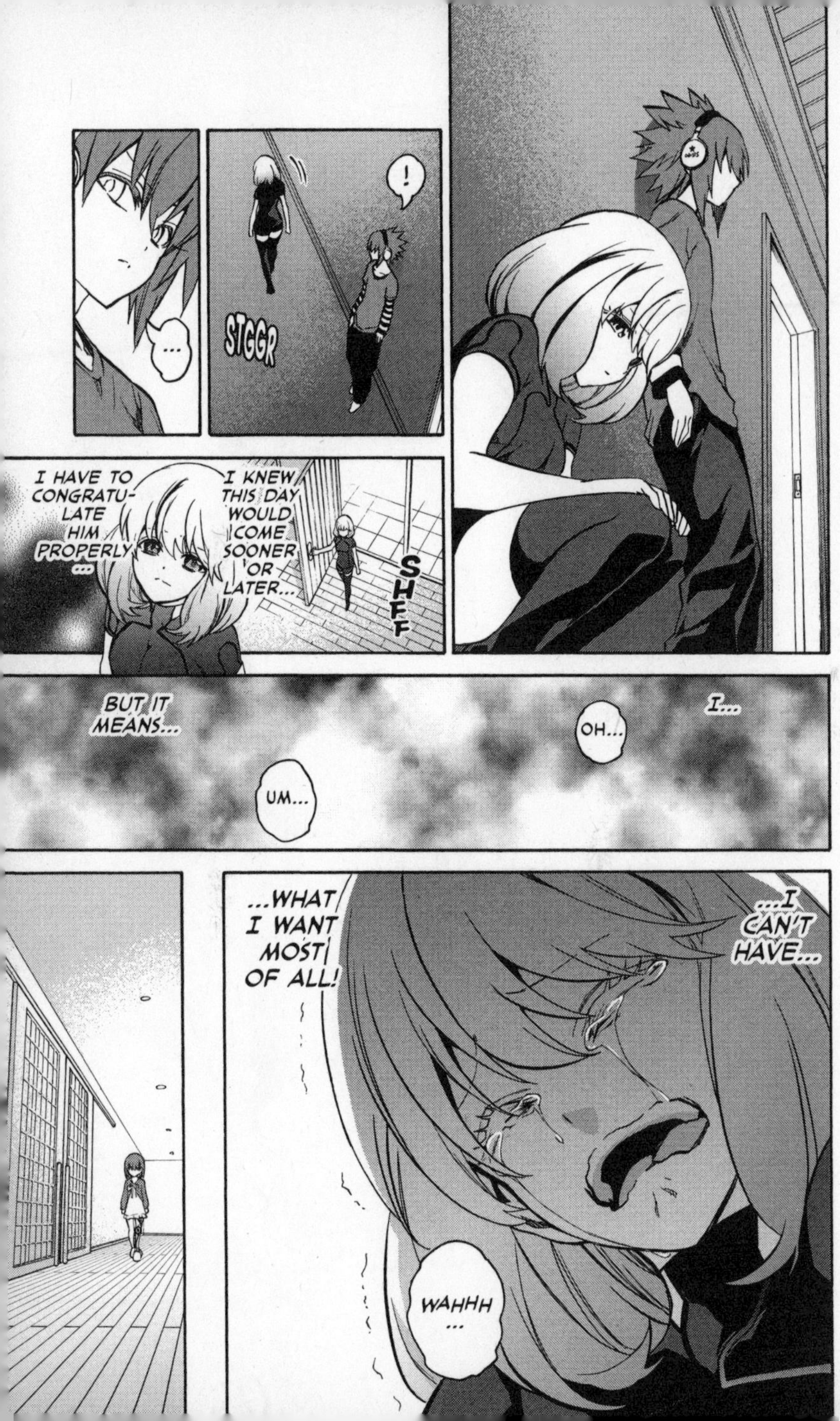
!
STGGR
...
I KNEW THIS DAY WOULD COME SOONER OR LATER...
SHFF
I HAVE TO CONGRATULATE HIM PROPERLY...
I...
OH...
UM...
BUT IT MEANS...
...I CAN'T HAVE...
...WHAT I WANT MOST OF ALL!
WAHHH...

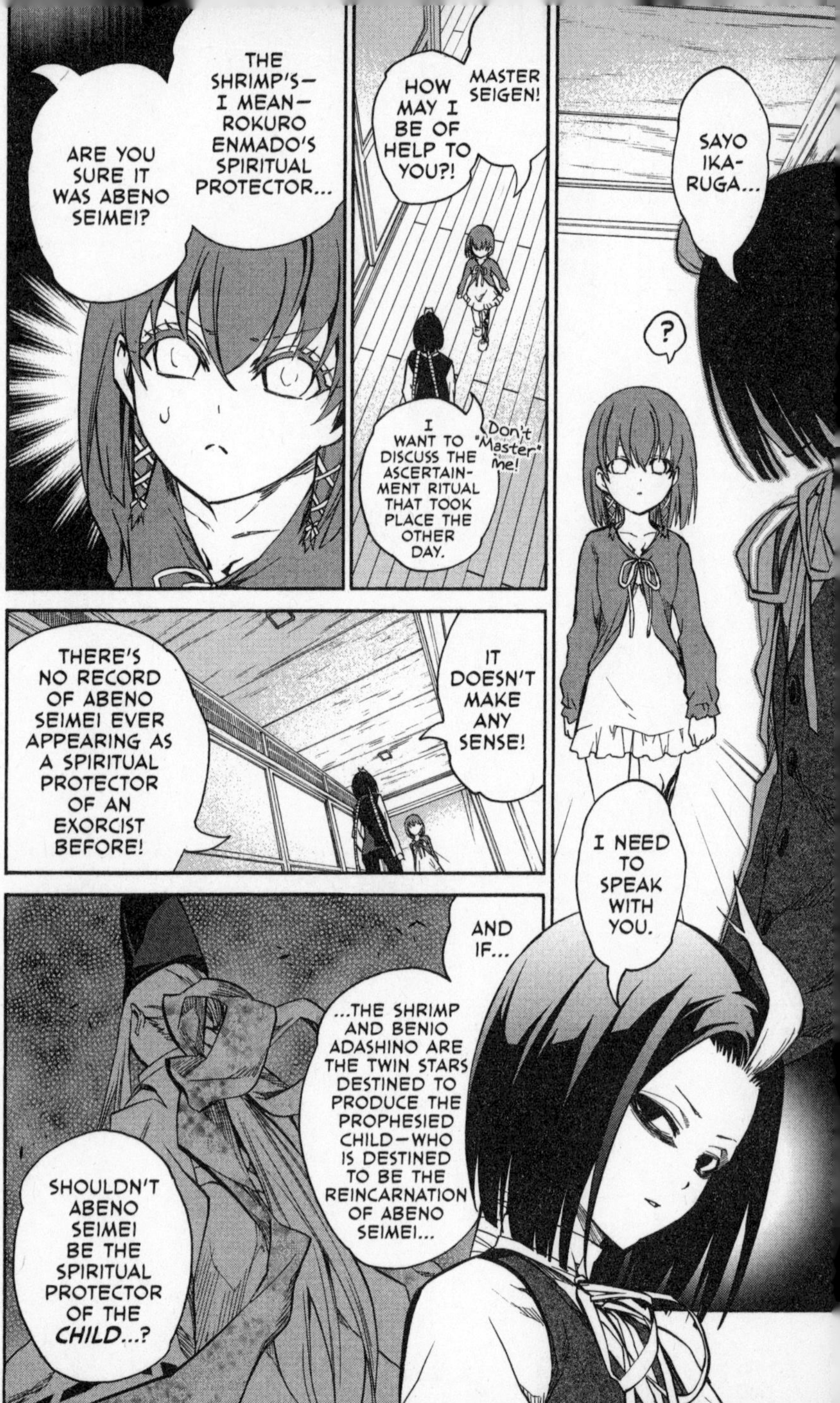
SAYO IKARUGA...
?
I NEED TO SPEAK WITH YOU.
MASTER SEIGEN!
HOW MAY I BE OF HELP TO YOU?!
I WANT TO DISCUSS THE ASCERTAINMENT RITUAL THAT TOOK PLACE THE OTHER DAY.
Don't "Master" me!
THE SHRIMP'S— I MEAN— ROKURO ENMADO'S SPIRITUAL PROTECTOR...
ARE YOU SURE IT WAS ABENO SEIMEI?
IT DOESN'T MAKE ANY SENSE!
THERE'S NO RECORD OF ABENO SEIMEI EVER APPEARING AS A SPIRITUAL PROTECTOR OF AN EXORCIST BEFORE!
AND IF...
...THE SHRIMP AND BENIO ADASHINO ARE THE TWIN STARS DESTINED TO PRODUCE THE PROPHESIED CHILD—WHO IS DESTINED TO BE THE REINCARNATION OF ABENO SEIMEI...
SHOULDN'T ABENO SEIMEI BE THE SPIRITUAL PROTECTOR OF THE *CHILD*...?

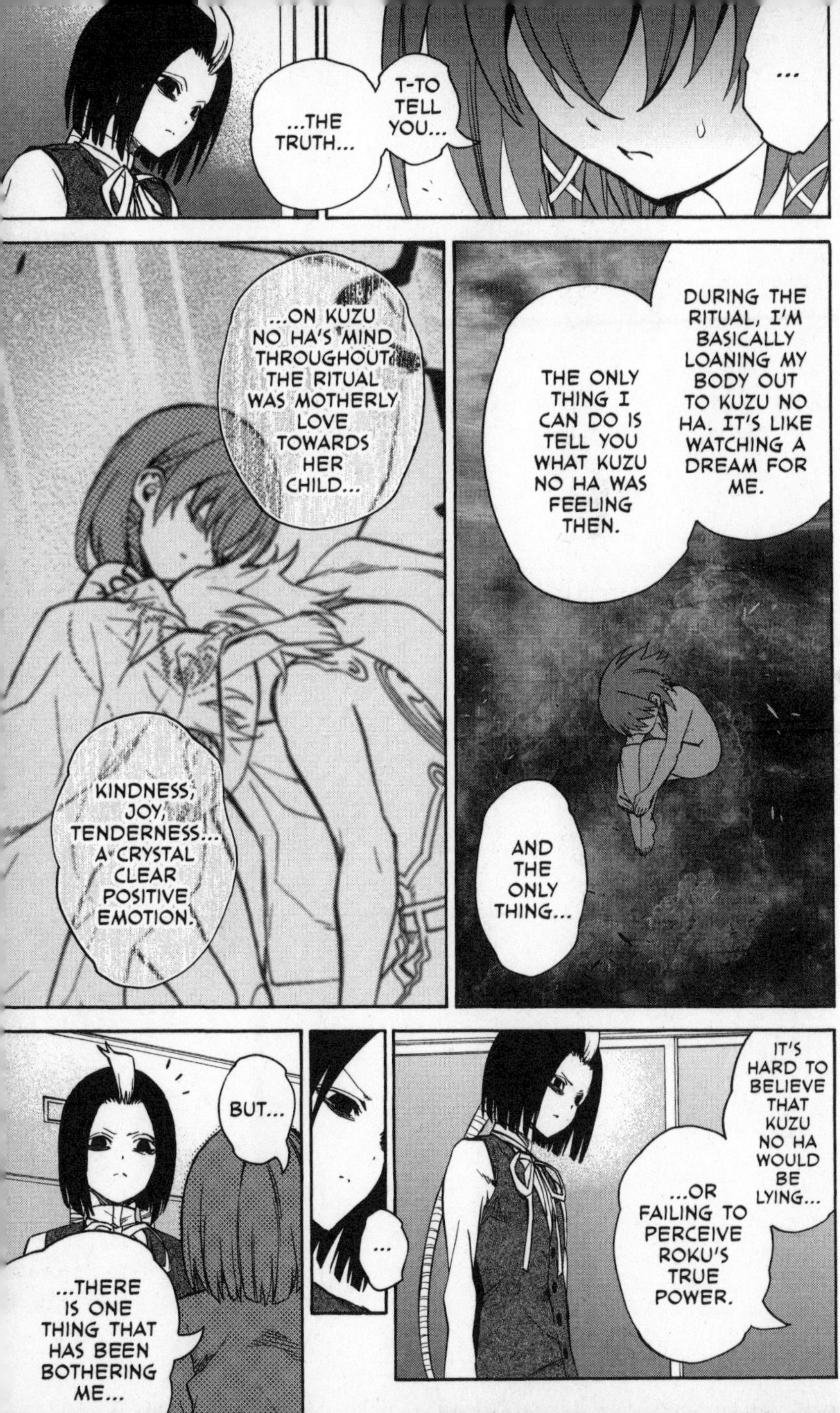
...
T-TO TELL YOU...
...THE TRUTH...
DURING THE RITUAL, I'M BASICALLY LOANING MY BODY OUT TO KUZU NO HA. IT'S LIKE WATCHING A DREAM FOR ME.
THE ONLY THING I CAN DO IS TELL YOU WHAT KUZU NO HA WAS FEELING THEN.
AND THE ONLY THING...
...ON KUZU NO HA'S MIND THROUGHOUT THE RITUAL WAS MOTHERLY LOVE TOWARDS HER CHILD...
KINDNESS, JOY, TENDERNESS... A CRYSTAL CLEAR POSITIVE EMOTION.
IT'S HARD TO BELIEVE THAT KUZU NO HA WOULD BE LYING...
...OR FAILING TO PERCEIVE ROKU'S TRUE POWER.
...
BUT...
...THERE IS ONE THING THAT HAS BEEN BOTHERING ME...

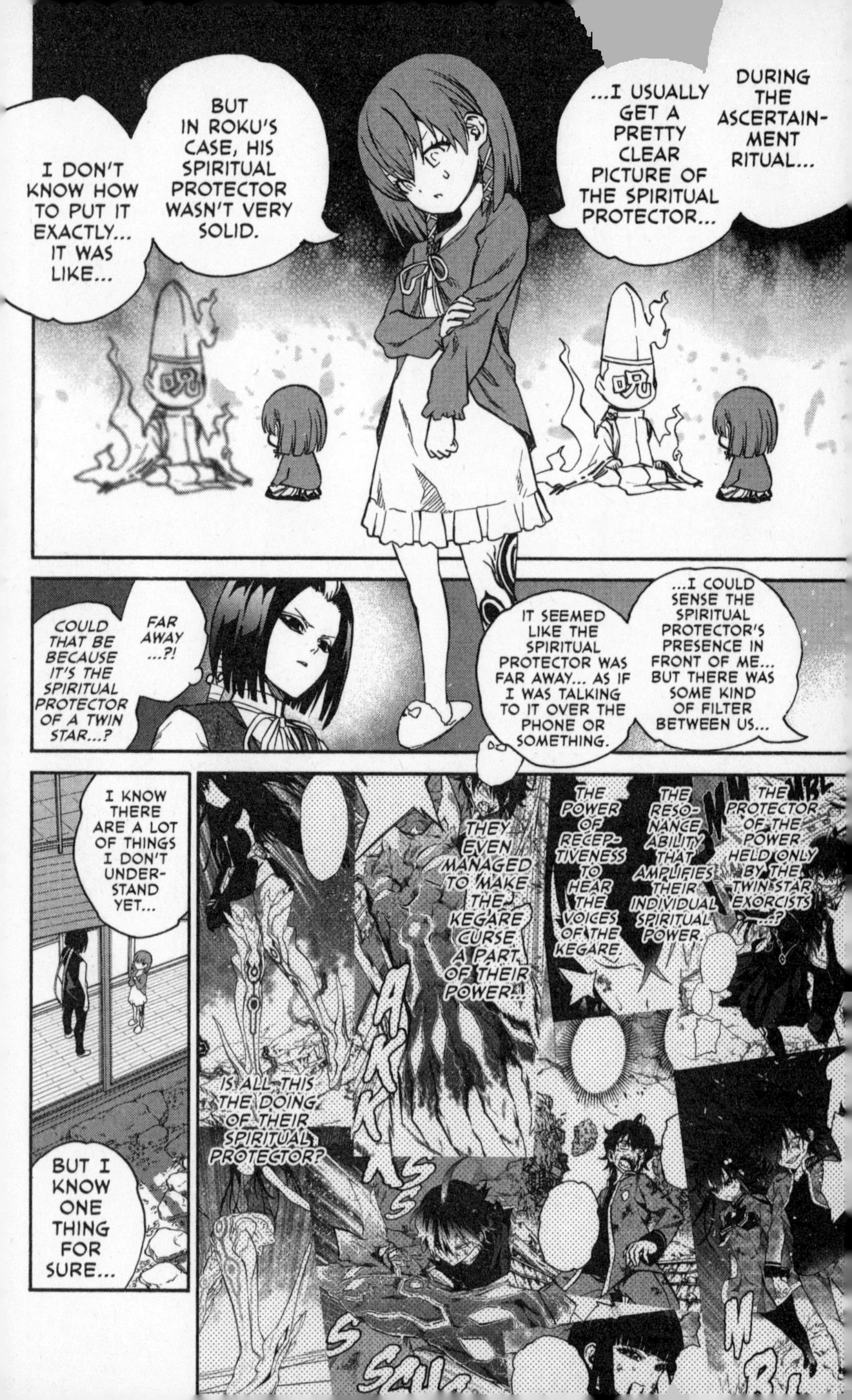
DURING THE ASCERTAINMENT RITUAL...
...I USUALLY GET A PRETTY CLEAR PICTURE OF THE SPIRITUAL PROTECTOR...
BUT IN ROKU'S CASE, HIS SPIRITUAL PROTECTOR WASN'T VERY SOLID.
I DON'T KNOW HOW TO PUT IT EXACTLY... IT WAS LIKE...
...I COULD SENSE THE SPIRITUAL PROTECTOR'S PRESENCE IN FRONT OF ME... BUT THERE WAS SOME KIND OF FILTER BETWEEN US...
IT SEEMED LIKE THE SPIRITUAL PROTECTOR WAS FAR AWAY... AS IF I WAS TALKING TO IT OVER THE PHONE OR SOMETHING.
FAR AWAY ...?!
COULD THAT BE BECAUSE IT'S THE SPIRITUAL PROTECTOR OF A TWIN STAR...?
THE PROTECTOR OF THE POWER HELD ONLY BY THE TWIN STAR EXORCISTS...?
THE RESONANCE ABILITY THAT AMPLIFIES THEIR INDIVIDUAL SPIRITUAL POWER.
THE POWER OF RECEPTIVENESS TO HEAR THE VOICES OF THE KEGARE.
THEY EVEN MANAGED TO MAKE THE KEGARE CURSE A PART OF THEIR POWER..!
IS ALL THIS THE DOING OF THEIR SPIRITUAL PROTECTOR?
I KNOW THERE ARE A LOT OF THINGS I DON'T UNDERSTAND YET...
BUT I KNOW ONE THING FOR SURE...

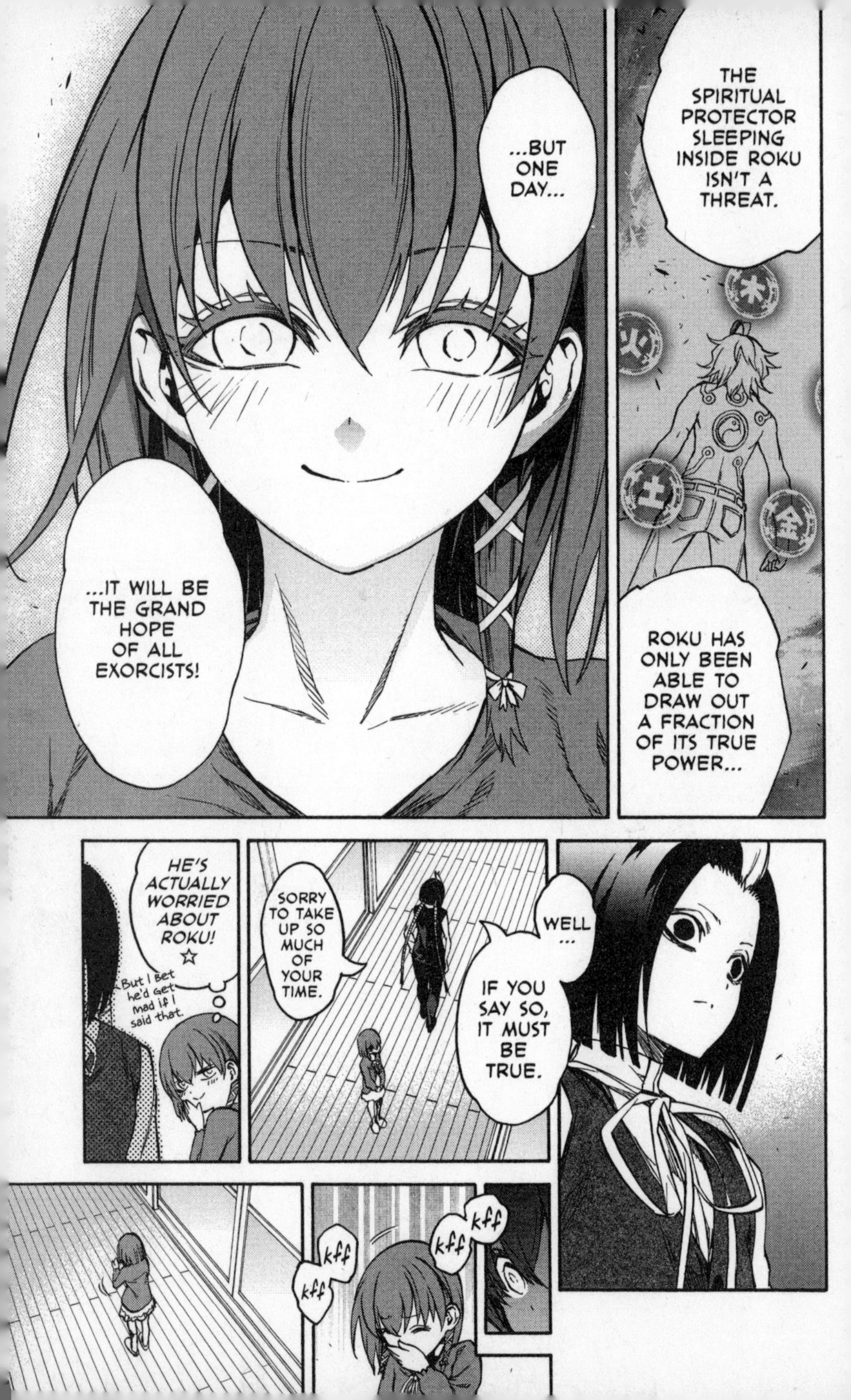
THE SPIRITUAL PROTECTOR SLEEPING INSIDE ROKU ISN'T A THREAT.
ROKU HAS ONLY BEEN ABLE TO DRAW OUT A FRACTION OF ITS TRUE POWER...
...BUT ONE DAY...
...IT WILL BE THE GRAND HOPE OF ALL EXORCISTS!
WELL...
IF YOU SAY SO, IT MUST BE TRUE.
SORRY TO TAKE UP SO MUCH OF YOUR TIME.
HE'S ACTUALLY WORRIED ABOUT ROKU! ☆
But I bet he'd get mad if I said that.
kff
kff
kff
kff

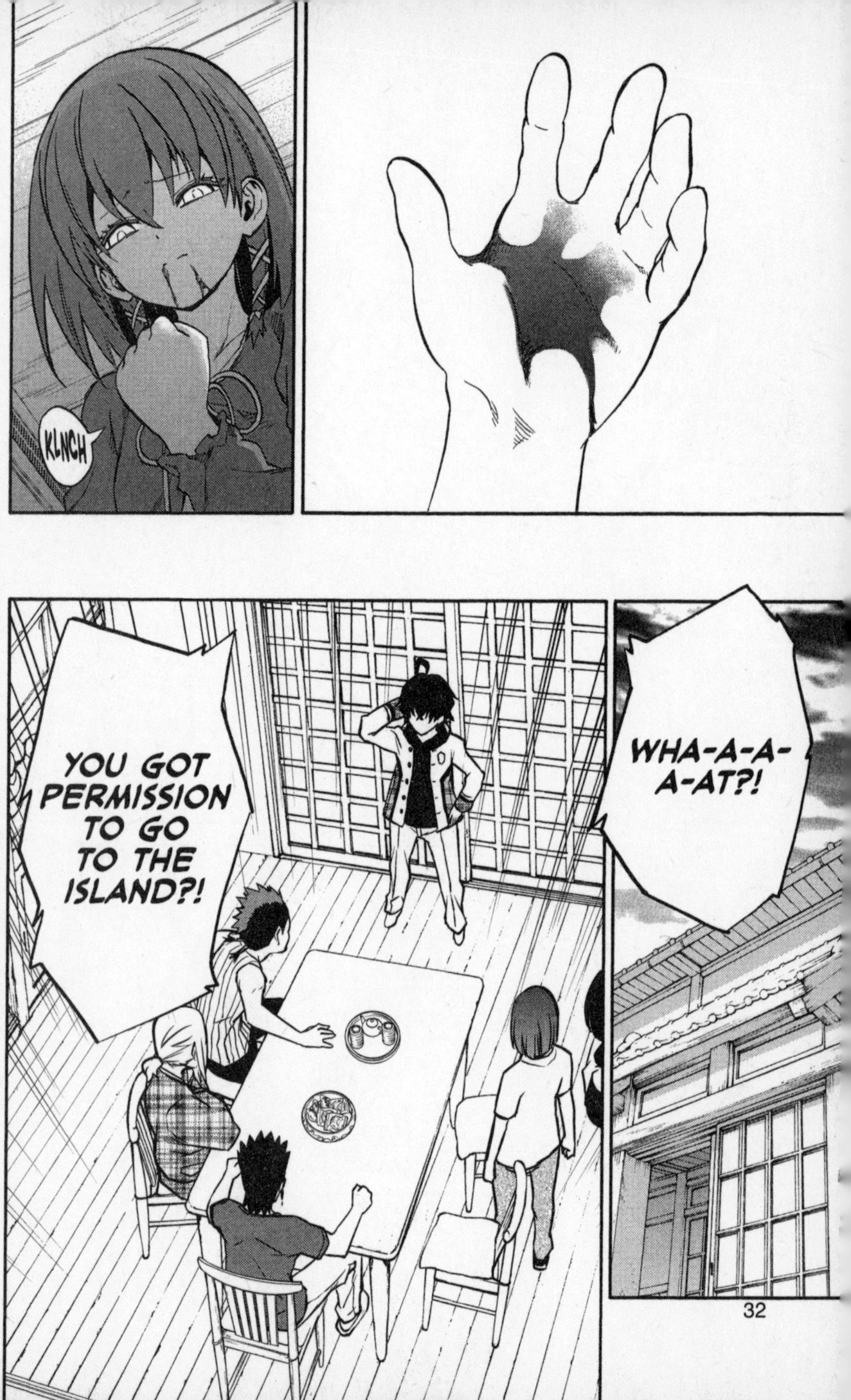
KLNCH
WHA-A-A-A-AT?!
YOU GOT PERMISSION TO GO TO THE ISLAND?!

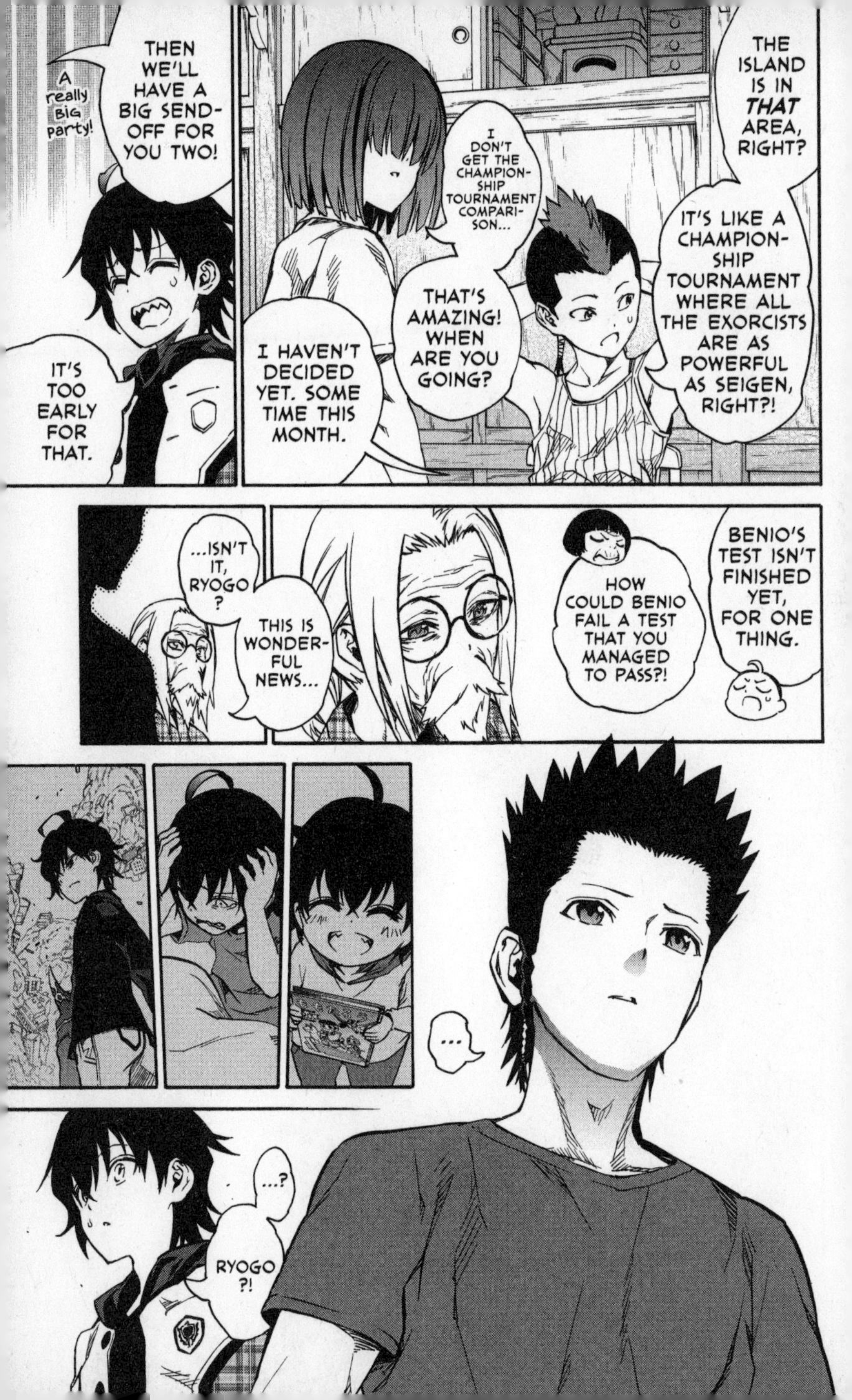
THE ISLAND IS IN *THAT* AREA, RIGHT?
IT'S LIKE A CHAMPIONSHIP TOURNAMENT WHERE ALL THE EXORCISTS ARE AS POWERFUL AS SEIGEN, RIGHT?!
I DON'T GET THE CHAMPIONSHIP TOURNAMENT COMPARISON...
THAT'S AMAZING! WHEN ARE YOU GOING?
I HAVEN'T DECIDED YET. SOME TIME THIS MONTH.
THEN WE'LL HAVE A BIG SEND-OFF FOR YOU TWO!
A really BIG party!
IT'S TOO EARLY FOR THAT.
BENIO'S TEST ISN'T FINISHED YET, FOR ONE THING.
HOW COULD BENIO FAIL A TEST THAT YOU MANAGED TO PASS?!
THIS IS WONDERFUL NEWS...
...ISN'T IT, RYOGO?
...
...?
RYOGO?!

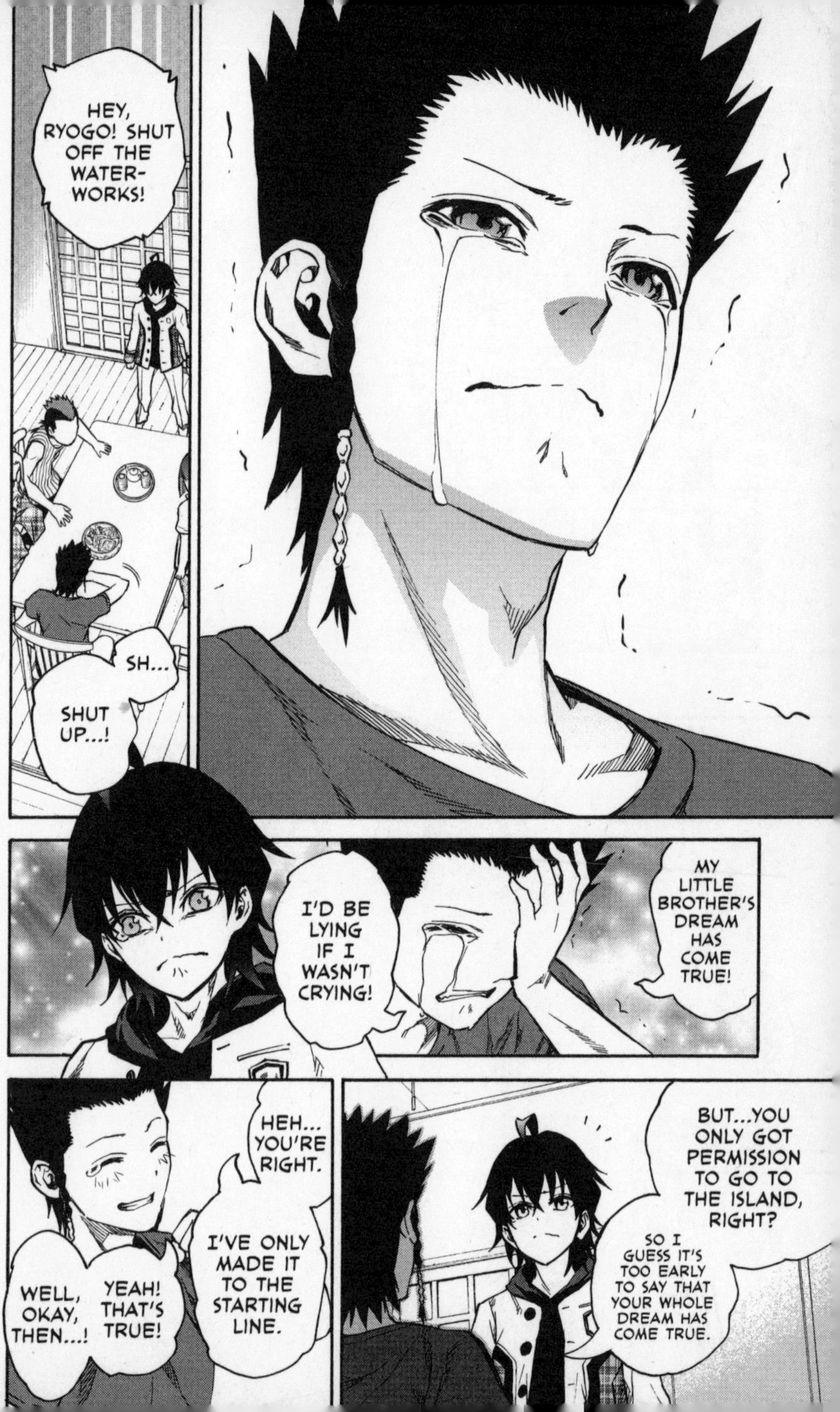
HEY, RYOGO! SHUT OFF THE WATER-WORKS!
SH... SHUT UP...!
MY LITTLE BROTHER'S DREAM HAS COME TRUE!
I'D BE LYING IF I WASN'T CRYING!
BUT...YOU ONLY GOT PERMISSION TO GO TO THE ISLAND, RIGHT?
SO I GUESS IT'S TOO EARLY TO SAY THAT YOUR WHOLE DREAM HAS COME TRUE.
HEH... YOU'RE RIGHT.
I'VE ONLY MADE IT TO THE STARTING LINE.
YEAH! THAT'S TRUE!
WELL, OKAY, THEN...!

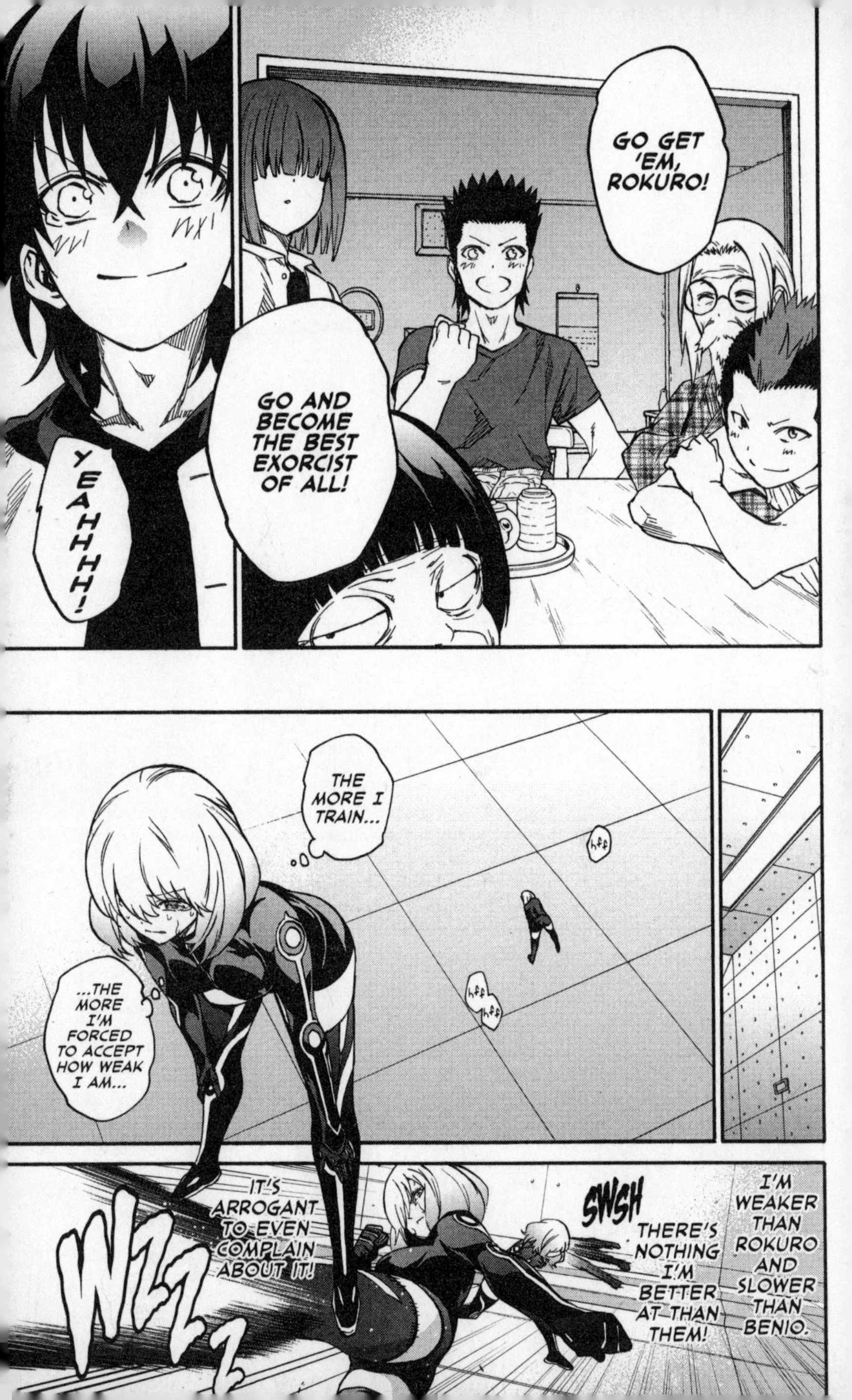
GO GET 'EM, ROKURO!
GO AND BECOME THE BEST EXORCIST OF ALL!
YEAHHHH!
THE MORE I TRAIN...
hff
hff
hff
...THE MORE I'M FORCED TO ACCEPT HOW WEAK I AM...
I'M WEAKER THAN ROKURO AND SLOWER THAN BENIO.
THERE'S NOTHING I'M BETTER AT THAN THEM!
SWSH
IT'S ARROGANT TO EVEN COMPLAIN ABOUT IT!
WZZZ

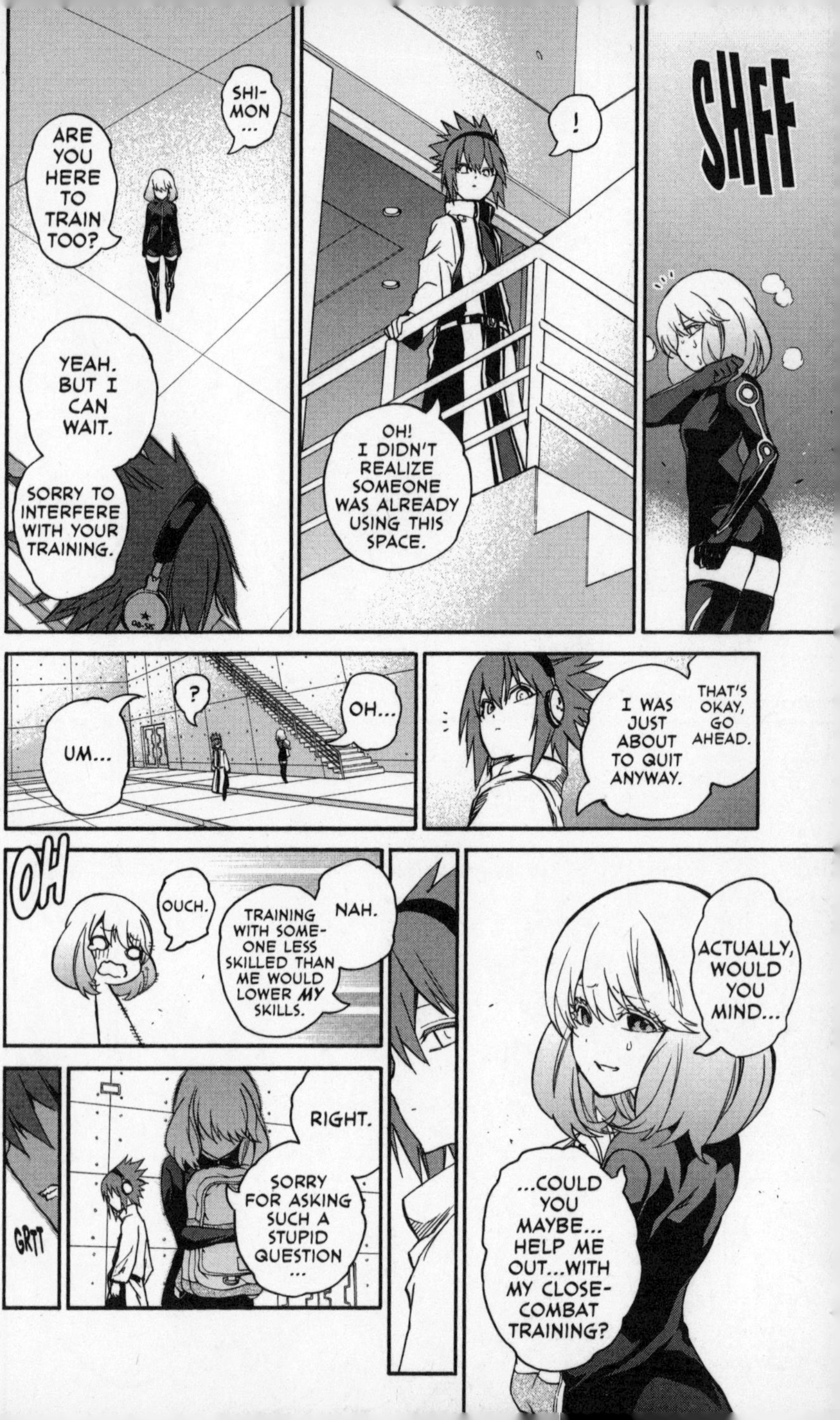
SHFF
!
OH! I DIDN'T REALIZE SOMEONE WAS ALREADY USING THIS SPACE.
SHI-MON...
ARE YOU HERE TO TRAIN TOO?
YEAH. BUT I CAN WAIT.
SORRY TO INTERFERE WITH YOUR TRAINING.
THAT'S OKAY, GO AHEAD.
I WAS JUST ABOUT TO QUIT ANYWAY.
OH...
?
UM...
ACTUALLY, WOULD YOU MIND...
...COULD YOU MAYBE... HELP ME OUT...WITH MY CLOSE-COMBAT TRAINING?
NAH.
TRAINING WITH SOME-ONE LESS SKILLED THAN ME WOULD LOWER *MY* SKILLS.
OUCH.
OH
RIGHT.
SORRY FOR ASKING SUCH A STUPID QUESTION...
GRTT

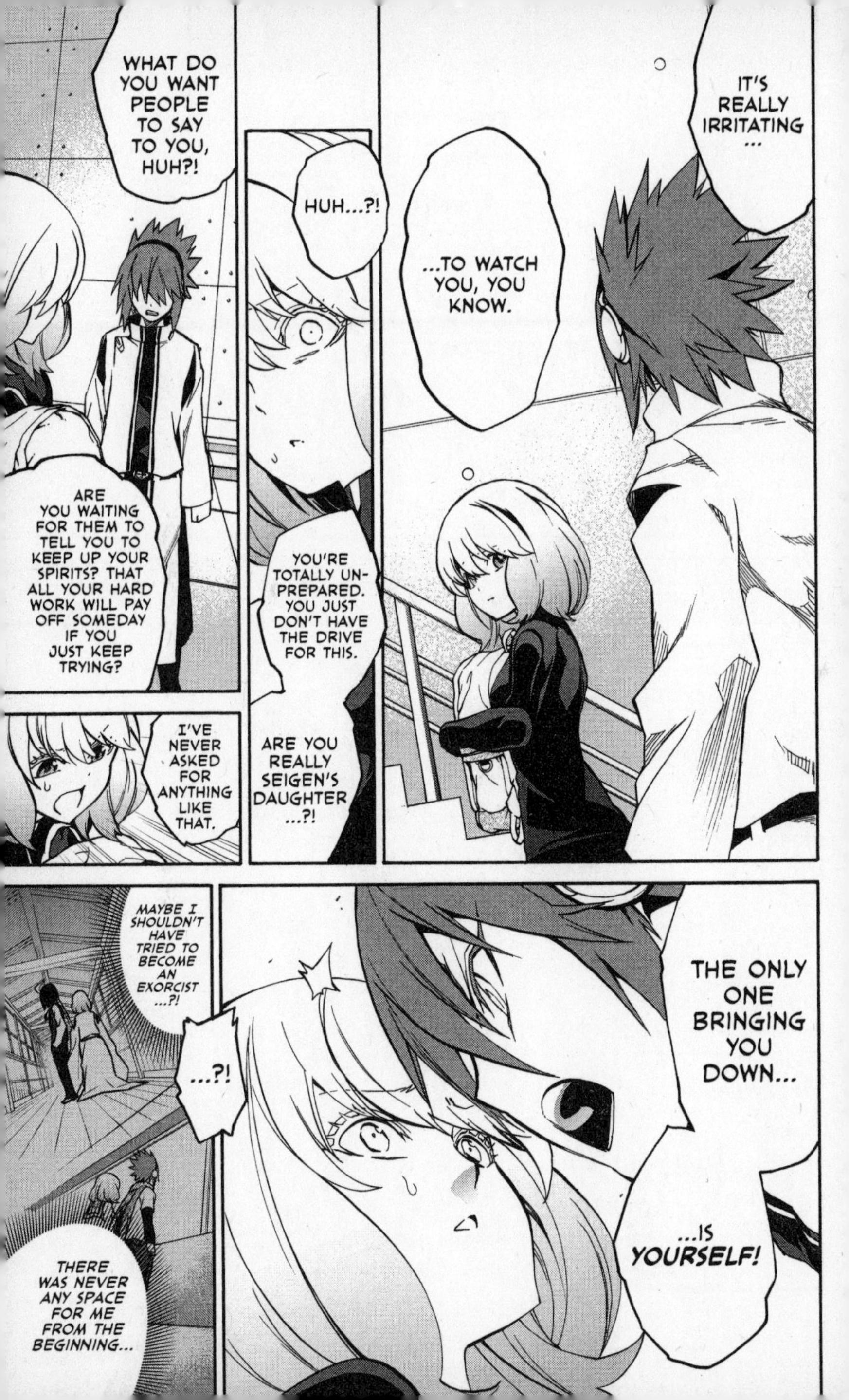
IT'S REALLY IRRITATING...
...TO WATCH YOU, YOU KNOW.
HUH...?!
YOU'RE TOTALLY UN-PREPARED. YOU JUST DON'T HAVE THE DRIVE FOR THIS.
ARE YOU REALLY SEIGEN'S DAUGHTER...?!
WHAT DO YOU WANT PEOPLE TO SAY TO YOU, HUH?!
ARE YOU WAITING FOR THEM TO TELL YOU TO KEEP UP YOUR SPIRITS? THAT ALL YOUR HARD WORK WILL PAY OFF SOMEDAY IF YOU JUST KEEP TRYING?
I'VE NEVER ASKED FOR ANYTHING LIKE THAT.
THE ONLY ONE BRINGING YOU DOWN...
...?!
...IS *YOURSELF!*
MAYBE I SHOULDN'T HAVE TRIED TO BECOME AN EXORCIST...?!
THERE WAS NEVER ANY SPACE FOR ME FROM THE BEGINNING...

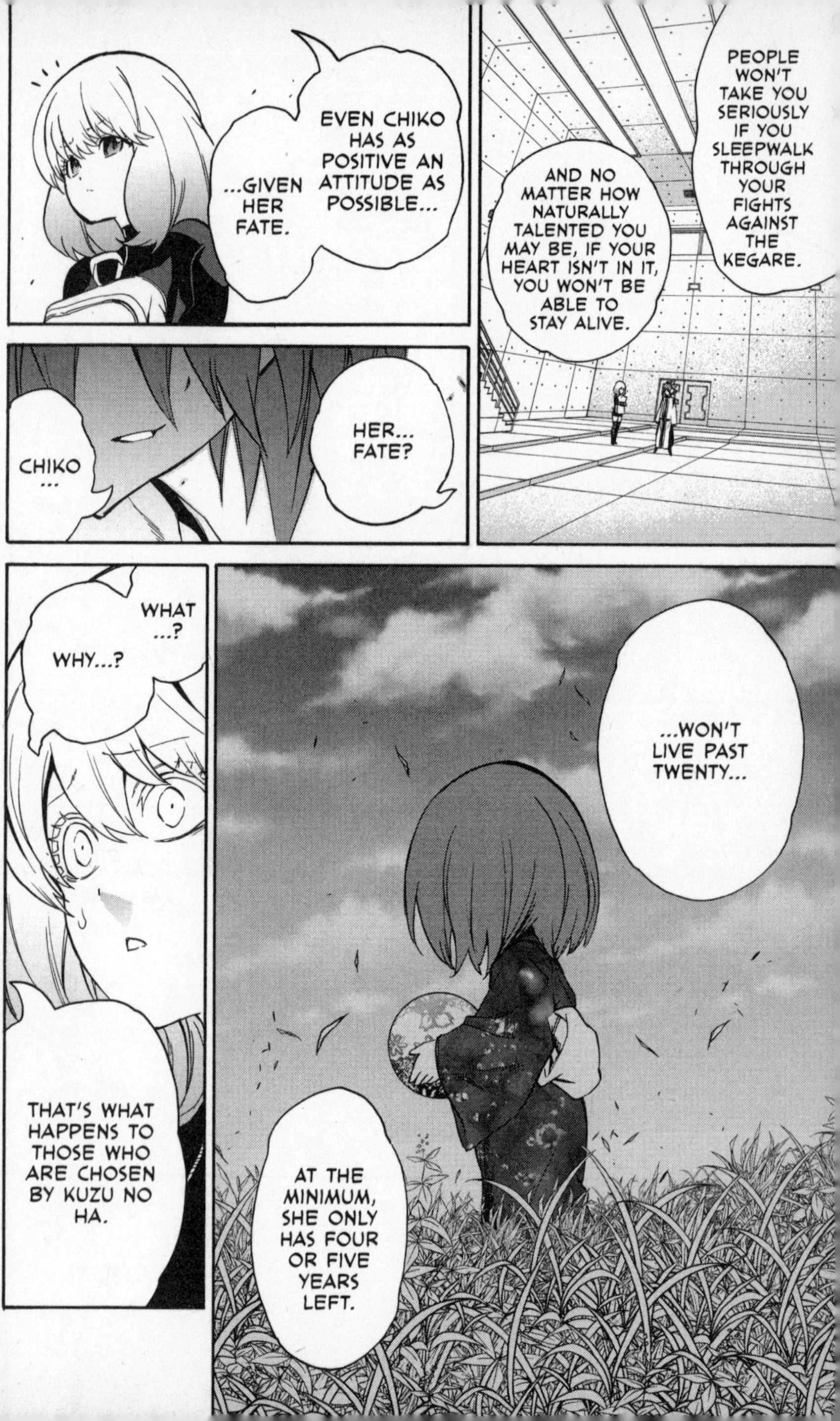
PEOPLE WON'T TAKE YOU SERIOUSLY IF YOU SLEEPWALK THROUGH YOUR FIGHTS AGAINST THE KEGARE.
AND NO MATTER HOW NATURALLY TALENTED YOU MAY BE, IF YOUR HEART ISN'T IN IT, YOU WON'T BE ABLE TO STAY ALIVE.
EVEN CHIKO HAS AS POSITIVE AN ATTITUDE AS POSSIBLE...
...GIVEN HER FATE.
HER... FATE?
CHIKO...
...WON'T LIVE PAST TWENTY...
AT THE MINIMUM, SHE ONLY HAS FOUR OR FIVE YEARS LEFT.
WHAT...?
WHY...?
THAT'S WHAT HAPPENS TO THOSE WHO ARE CHOSEN BY KUZU NO HA.

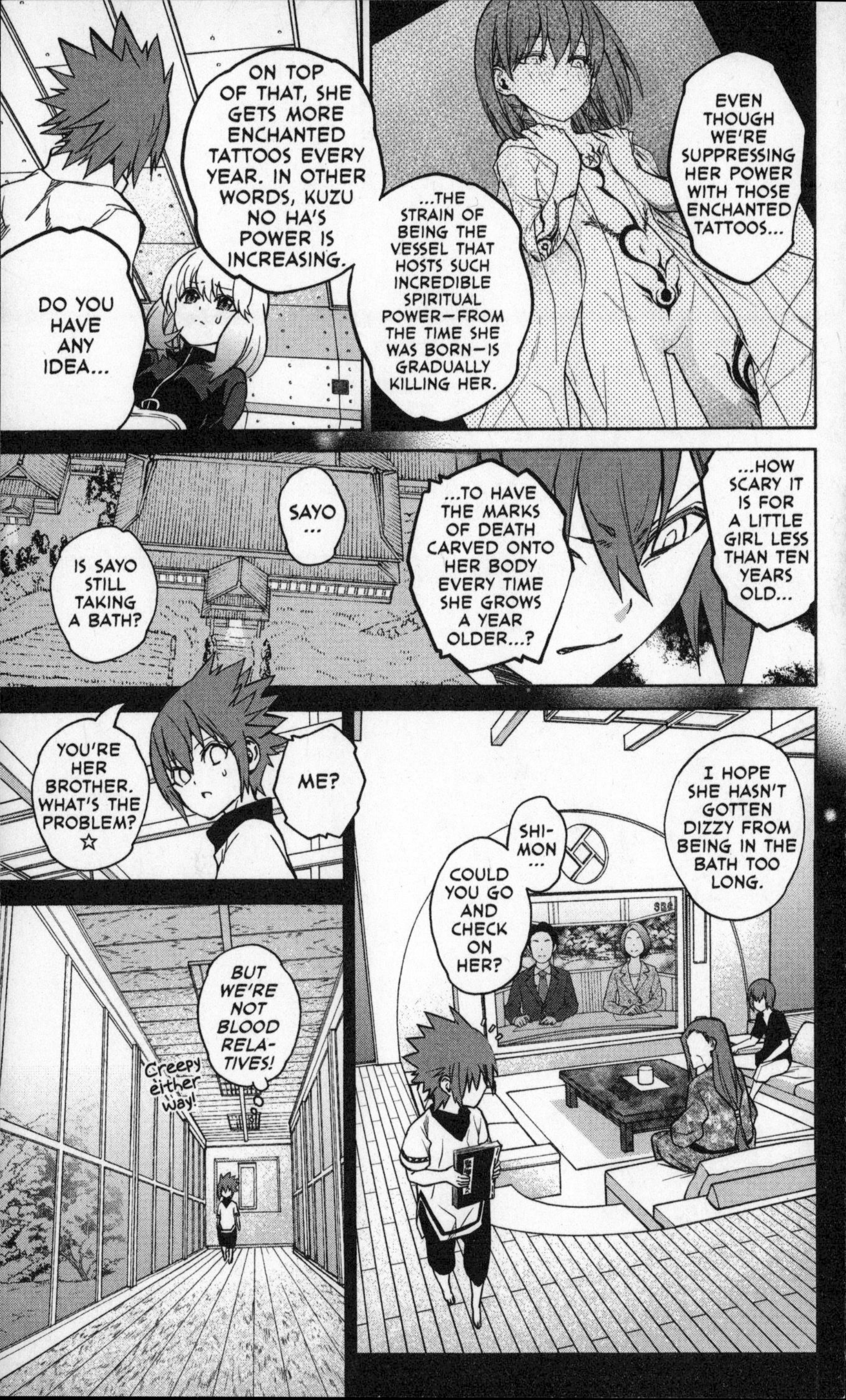
EVEN THOUGH WE'RE SUPPRESSING HER POWER WITH THOSE ENCHANTED TATTOOS...
...THE STRAIN OF BEING THE VESSEL THAT HOSTS SUCH INCREDIBLE SPIRITUAL POWER—FROM THE TIME SHE WAS BORN—IS GRADUALLY KILLING HER.
ON TOP OF THAT, SHE GETS MORE ENCHANTED TATTOOS EVERY YEAR. IN OTHER WORDS, KUZU NO HA'S POWER IS INCREASING.
DO YOU HAVE ANY IDEA...
...HOW SCARY IT IS FOR A LITTLE GIRL LESS THAN TEN YEARS OLD...
...TO HAVE THE MARKS OF DEATH CARVED ONTO HER BODY EVERY TIME SHE GROWS A YEAR OLDER...?
SAYO...
IS SAYO STILL TAKING A BATH?
I HOPE SHE HASN'T GOTTEN DIZZY FROM BEING IN THE BATH TOO LONG.
SHI-MON...
COULD YOU GO AND CHECK ON HER?
ME?
YOU'RE HER BROTHER. WHAT'S THE PROBLEM? ☆
BUT WE'RE NOT BLOOD RELATIVES!
Creepy either way!

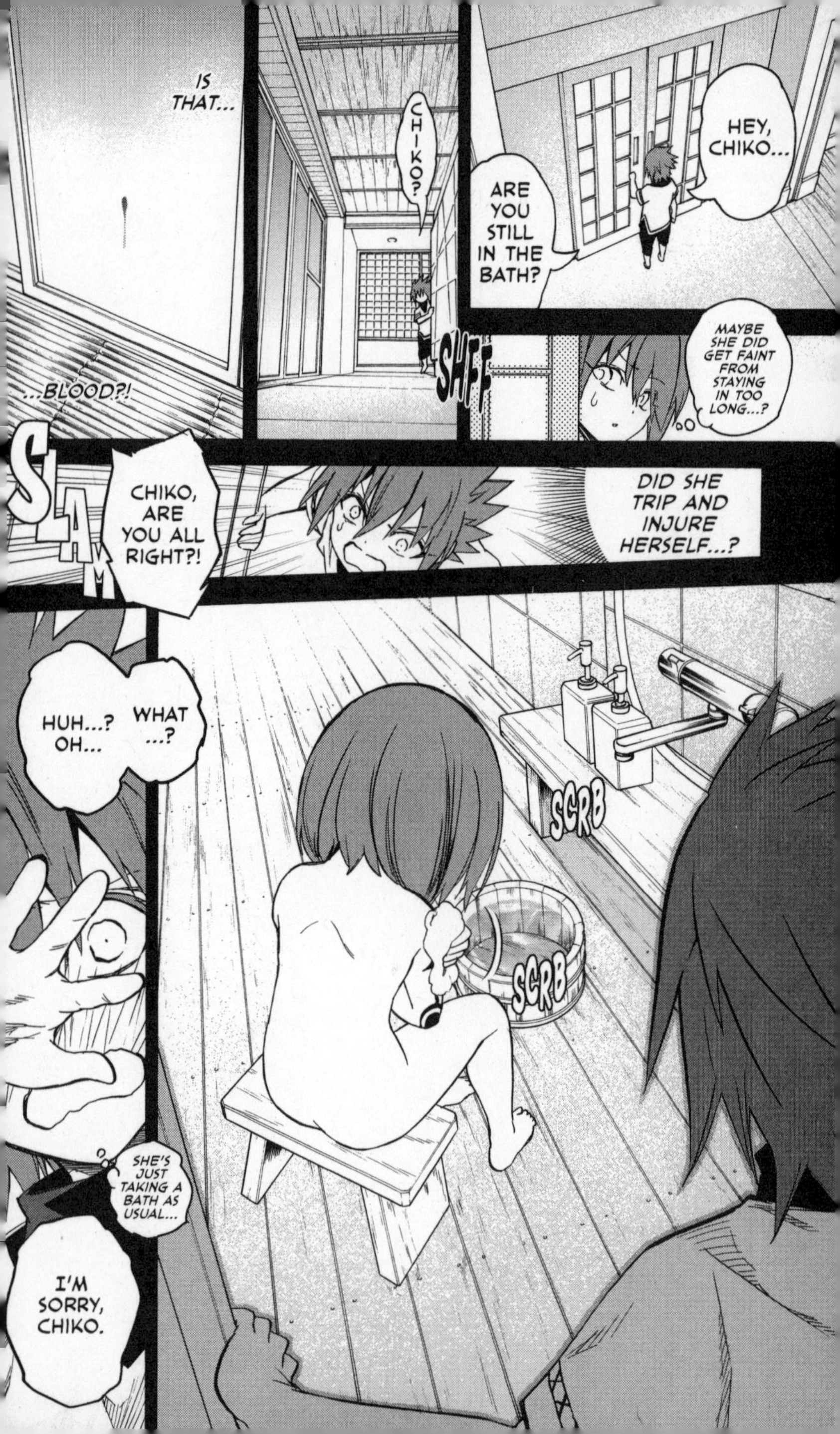
HEY, CHIKO...
ARE YOU STILL IN THE BATH?
MAYBE SHE DID GET FAINT FROM STAYING IN TOO LONG...?
CHIKO?
SHFF
IS THAT...
...BLOOD?!
DID SHE TRIP AND INJURE HERSELF...?
CHIKO, ARE YOU ALL RIGHT?!
SLAM
SCRB
SCRB
WHAT ...?
HUH...? OH...
SHE'S JUST TAKING A BATH AS USUAL...
I'M SORRY, CHIKO.

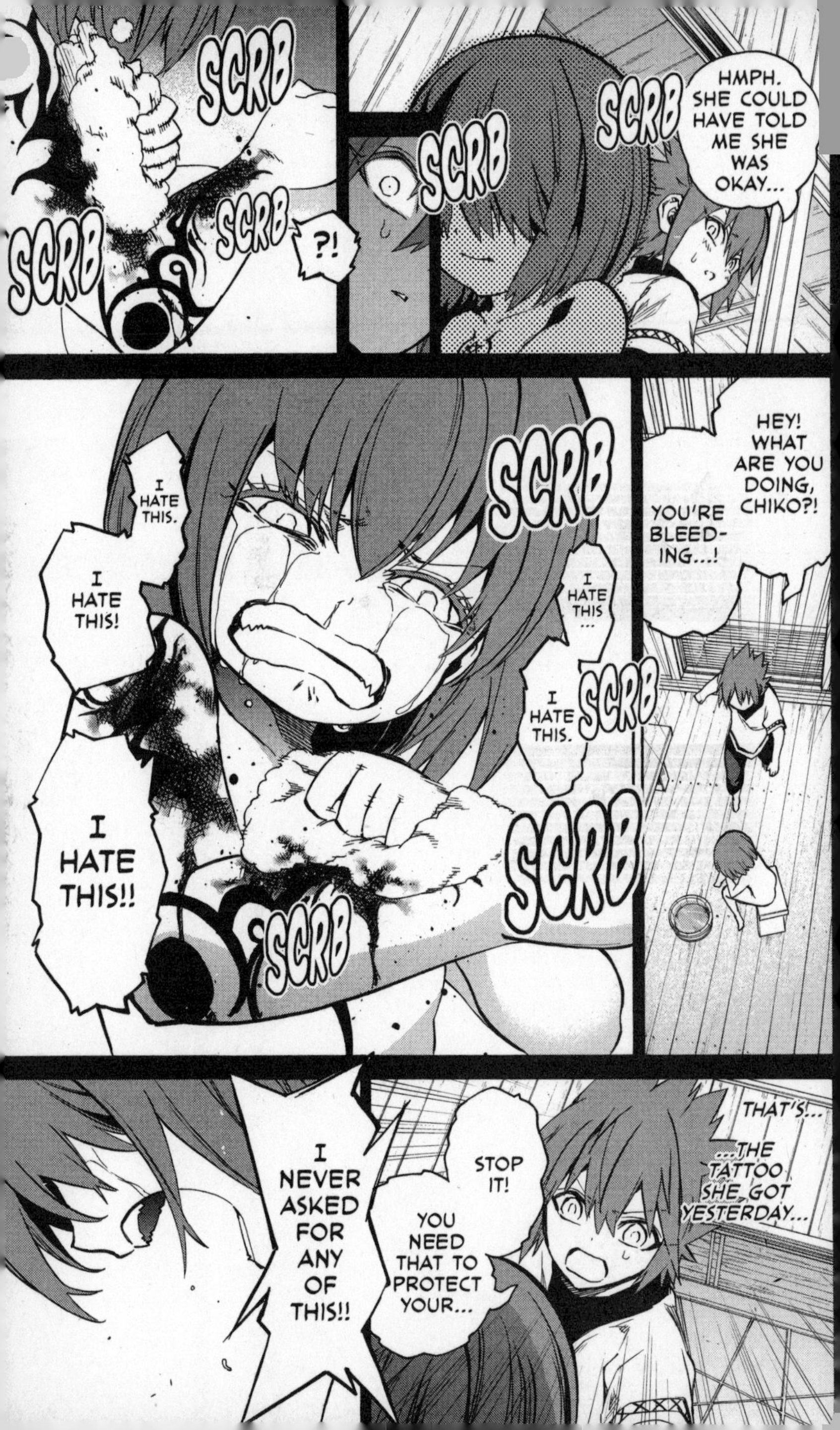
HMPH. SHE COULD HAVE TOLD ME SHE WAS OKAY...
SCRB
SCRB
?!
SCRB
SCRB
SCRB
HEY! WHAT ARE YOU DOING, CHIKO?!
YOU'RE BLEED-ING...!
SCRB
I HATE THIS...
I HATE THIS.
SCRB
SCRB
I HATE THIS.
I HATE THIS!
I HATE THIS!!
SCRB
THAT'S...
...THE TATTOO SHE GOT YESTERDAY...
STOP IT!
YOU NEED THAT TO PROTECT YOUR...
I NEVER ASKED FOR ANY OF THIS!!

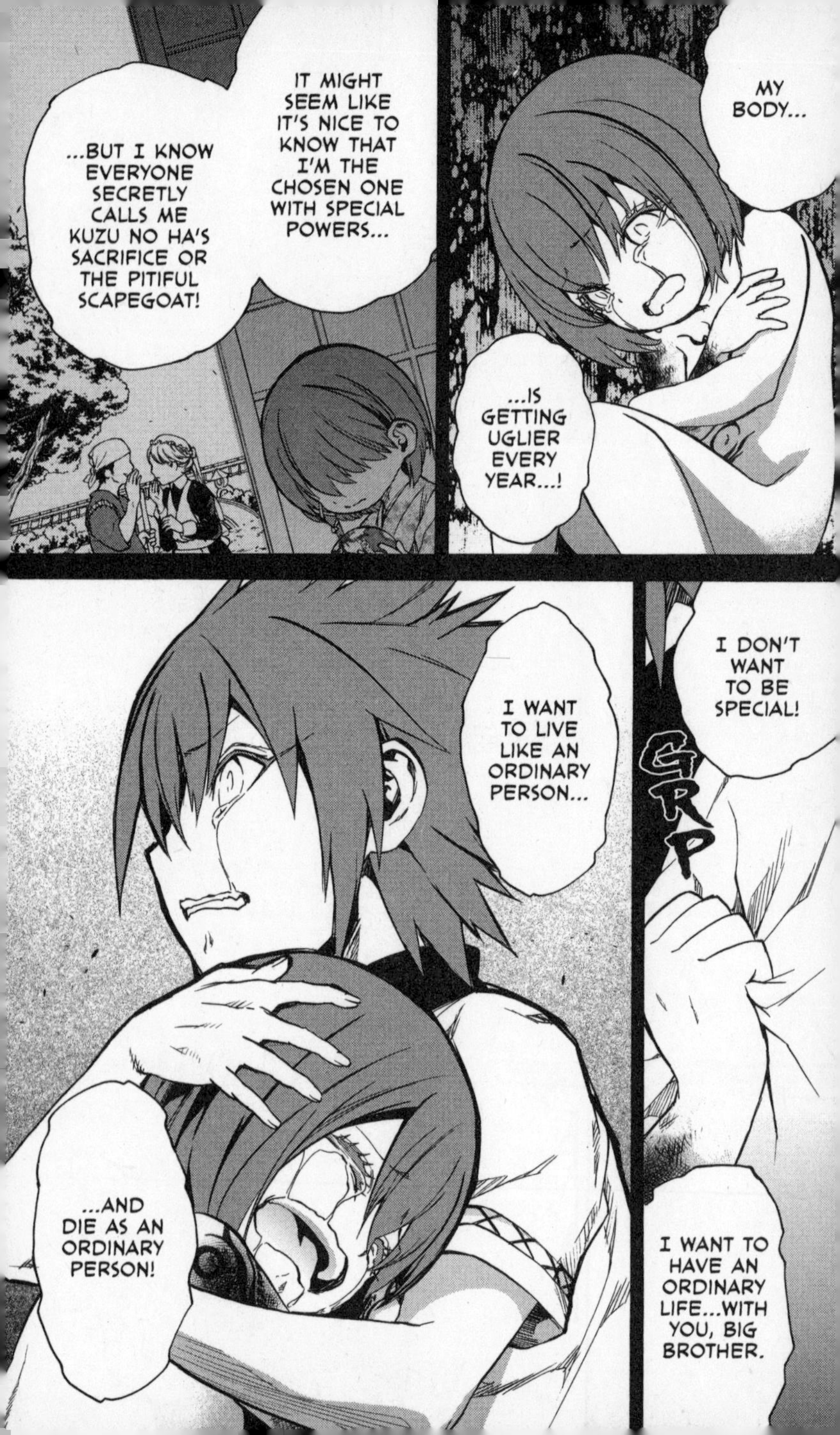
MY BODY...
...IS GETTING UGLIER EVERY YEAR...!
IT MIGHT SEEM LIKE IT'S NICE TO KNOW THAT I'M THE CHOSEN ONE WITH SPECIAL POWERS...
...BUT I KNOW EVERYONE SECRETLY CALLS ME KUZU NO HA'S SACRIFICE OR THE PITIFUL SCAPEGOAT!
I DON'T WANT TO BE SPECIAL!
GRP
I WANT TO HAVE AN ORDINARY LIFE...WITH YOU, BIG BROTHER.
I WANT TO LIVE LIKE AN ORDINARY PERSON...
...AND DIE AS AN ORDINARY PERSON!

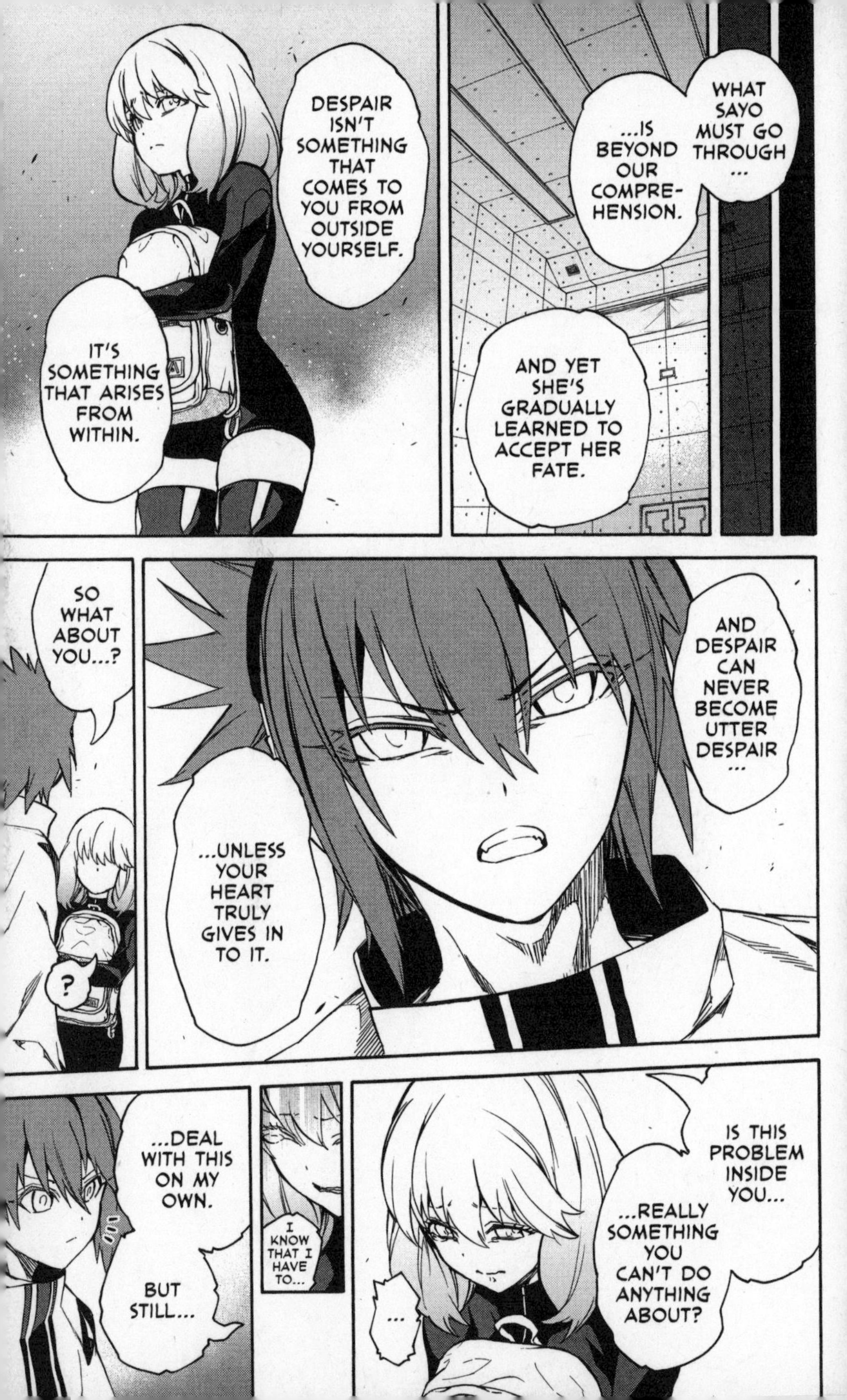
WHAT SAYO MUST GO THROUGH...
...IS BEYOND OUR COMPREHENSION.
AND YET SHE'S GRADUALLY LEARNED TO ACCEPT HER FATE.
DESPAIR ISN'T SOMETHING THAT COMES TO YOU FROM OUTSIDE YOURSELF.
IT'S SOMETHING THAT ARISES FROM WITHIN.
AND DESPAIR CAN NEVER BECOME UTTER DESPAIR...
...UNLESS YOUR HEART TRULY GIVES IN TO IT.
SO WHAT ABOUT YOU...?
?
IS THIS PROBLEM INSIDE YOU...
...REALLY SOMETHING YOU CAN'T DO ANYTHING ABOUT?
...
I KNOW THAT I HAVE TO...
...DEAL WITH THIS ON MY OWN.
BUT STILL...

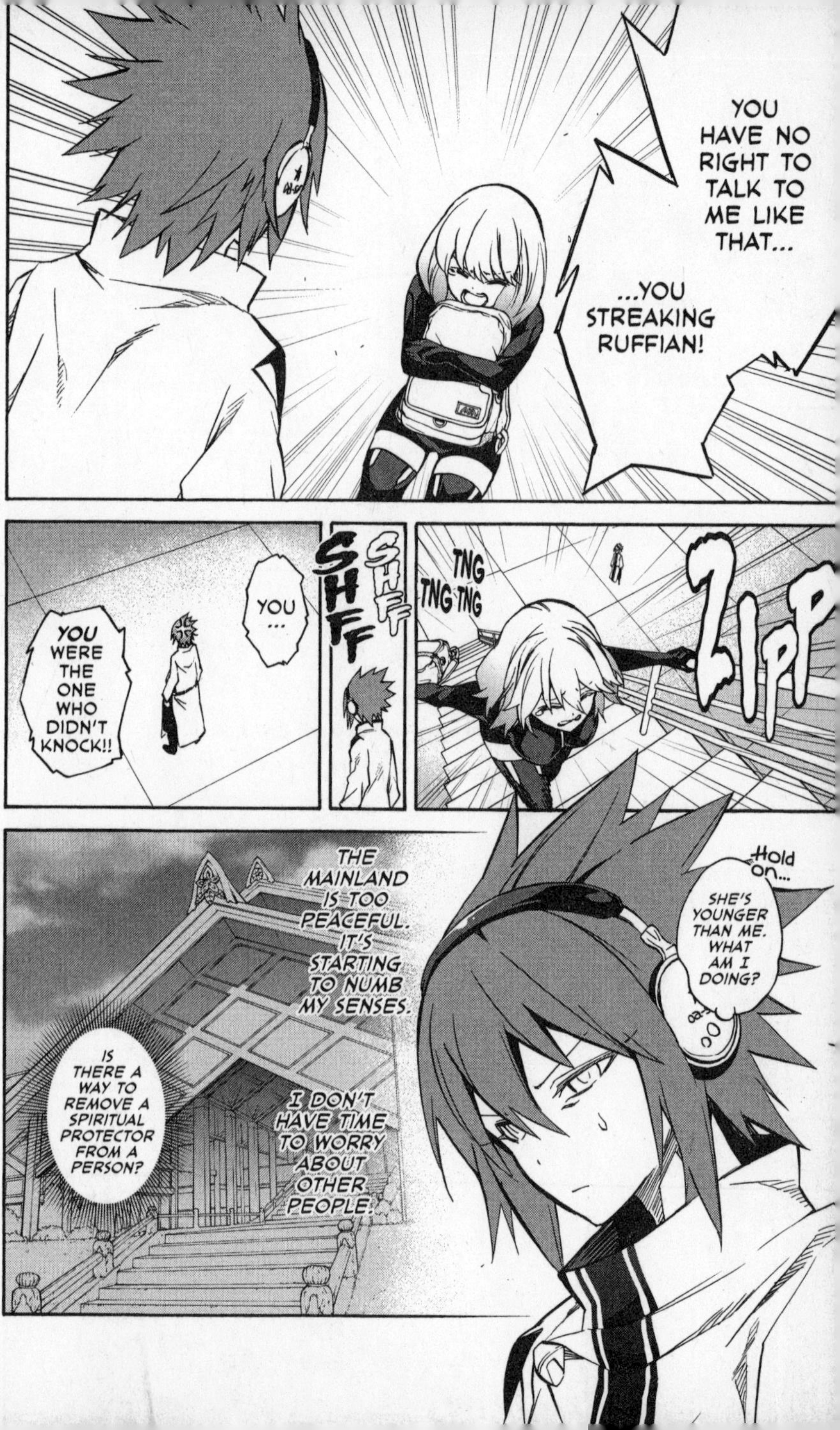
YOU HAVE NO RIGHT TO TALK TO ME LIKE THAT...
...YOU STREAKING RUFFIAN!
TNG TNG TNG
ZIPP
SHFF SHFF
YOU ...
YOU WERE THE ONE WHO DIDN'T KNOCK!!
Hold on...
SHE'S YOUNGER THAN ME. WHAT AM I DOING?
THE MAINLAND IS TOO PEACEFUL. IT'S STARTING TO NUMB MY SENSES.
I DON'T HAVE TIME TO WORRY ABOUT OTHER PEOPLE.
IS THERE A WAY TO REMOVE A SPIRITUAL PROTECTOR FROM A PERSON?

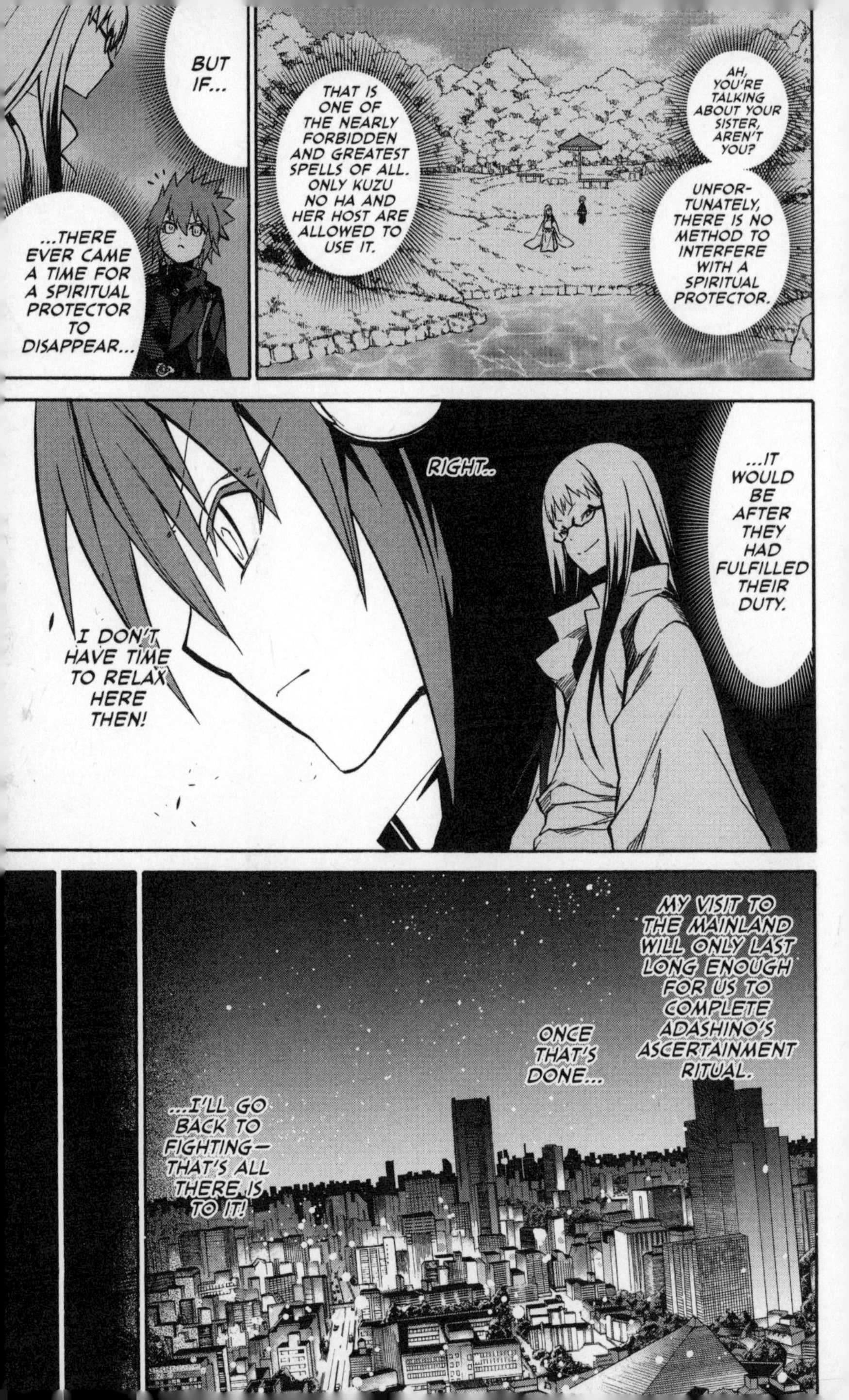
AH, YOU'RE TALKING ABOUT YOUR SISTER, AREN'T YOU?
UNFOR-TUNATELY, THERE IS NO METHOD TO INTERFERE WITH A SPIRITUAL PROTECTOR.
THAT IS ONE OF THE NEARLY FORBIDDEN AND GREATEST SPELLS OF ALL. ONLY KUZU NO HA AND HER HOST ARE ALLOWED TO USE IT.
BUT IF...
...THERE EVER CAME A TIME FOR A SPIRITUAL PROTECTOR TO DISAPPEAR...
...IT WOULD BE AFTER THEY HAD FULFILLED THEIR DUTY.
RIGHT..
I DON'T HAVE TIME TO RELAX HERE THEN!
MY VISIT TO THE MAINLAND WILL ONLY LAST LONG ENOUGH FOR US TO COMPLETE ADASHINO'S ASCERTAINMENT RITUAL.
ONCE THAT'S DONE...
...I'LL GO BACK TO FIGHTING—THAT'S ALL THERE IS TO IT!

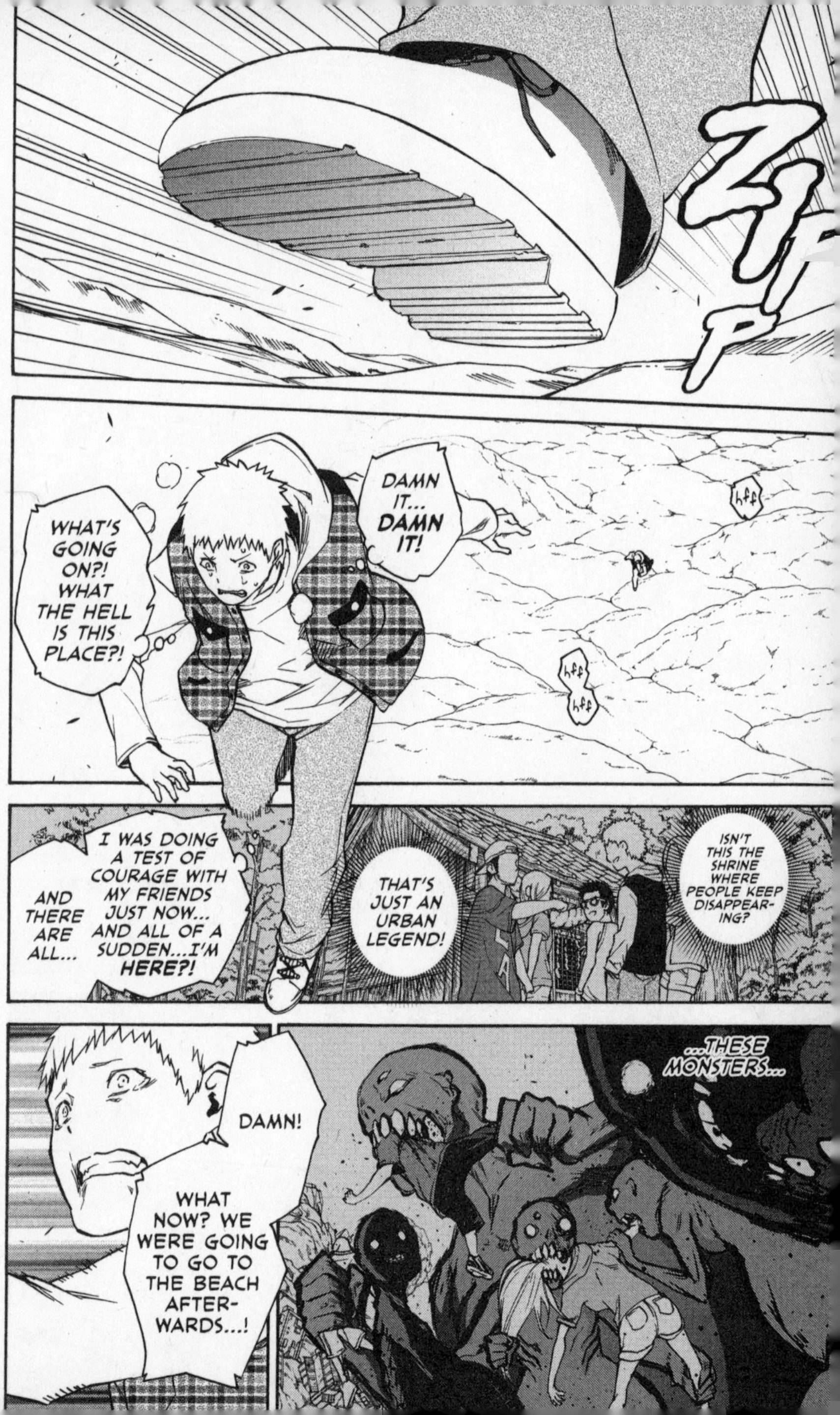
ZIP
DAMN IT... DAMN IT!
WHAT'S GOING ON?! WHAT THE HELL IS THIS PLACE?!
hff
hff
hff
I WAS DOING A TEST OF COURAGE WITH MY FRIENDS JUST NOW... AND ALL OF A SUDDEN...I'M HERE?!
ISN'T THIS THE SHRINE WHERE PEOPLE KEEP DISAPPEAR-ING?
THAT'S JUST AN URBAN LEGEND!
AND THERE ARE ALL...
...THESE MONSTERS...
DAMN!
WHAT NOW? WE WERE GOING TO GO TO THE BEACH AFTER-WARDS...!

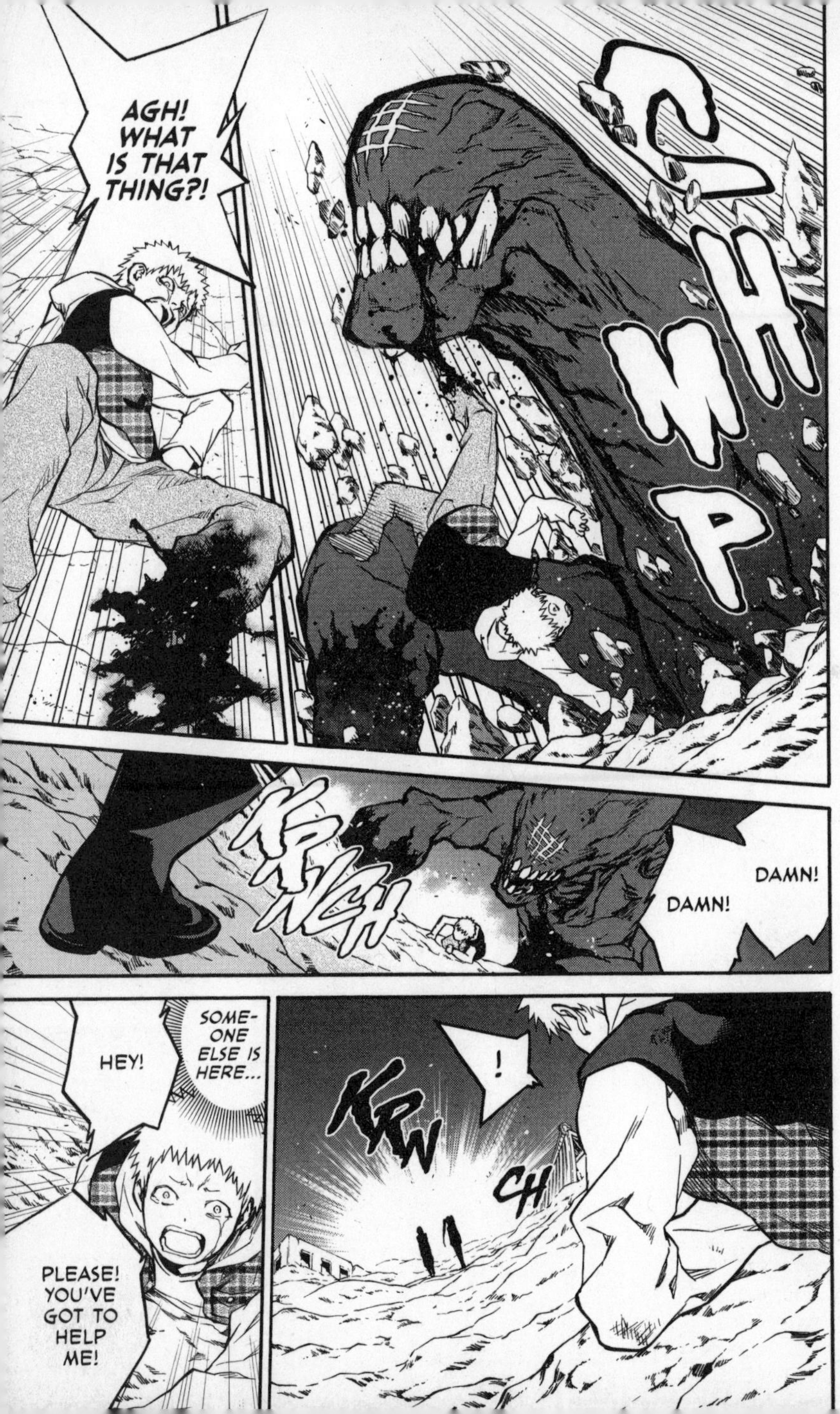
CHOMP
AGH! WHAT IS THAT THING?!
DAMN!
DAMN!
KRUNCH
!
KRUNCH
SOME-ONE ELSE IS HERE...
HEY!
PLEASE! YOU'VE GOT TO HELP ME!

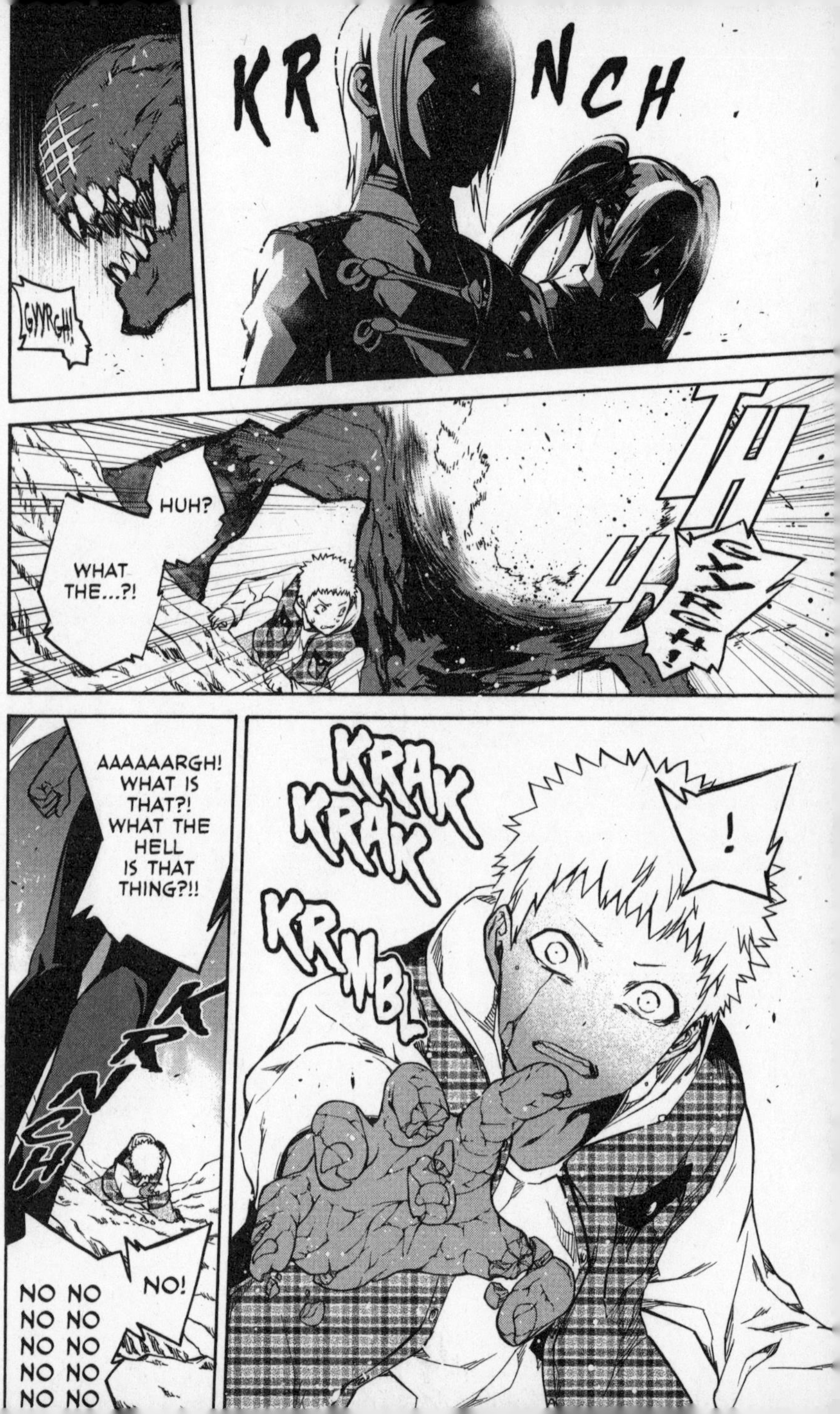
KR NCH
GYYRGH!
TH
U
GYYAAH!!
HUH?
WHAT THE...?!
!
KRAK KRAK
KRMBL
AAAAAARGH! WHAT IS THAT?! WHAT THE HELL IS THAT THING?!!
NRK
CH
NO!
NO NO NO NO NO NO NO NO NO NO

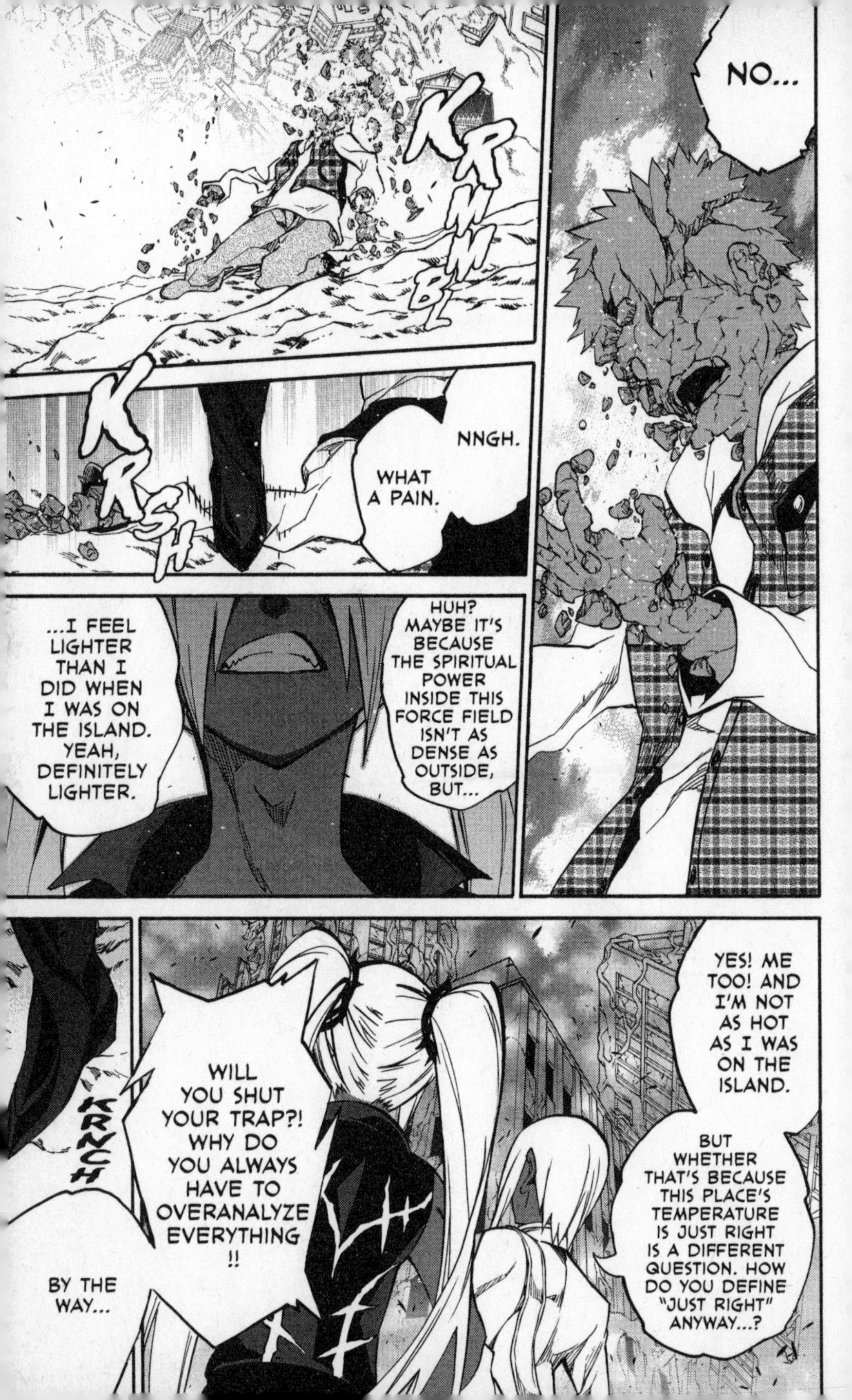
NO...
KRMMBL
KRSH
NNGH.
WHAT A PAIN.
HUH? MAYBE IT'S BECAUSE THE SPIRITUAL POWER INSIDE THIS FORCE FIELD ISN'T AS DENSE AS OUTSIDE, BUT...
...I FEEL LIGHTER THAN I DID WHEN I WAS ON THE ISLAND. YEAH, DEFINITELY LIGHTER.
YES! ME TOO! AND I'M NOT AS HOT AS I WAS ON THE ISLAND.
BUT WHETHER THAT'S BECAUSE THIS PLACE'S TEMPERATURE IS JUST RIGHT IS A DIFFERENT QUESTION. HOW DO YOU DEFINE "JUST RIGHT" ANYWAY...?
WILL YOU SHUT YOUR TRAP?! WHY DO YOU ALWAYS HAVE TO OVERANALYZE EVERYTHING!!
KRNCH
BY THE WAY...

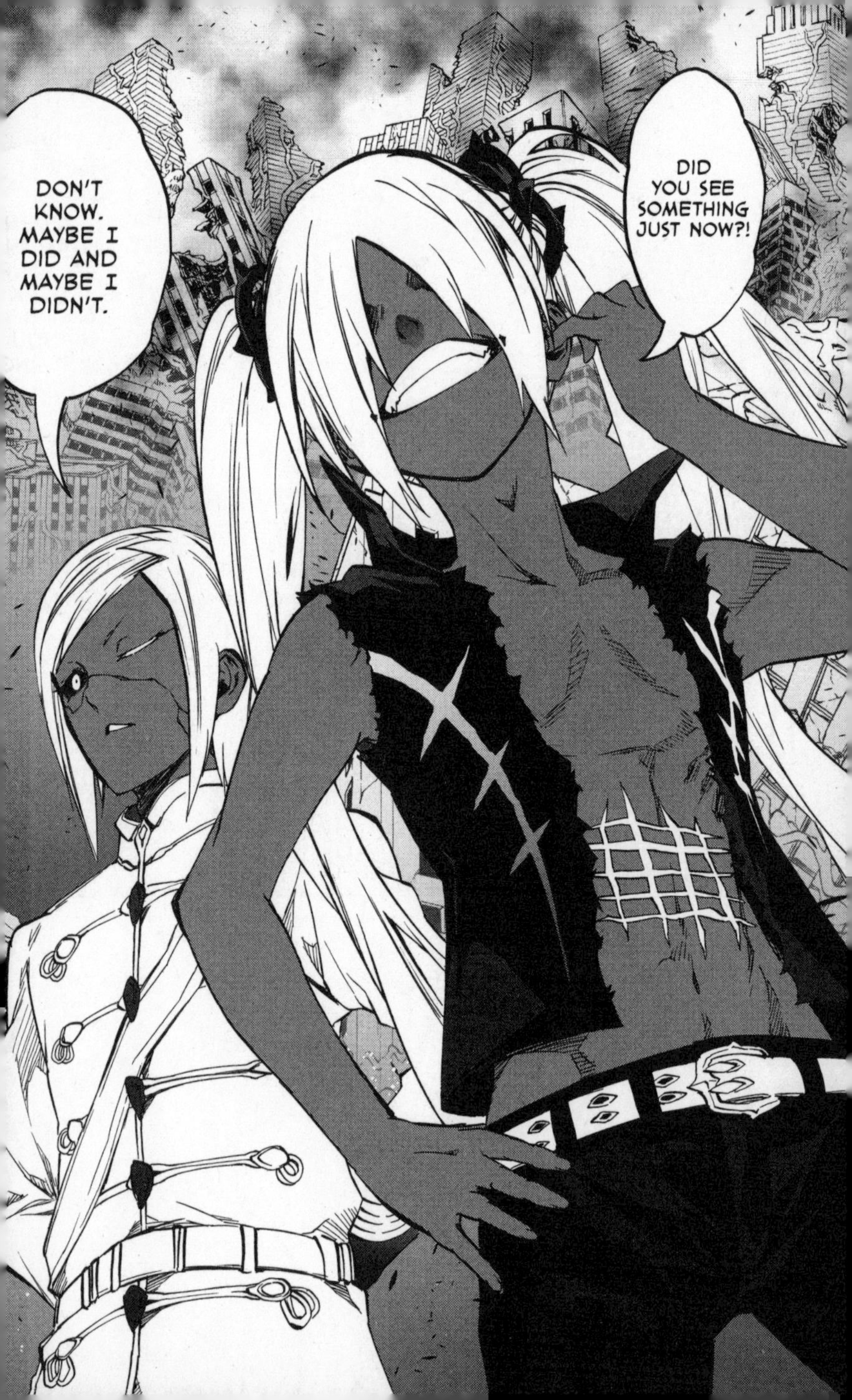
DID YOU SEE SOMETHING JUST NOW?!
DON'T KNOW. MAYBE I DID AND MAYBE I DIDN'T.

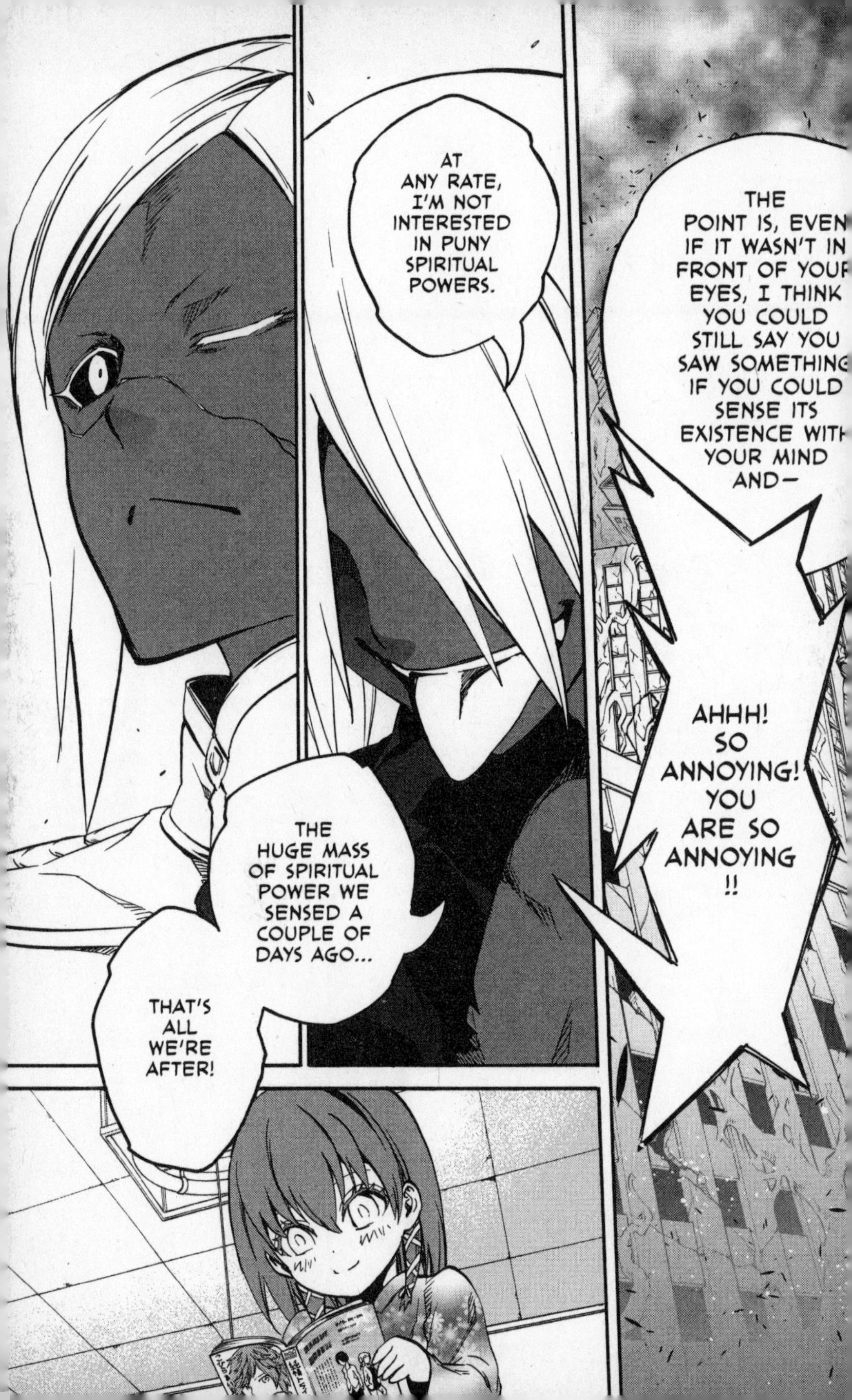
THE POINT IS, EVEN IF IT WASN'T IN FRONT OF YOUR EYES, I THINK YOU COULD STILL SAY YOU SAW SOMETHING IF YOU COULD SENSE ITS EXISTENCE WITH YOUR MIND AND—
AHHH! SO ANNOYING! YOU ARE SO ANNOYING !!
AT ANY RATE, I'M NOT INTERESTED IN PUNY SPIRITUAL POWERS.
THE HUGE MASS OF SPIRITUAL POWER WE SENSED A COUPLE OF DAYS AGO...
THAT'S ALL WE'RE AFTER!

Column ⑮ Kuzu no Ha

I've talked a little bit about her in the story already. She's Abeno Seimei's mother. Legend has it that Abeno Yasuna saved Kuzu no Ha from a thug when she was in mortal form. They fell in love and had a child, and that child was Seimei. Then again, this is based on books and entertainments of that time, so some say the story about Seimei being the child of a fox is a work of fiction. Well, obviously.

However, while there are many stories about the mother being a fox, there are no records of Seimei's real mother in historical documents, so perhaps a huge secret was being obfuscated? And if his mother really was a fox, it could mean that if you removed the *eboshi* hat that he is often seen wearing in images...you would see furry fox ears underneath!

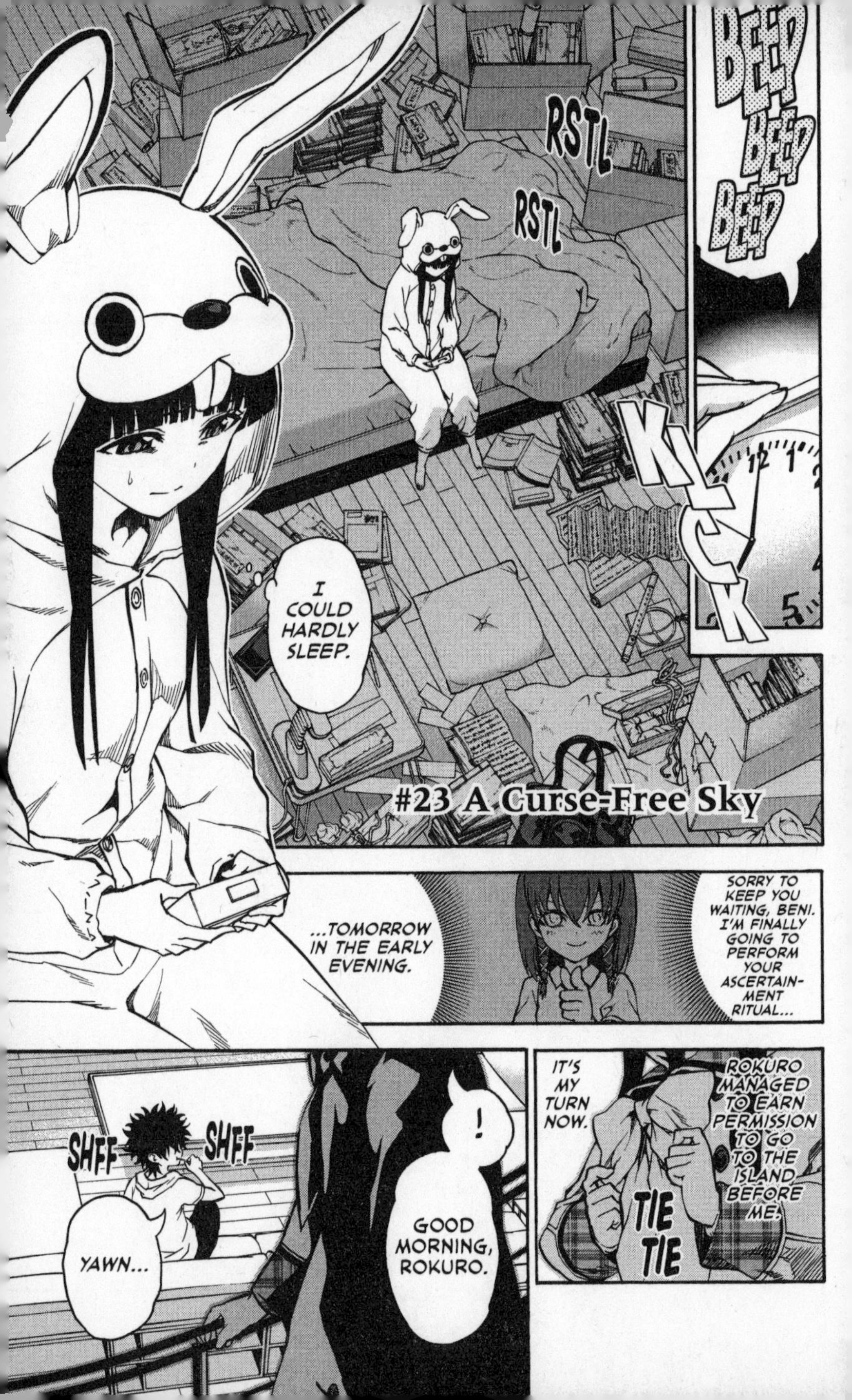

BEEP BEEP BEEP
KLICK
RSTL
RSTL
I COULD HARDLY SLEEP.
#23 A Curse-Free Sky
SORRY TO KEEP YOU WAITING, BENI. I'M FINALLY GOING TO PERFORM YOUR ASCERTAINMENT RITUAL...
...TOMORROW IN THE EARLY EVENING.
ROKURO MANAGED TO EARN PERMISSION TO GO TO THE ISLAND BEFORE ME.
IT'S MY TURN NOW.
TIE TIE
!
GOOD MORNING, ROKURO.
SHFF SHFF
YAWN...

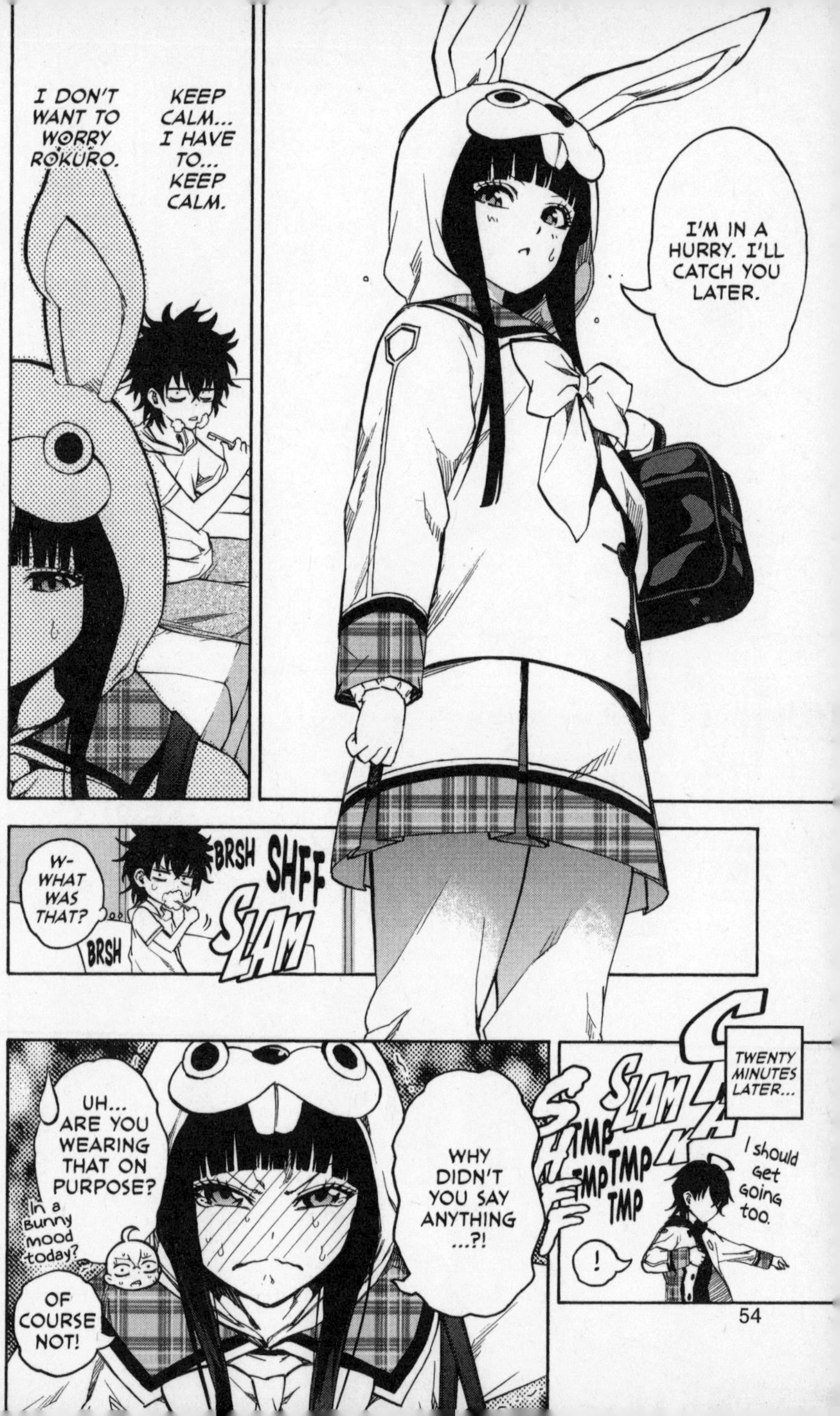
I'M IN A HURRY. I'LL CATCH YOU LATER.
KEEP CALM... I HAVE TO... KEEP CALM.
I DON'T WANT TO WORRY ROKURO.
SHFF
BRSH
SLAM
W-WHAT WAS THAT?
BRSH
TWENTY MINUTES LATER...
SLAM
SLAM
TMP TMP TMP TMP TMP TMP
I should Get Going too.
!
WHY DIDN'T YOU SAY ANYTHING ...?!
UH... ARE YOU WEARING THAT ON PURPOSE?
In a Bunny mood today?
OF COURSE NOT!

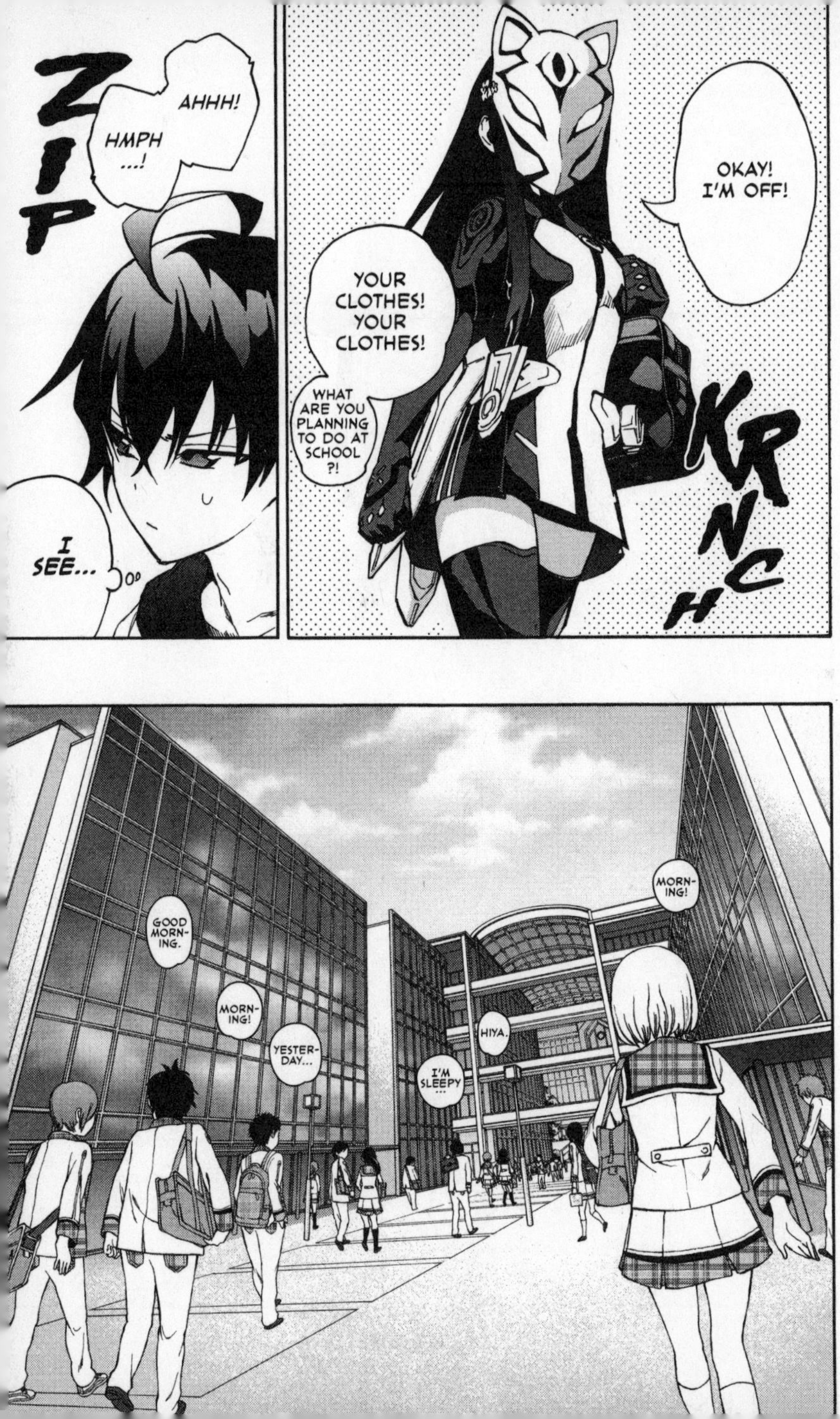
OKAY! I'M OFF!
KRNCH
YOUR CLOTHES! YOUR CLOTHES!
WHAT ARE YOU PLANNING TO DO AT SCHOOL?!
ZIP
AHHH!
HMPH ...!
I SEE...
MORN-ING!
HIYA.
I'M SLEEPY ...
YESTER-DAY...
MORN-ING!
GOOD MORN-ING.

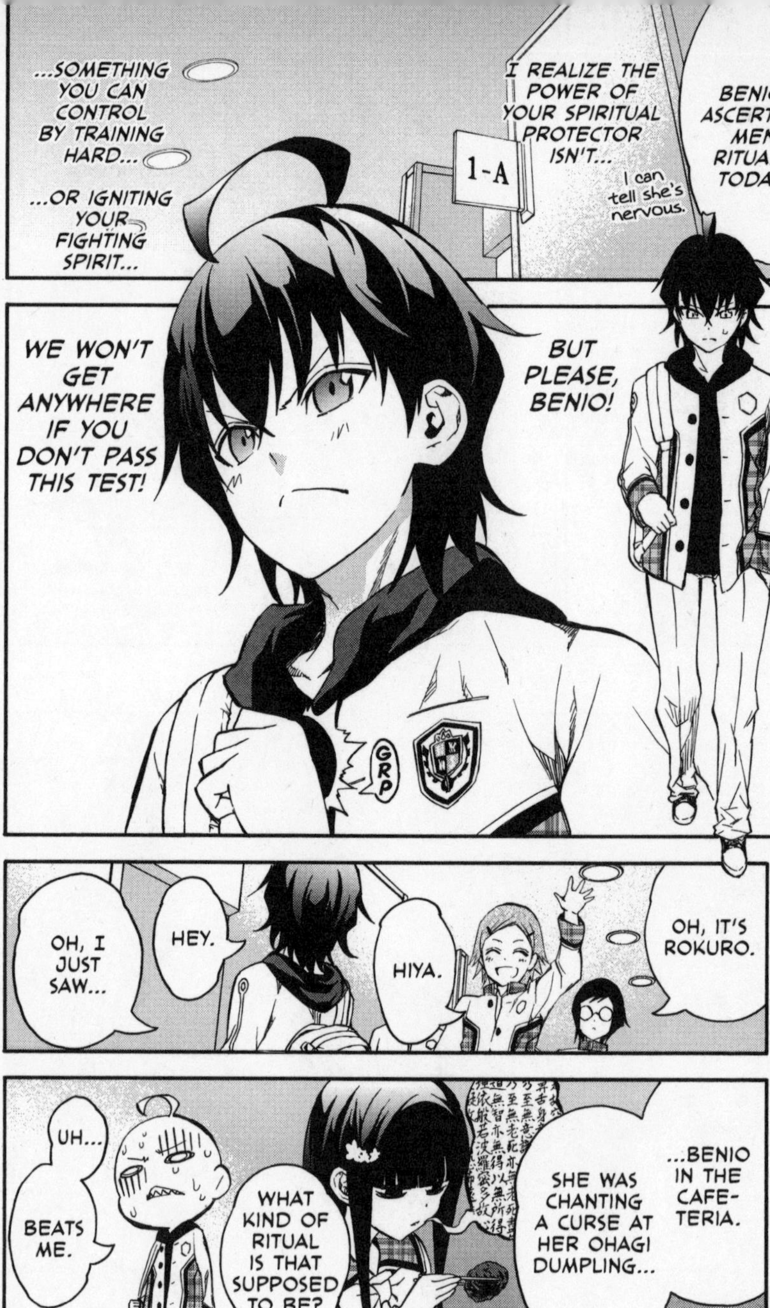
BENIO'S ASCERTAIN-MENT RITUAL IS TODAY...
I can tell she's nervous.
I REALIZE THE POWER OF YOUR SPIRITUAL PROTECTOR ISN'T...
...SOMETHING YOU CAN CONTROL BY TRAINING HARD...
...OR IGNITING YOUR FIGHTING SPIRIT...
1-A
BUT PLEASE, BENIO!
WE WON'T GET ANYWHERE IF YOU DON'T PASS THIS TEST!
GRP
OH, IT'S ROKURO.
HIYA.
HEY.
OH, I JUST SAW...
...BENIO IN THE CAFE-TERIA.
SHE WAS CHANTING A CURSE AT HER OHAGI DUMPLING...
WHAT KIND OF RITUAL IS THAT SUPPOSED TO BE?
UH...
BEATS ME.

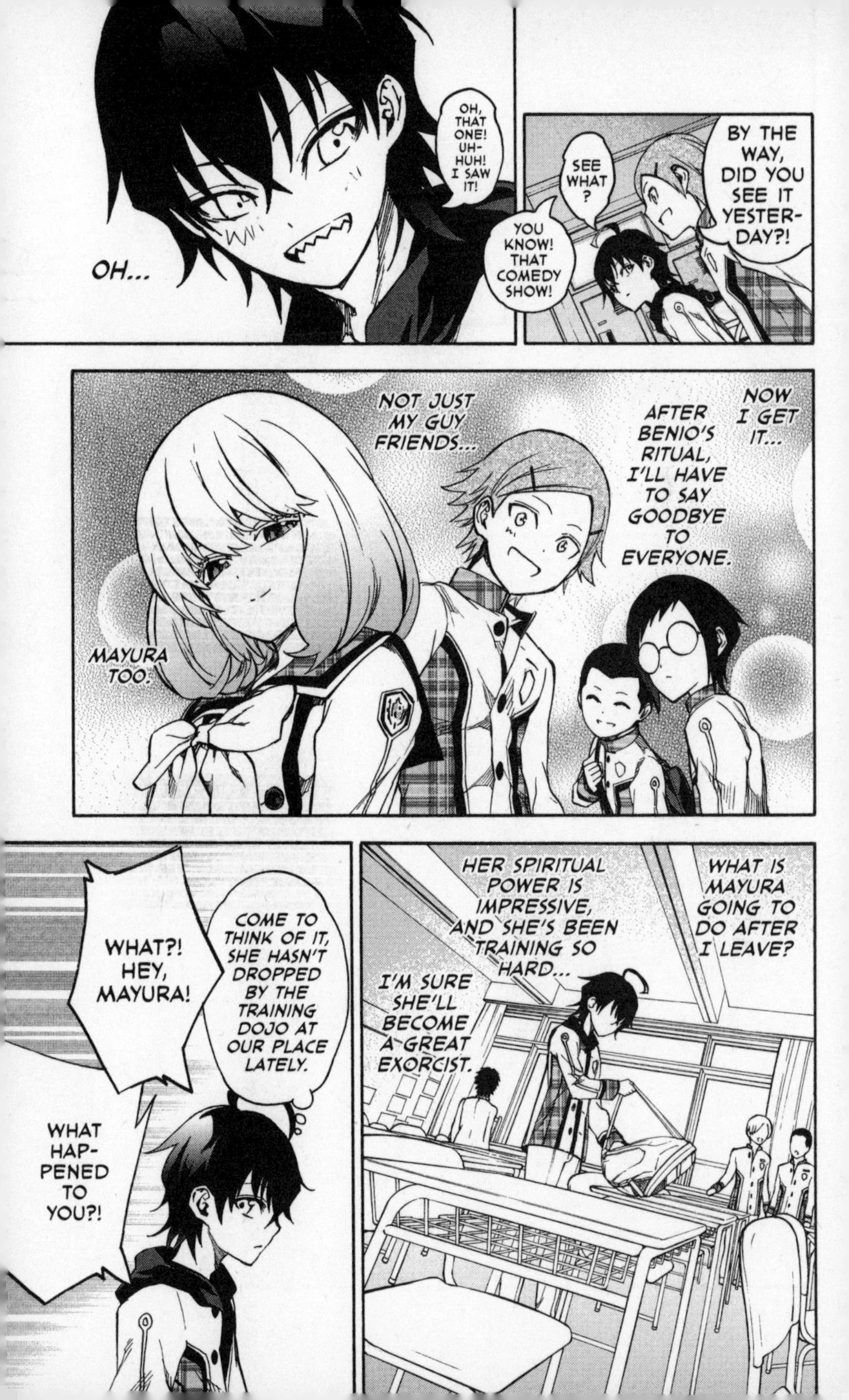
BY THE WAY, DID YOU SEE IT YESTERDAY?!
SEE WHAT?
YOU KNOW! THAT COMEDY SHOW!
OH, THAT ONE! UH-HUH! I SAW IT!
OH...
NOW I GET IT...
AFTER BENIO'S RITUAL, I'LL HAVE TO SAY GOODBYE TO EVERYONE.
NOT JUST MY GUY FRIENDS...
MAYURA TOO.
WHAT IS MAYURA GOING TO DO AFTER I LEAVE?
HER SPIRITUAL POWER IS IMPRESSIVE, AND SHE'S BEEN TRAINING SO HARD...
I'M SURE SHE'LL BECOME A GREAT EXORCIST.
COME TO THINK OF IT, SHE HASN'T DROPPED BY THE TRAINING DOJO AT OUR PLACE LATELY.
WHAT?! HEY, MAYURA!
WHAT HAPPENED TO YOU?!

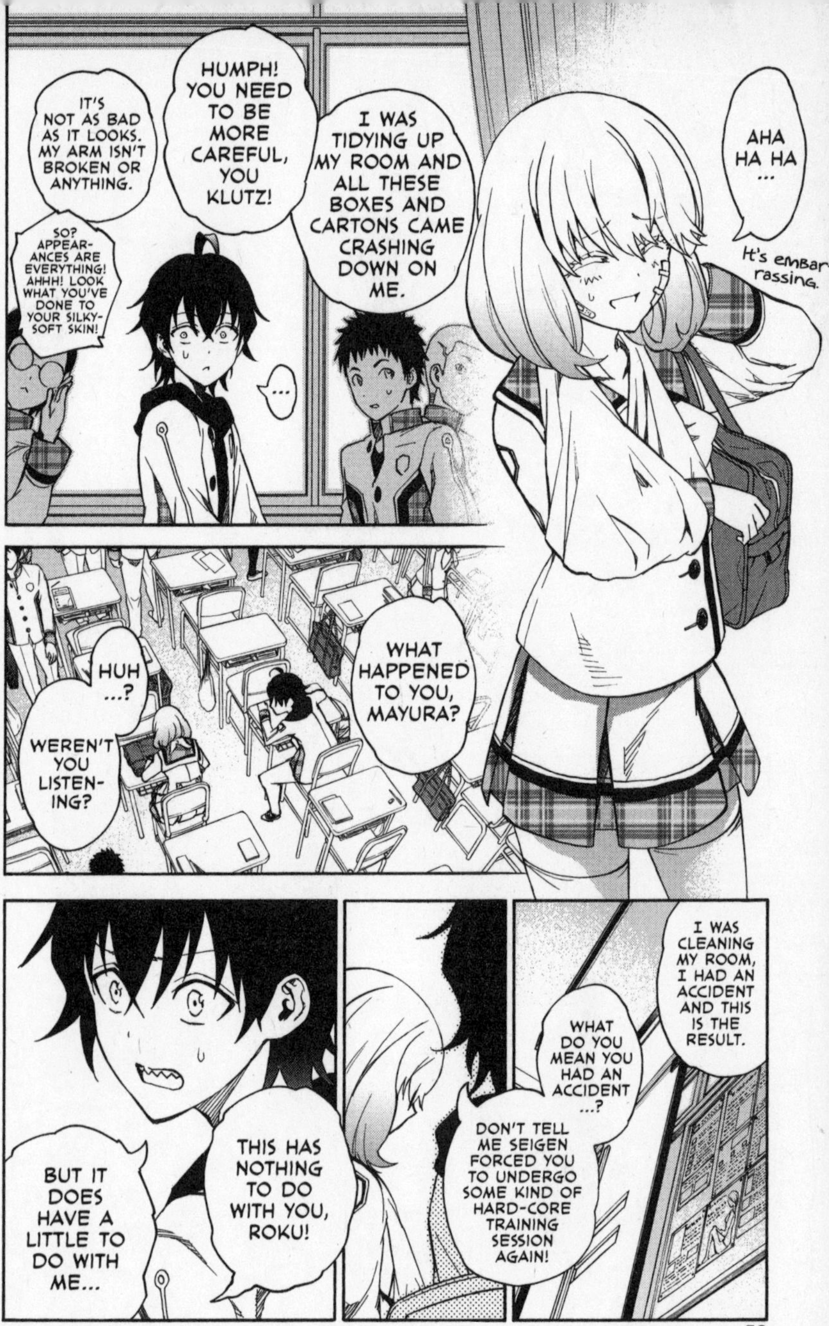
AHA HA HA ...
It's embarrassing.
I WAS TIDYING UP MY ROOM AND ALL THESE BOXES AND CARTONS CAME CRASHING DOWN ON ME.
HUMPH! YOU NEED TO BE MORE CAREFUL, YOU KLUTZ!
IT'S NOT AS BAD AS IT LOOKS. MY ARM ISN'T BROKEN OR ANYTHING.
SO? APPEAR-ANCES ARE EVERYTHING! AHHH! LOOK WHAT YOU'VE DONE TO YOUR SILKY-SOFT SKIN!
...
WHAT HAPPENED TO YOU, MAYURA?
HUH ...?
WEREN'T YOU LISTEN-ING?
I WAS CLEANING MY ROOM, I HAD AN ACCIDENT AND THIS IS THE RESULT.
WHAT DO YOU MEAN YOU HAD AN ACCIDENT ...?
DON'T TELL ME SEIGEN FORCED YOU TO UNDERGO SOME KIND OF HARD-CORE TRAINING SESSION AGAIN!
THIS HAS NOTHING TO DO WITH YOU, ROKU!
BUT IT DOES HAVE A LITTLE TO DO WITH ME...

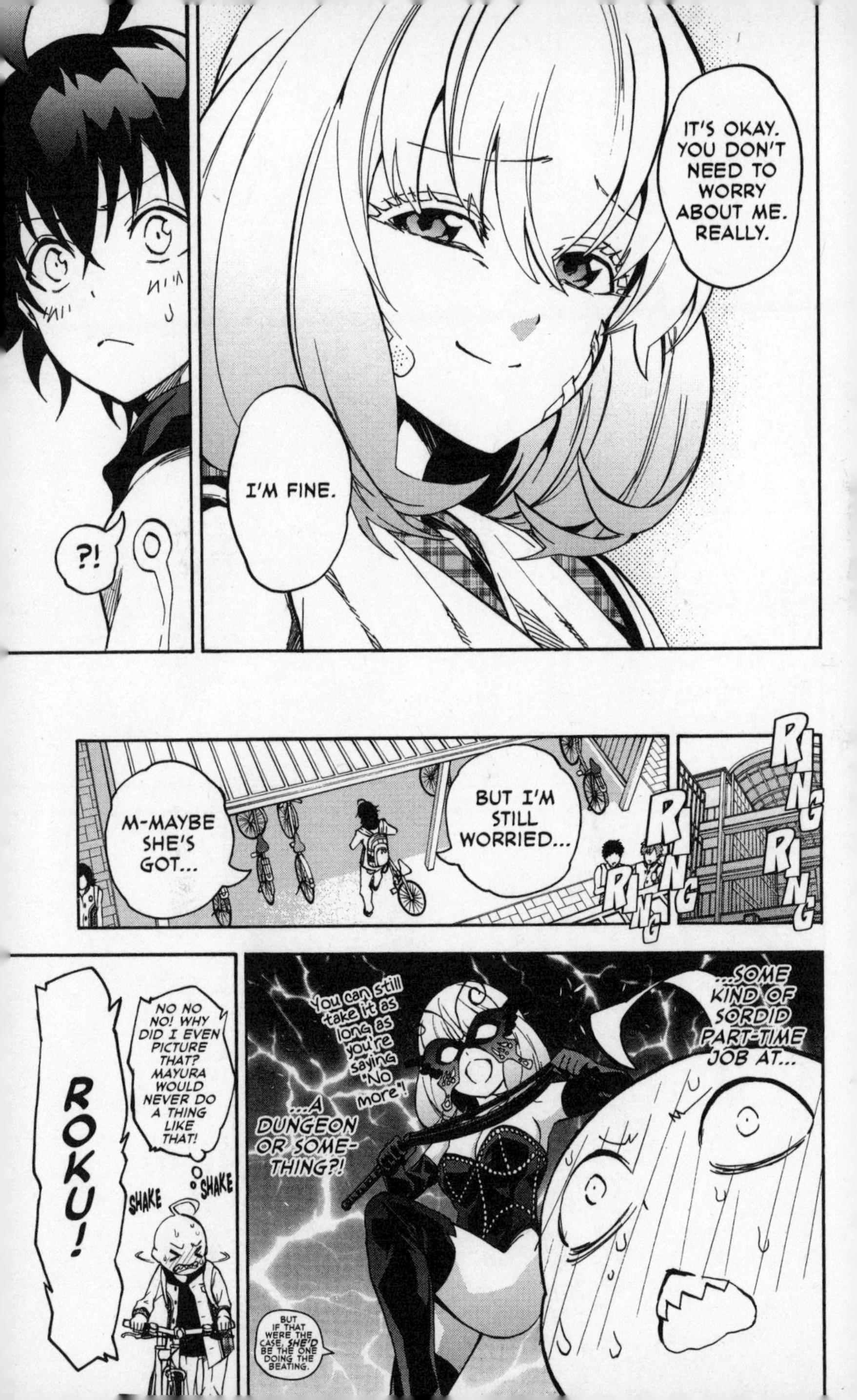
IT'S OKAY. YOU DON'T NEED TO WORRY ABOUT ME. REALLY.
I'M FINE.
?!
RING RING RING RING
BUT I'M STILL WORRIED...
M-MAYBE SHE'S GOT...
...SOME KIND OF SORDID PART-TIME JOB AT...
You can still take it as long as you're saying 'No more'!
...A DUNGEON OR SOME-THING?!
BUT IF THAT WERE THE CASE, SHE'D BE THE ONE DOING THE BEATING.
ROKU!
NO NO NO! WHY DID I EVEN PICTURE THAT? MAYURA WOULD NEVER DO A THING LIKE THAT!
SHAKE
SHAKE

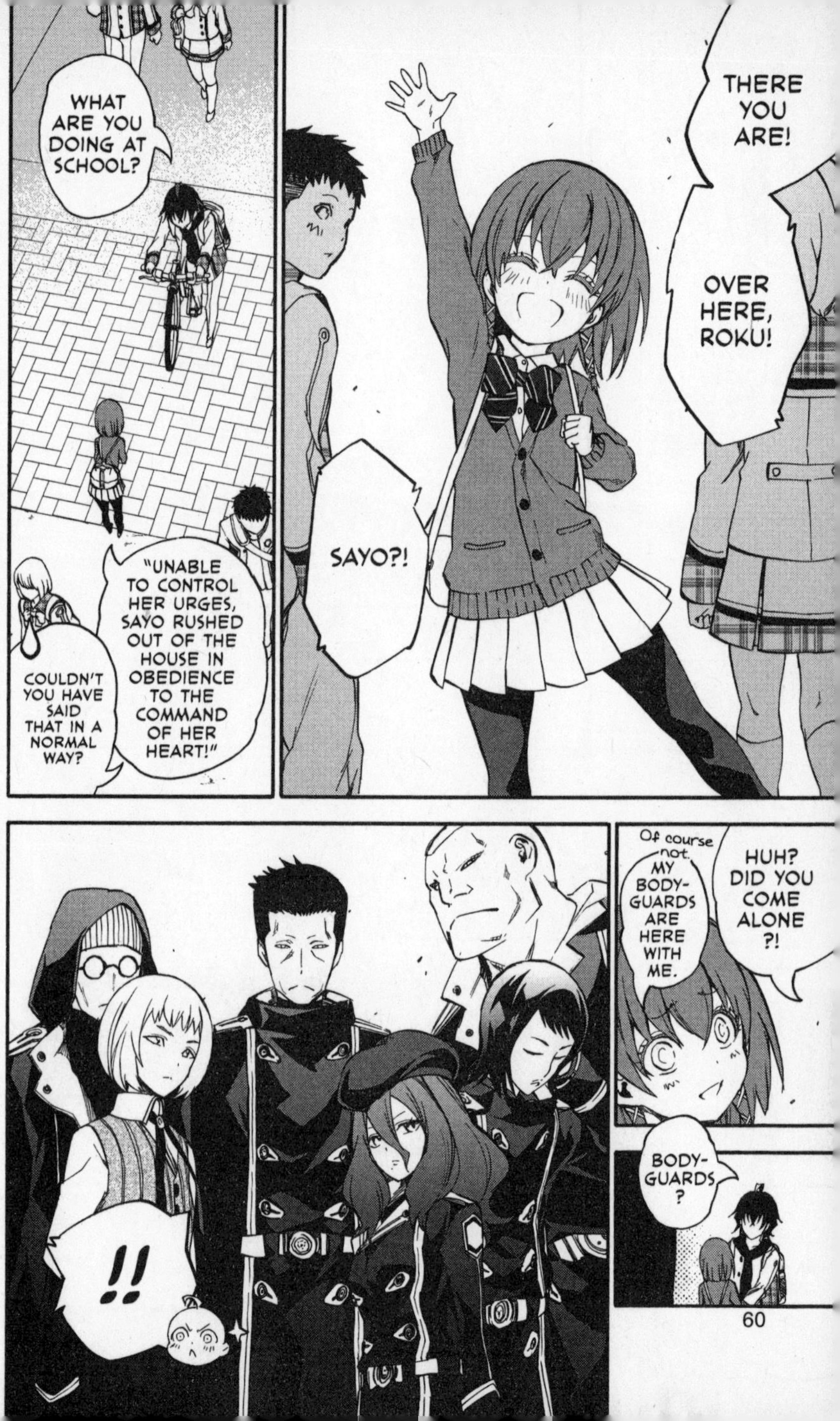
THERE YOU ARE!
OVER HERE, ROKU!
SAYO?!
WHAT ARE YOU DOING AT SCHOOL?
"UNABLE TO CONTROL HER URGES, SAYO RUSHED OUT OF THE HOUSE IN OBEDIENCE TO THE COMMAND OF HER HEART!"
COULDN'T YOU HAVE SAID THAT IN A NORMAL WAY?
HUH? DID YOU COME ALONE?!
Of course not. MY BODY-GUARDS ARE HERE WITH ME.
BODY-GUARDS?
!!

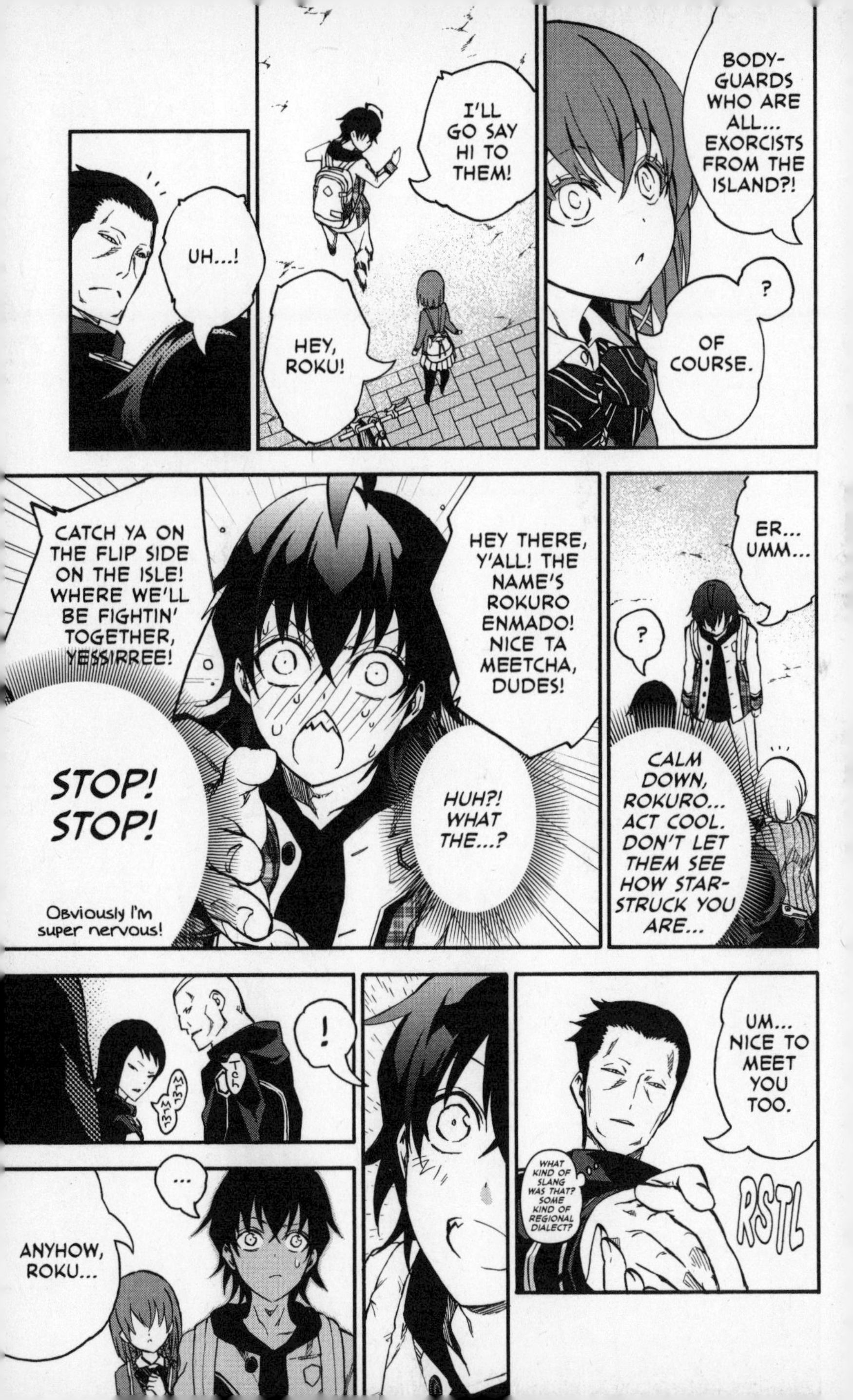
BODY-GUARDS WHO ARE ALL... EXORCISTS FROM THE ISLAND?!
?
OF COURSE.
I'LL GO SAY HI TO THEM!
HEY, ROKU!
UH...!
ER... UMM...
?
CALM DOWN, ROKURO... ACT COOL. DON'T LET THEM SEE HOW STAR-STRUCK YOU ARE...
HEY THERE, Y'ALL! THE NAME'S ROKURO ENMADO! NICE TA MEETCHA, DUDES!
CATCH YA ON THE FLIP SIDE ON THE ISLE! WHERE WE'LL BE FIGHTIN' TOGETHER, YESSIRREE!
HUH?! WHAT THE...?
STOP! STOP!
Obviously I'm super nervous!
UM... NICE TO MEET YOU TOO.
WHAT KIND OF SLANG WAS THAT? SOME KIND OF REGIONAL DIALECT?
RSTL
!
Tch
...
ANYHOW, ROKU...

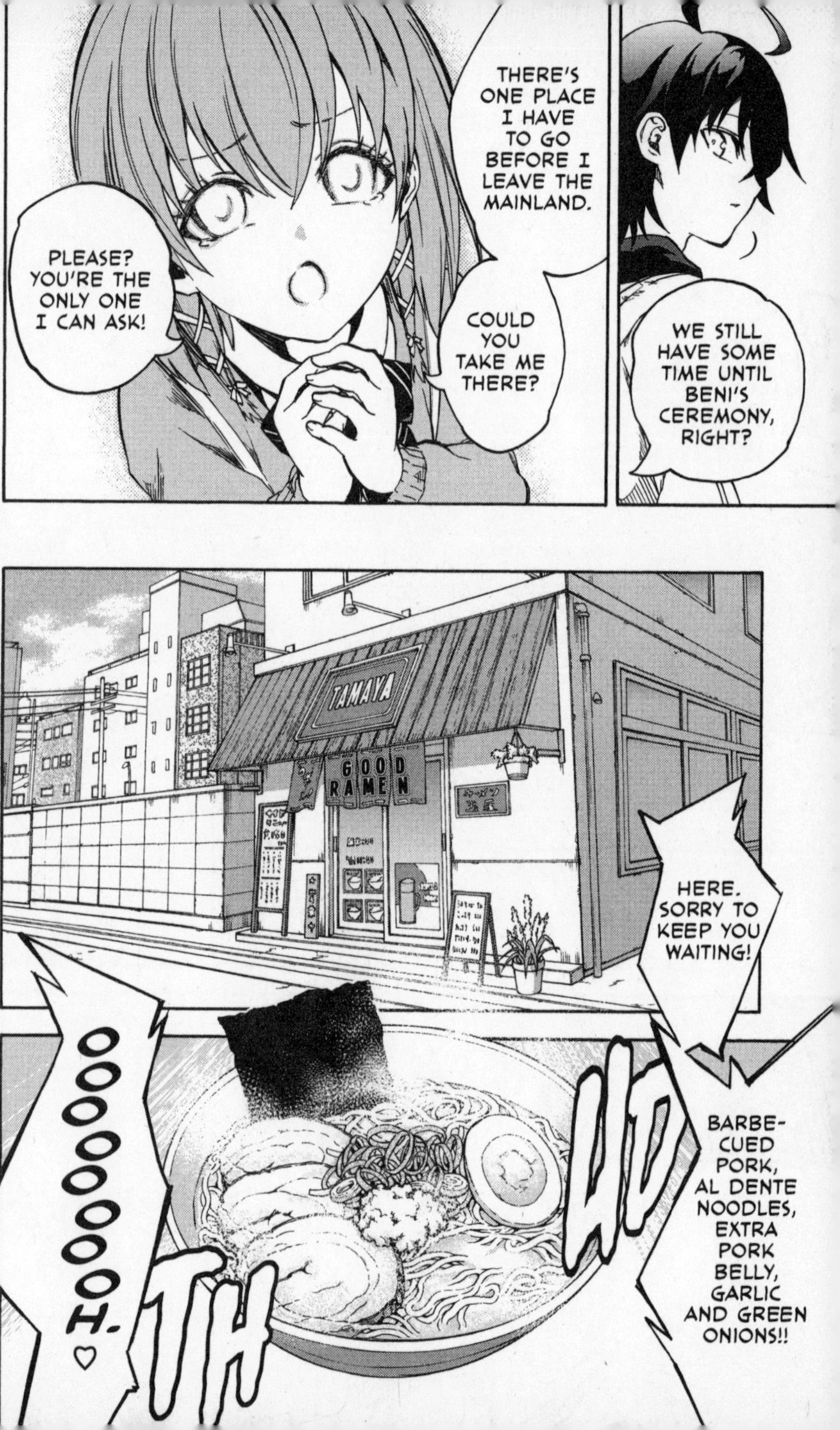
WE STILL HAVE SOME TIME UNTIL BENI'S CEREMONY, RIGHT?
THERE'S ONE PLACE I HAVE TO GO BEFORE I LEAVE THE MAINLAND.
COULD YOU TAKE ME THERE?
PLEASE? YOU'RE THE ONLY ONE I CAN ASK!
TAMAYA
GOOD RAMEN
HERE. SORRY TO KEEP YOU WAITING!
BARBE-CUED PORK, AL DENTE NOODLES, EXTRA PORK BELLY, GARLIC AND GREEN ONIONS!!
THUD
OOOOOOOOOH-♡

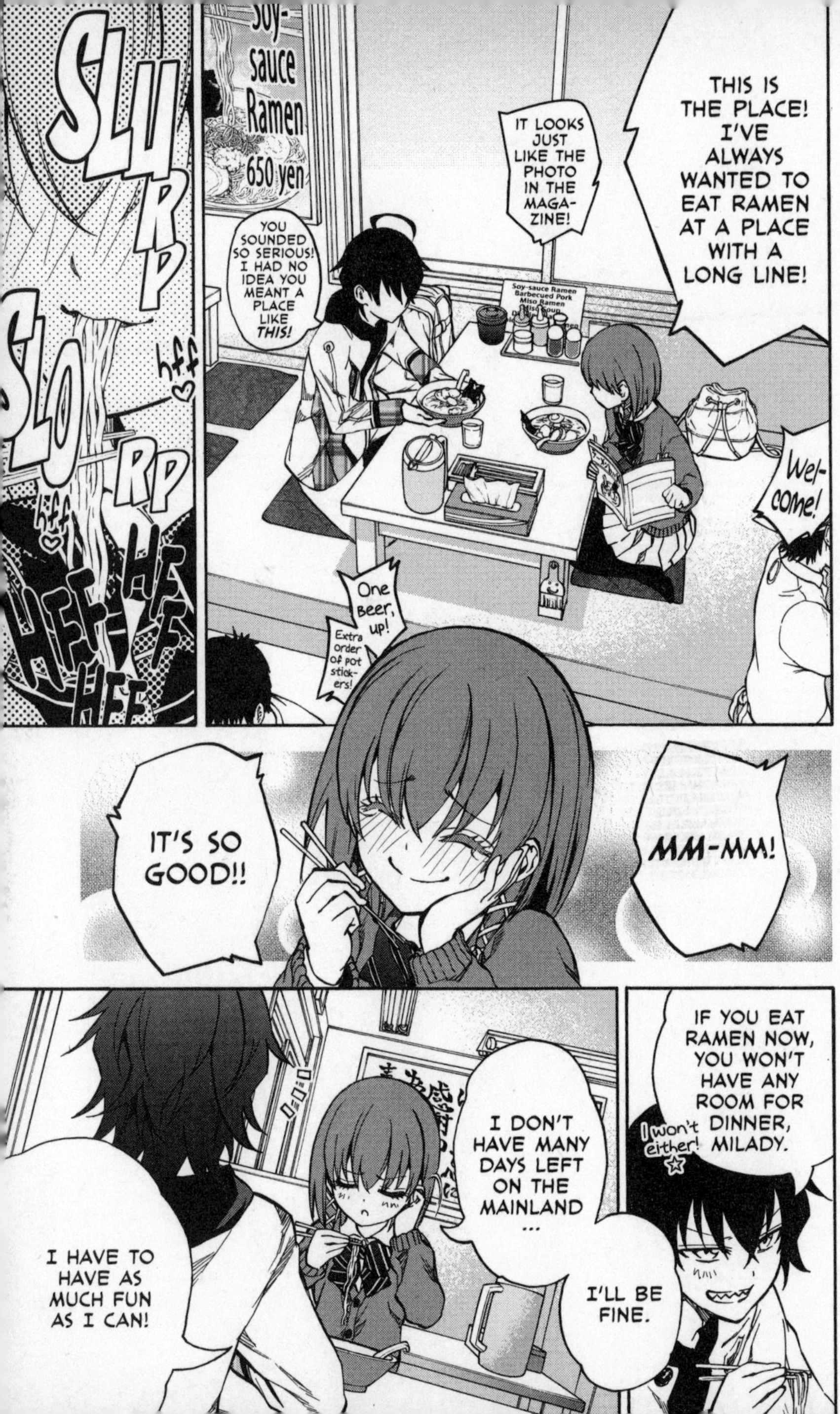

THIS IS THE PLACE! I'VE ALWAYS WANTED TO EAT RAMEN AT A PLACE WITH A LONG LINE!
IT LOOKS JUST LIKE THE PHOTO IN THE MAGAZINE!
Soy-sauce Ramen 650 yen
YOU SOUNDED SO SERIOUS! I HAD NO IDEA YOU MEANT A PLACE LIKE *THIS!*
Soy-sauce Ramen
Barbecued Pork
Miso Ramen
Wel-come!
One beer, up!
Extra order of pot stickers!
SLURRP
SLORP
hff
hff
HEF HEF HEF HEF
MM-MM!
IT'S SO GOOD!!
IF YOU EAT RAMEN NOW, YOU WON'T HAVE ANY ROOM FOR DINNER, MILADY.
I won't either!
I'LL BE FINE.
I DON'T HAVE MANY DAYS LEFT ON THE MAINLAND ...
I HAVE TO HAVE AS MUCH FUN AS I CAN!

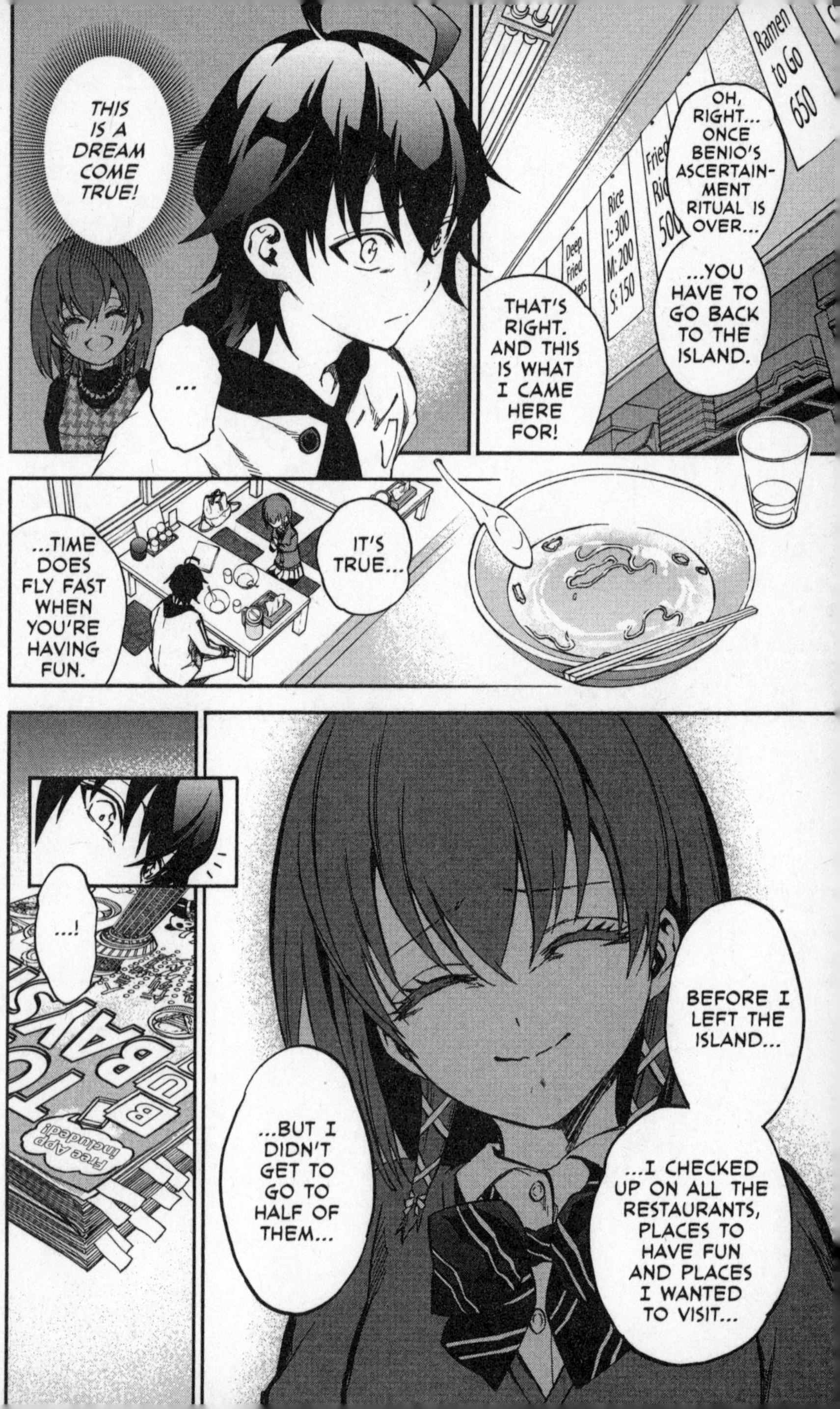
Ramen to Go 650
Rice L:300 M:200 S:150
OH, RIGHT... ONCE BENIO'S ASCERTAINMENT RITUAL IS OVER...
...YOU HAVE TO GO BACK TO THE ISLAND.
THAT'S RIGHT. AND THIS IS WHAT I CAME HERE FOR!
THIS IS A DREAM COME TRUE!
...
IT'S TRUE...
...TIME DOES FLY FAST WHEN YOU'RE HAVING FUN.
BEFORE I LEFT THE ISLAND...
...I CHECKED UP ON ALL THE RESTAURANTS, PLACES TO HAVE FUN AND PLACES I WANTED TO VISIT...
...BUT I DIDN'T GET TO GO TO HALF OF THEM...
...!
Free App Included!

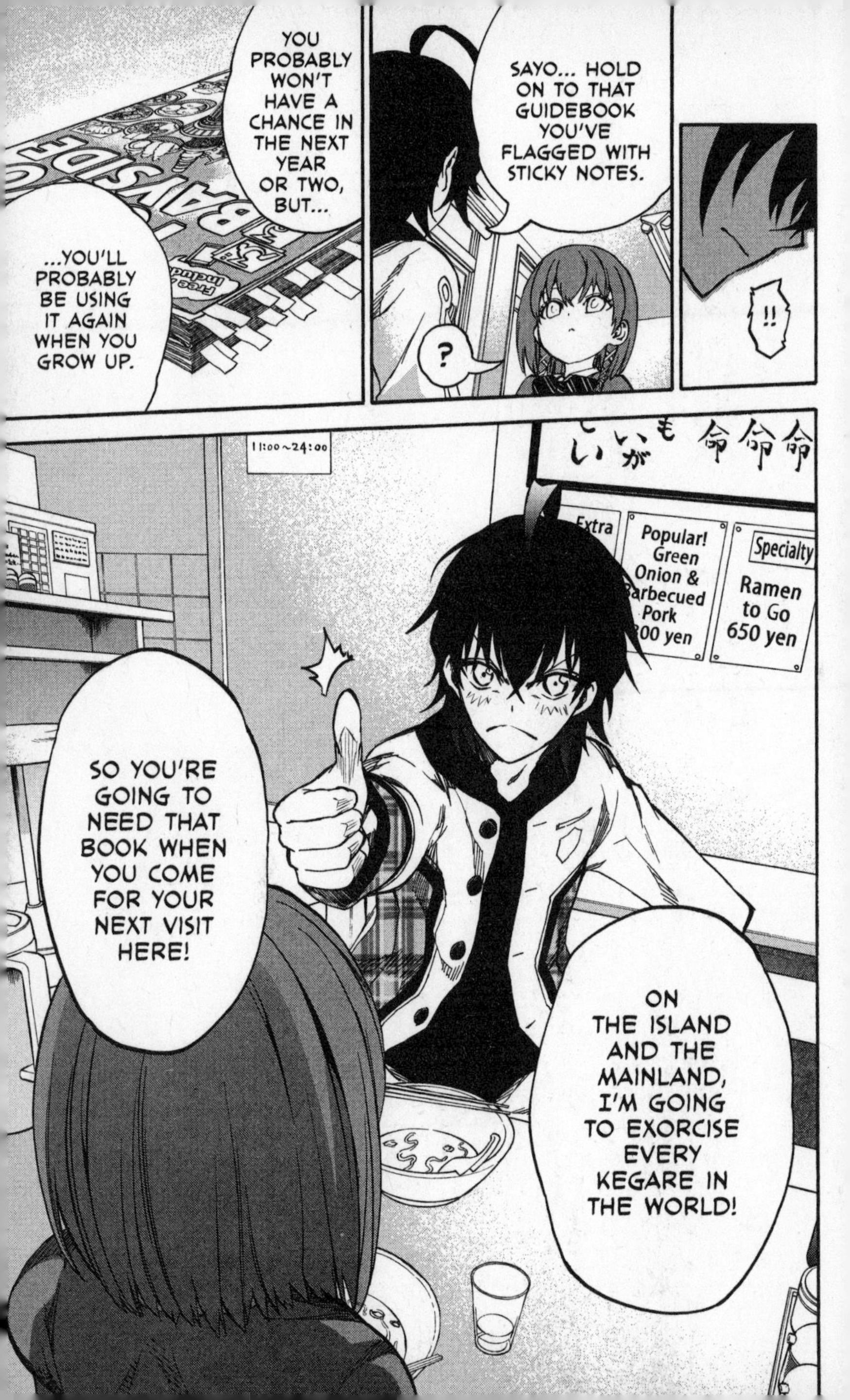
!!
SAYO... HOLD ON TO THAT GUIDEBOOK YOU'VE FLAGGED WITH STICKY NOTES.
?
YOU PROBABLY WON'T HAVE A CHANCE IN THE NEXT YEAR OR TWO, BUT...
...YOU'LL PROBABLY BE USING IT AGAIN WHEN YOU GROW UP.
11:00~24:00
Specialty
Ramen to Go 650 yen
ON THE ISLAND AND THE MAINLAND, I'M GOING TO EXORCISE EVERY KEGARE IN THE WORLD!
SO YOU'RE GOING TO NEED THAT BOOK WHEN YOU COME FOR YOUR NEXT VISIT HERE!

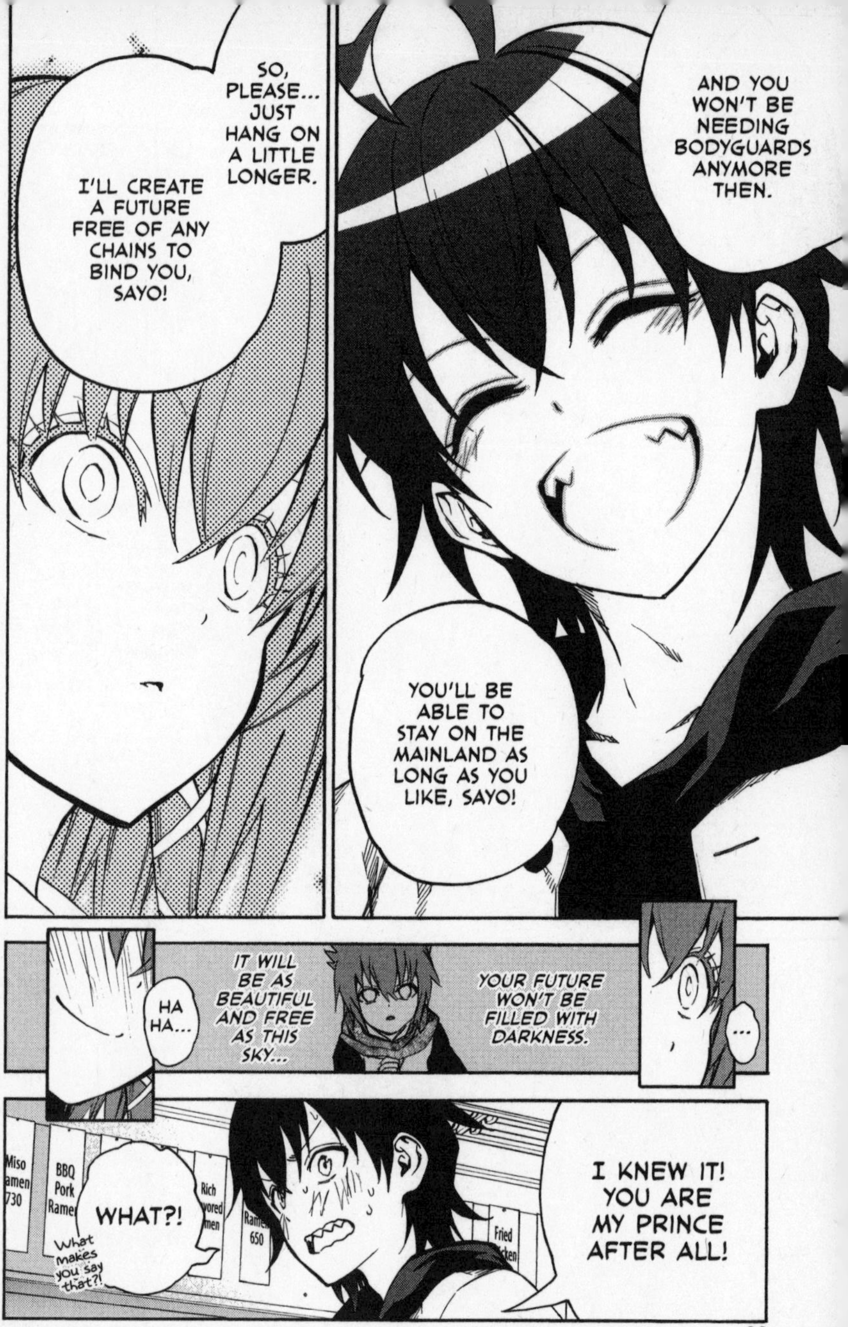
AND YOU WON'T BE NEEDING BODYGUARDS ANYMORE THEN.
YOU'LL BE ABLE TO STAY ON THE MAINLAND AS LONG AS YOU LIKE, SAYO!
SO, PLEASE... JUST HANG ON A LITTLE LONGER.
I'LL CREATE A FUTURE FREE OF ANY CHAINS TO BIND YOU, SAYO!
...
YOUR FUTURE WON'T BE FILLED WITH DARKNESS.
IT WILL BE AS BEAUTIFUL AND FREE AS THIS SKY...
HA HA...
I KNEW IT! YOU ARE MY PRINCE AFTER ALL!
WHAT?!
What makes you say that?!

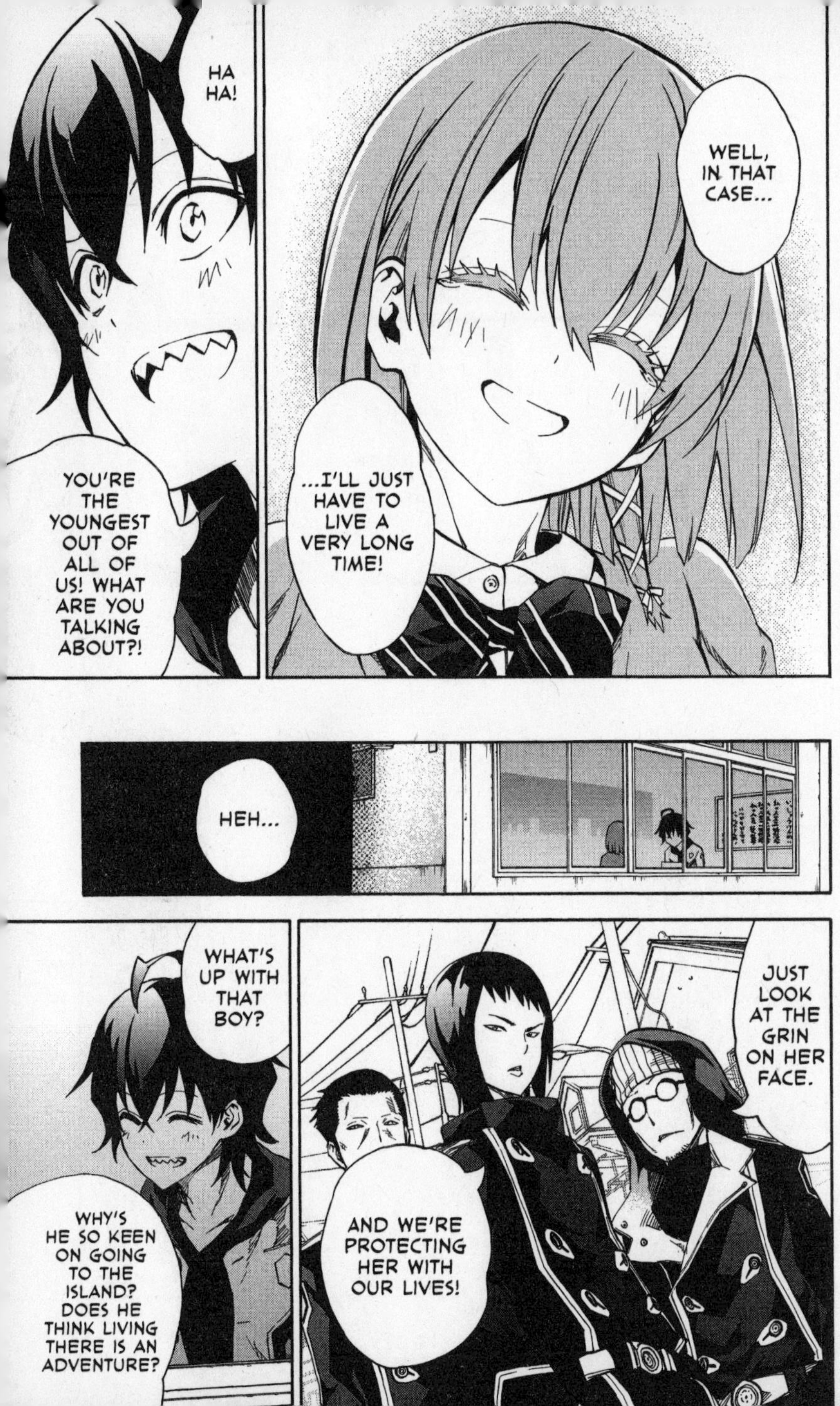
WELL, IN THAT CASE...
...I'LL JUST HAVE TO LIVE A VERY LONG TIME!
HA HA!
YOU'RE THE YOUNGEST OUT OF ALL OF US! WHAT ARE YOU TALKING ABOUT?!
HEH...
JUST LOOK AT THE GRIN ON HER FACE.
AND WE'RE PROTECTING HER WITH OUR LIVES!
WHAT'S UP WITH THAT BOY?
WHY'S HE SO KEEN ON GOING TO THE ISLAND? DOES HE THINK LIVING THERE IS AN ADVENTURE?

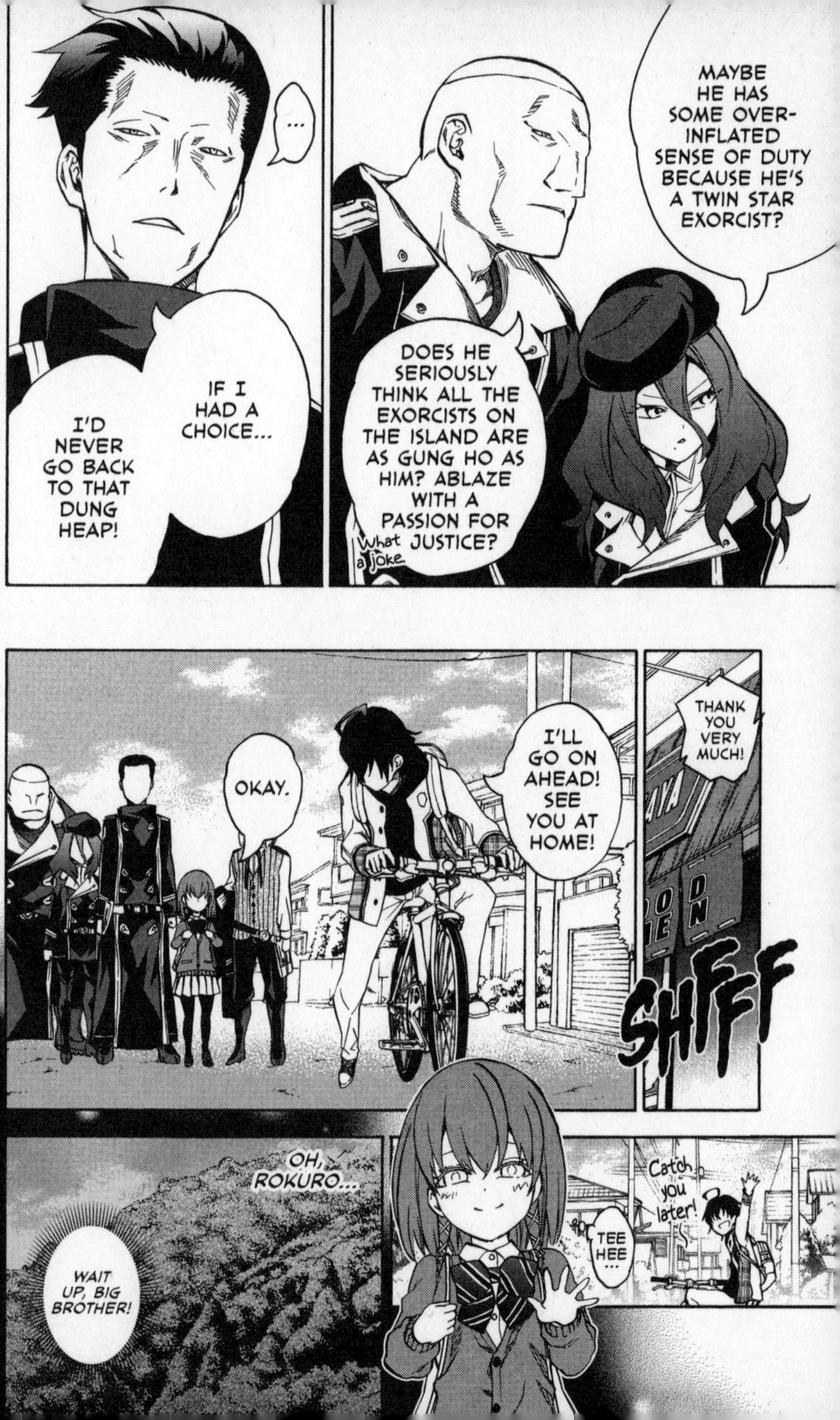
MAYBE HE HAS SOME OVER-INFLATED SENSE OF DUTY BECAUSE HE'S A TWIN STAR EXORCIST?
DOES HE SERIOUSLY THINK ALL THE EXORCISTS ON THE ISLAND ARE AS GUNG HO AS HIM? ABLAZE WITH A PASSION FOR JUSTICE?
What a joke.
...
IF I HAD A CHOICE...
I'D NEVER GO BACK TO THAT DUNG HEAP!
THANK YOU VERY MUCH!
SHFF
I'LL GO ON AHEAD! SEE YOU AT HOME!
OKAY.
Catch you later!
TEE HEE...
OH, ROKURO...
WAIT UP, BIG BROTHER!

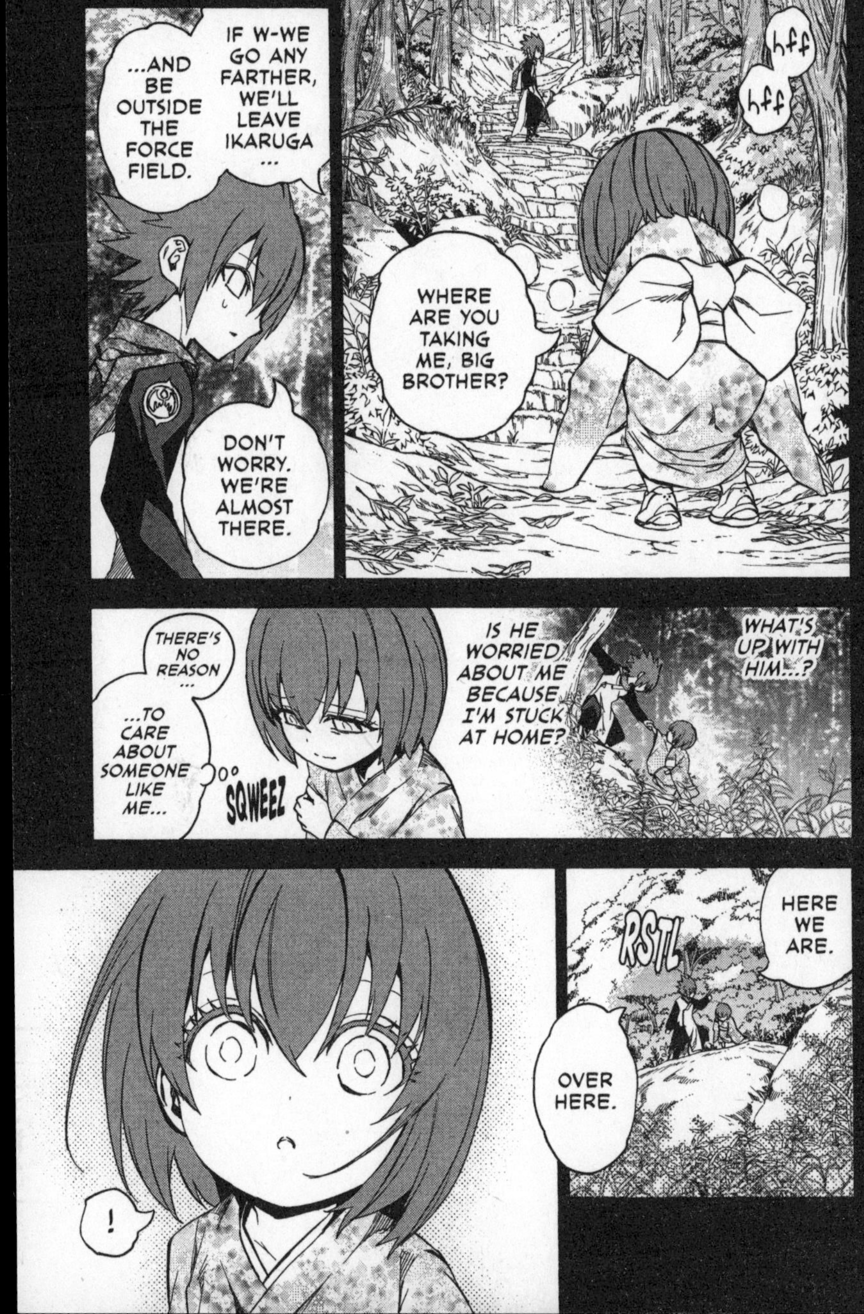
hff
hff
WHERE ARE YOU TAKING ME, BIG BROTHER?
IF W-WE GO ANY FARTHER, WE'LL LEAVE IKARUGA ...
...AND BE OUTSIDE THE FORCE FIELD.
DON'T WORRY. WE'RE ALMOST THERE.
WHAT'S UP WITH HIM...?
IS HE WORRIED ABOUT ME BECAUSE I'M STUCK AT HOME?
THERE'S NO REASON ...
...TO CARE ABOUT SOMEONE LIKE ME...
SQWEEZ
RSTL
HERE WE ARE.
OVER HERE.
!

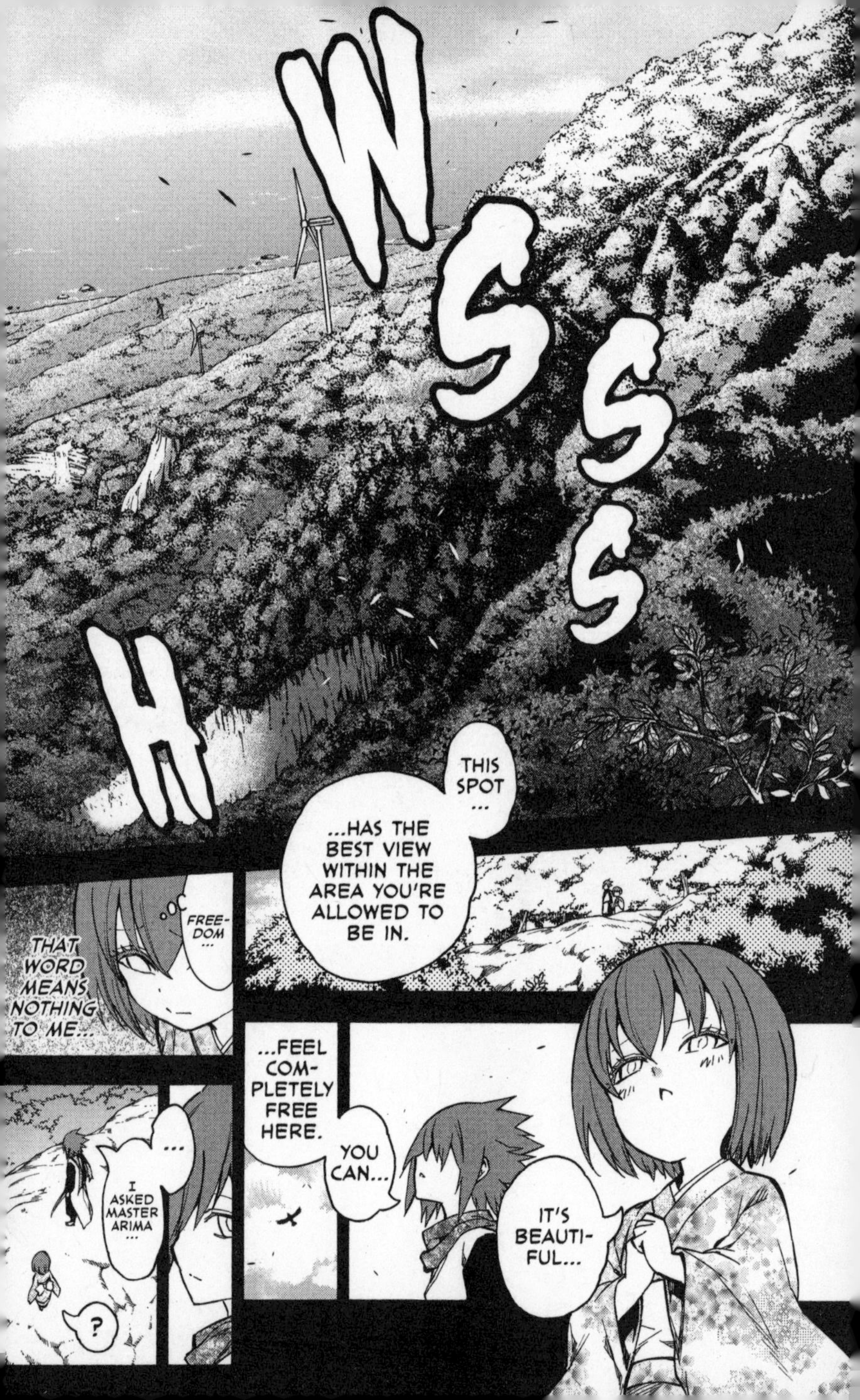
WSSSH
THIS SPOT...
...HAS THE BEST VIEW WITHIN THE AREA YOU'RE ALLOWED TO BE IN.
FREE-DOM...
THAT WORD MEANS NOTHING TO ME...
IT'S BEAUTI-FUL...
YOU CAN...
...FEEL COM-PLETELY FREE HERE.
...
I ASKED MASTER ARIMA...
?

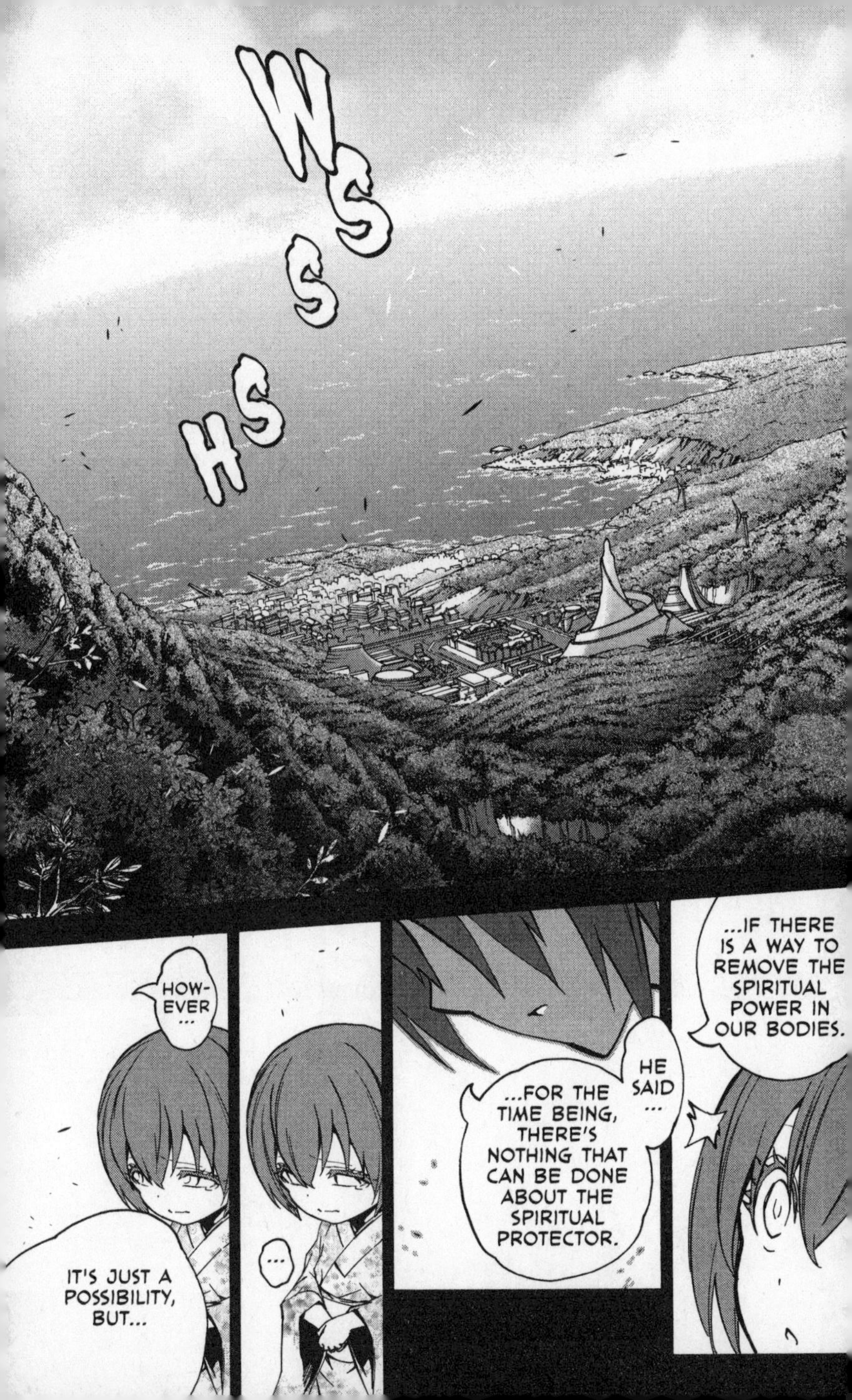
WSSSH
...IF THERE IS A WAY TO REMOVE THE SPIRITUAL POWER IN OUR BODIES.
HE SAID...
...FOR THE TIME BEING, THERE'S NOTHING THAT CAN BE DONE ABOUT THE SPIRITUAL PROTECTOR.
...
HOW-EVER...
IT'S JUST A POSSIBILITY, BUT...

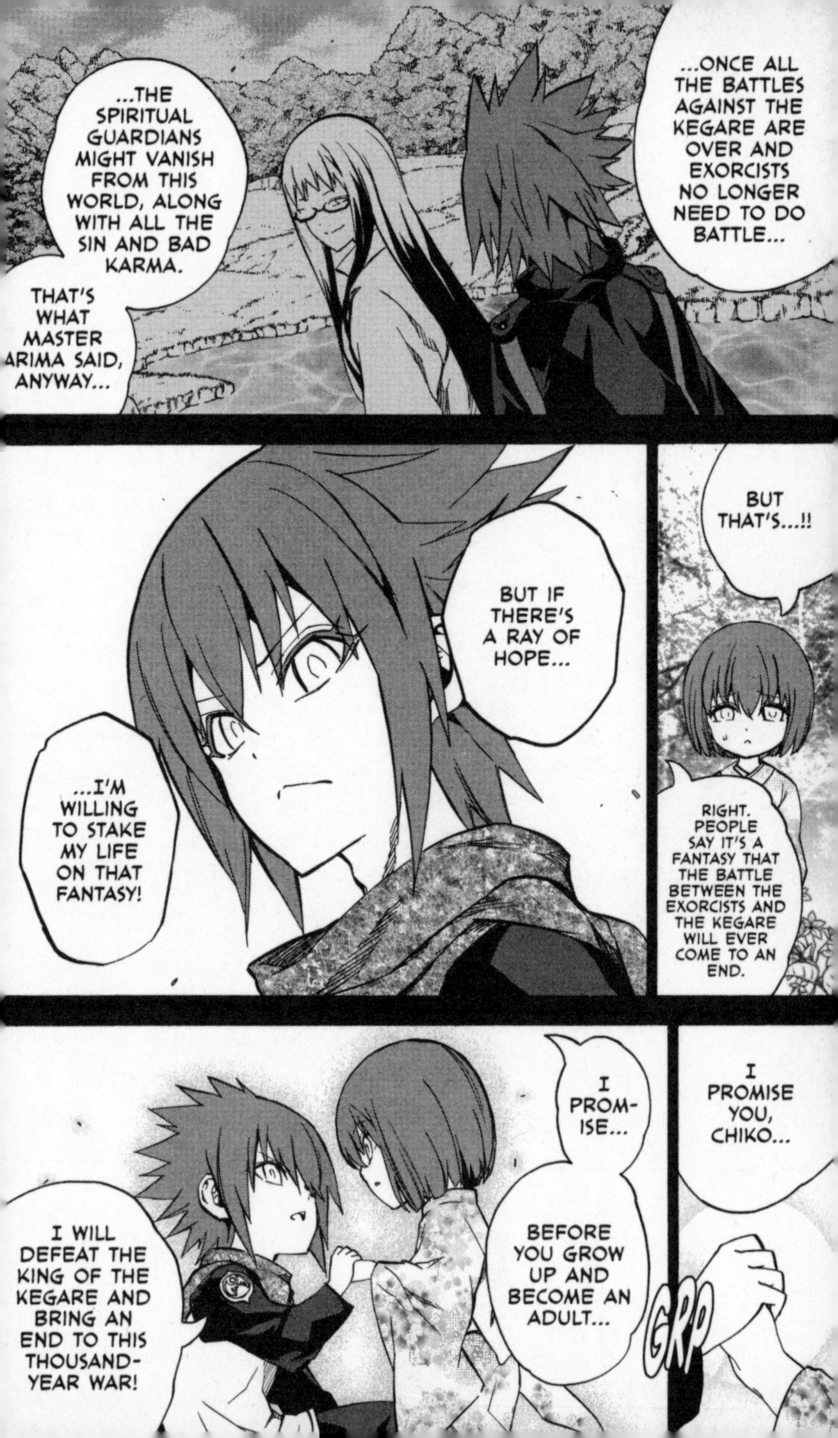
...ONCE ALL THE BATTLES AGAINST THE KEGARE ARE OVER AND EXORCISTS NO LONGER NEED TO DO BATTLE...
...THE SPIRITUAL GUARDIANS MIGHT VANISH FROM THIS WORLD, ALONG WITH ALL THE SIN AND BAD KARMA.
THAT'S WHAT MASTER ARIMA SAID, ANYWAY...
BUT THAT'S...!!
RIGHT. PEOPLE SAY IT'S A FANTASY THAT THE BATTLE BETWEEN THE EXORCISTS AND THE KEGARE WILL EVER COME TO AN END.
BUT IF THERE'S A RAY OF HOPE...
...I'M WILLING TO STAKE MY LIFE ON THAT FANTASY!
I PROMISE YOU, CHIKO...
GRP
I PROM-ISE...
BEFORE YOU GROW UP AND BECOME AN ADULT...
I WILL DEFEAT THE KING OF THE KEGARE AND BRING AN END TO THIS THOUSAND-YEAR WAR!

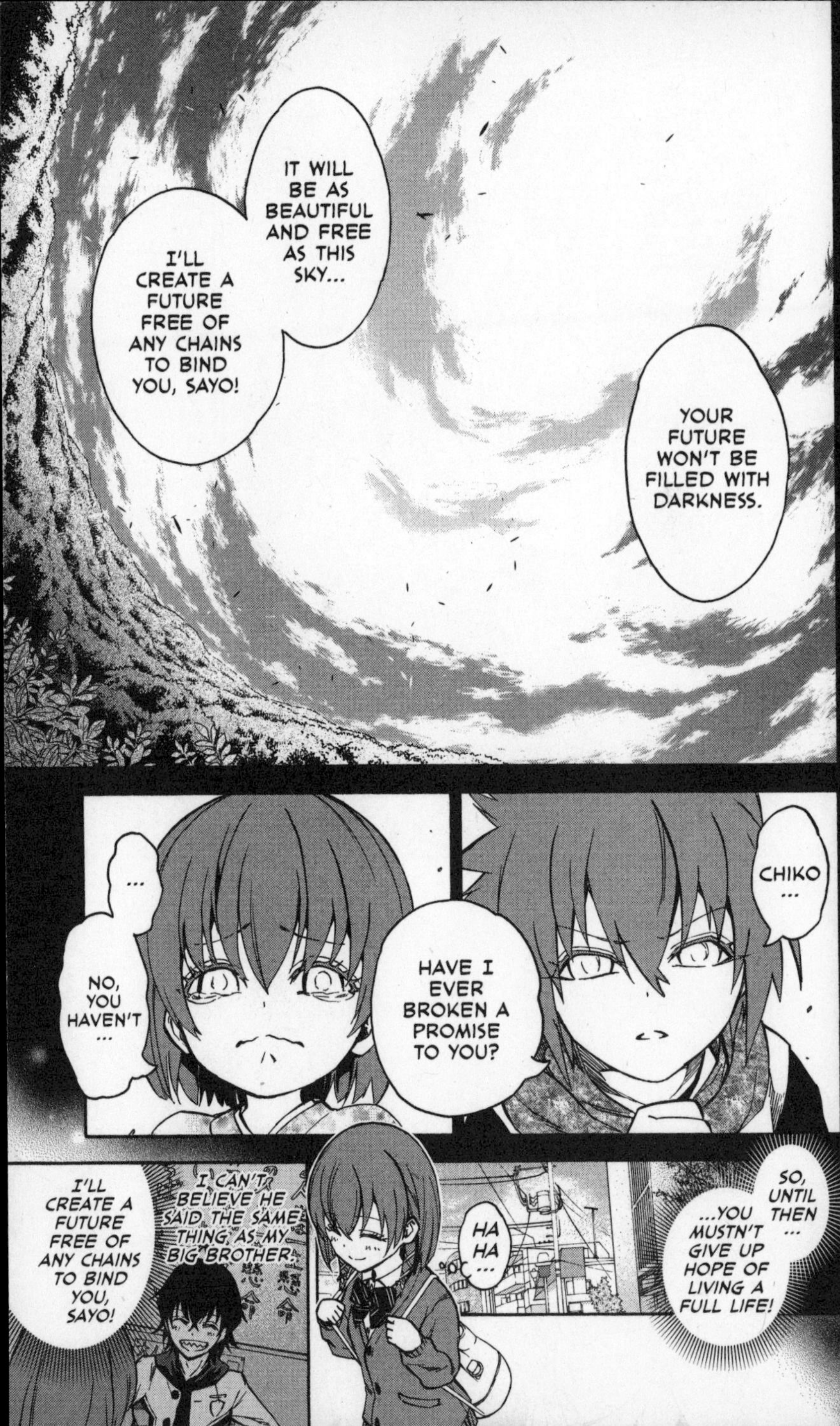
YOUR FUTURE WON'T BE FILLED WITH DARKNESS.
IT WILL BE AS BEAUTIFUL AND FREE AS THIS SKY...
I'LL CREATE A FUTURE FREE OF ANY CHAINS TO BIND YOU, SAYO!
CHIKO ...
HAVE I EVER BROKEN A PROMISE TO YOU?
...
NO, YOU HAVEN'T ...
SO, UNTIL THEN ...
...YOU MUSTN'T GIVE UP HOPE OF LIVING A FULL LIFE!
HA HA ...
I CAN'T BELIEVE HE SAID THE SAME THING AS MY BIG BROTHER.
I'LL CREATE A FUTURE FREE OF ANY CHAINS TO BIND YOU, SAYO!

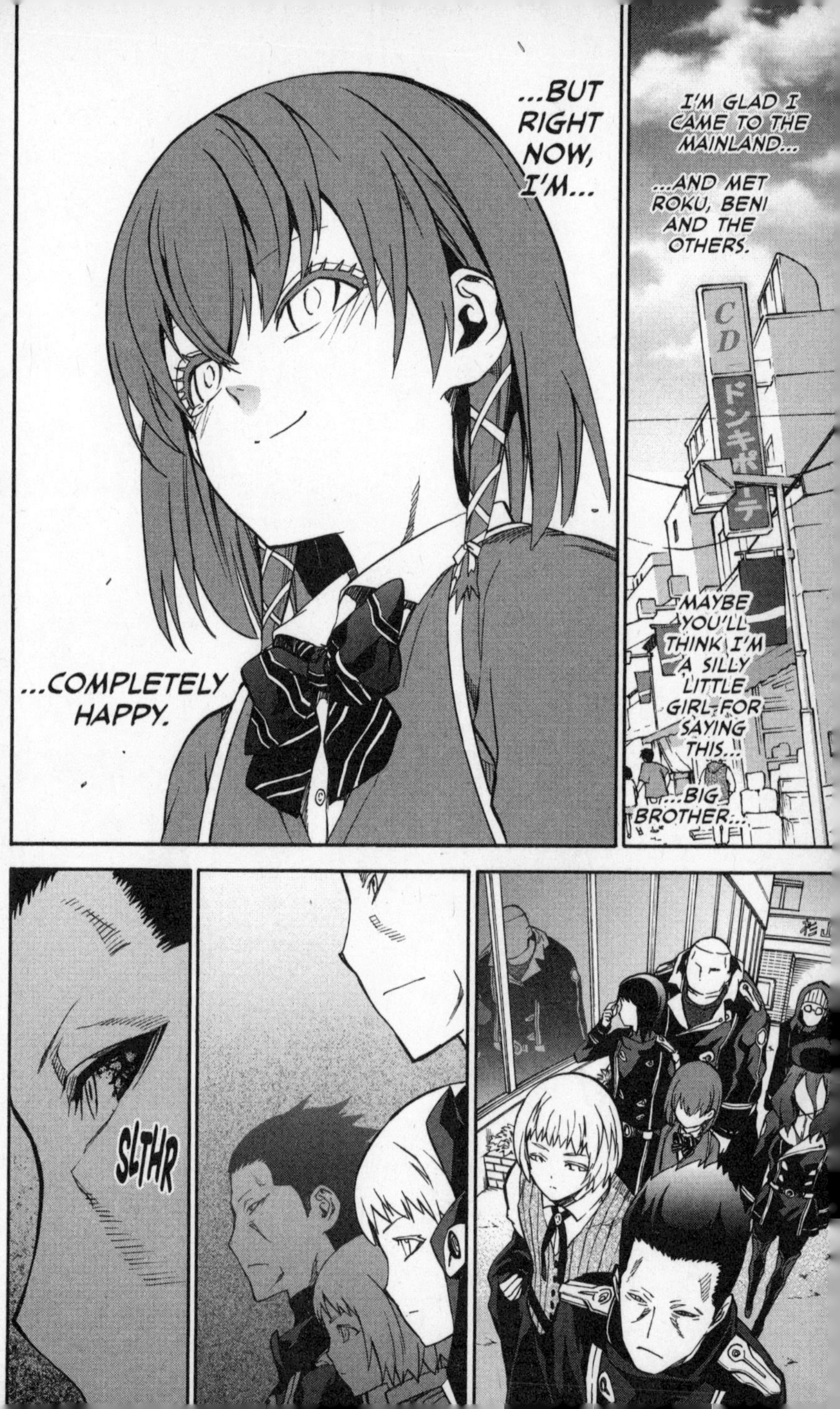
I'M GLAD I CAME TO THE MAINLAND...
...AND MET ROKU, BENI AND THE OTHERS.
CD
ドンキポーテ
MAYBE YOU'LL THINK I'M A SILLY LITTLE GIRL FOR SAYING THIS...
...BIG BROTHER...
...BUT RIGHT NOW, I'M...
...COMPLETELY HAPPY.
SLTHR

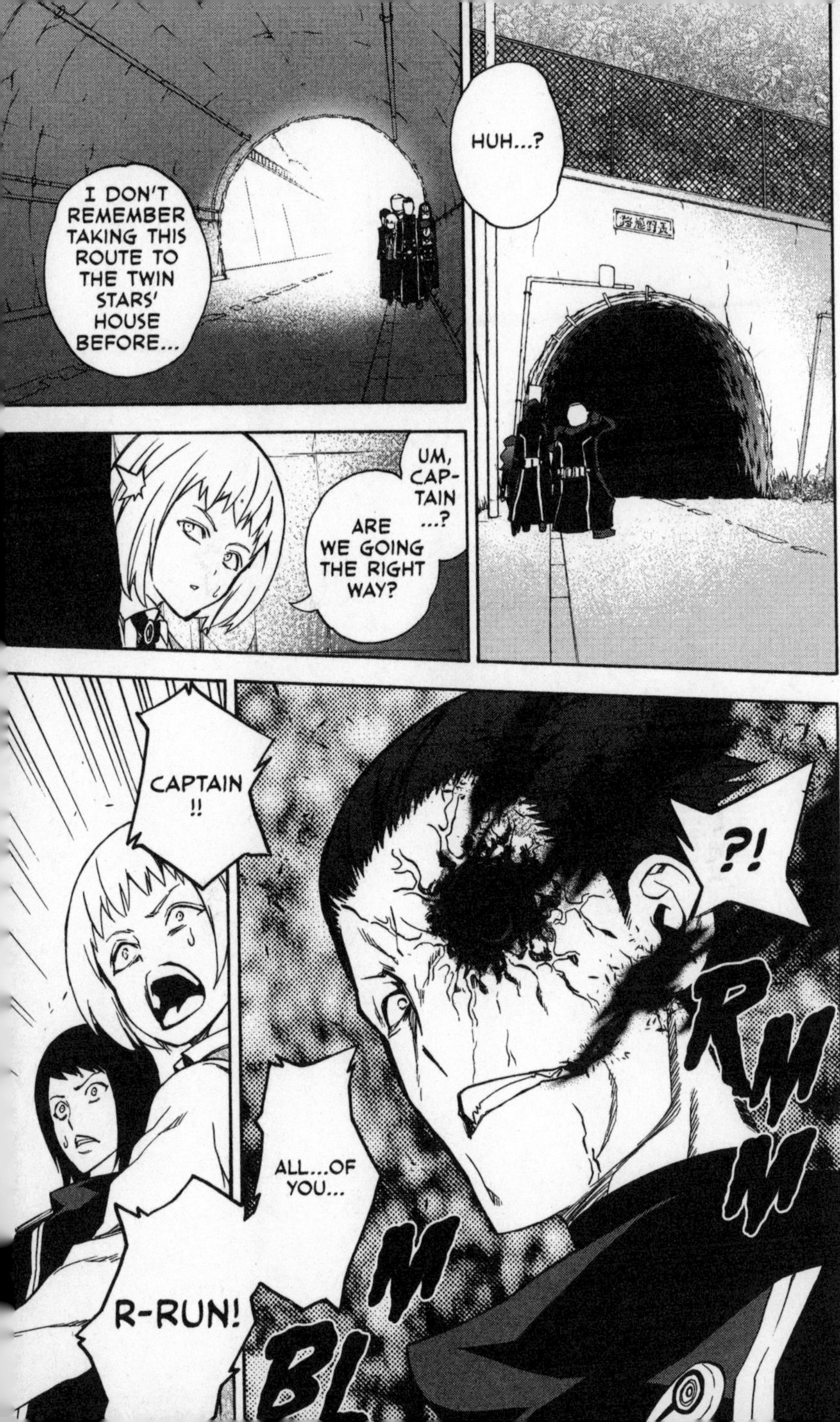
HUH...?
I DON'T REMEMBER TAKING THIS ROUTE TO THE TWIN STARS' HOUSE BEFORE...
UM, CAPTAIN...?
ARE WE GOING THE RIGHT WAY?
?!
RMM
ALL...OF YOU...
BLMM
CAPTAIN!!
R-RUN!

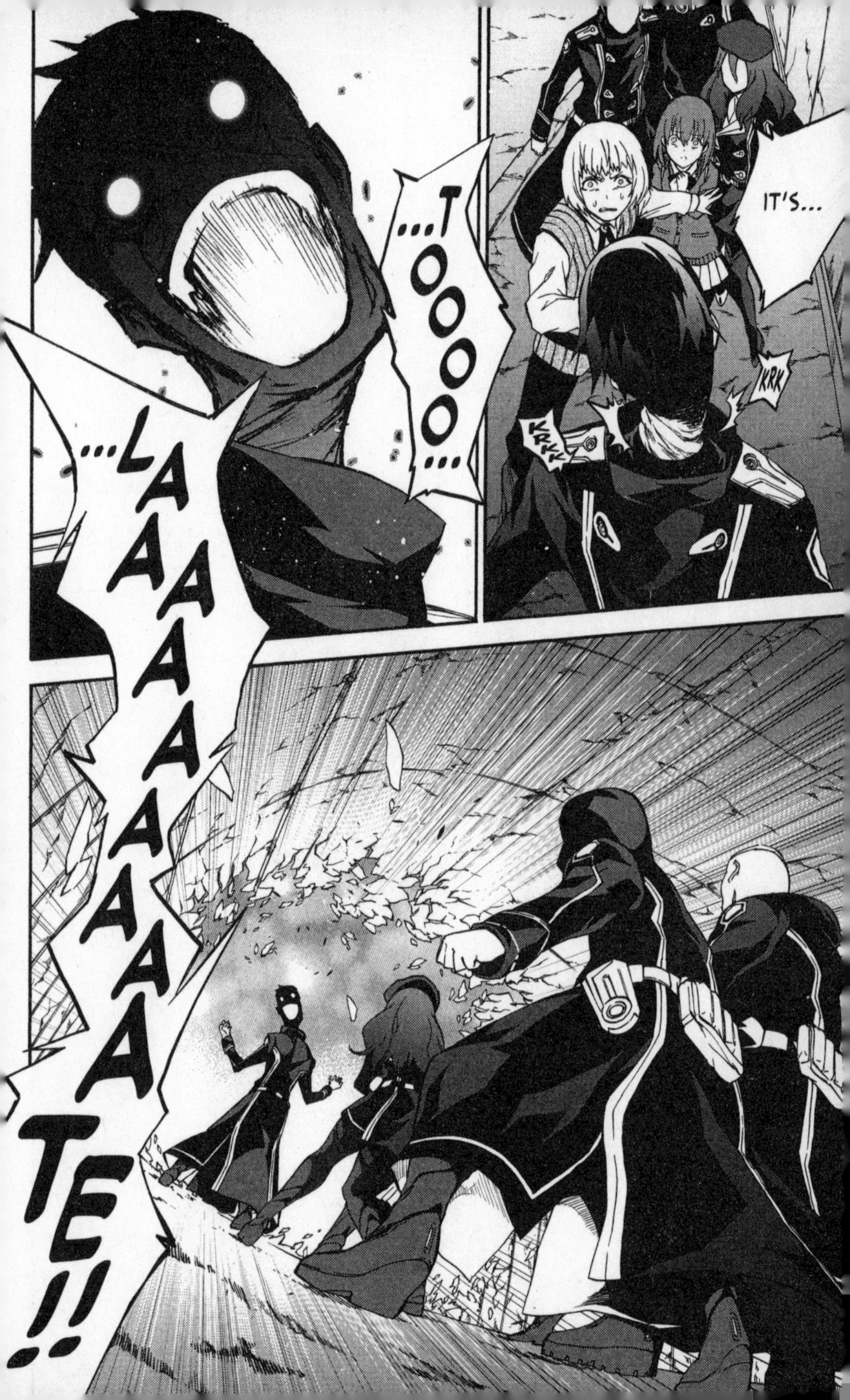
IT'S...
KRK
KRKK
...TOOOO...
...LAAAAAAAAATE!!

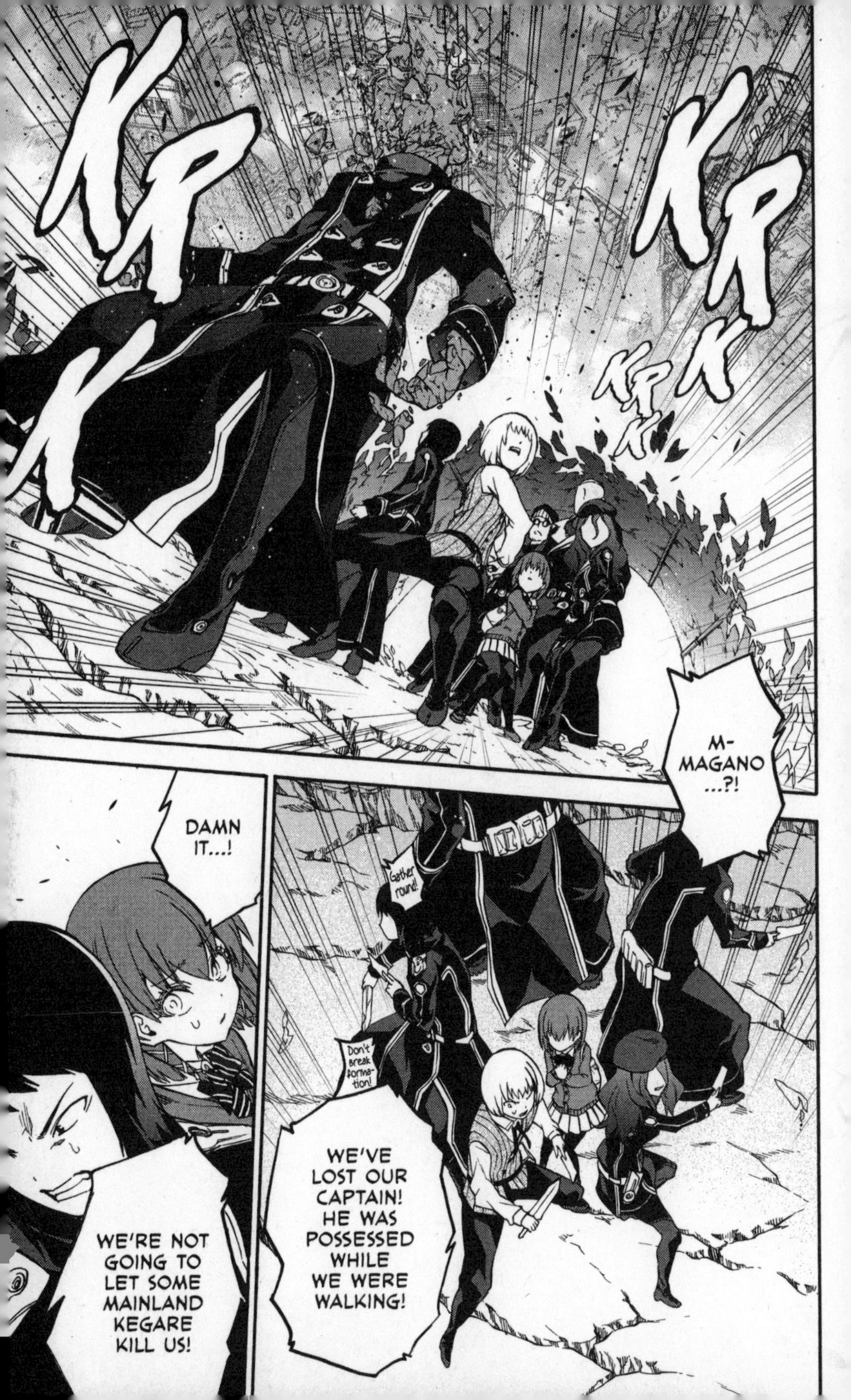
M-MAGANO...?!
Gather round!
Don't break formation!
WE'VE LOST OUR CAPTAIN! HE WAS POSSESSED WHILE WE WERE WALKING!
DAMN IT...!
WE'RE NOT GOING TO LET SOME MAINLAND KEGARE KILL US!

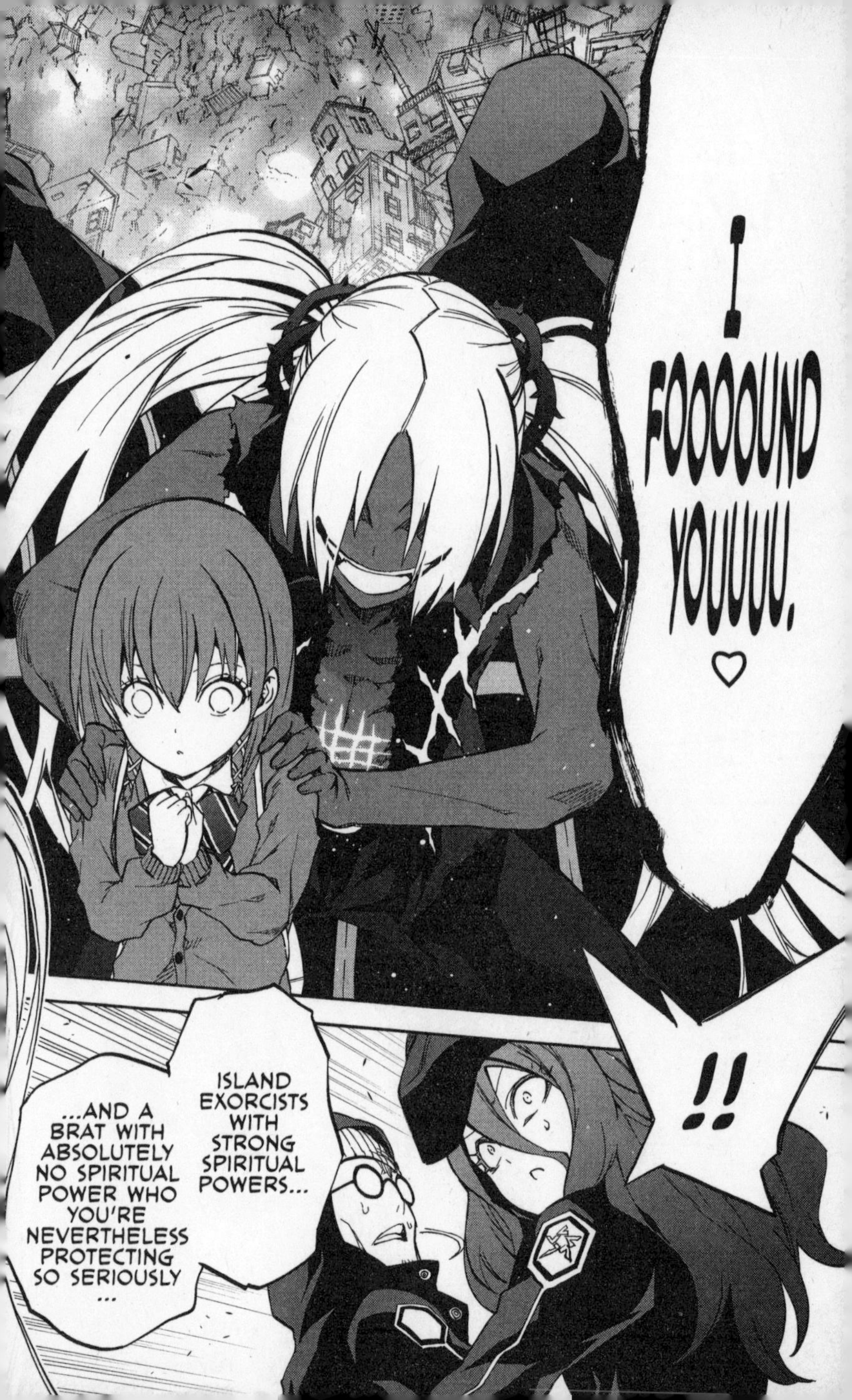
I FOOOOUND YOUUUU. ♥
!!
ISLAND EXORCISTS WITH STRONG SPIRITUAL POWERS...
...AND A BRAT WITH ABSOLUTELY NO SPIRITUAL POWER WHO YOU'RE NEVERTHELESS PROTECTING SO SERIOUSLY...

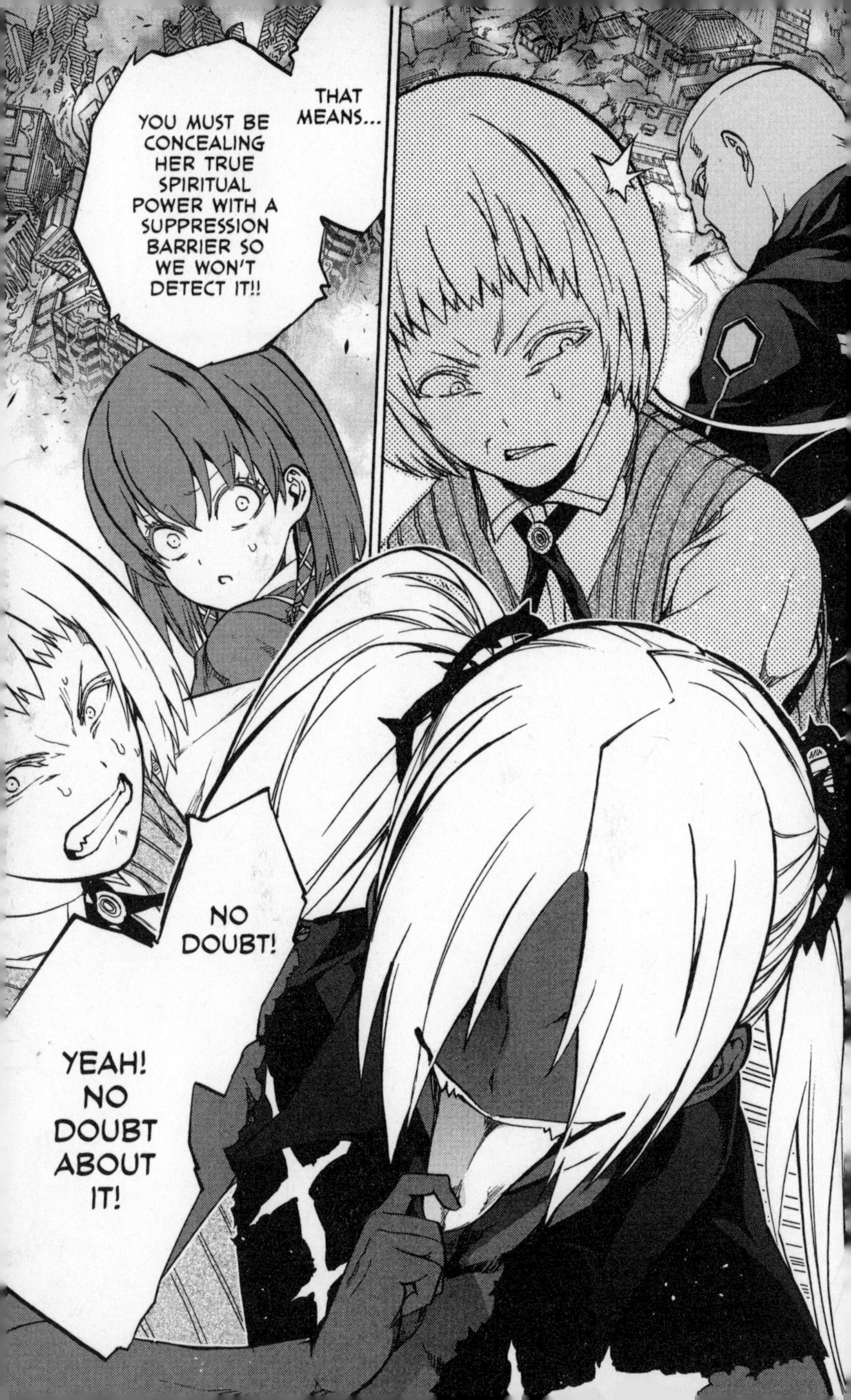
THAT MEANS...
YOU MUST BE CONCEALING HER TRUE SPIRITUAL POWER WITH A SUPPRESSION BARRIER SO WE WON'T DETECT IT!!
NO DOUBT!
YEAH! NO DOUBT ABOUT IT!

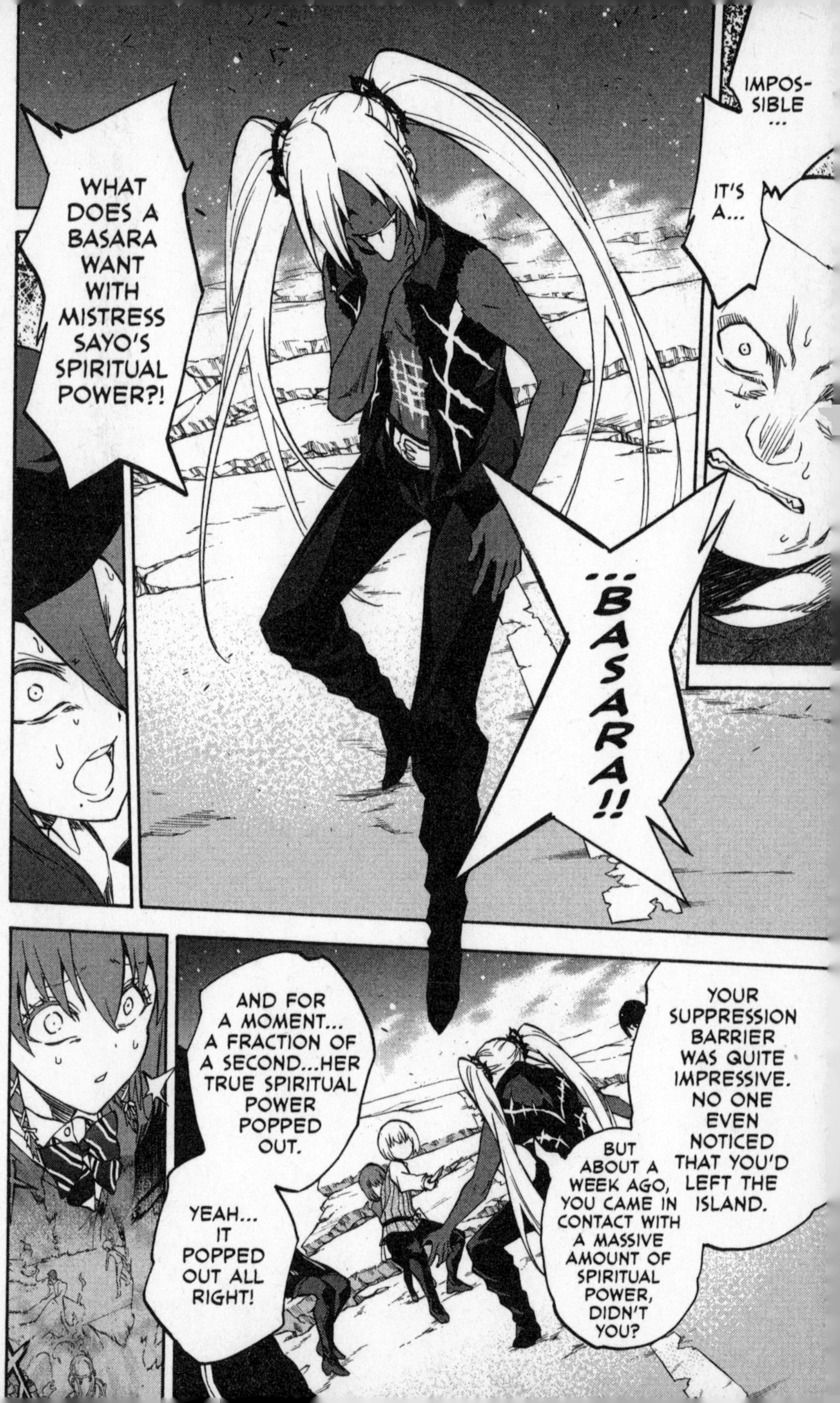
IMPOSSIBLE...
IT'S A...
...BASARA!!
WHAT DOES A BASARA WANT WITH MISTRESS SAYO'S SPIRITUAL POWER?!
YOUR SUPPRESSION BARRIER WAS QUITE IMPRESSIVE. NO ONE EVEN NOTICED THAT YOU'D LEFT THE ISLAND.
BUT ABOUT A WEEK AGO, YOU CAME IN CONTACT WITH A MASSIVE AMOUNT OF SPIRITUAL POWER, DIDN'T YOU?
AND FOR A MOMENT... A FRACTION OF A SECOND...HER TRUE SPIRITUAL POWER POPPED OUT.
YEAH... IT POPPED OUT ALL RIGHT!

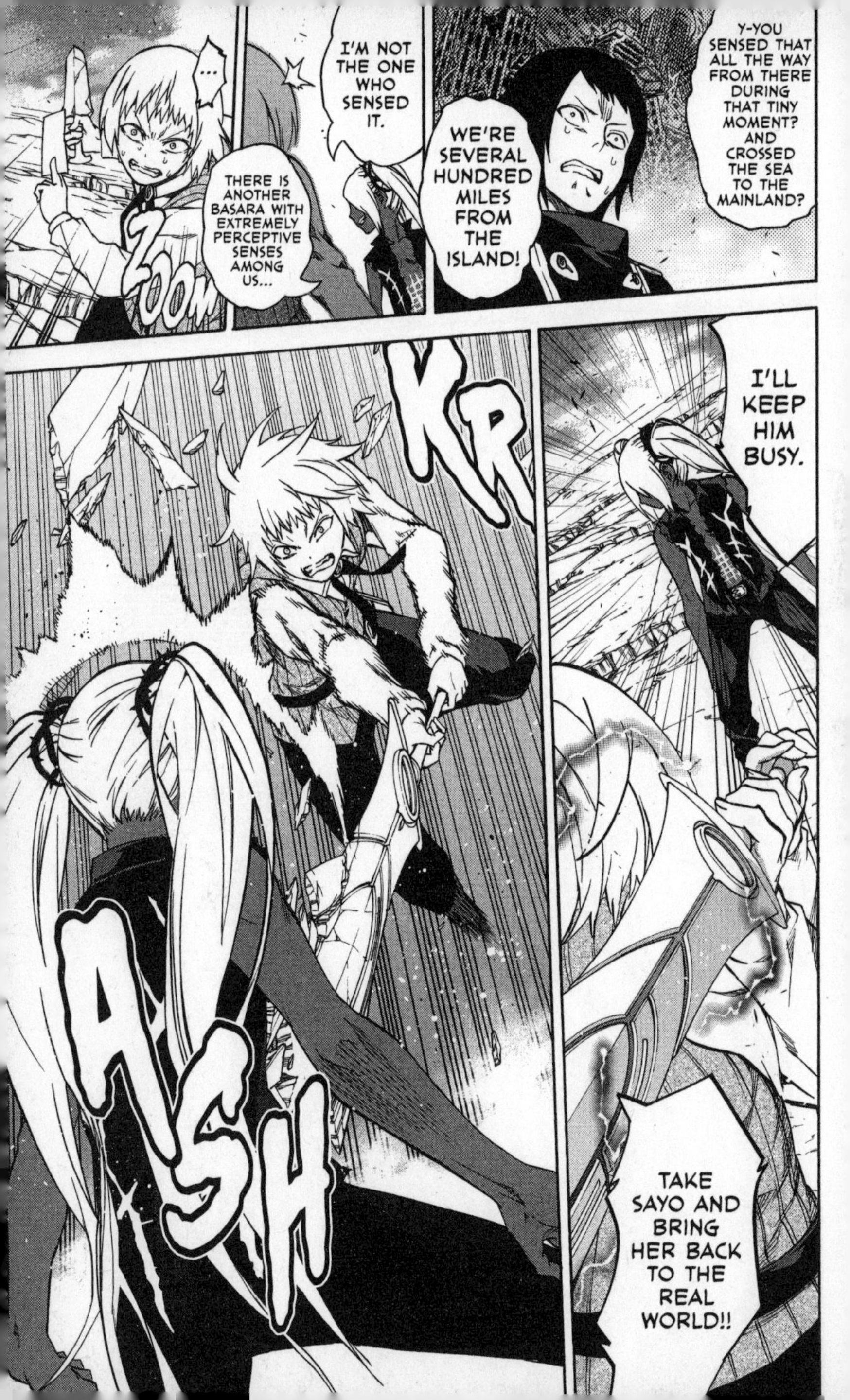

Y-YOU SENSED THAT ALL THE WAY FROM THERE DURING THAT TINY MOMENT? AND CROSSED THE SEA TO THE MAINLAND?
WE'RE SEVERAL HUNDRED MILES FROM THE ISLAND!
I'M NOT THE ONE WHO SENSED IT.
THERE IS ANOTHER BASARA WITH EXTREMELY PERCEPTIVE SENSES AMONG US...
...
ZOOOM
I'LL KEEP HIM BUSY.
TAKE SAYO AND BRING HER BACK TO THE REAL WORLD!!
KR
ASH

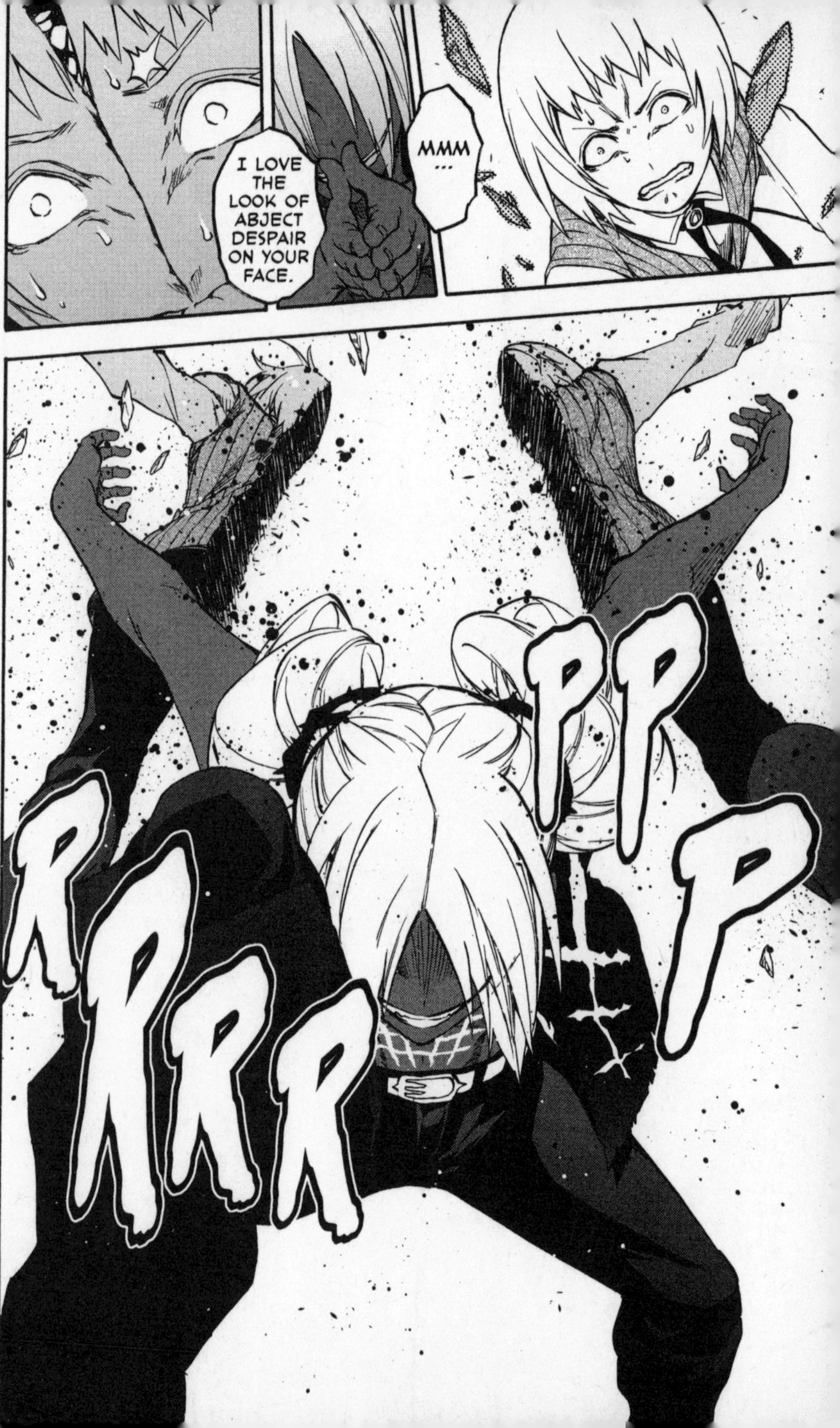
MMM...
I LOVE THE LOOK OF ABJECT DESPAIR ON YOUR FACE.
RRRRPPP

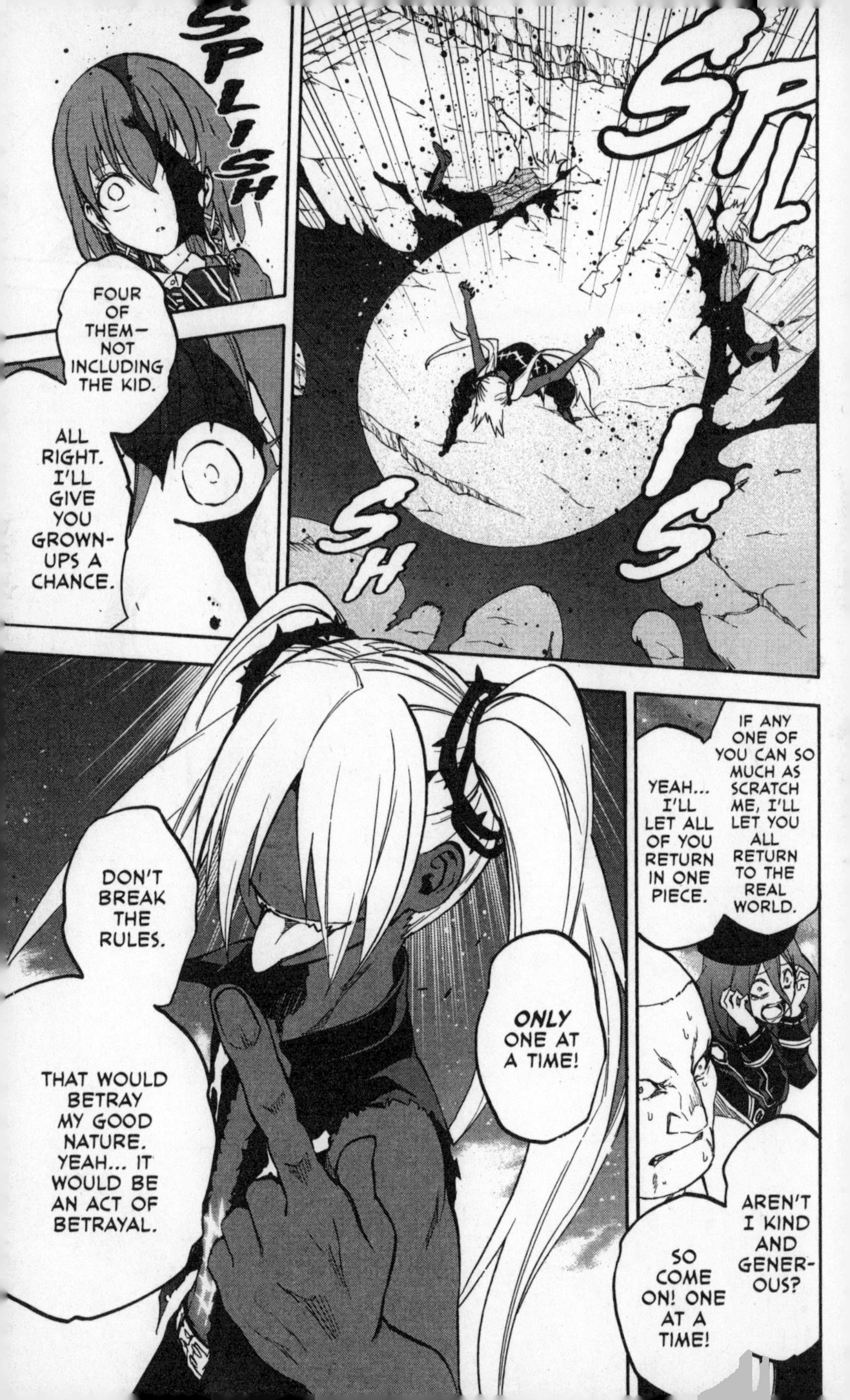
SPLISH
SPLISH
FOUR OF THEM— NOT INCLUDING THE KID.
ALL RIGHT. I'LL GIVE YOU GROWN-UPS A CHANCE.
IF ANY ONE OF YOU CAN SO MUCH AS SCRATCH ME, I'LL LET YOU ALL RETURN TO THE REAL WORLD.
YEAH... I'LL LET ALL OF YOU RETURN IN ONE PIECE.
AREN'T I KIND AND GENER-OUS?
SO COME ON! ONE AT A TIME!
ONLY ONE AT A TIME!
DON'T BREAK THE RULES.
THAT WOULD BETRAY MY GOOD NATURE. YEAH... IT WOULD BE AN ACT OF BETRAYAL.

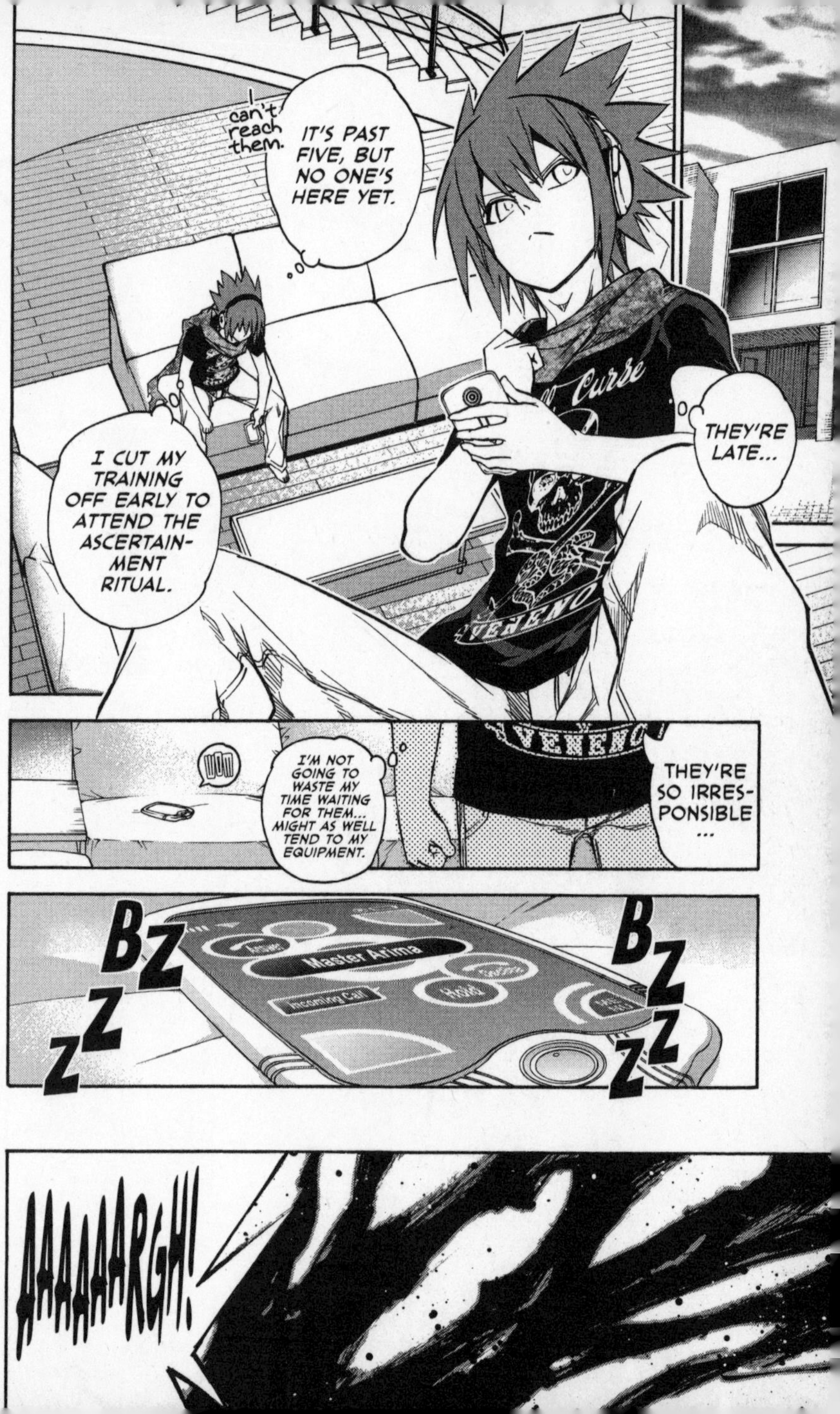
IT'S PAST FIVE, BUT NO ONE'S HERE YET.
I can't reach them.
THEY'RE LATE...
I CUT MY TRAINING OFF EARLY TO ATTEND THE ASCERTAINMENT RITUAL.
THEY'RE SO IRRESPONSIBLE...
I'M NOT GOING TO WASTE MY TIME WAITING FOR THEM... MIGHT AS WELL TEND TO MY EQUIPMENT.
BZZZ
BZZZ
Master Arima
Incoming Call
Hold
AAAAARGH!

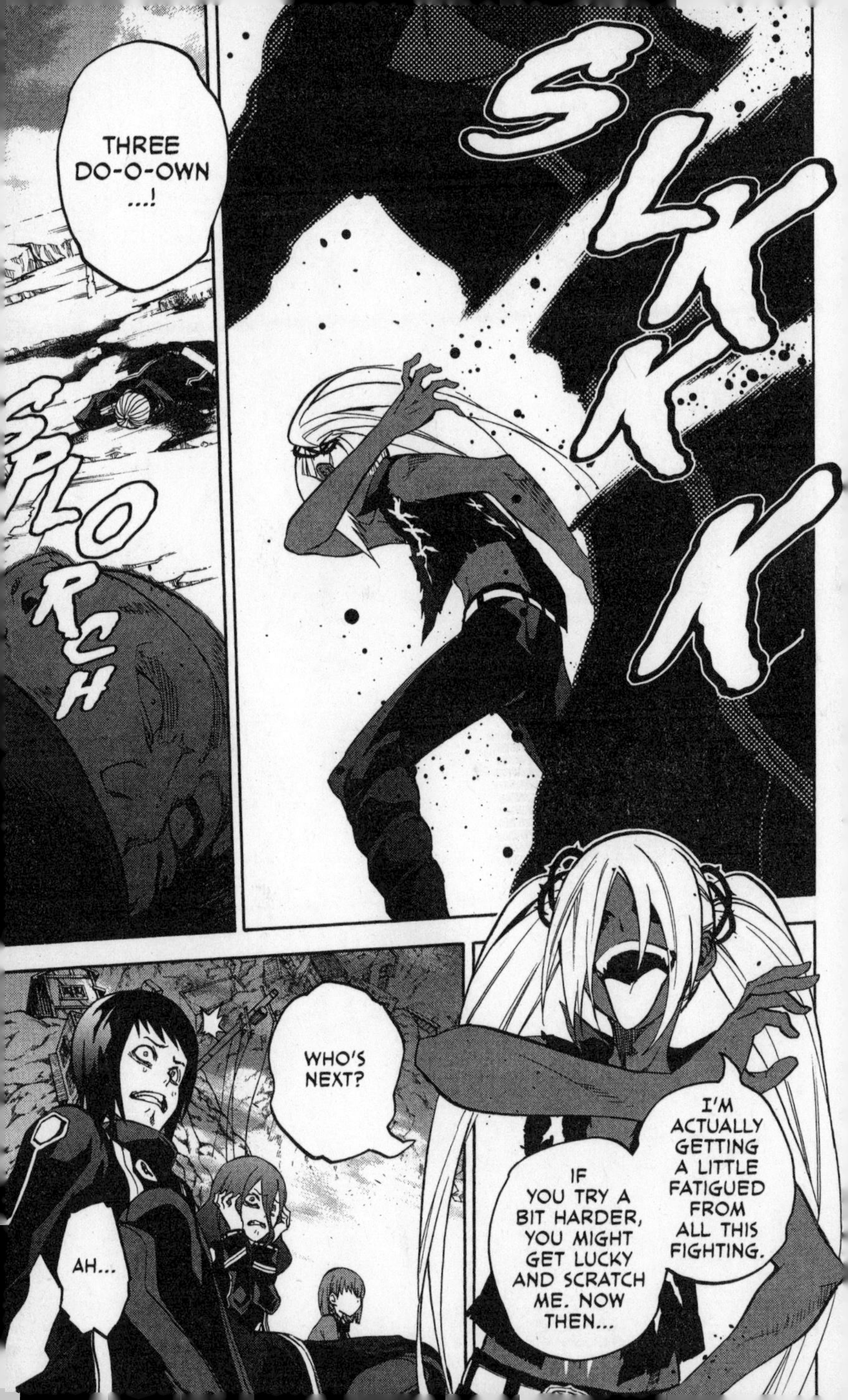

SLKKK
THREE DO-O-OWN ...!
SPLORCH
I'M ACTUALLY GETTING A LITTLE FATIGUED FROM ALL THIS FIGHTING.
IF YOU TRY A BIT HARDER, YOU MIGHT GET LUCKY AND SCRATCH ME. NOW THEN...
WHO'S NEXT?
AH...

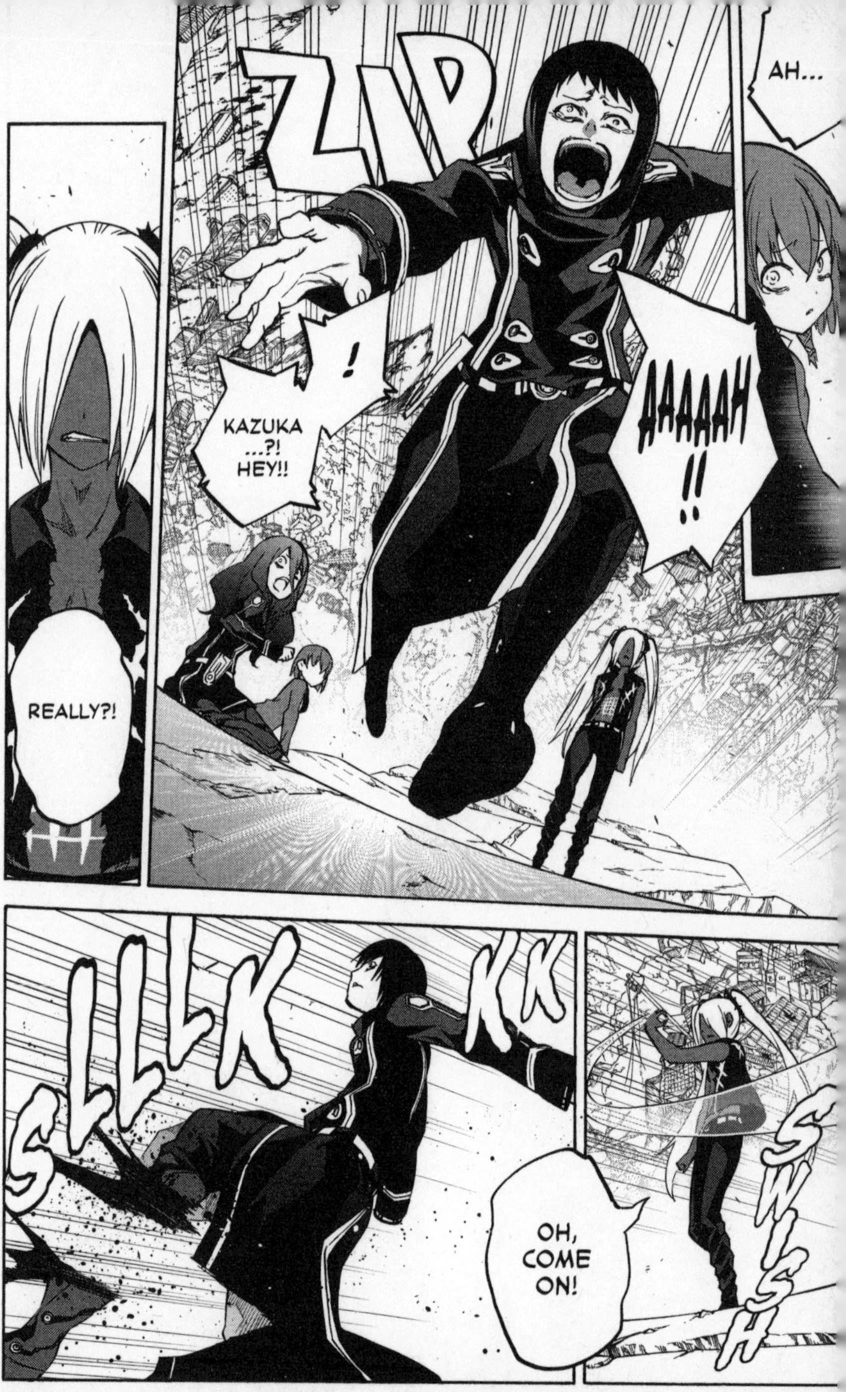
AH...
ZIP
AAAAAH!!
!
KAZUKA...?! HEY!!
REALLY?!
SWISH
OH, COME ON!
SLLLKKK

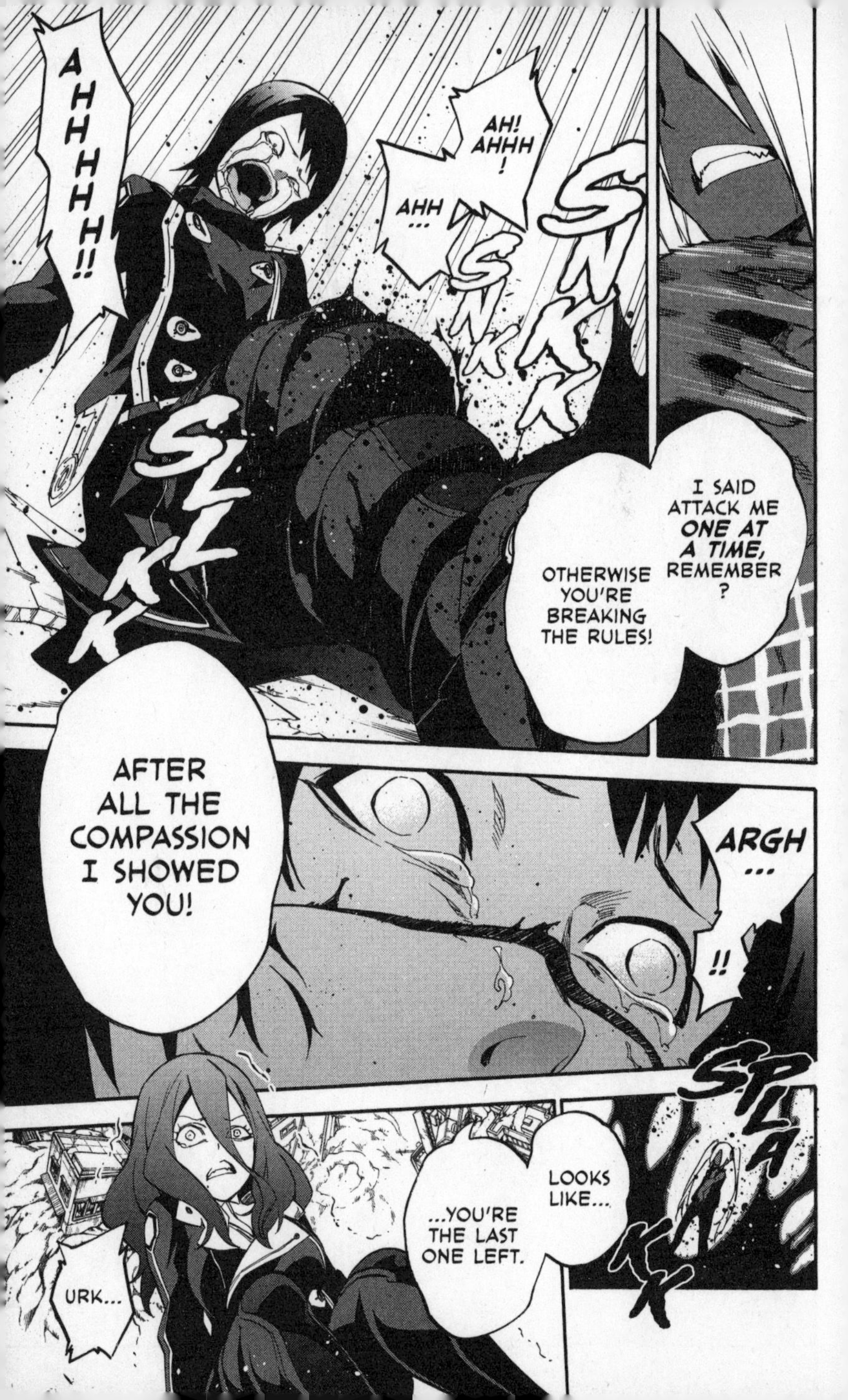
SNKK
AH! AHHH!
AHH...
SNKK
AHHHHHH!!
SLKK
I SAID ATTACK ME *ONE AT A TIME,* REMEMBER?
OTHERWISE YOU'RE BREAKING THE RULES!
ARGH... !!
AFTER ALL THE COMPASSION I SHOWED YOU!
SPLAKK
LOOKS LIKE...
...YOU'RE THE LAST ONE LEFT.
URK...

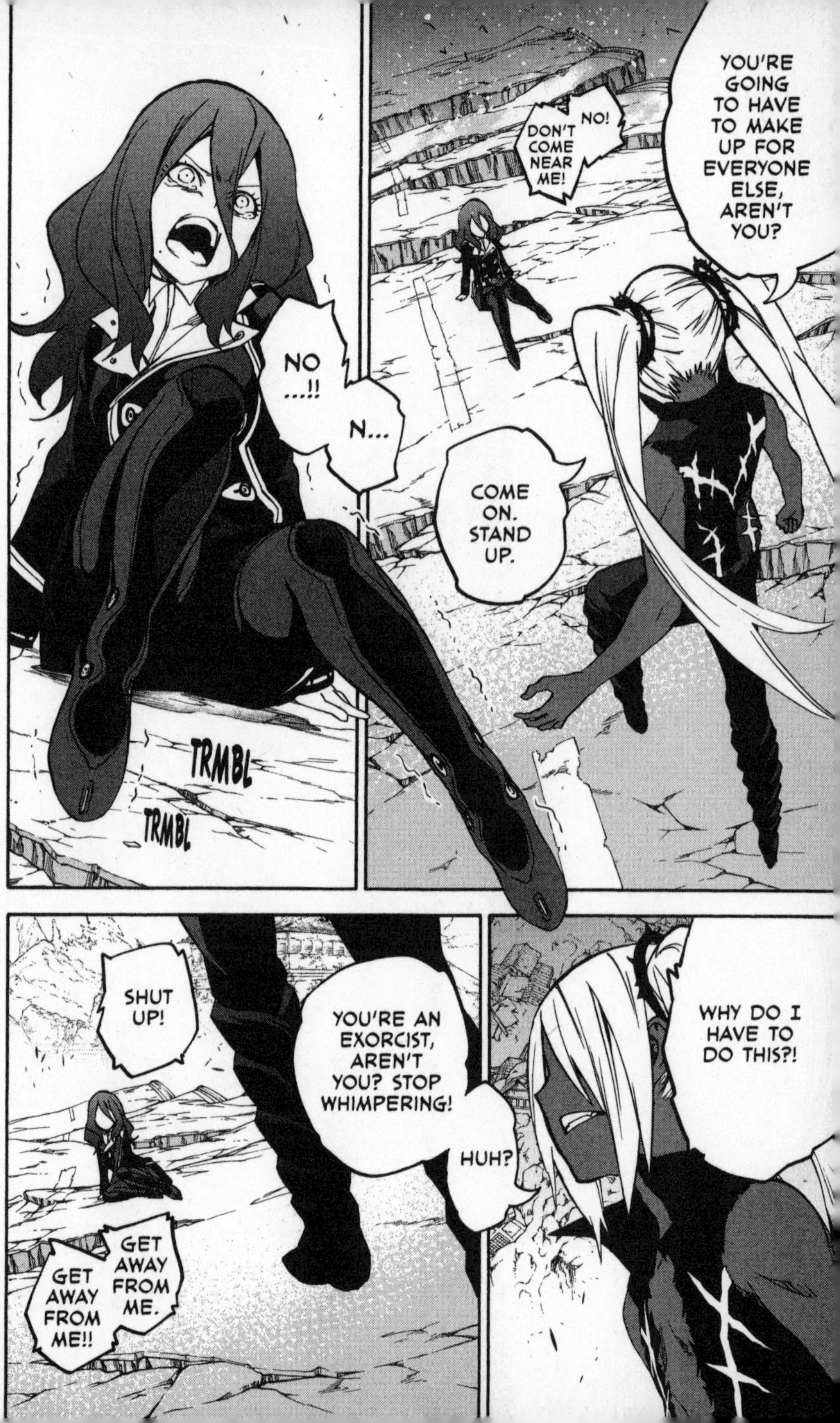
YOU'RE GOING TO HAVE TO MAKE UP FOR EVERYONE ELSE, AREN'T YOU?
NO! DON'T COME NEAR ME!
COME ON. STAND UP.
NO ...!!
N...
TRMBL
TRMBL
WHY DO I HAVE TO DO THIS?!
YOU'RE AN EXORCIST, AREN'T YOU? STOP WHIMPERING!
HUH?
SHUT UP!
GET AWAY FROM ME.
GET AWAY FROM ME!!

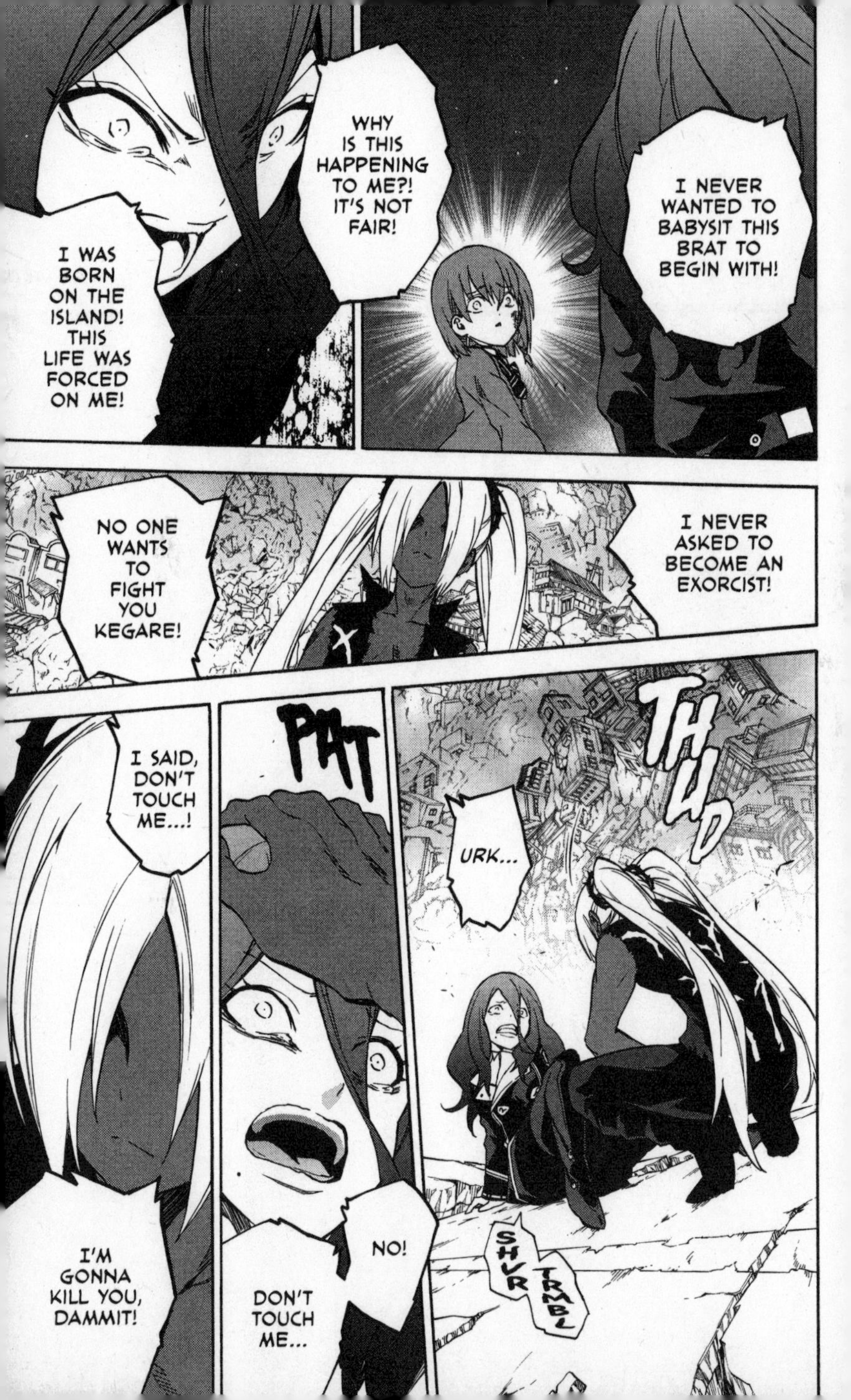
I NEVER WANTED TO BABYSIT THIS BRAT TO BEGIN WITH!
WHY IS THIS HAPPENING TO ME?! IT'S NOT FAIR!
I WAS BORN ON THE ISLAND! THIS LIFE WAS FORCED ON ME!
I NEVER ASKED TO BECOME AN EXORCIST!
NO ONE WANTS TO FIGHT YOU KEGARE!
THUD
URK...
SHUR
TRMBL
PAT
NO!
DON'T TOUCH ME...
I SAID, DON'T TOUCH ME...!
I'M GONNA KILL YOU, DAMMIT!

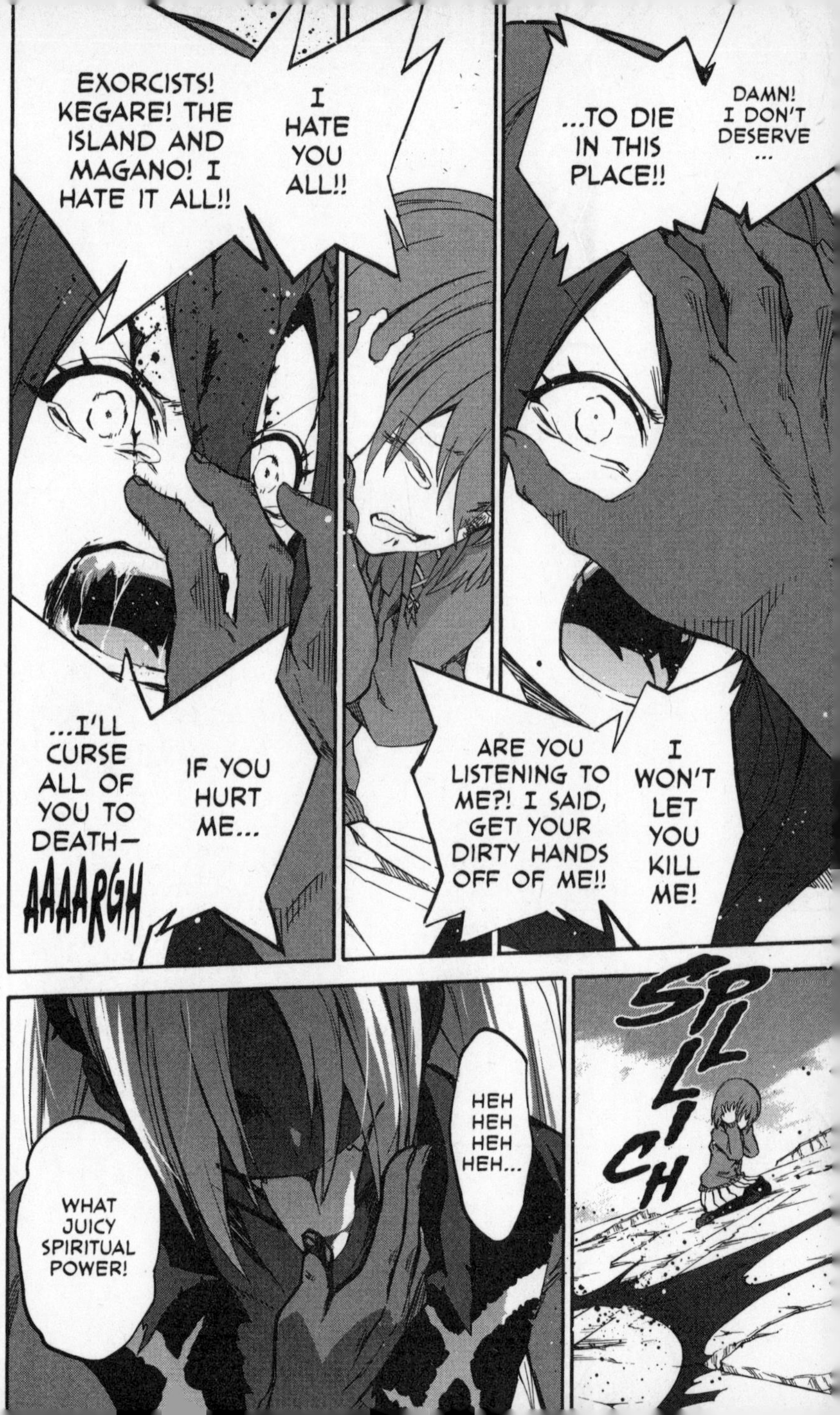
DAMN! I DON'T DESERVE...
...TO DIE IN THIS PLACE!!
I WON'T LET YOU KILL ME!
ARE YOU LISTENING TO ME?! I SAID, GET YOUR DIRTY HANDS OFF OF ME!!
I HATE YOU ALL!!
EXORCISTS! KEGARE! THE ISLAND AND MAGANO! I HATE IT ALL!!
IF YOU HURT ME...
...I'LL CURSE ALL OF YOU TO DEATH—
AAAARGH
SPLLLICH
HEH HEH HEH HEH...
WHAT JUICY SPIRITUAL POWER!

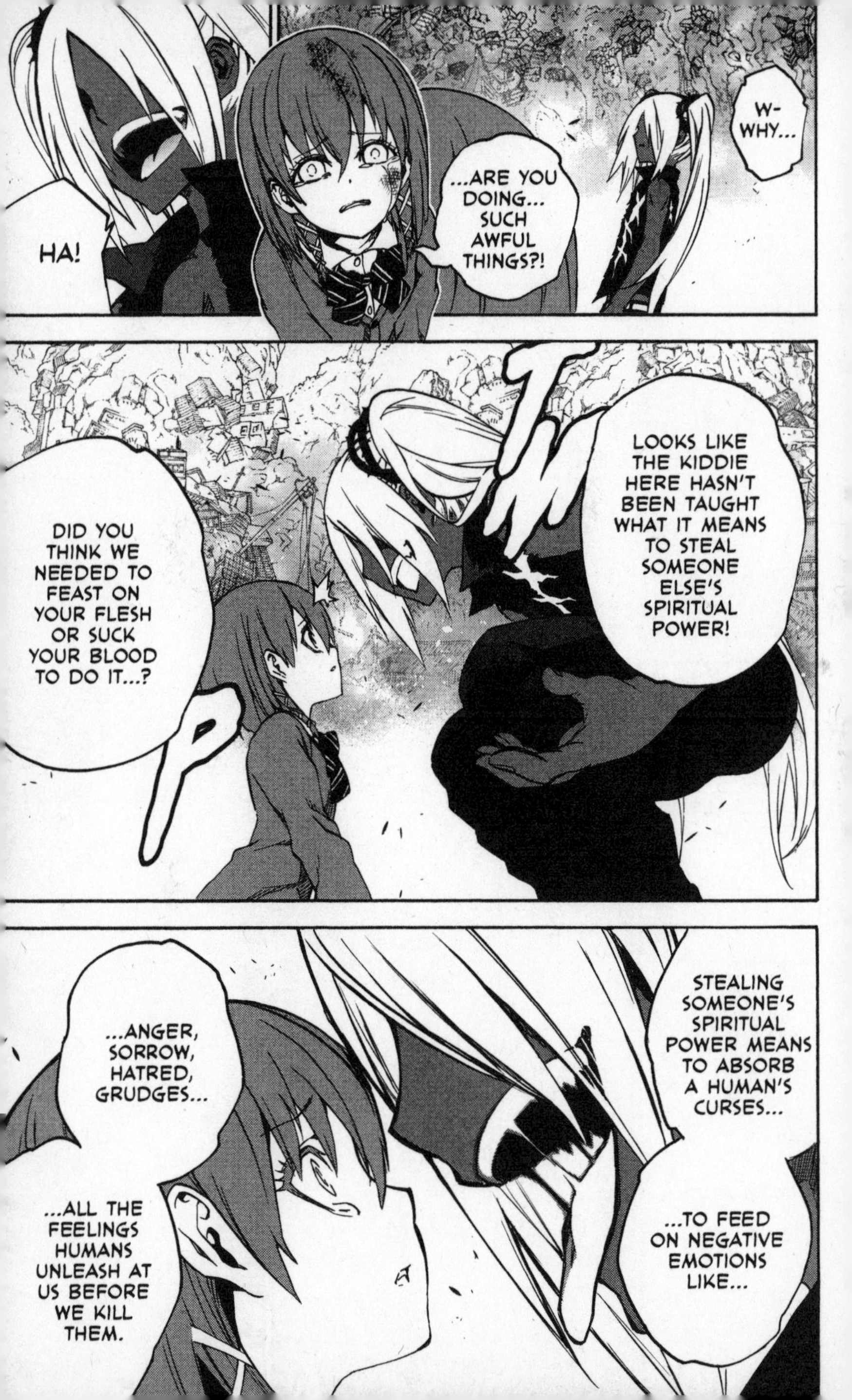
W- WHY...
...ARE YOU DOING... SUCH AWFUL THINGS?!
HA!
LOOKS LIKE THE KIDDIE HERE HASN'T BEEN TAUGHT WHAT IT MEANS TO STEAL SOMEONE ELSE'S SPIRITUAL POWER!
DID YOU THINK WE NEEDED TO FEAST ON YOUR FLESH OR SUCK YOUR BLOOD TO DO IT...?
STEALING SOMEONE'S SPIRITUAL POWER MEANS TO ABSORB A HUMAN'S CURSES...
...TO FEED ON NEGATIVE EMOTIONS LIKE...
...ANGER, SORROW, HATRED, GRUDGES...
...ALL THE FEELINGS HUMANS UNLEASH AT US BEFORE WE KILL THEM.

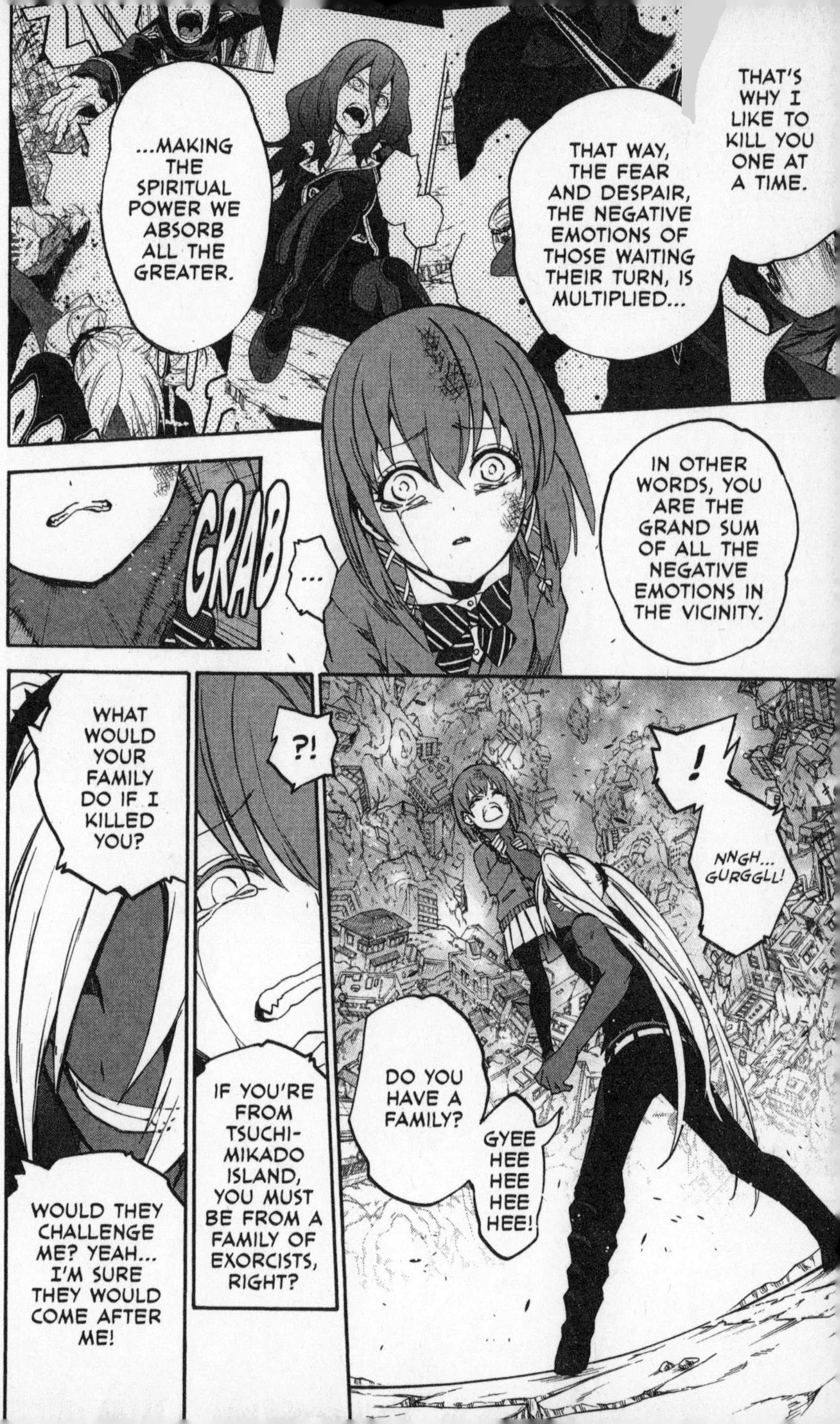
THAT'S WHY I LIKE TO KILL YOU ONE AT A TIME.
THAT WAY, THE FEAR AND DESPAIR, THE NEGATIVE EMOTIONS OF THOSE WAITING THEIR TURN, IS MULTIPLIED...
...MAKING THE SPIRITUAL POWER WE ABSORB ALL THE GREATER.
IN OTHER WORDS, YOU ARE THE GRAND SUM OF ALL THE NEGATIVE EMOTIONS IN THE VICINITY.
...
GRAB
!
NNGH... GURGGLL!
DO YOU HAVE A FAMILY?
GYEE HEE HEE HEE HEE!
?!
IF YOU'RE FROM TSUCHI-MIKADO ISLAND, YOU MUST BE FROM A FAMILY OF EXORCISTS, RIGHT?
WHAT WOULD YOUR FAMILY DO IF I KILLED YOU?
WOULD THEY CHALLENGE ME? YEAH... I'M SURE THEY WOULD COME AFTER ME!

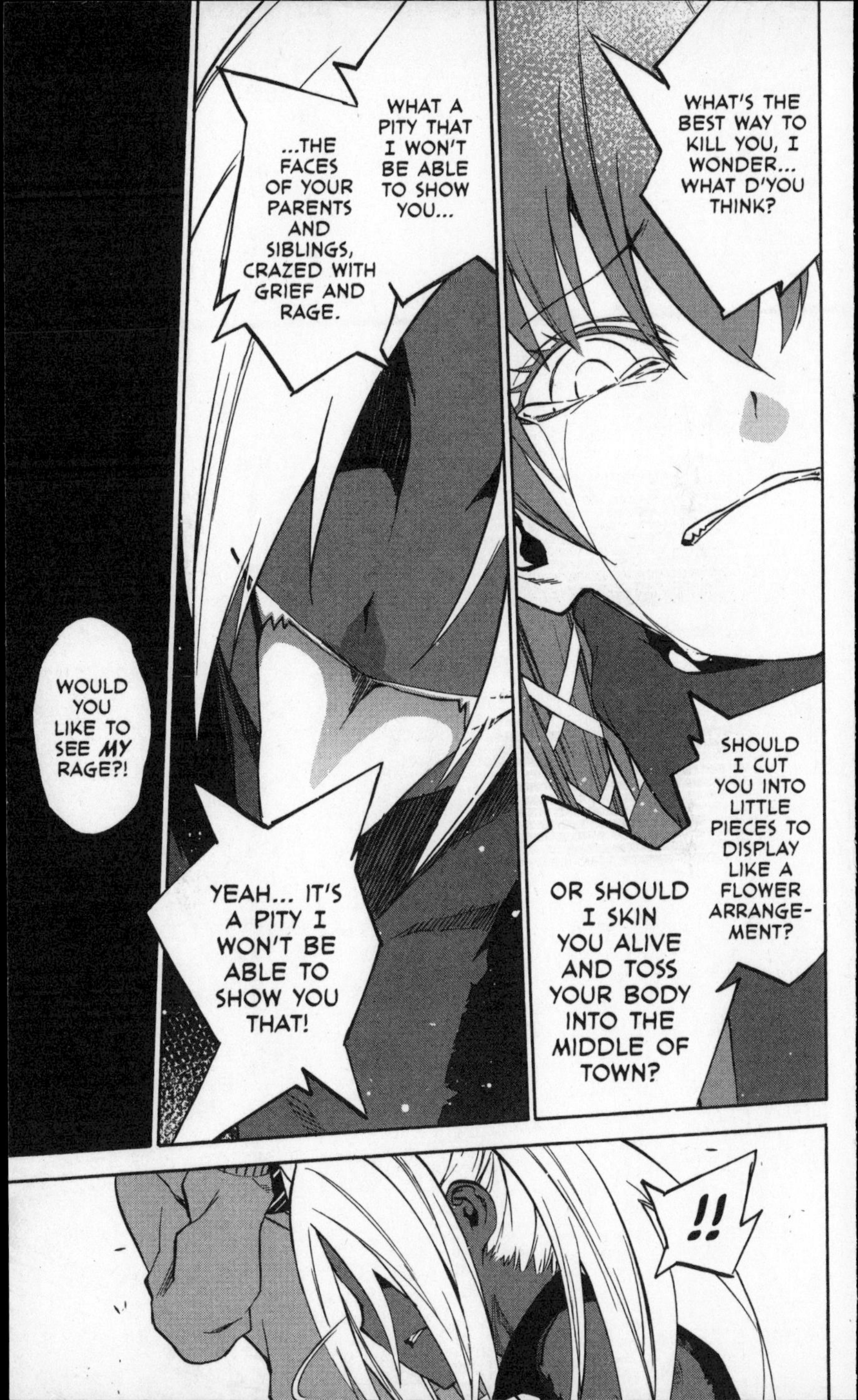
WHAT'S THE BEST WAY TO KILL YOU, I WONDER... WHAT D'YOU THINK?
WHAT A PITY THAT I WON'T BE ABLE TO SHOW YOU...
...THE FACES OF YOUR PARENTS AND SIBLINGS, CRAZED WITH GRIEF AND RAGE.
SHOULD I CUT YOU INTO LITTLE PIECES TO DISPLAY LIKE A FLOWER ARRANGE-MENT?
OR SHOULD I SKIN YOU ALIVE AND TOSS YOUR BODY INTO THE MIDDLE OF TOWN?
YEAH... IT'S A PITY I WON'T BE ABLE TO SHOW YOU THAT!
WOULD YOU LIKE TO SEE *MY* RAGE?!
!!

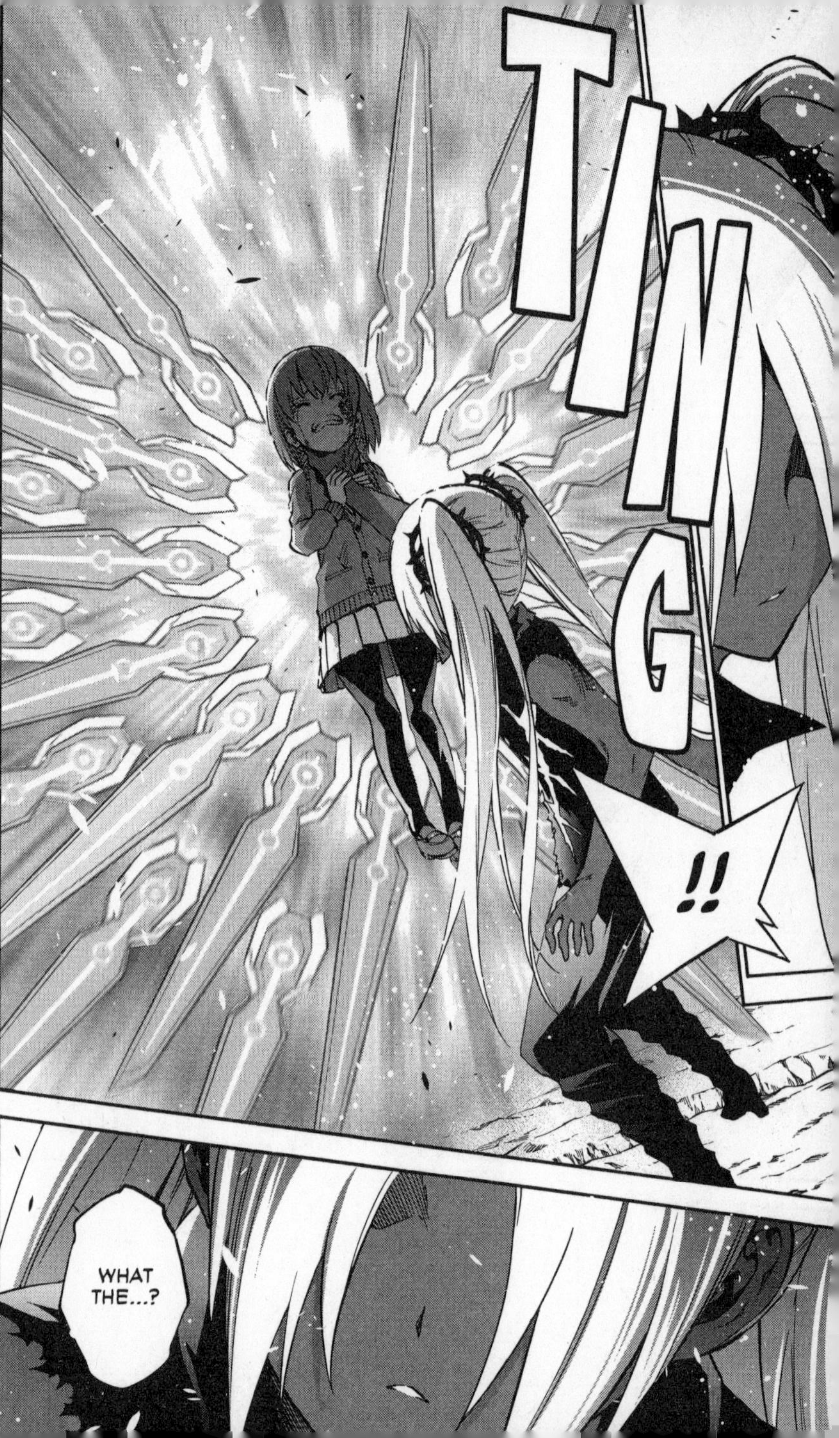
TING
!!
WHAT THE...?

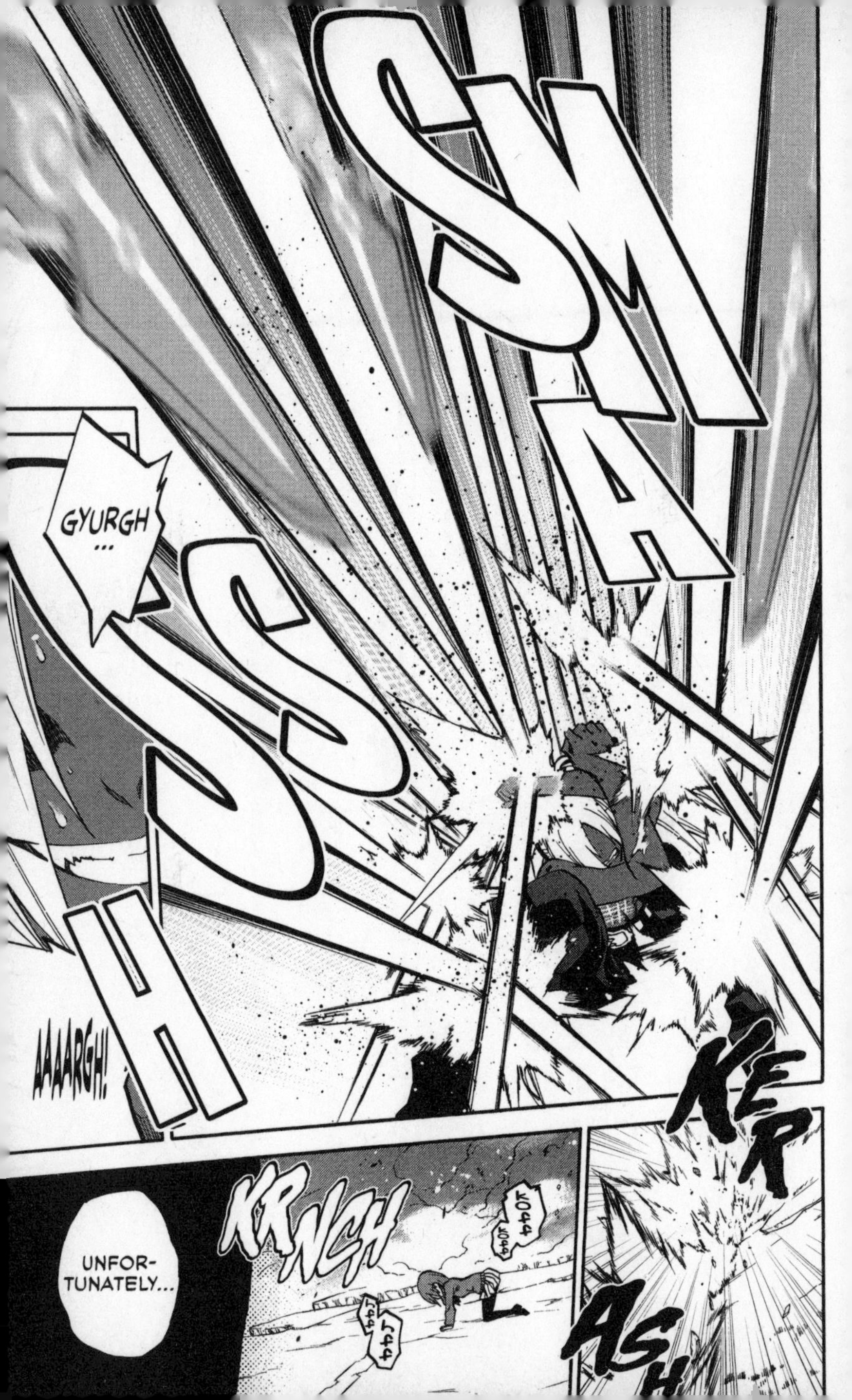
GYURGH ...
SMASH
AAAARGH!
KERASH
KRNCH
KOFF KOFF
UNFORTUNATELY...

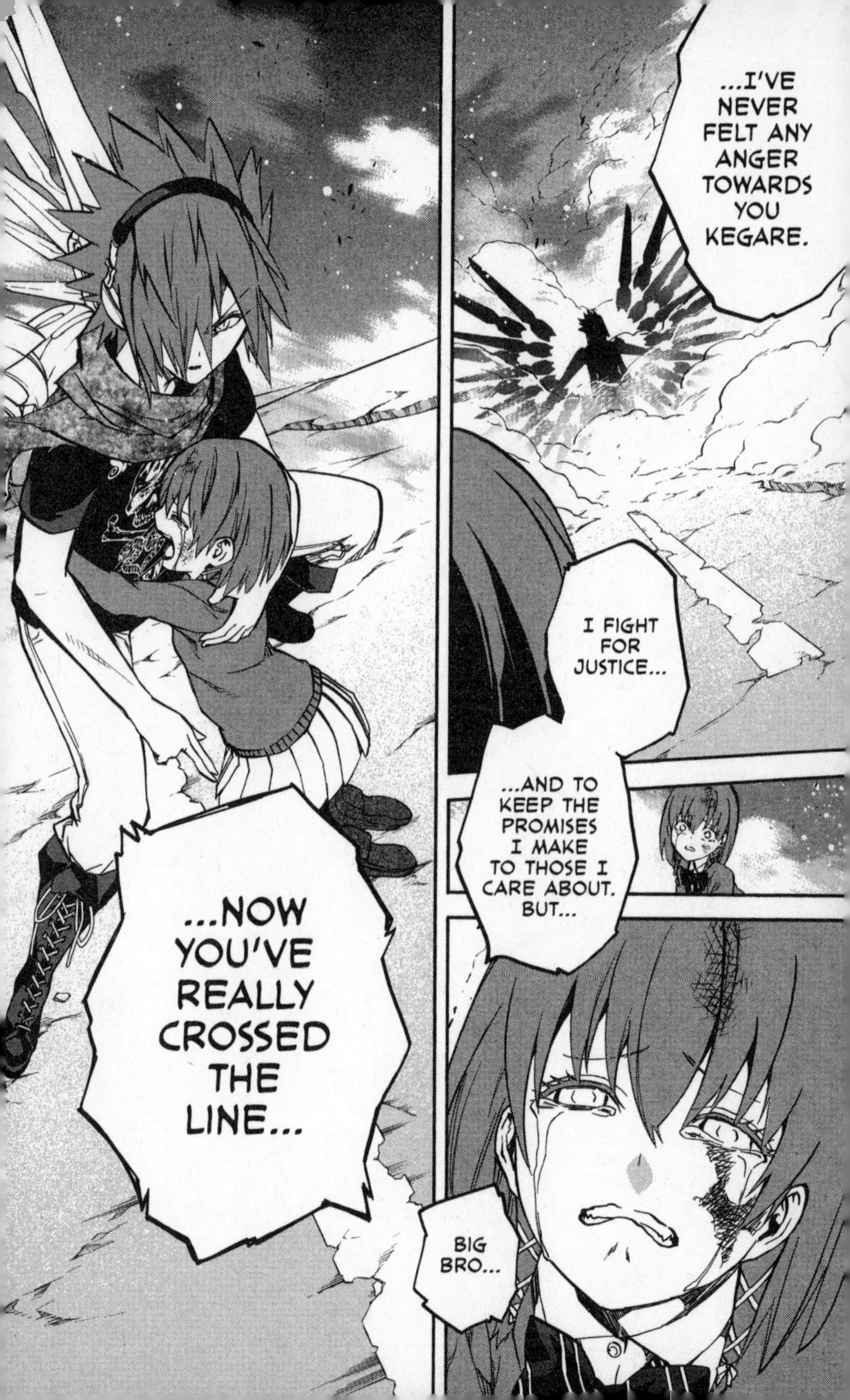
...I'VE NEVER FELT ANY ANGER TOWARDS YOU KEGARE.
I FIGHT FOR JUSTICE...
...AND TO KEEP THE PROMISES I MAKE TO THOSE I CARE ABOUT. BUT...
BIG BRO...
...NOW YOU'VE REALLY CROSSED THE LINE...

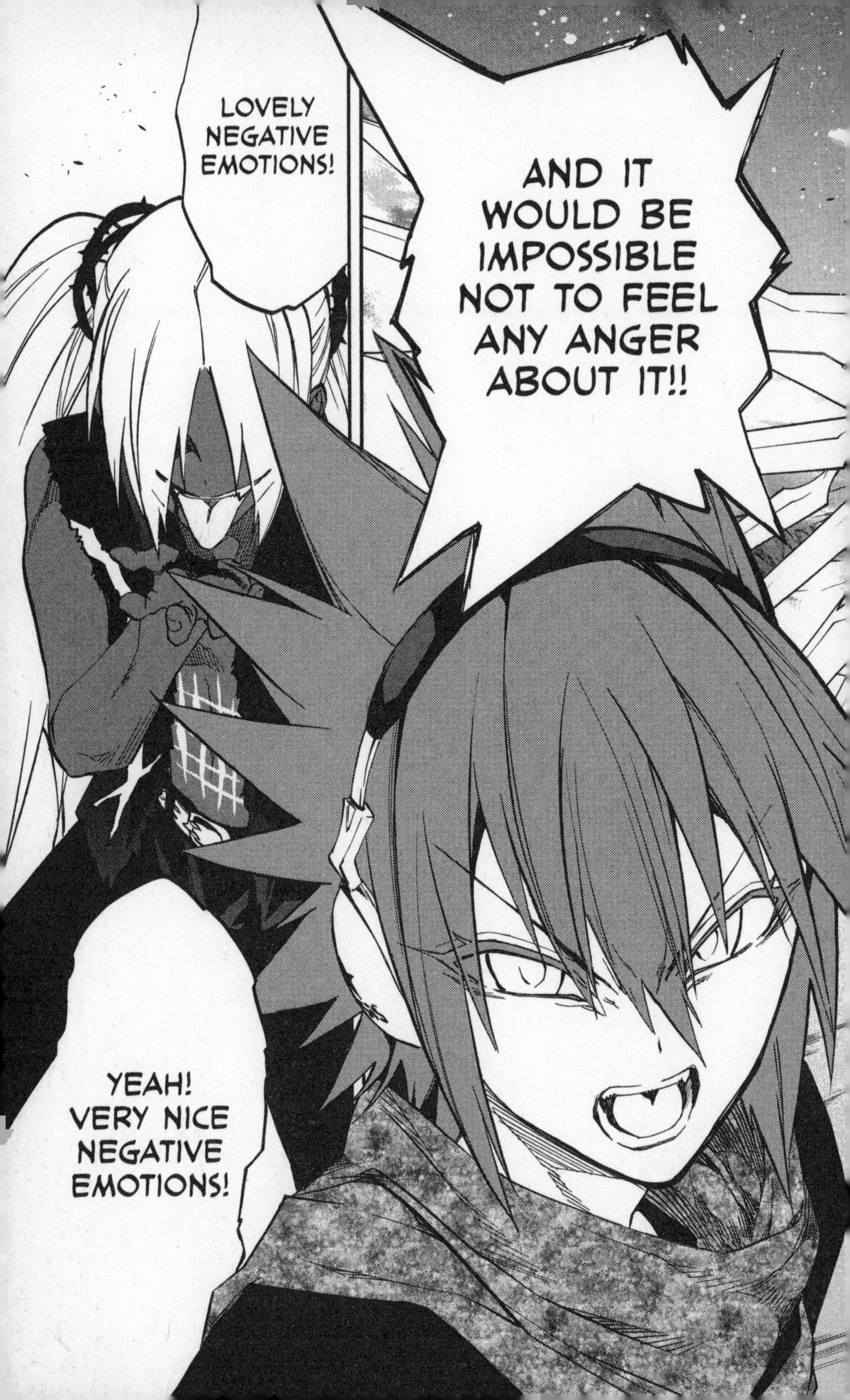
AND IT WOULD BE IMPOSSIBLE NOT TO FEEL ANY ANGER ABOUT IT!!
LOVELY NEGATIVE EMOTIONS!
YEAH! VERY NICE NEGATIVE EMOTIONS!

ROKURO'S FRIENDS

I don't think I'll get the opportunity later if I don't draw them now.

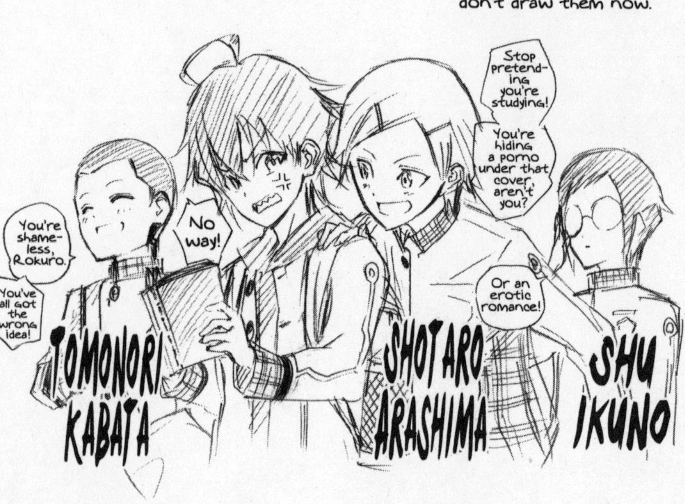
Stop pretend-ing you're studying!
You're hiding a porno under that cover, aren't you?
Or an erotic romance!
SHU IKUNO
SHOTARO ARASHIMA
No way!
You're shame-less, Rokuro.
You've all got the wrong idea!
TOMONORI KABATA

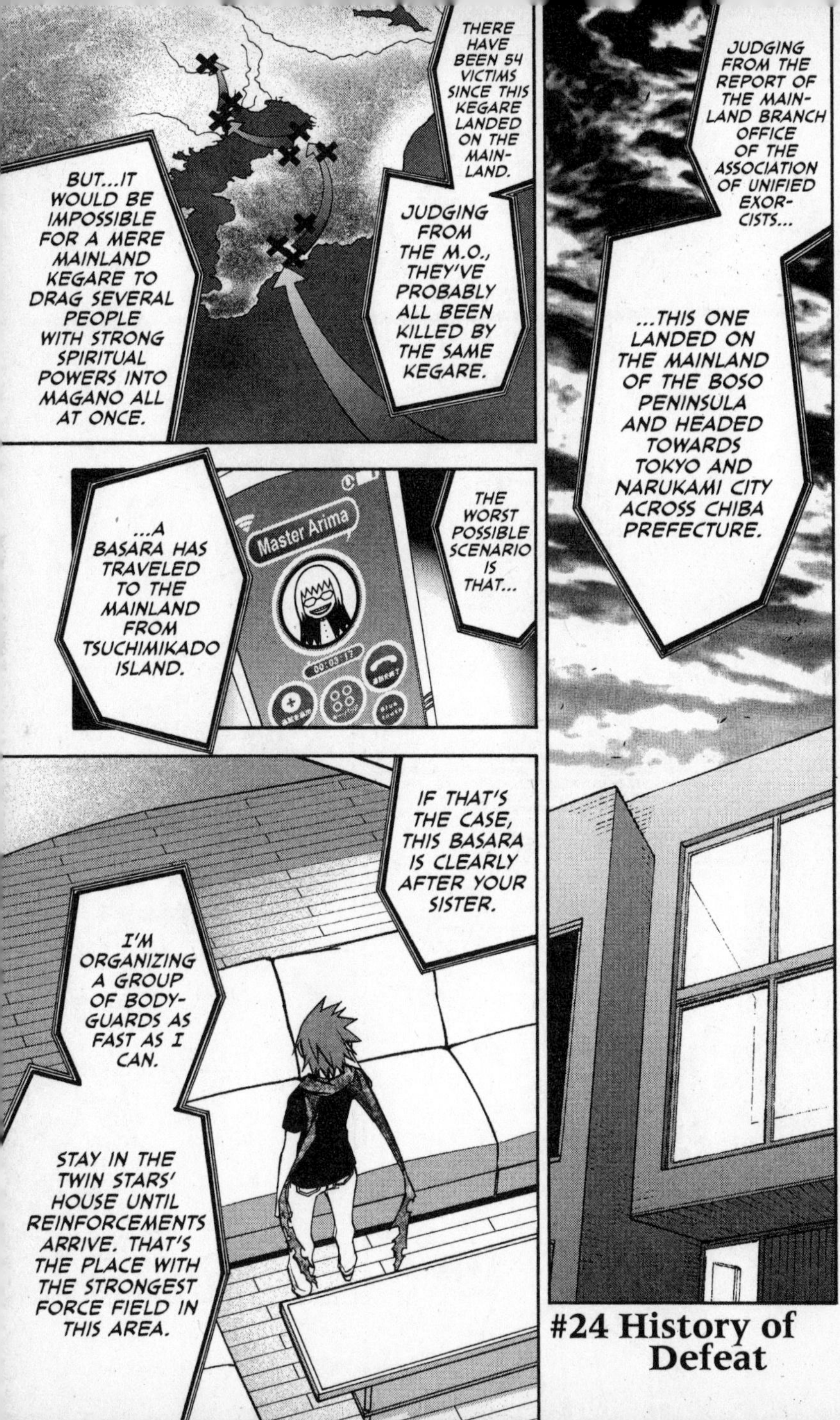
JUDGING FROM THE REPORT OF THE MAIN-LAND BRANCH OFFICE OF THE ASSOCIATION OF UNIFIED EXOR-CISTS...
...THIS ONE LANDED ON THE MAINLAND OF THE BOSO PENINSULA AND HEADED TOWARDS TOKYO AND NARUKAMI CITY ACROSS CHIBA PREFECTURE.
THERE HAVE BEEN 54 VICTIMS SINCE THIS KEGARE LANDED ON THE MAIN-LAND.
JUDGING FROM THE M.O., THEY'VE PROBABLY ALL BEEN KILLED BY THE SAME KEGARE.
BUT...IT WOULD BE IMPOSSIBLE FOR A MERE MAINLAND KEGARE TO DRAG SEVERAL PEOPLE WITH STRONG SPIRITUAL POWERS INTO MAGANO ALL AT ONCE.
THE WORST POSSIBLE SCENARIO IS THAT...
Master Arima
...A BASARA HAS TRAVELED TO THE MAINLAND FROM TSUCHIMIKADO ISLAND.
IF THAT'S THE CASE, THIS BASARA IS CLEARLY AFTER YOUR SISTER.
I'M ORGANIZING A GROUP OF BODY-GUARDS AS FAST AS I CAN.
STAY IN THE TWIN STARS' HOUSE UNTIL REINFORCEMENTS ARRIVE. THAT'S THE PLACE WITH THE STRONGEST FORCE FIELD IN THIS AREA.

#24 History of Defeat

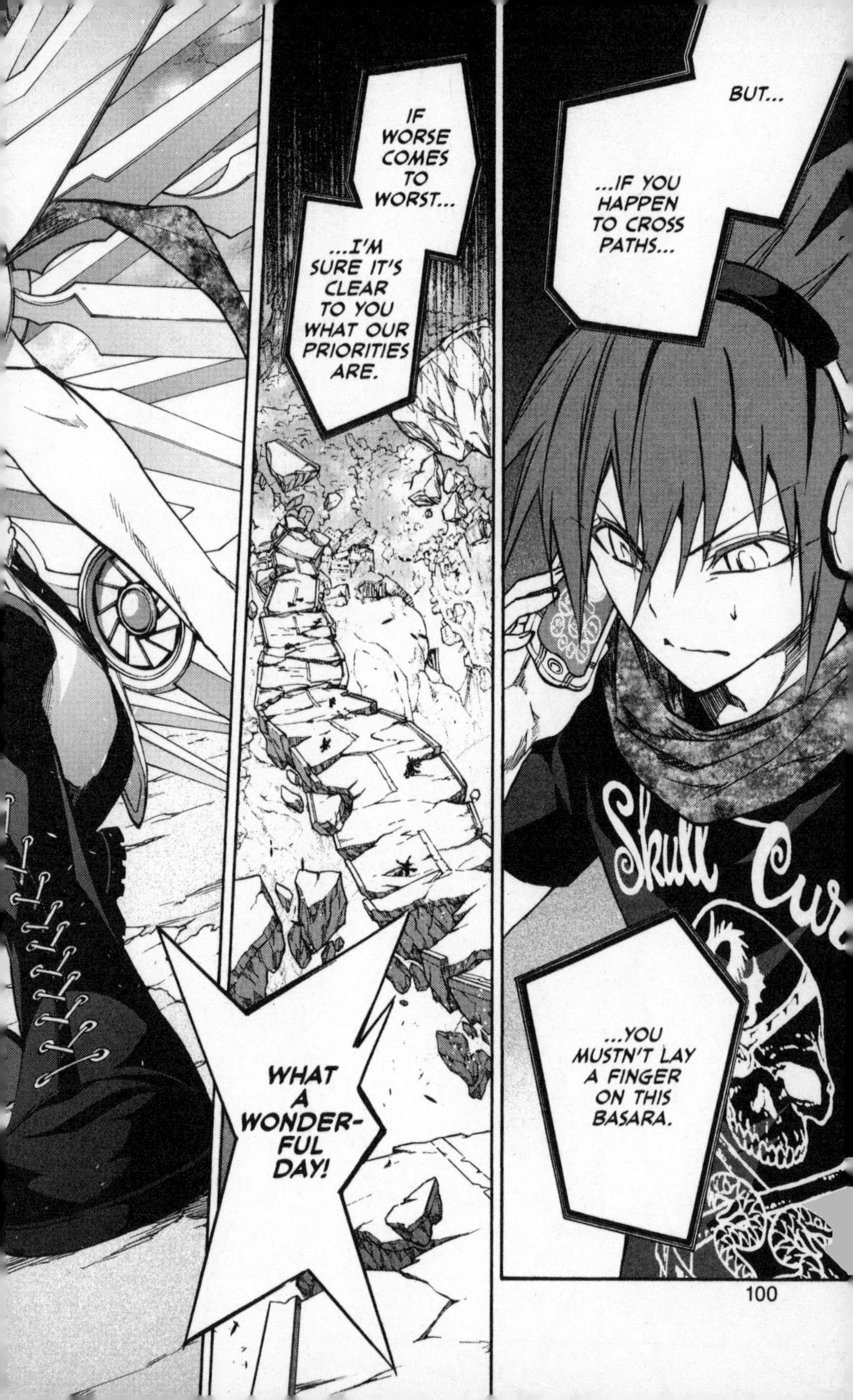
BUT...
...IF YOU HAPPEN TO CROSS PATHS...
...YOU MUSTN'T LAY A FINGER ON THIS BASARA.
IF WORSE COMES TO WORST...
...I'M SURE IT'S CLEAR TO YOU WHAT OUR PRIORITIES ARE.
WHAT A WONDERFUL DAY!

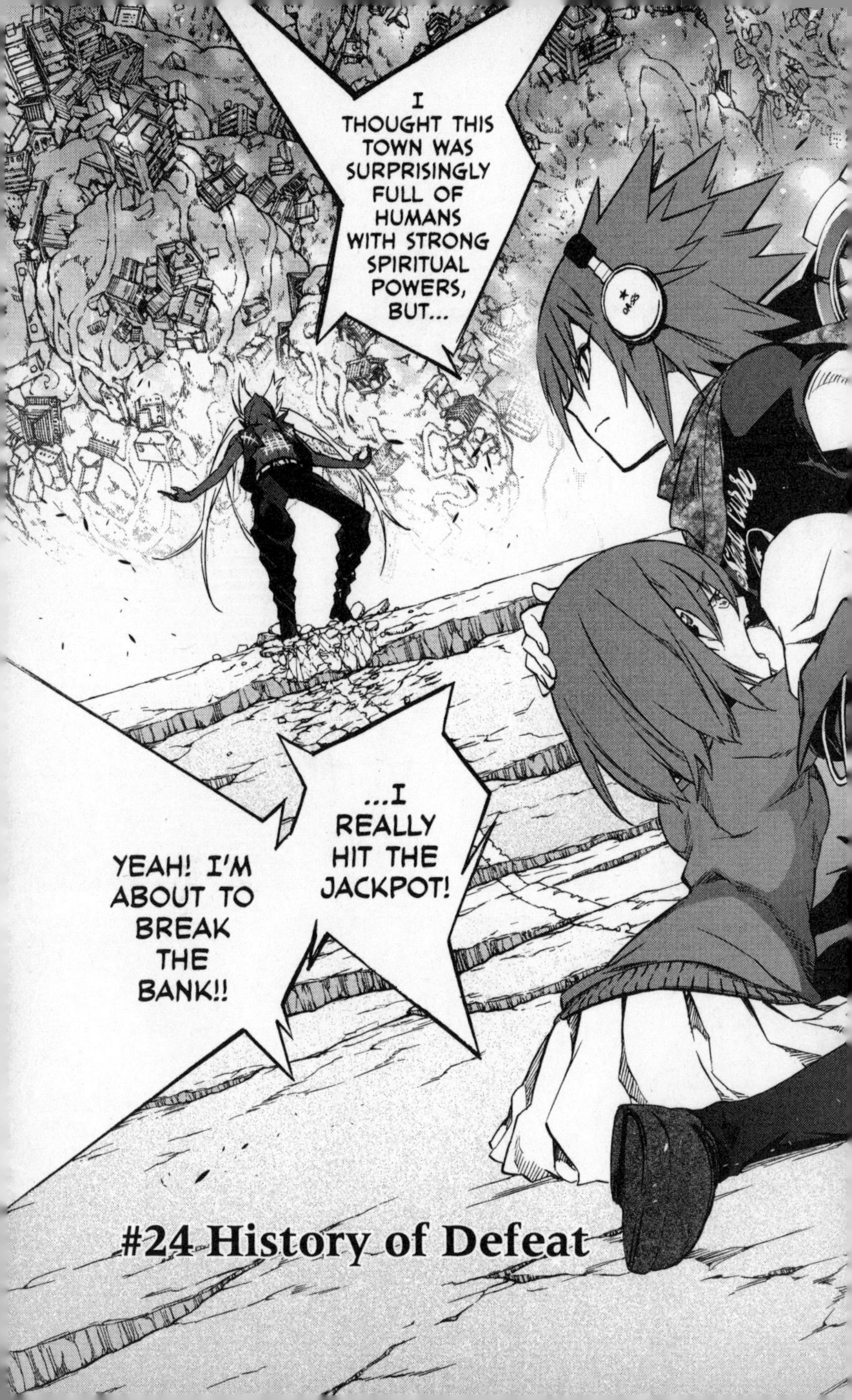
I THOUGHT THIS TOWN WAS SURPRISINGLY FULL OF HUMANS WITH STRONG SPIRITUAL POWERS, BUT...
...I REALLY HIT THE JACKPOT!
YEAH! I'M ABOUT TO BREAK THE BANK!!

#24 History of Defeat

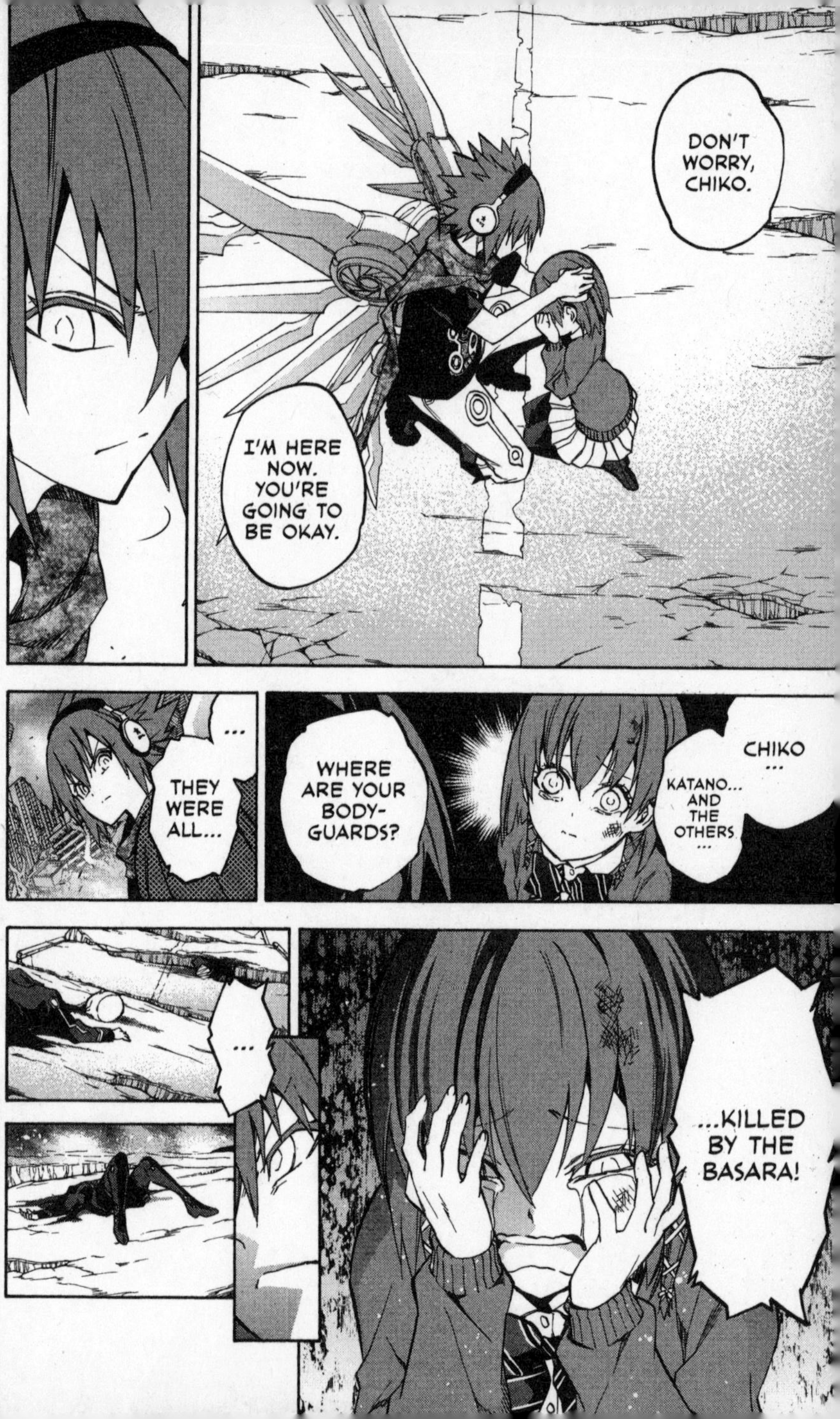
DON'T WORRY, CHIKO.
I'M HERE NOW. YOU'RE GOING TO BE OKAY.
CHIKO...
KATANO... AND THE OTHERS...
WHERE ARE YOUR BODY-GUARDS?
...
THEY WERE ALL...
...KILLED BY THE BASARA!
...

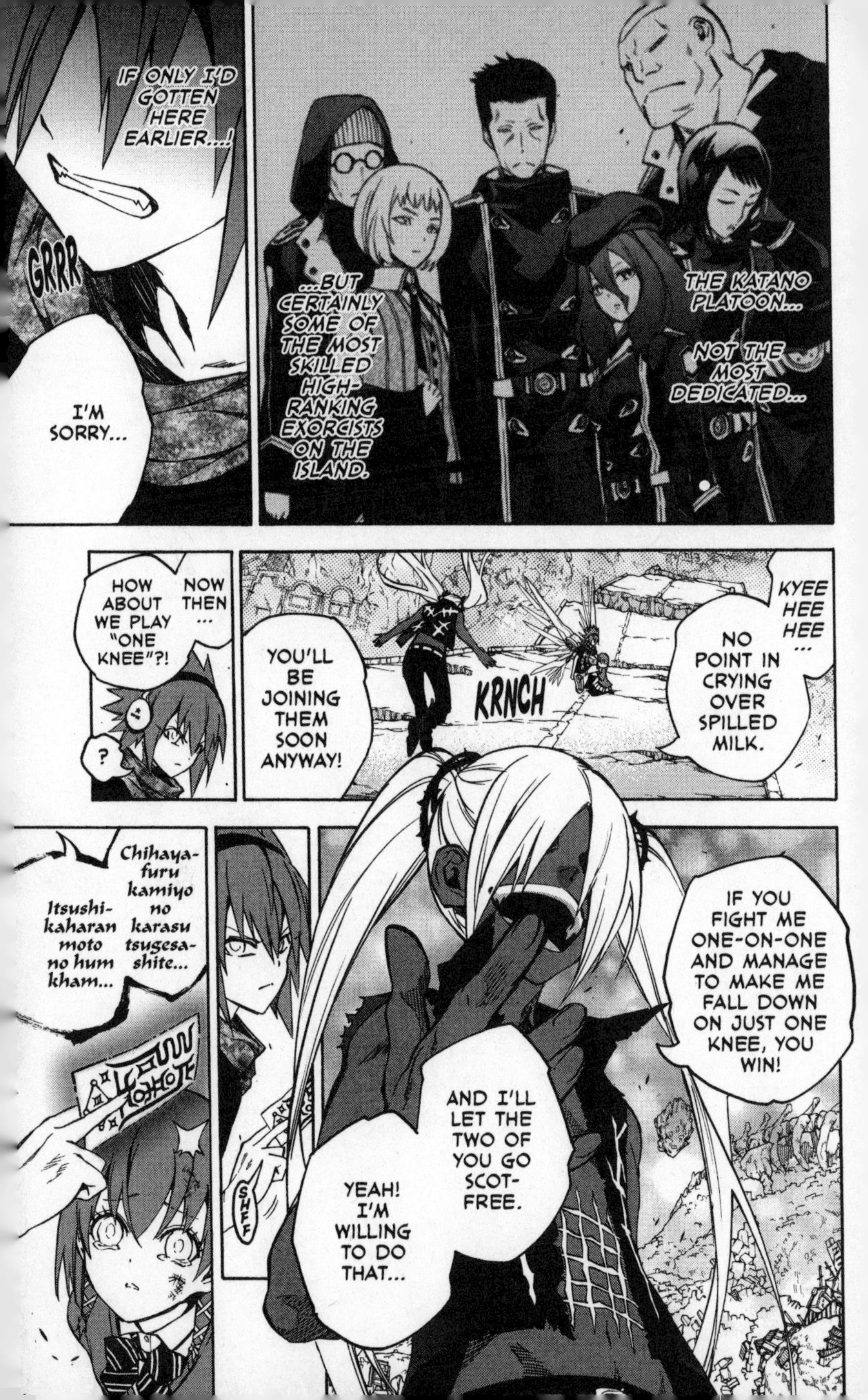
THE KATANO PLATOON...
NOT THE MOST DEDICATED...
...BUT CERTAINLY SOME OF THE MOST SKILLED HIGH-RANKING EXORCISTS ON THE ISLAND.
IF ONLY I'D GOTTEN HERE EARLIER...!
GRRR
I'M SORRY...
KYEE HEE HEE...
NO POINT IN CRYING OVER SPILLED MILK.
KRNCH
YOU'LL BE JOINING THEM SOON ANYWAY!
NOW THEN...
HOW ABOUT WE PLAY "ONE KNEE"?!
?
IF YOU FIGHT ME ONE-ON-ONE AND MANAGE TO MAKE ME FALL DOWN ON JUST ONE KNEE, YOU WIN!
AND I'LL LET THE TWO OF YOU GO SCOT-FREE.
YEAH! I'M WILLING TO DO THAT...
SHFF
Chihaya-furu kamiyo no karasu tsugesa-shite...
Itsushi-kaharan moto no hum kham...

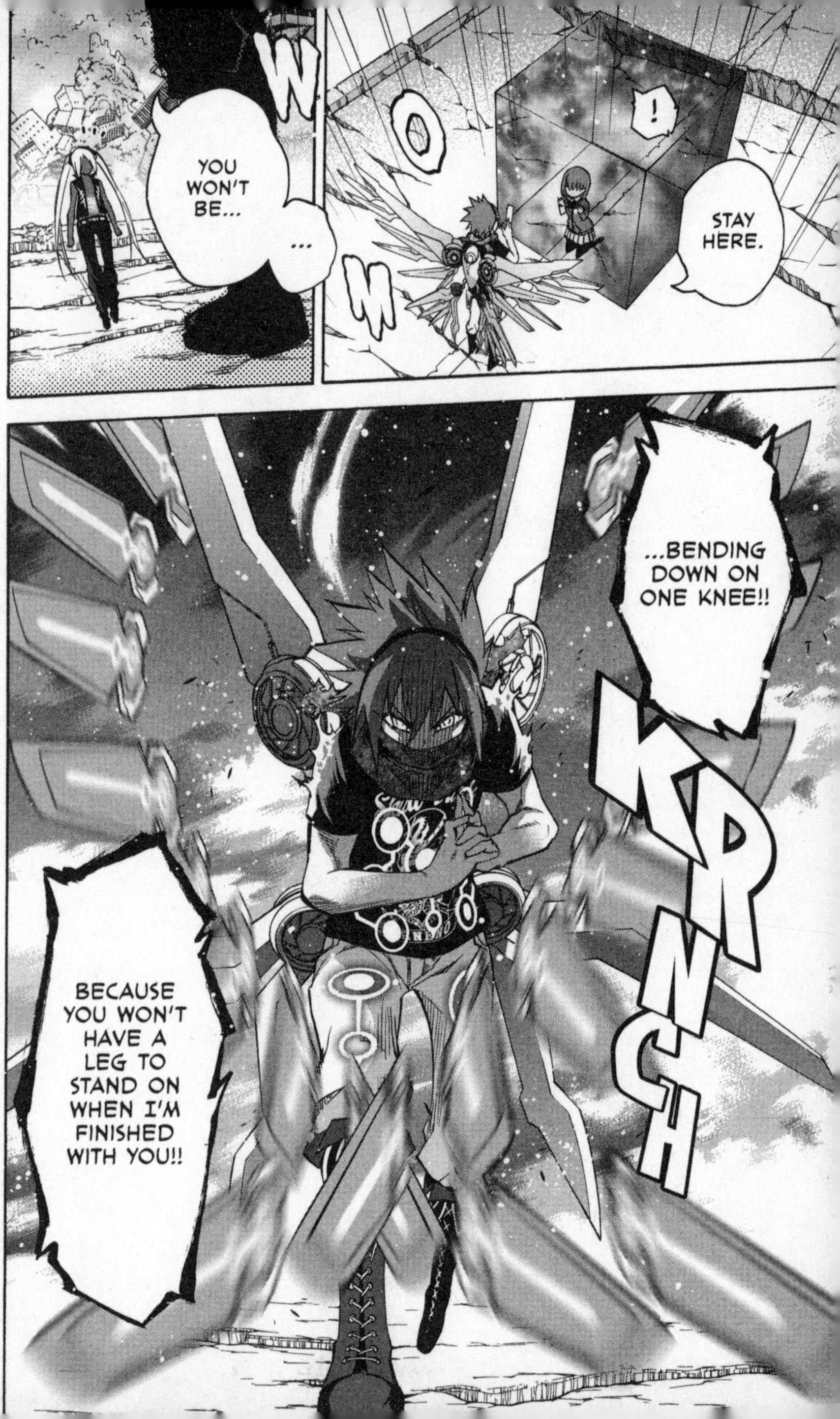
!
STAY HERE.
WOM
YOU WON'T BE...
...
...BENDING DOWN ON ONE KNEE!!
KRNCH
BECAUSE YOU WON'T HAVE A LEG TO STAND ON WHEN I'M FINISHED WITH YOU!!

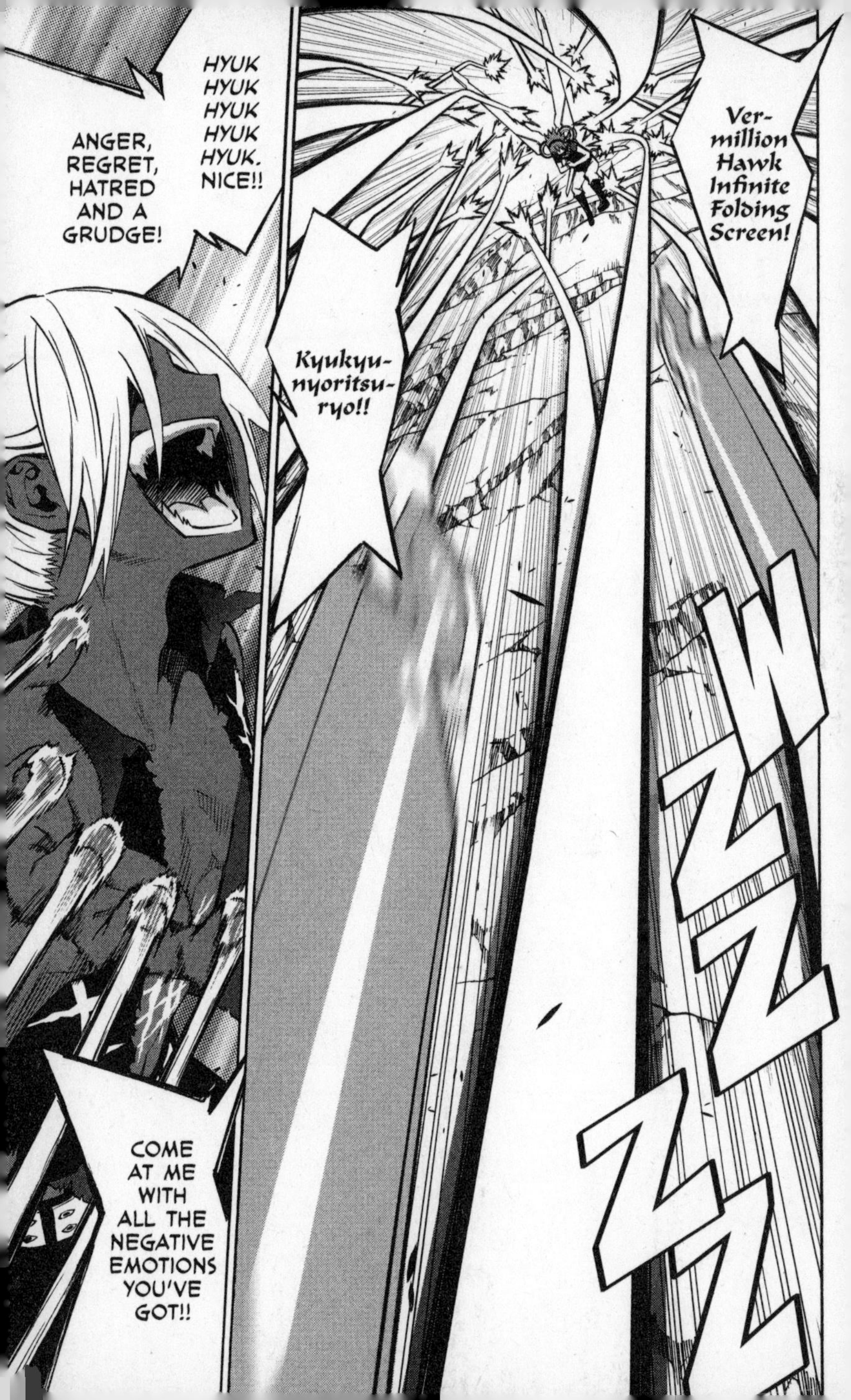
Vermillion Hawk Infinite Folding Screen!
Kyukyunyoritsuryo!!
ZZZW
HYUK HYUK HYUK HYUK HYUK. NICE!!
ANGER, REGRET, HATRED AND A GRUDGE!
COME AT ME WITH ALL THE NEGATIVE EMOTIONS YOU'VE GOT!!

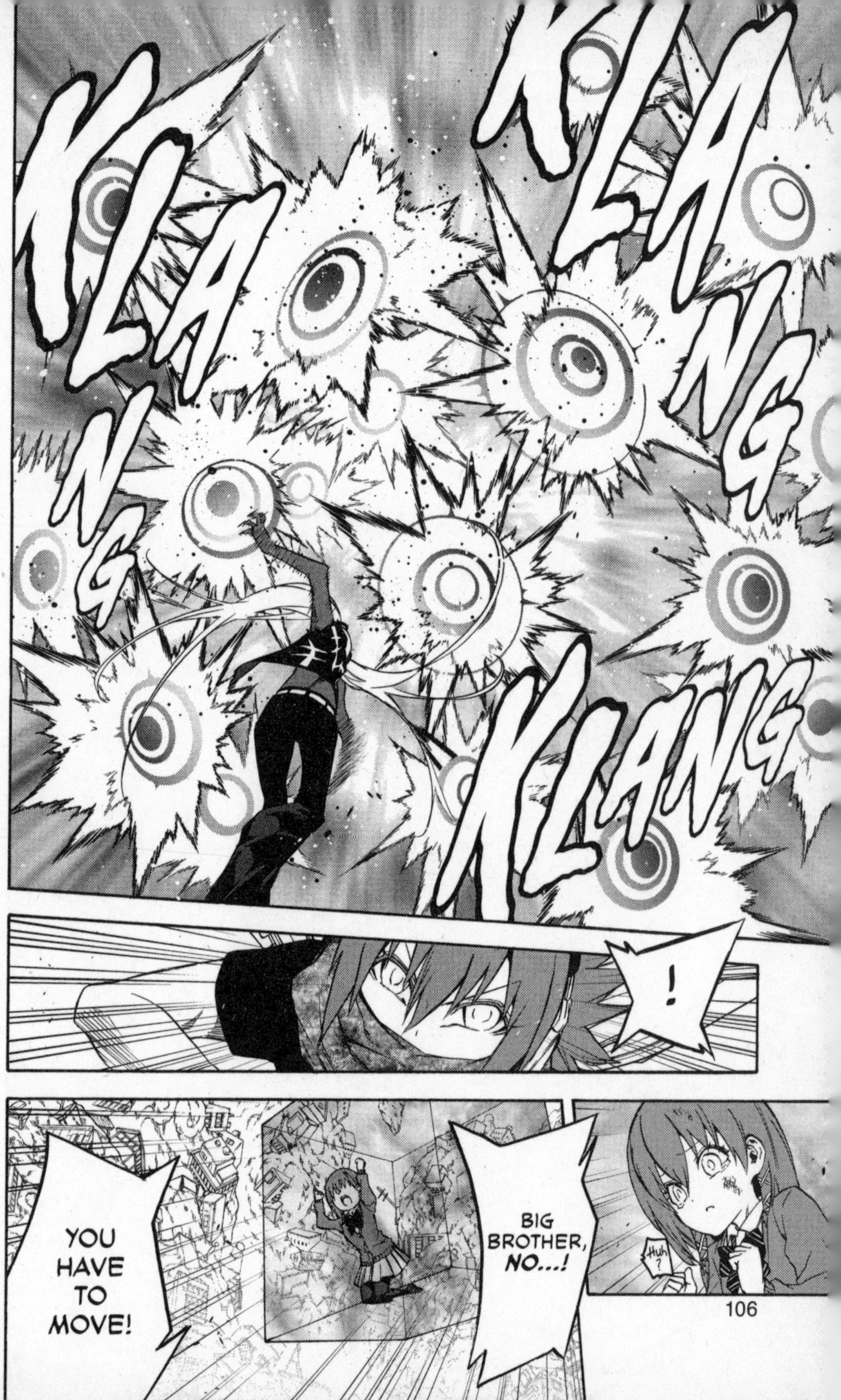
KLANG
KLANG
KLANG
!
Huh?
BIG BROTHER, NO...!
YOU HAVE TO MOVE!

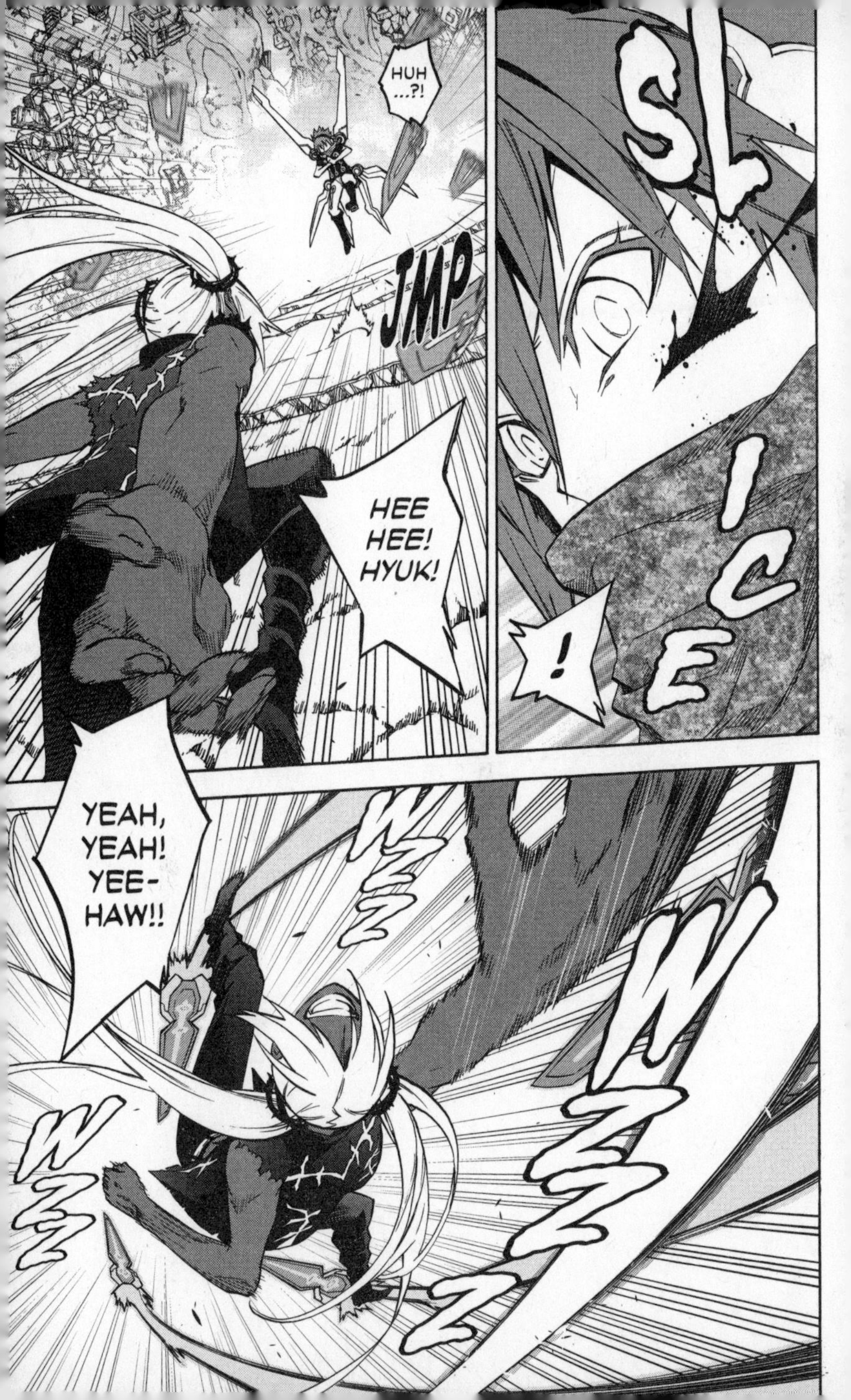
SLICE
!
HUH ...?!
JMP
HEE HEE! HYUK!
YEAH, YEAH! YEE-HAW!!

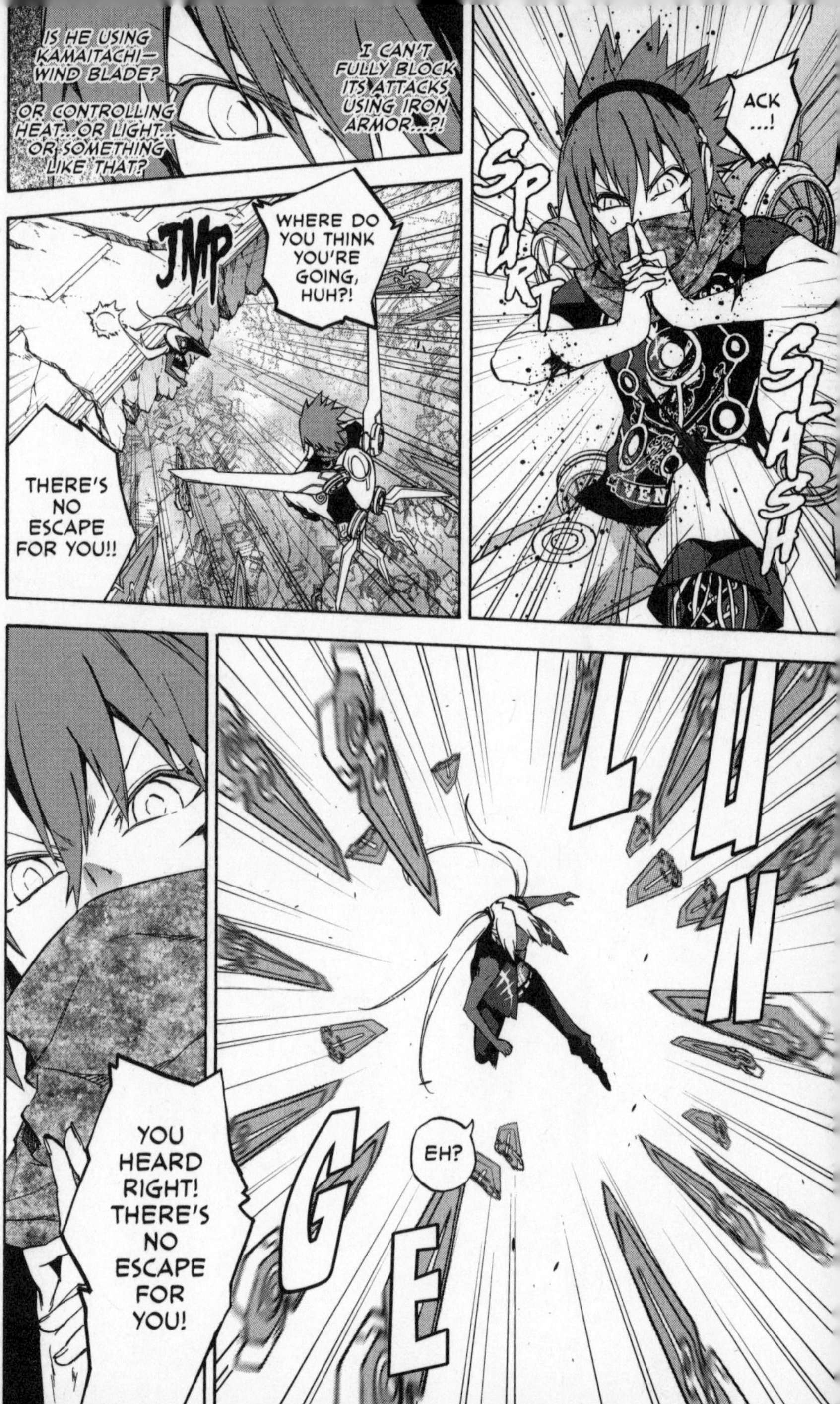
ACK ...!
SPLURT
SLASH
I CAN'T FULLY BLOCK ITS ATTACKS USING IRON ARMOR...?!
IS HE USING KAMAITACHI— WIND BLADE?
OR CONTROLLING HEAT...OR LIGHT... OR SOMETHING LIKE THAT?
WHERE DO YOU THINK YOU'RE GOING, HUH?!
JMP
THERE'S NO ESCAPE FOR YOU!!
LUNGE
EH?
YOU HEARD RIGHT! THERE'S NO ESCAPE FOR YOU!

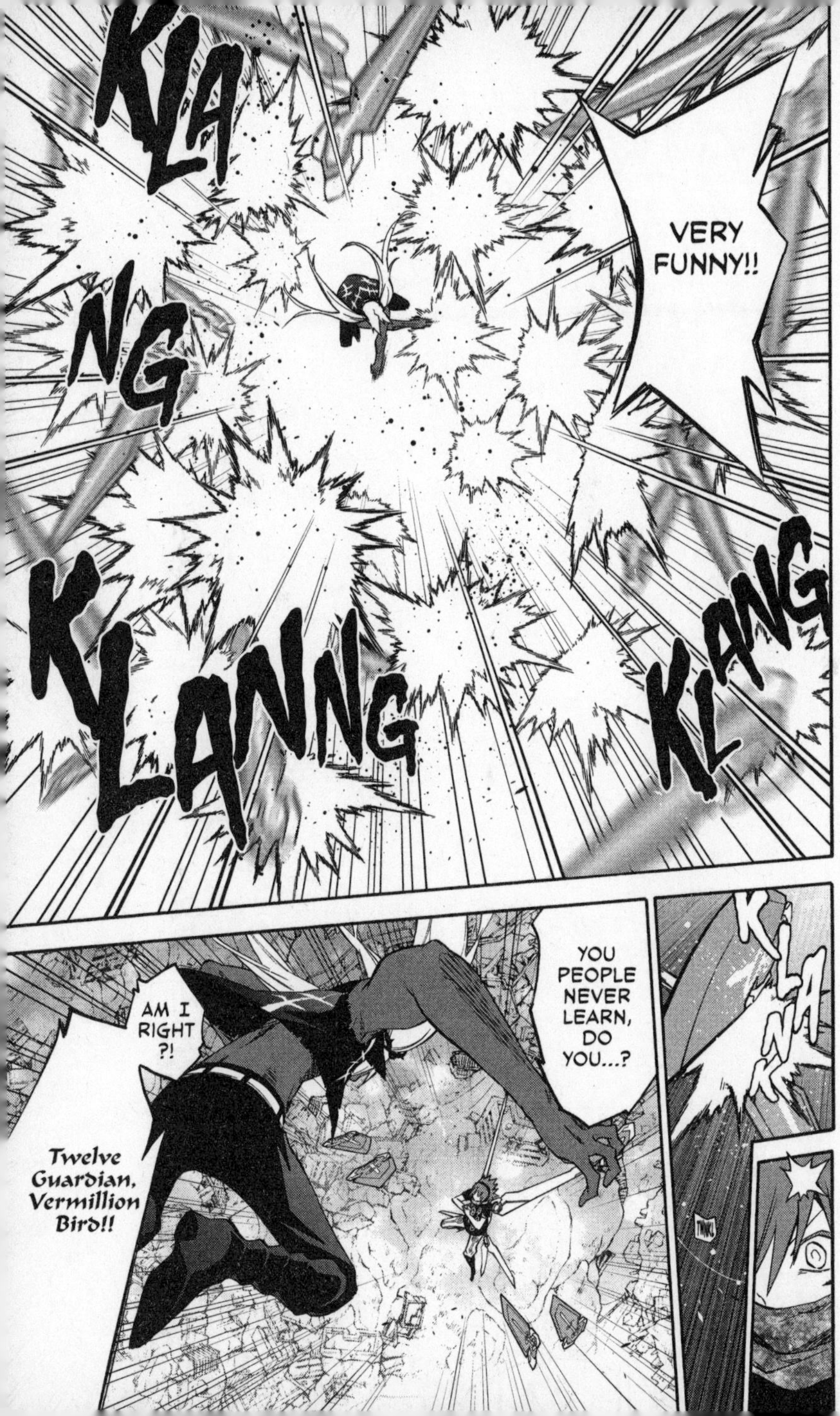
VERY FUNNY!!
KLANG
KLANG
KLANNG
KLANK
TWNK!
YOU PEOPLE NEVER LEARN, DO YOU...?
AM I RIGHT ?!
Twelve Guardian, Vermillion Bird!!

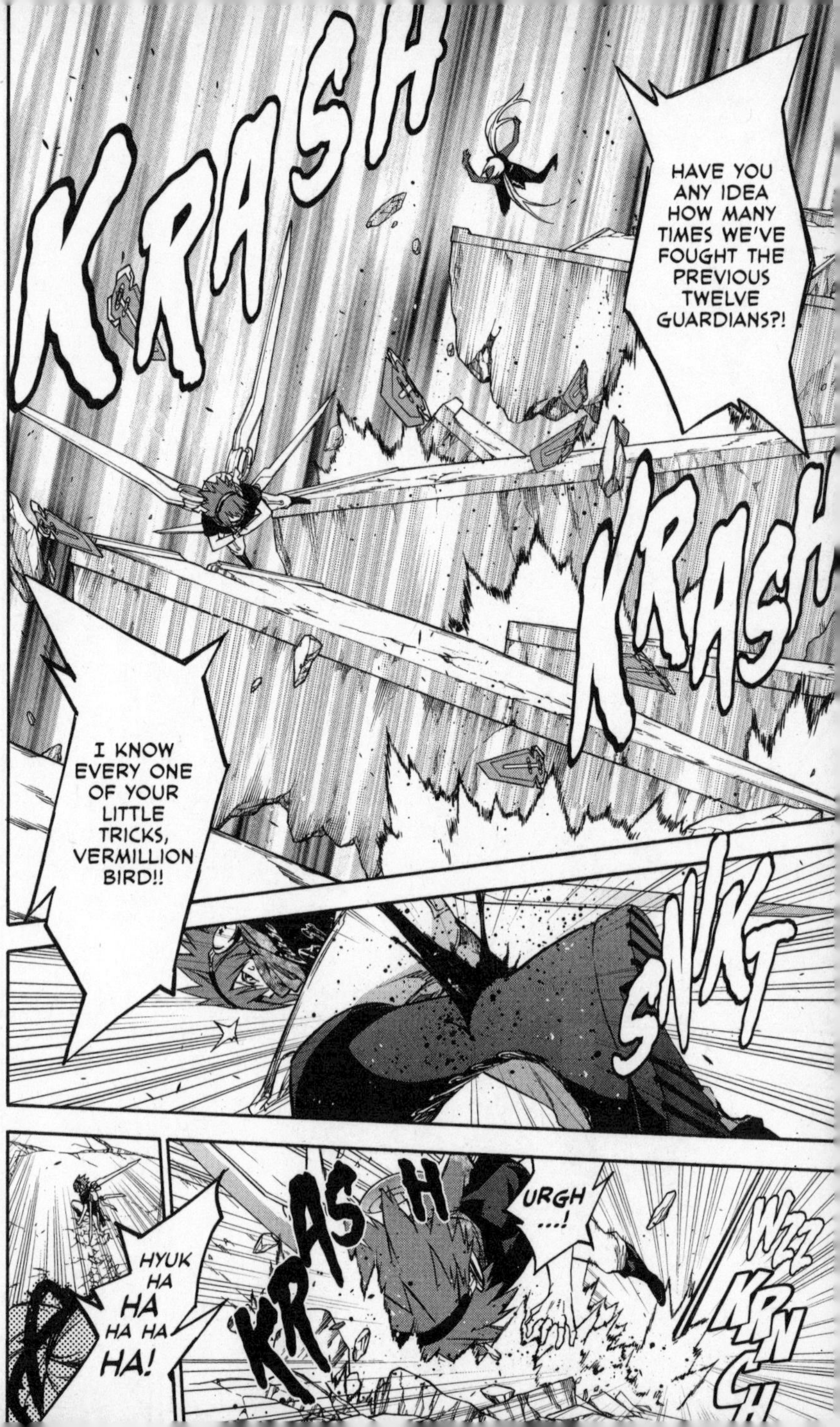
HAVE YOU ANY IDEA HOW MANY TIMES WE'VE FOUGHT THE PREVIOUS TWELVE GUARDIANS?!
KRASH
KRASH
I KNOW EVERY ONE OF YOUR LITTLE TRICKS, VERMILLION BIRD!!
SNIKT
WZZ
KRNCH
URGH ...!
KRASH
HYUK HA HA HA HA HA!

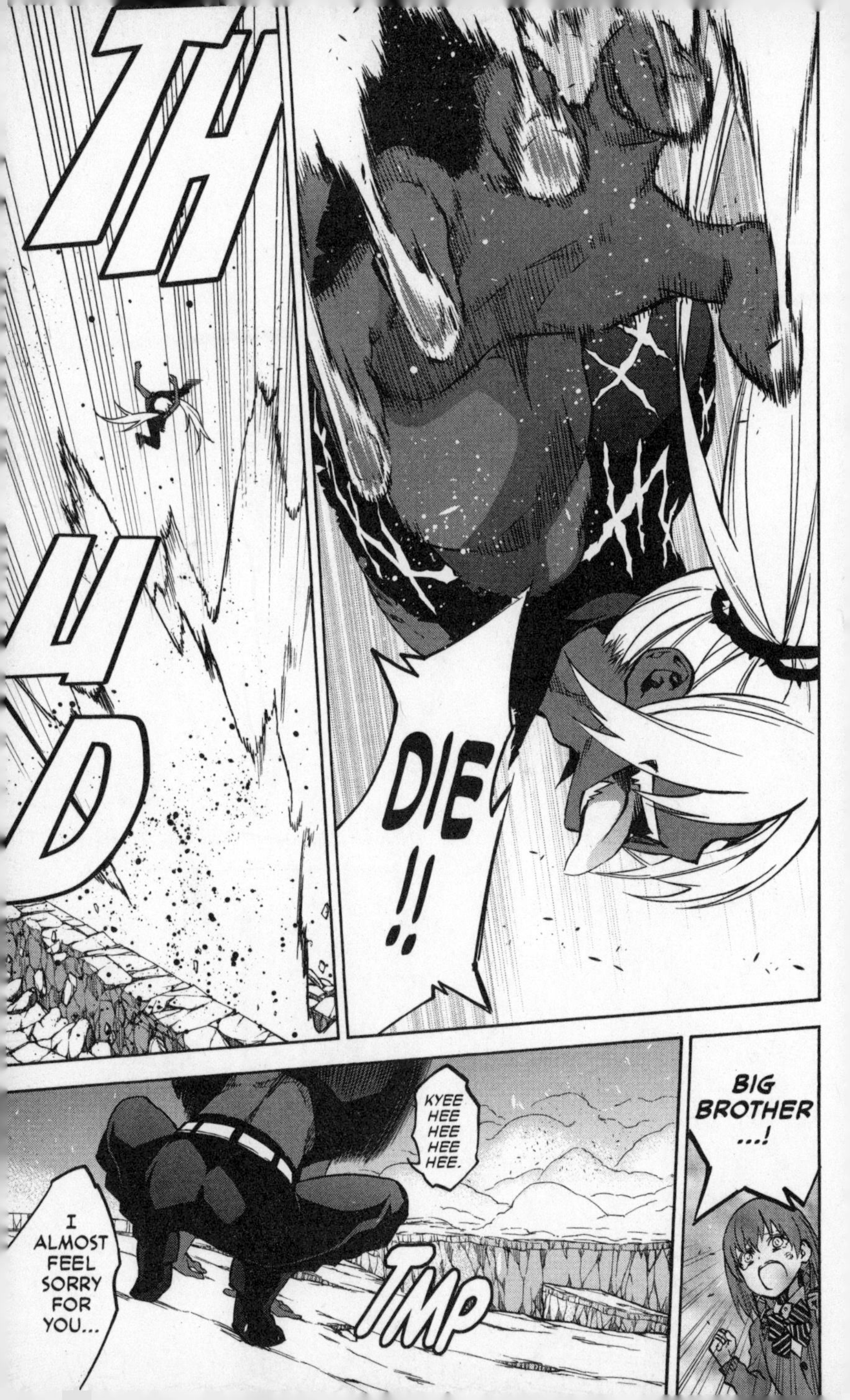
DIE!!
THUD
BIG BROTHER...!
KYEE HEE HEE HEE HEE.
I ALMOST FEEL SORRY FOR YOU...
TMP

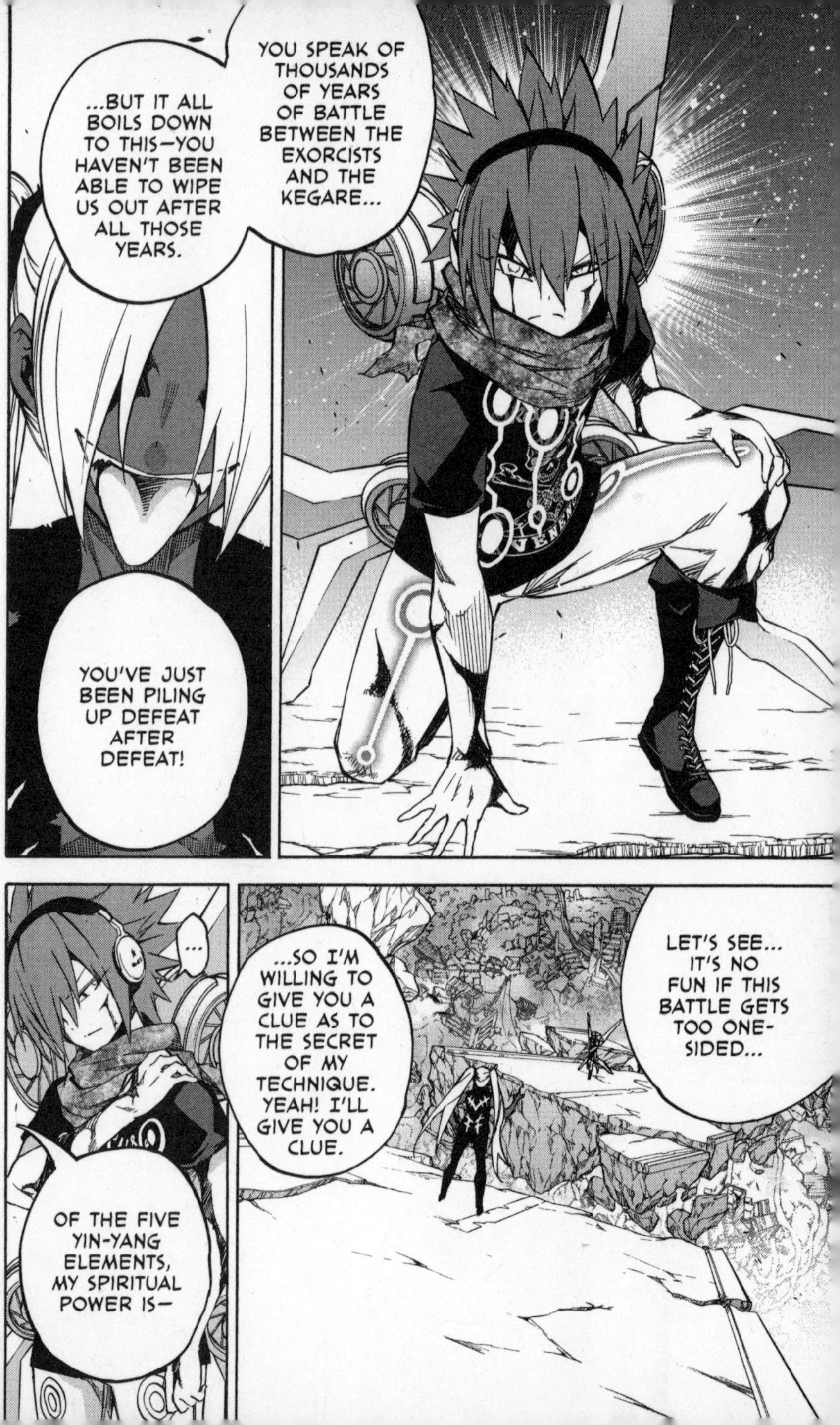
YOU SPEAK OF THOUSANDS OF YEARS OF BATTLE BETWEEN THE EXORCISTS AND THE KEGARE...
...BUT IT ALL BOILS DOWN TO THIS—YOU HAVEN'T BEEN ABLE TO WIPE US OUT AFTER ALL THOSE YEARS.
YOU'VE JUST BEEN PILING UP DEFEAT AFTER DEFEAT!
LET'S SEE... IT'S NO FUN IF THIS BATTLE GETS TOO ONE-SIDED...
...SO I'M WILLING TO GIVE YOU A CLUE AS TO THE SECRET OF MY TECHNIQUE. YEAH! I'LL GIVE YOU A CLUE.
...
OF THE FIVE YIN-YANG ELEMENTS, MY SPIRITUAL POWER IS—

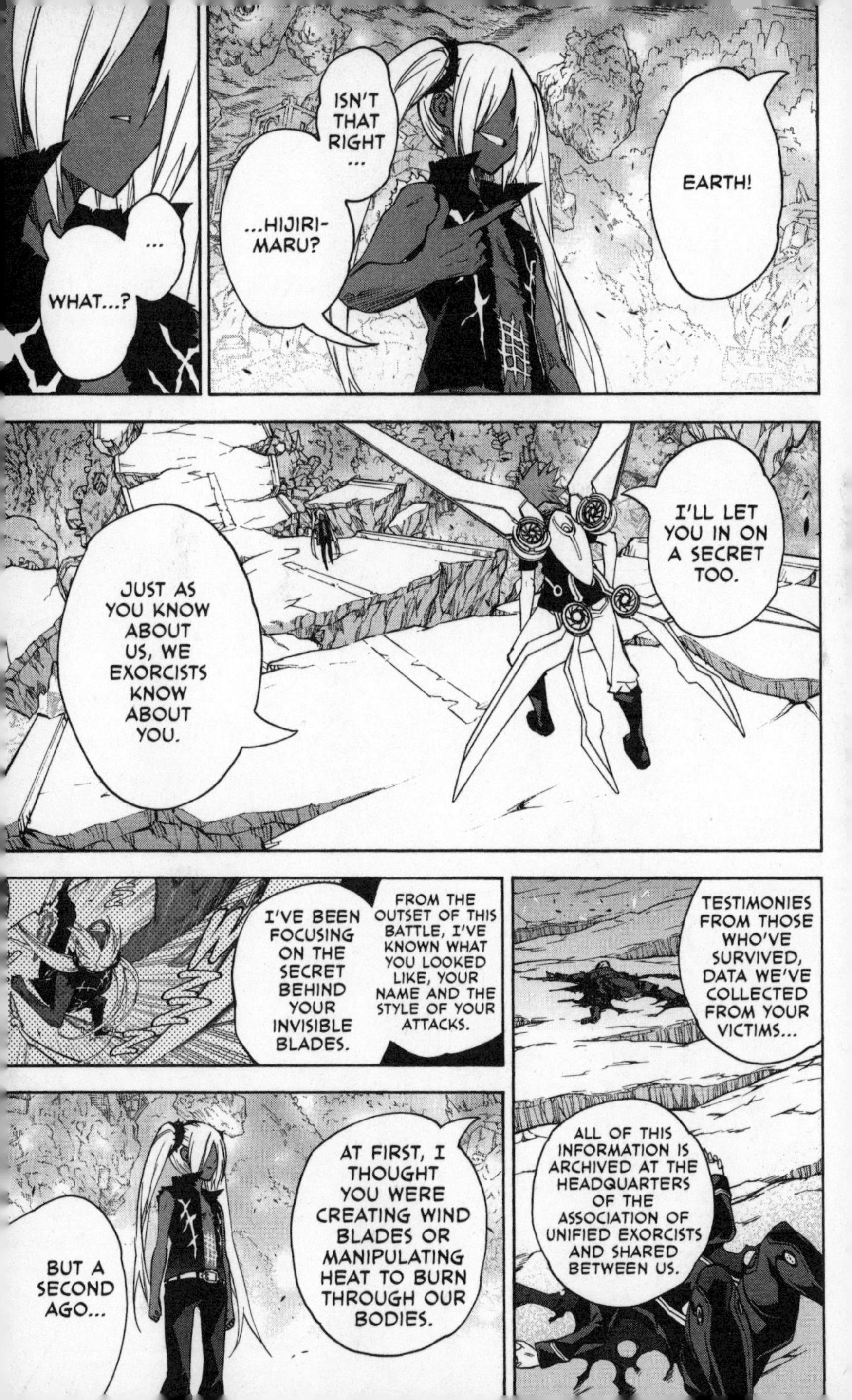
EARTH!
ISN'T THAT RIGHT ...
...HIJIRI-MARU?
...
WHAT...?
I'LL LET YOU IN ON A SECRET TOO.
JUST AS YOU KNOW ABOUT US, WE EXORCISTS KNOW ABOUT YOU.
TESTIMONIES FROM THOSE WHO'VE SURVIVED, DATA WE'VE COLLECTED FROM YOUR VICTIMS...
ALL OF THIS INFORMATION IS ARCHIVED AT THE HEADQUARTERS OF THE ASSOCIATION OF UNIFIED EXORCISTS AND SHARED BETWEEN US.
FROM THE OUTSET OF THIS BATTLE, I'VE KNOWN WHAT YOU LOOKED LIKE, YOUR NAME AND THE STYLE OF YOUR ATTACKS.
I'VE BEEN FOCUSING ON THE SECRET BEHIND YOUR INVISIBLE BLADES.
AT FIRST, I THOUGHT YOU WERE CREATING WIND BLADES OR MANIPULATING HEAT TO BURN THROUGH OUR BODIES.
BUT A SECOND AGO...

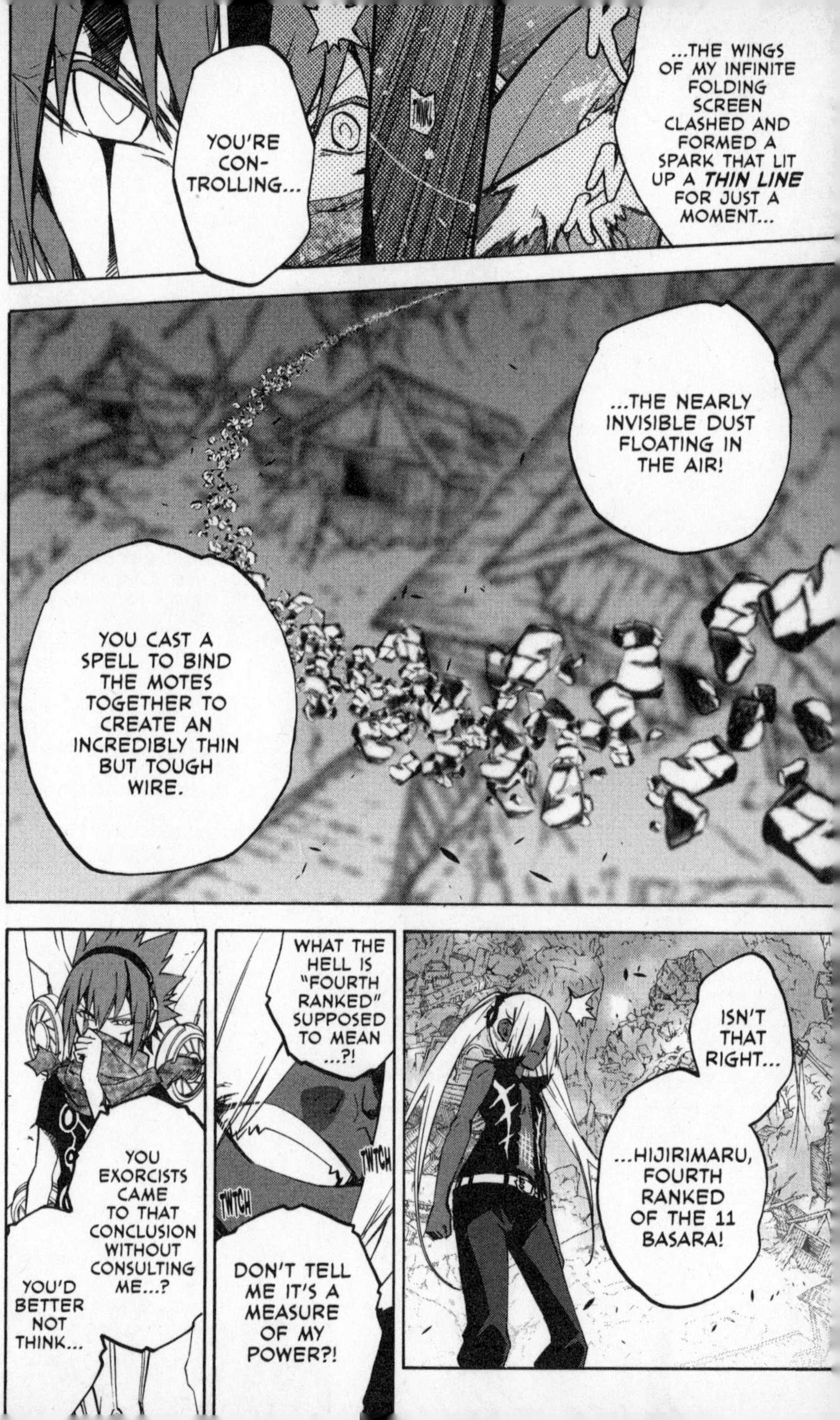
...THE WINGS OF MY INFINITE FOLDING SCREEN CLASHED AND FORMED A SPARK THAT LIT UP A *THIN LINE* FOR JUST A MOMENT...
YOU'RE CON-TROLLING...
...THE NEARLY INVISIBLE DUST FLOATING IN THE AIR!
YOU CAST A SPELL TO BIND THE MOTES TOGETHER TO CREATE AN INCREDIBLY THIN BUT TOUGH WIRE.
ISN'T THAT RIGHT...
...HIJIRIMARU, FOURTH RANKED OF THE 11 BASARA!
WHAT THE HELL IS "FOURTH RANKED" SUPPOSED TO MEAN ...?!
TWITCH
TWITCH
DON'T TELL ME IT'S A MEASURE OF MY POWER?!
YOU EXORCISTS CAME TO THAT CONCLUSION WITHOUT CONSULTING ME...?
YOU'D BETTER NOT THINK...

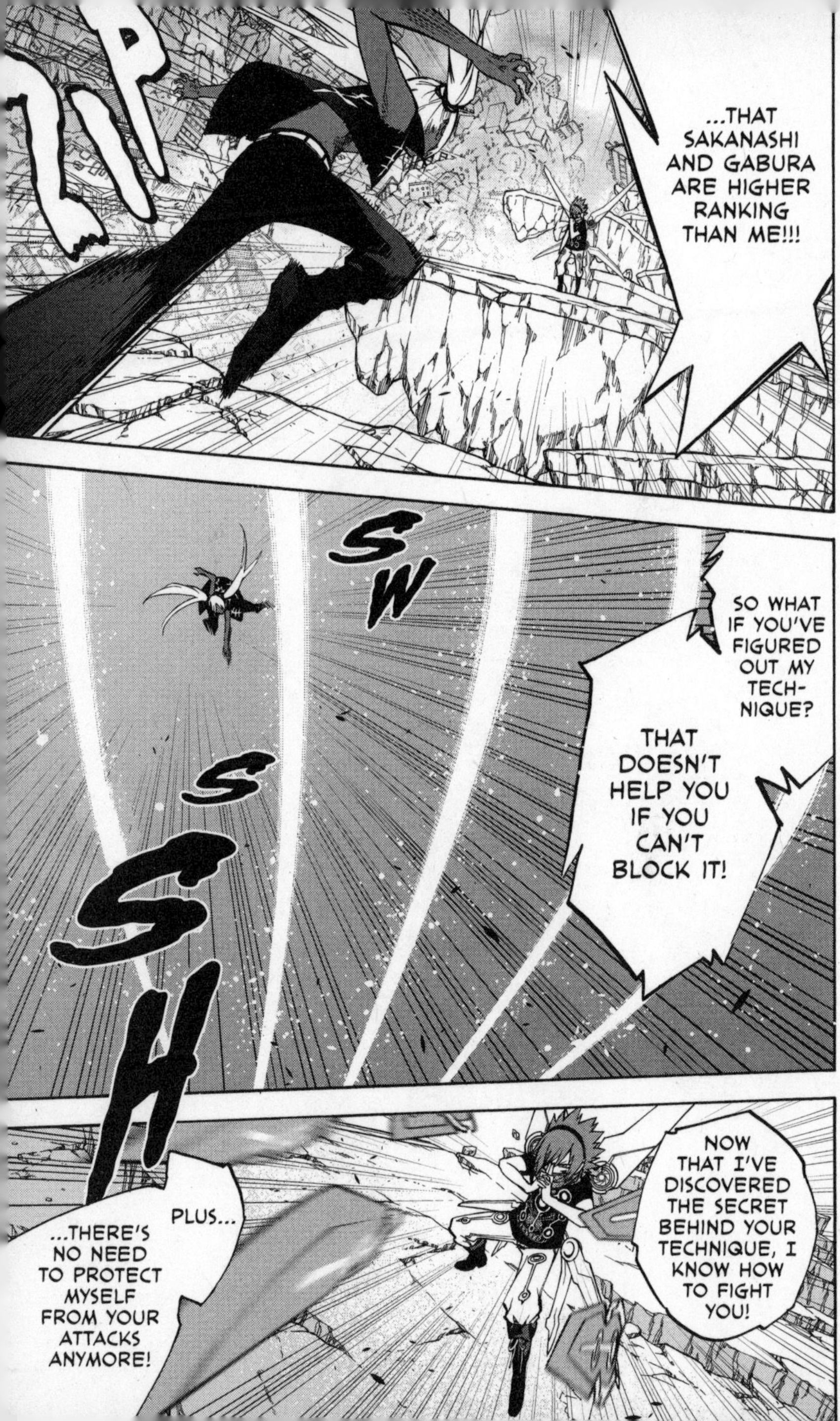
...THAT SAKANASHI AND GABURA ARE HIGHER RANKING THAN ME!!!
SO WHAT IF YOU'VE FIGURED OUT MY TECH-NIQUE?
THAT DOESN'T HELP YOU IF YOU CAN'T BLOCK IT!
SW
SSH
NOW THAT I'VE DISCOVERED THE SECRET BEHIND YOUR TECHNIQUE, I KNOW HOW TO FIGHT YOU!
PLUS...
...THERE'S NO NEED TO PROTECT MYSELF FROM YOUR ATTACKS ANYMORE!

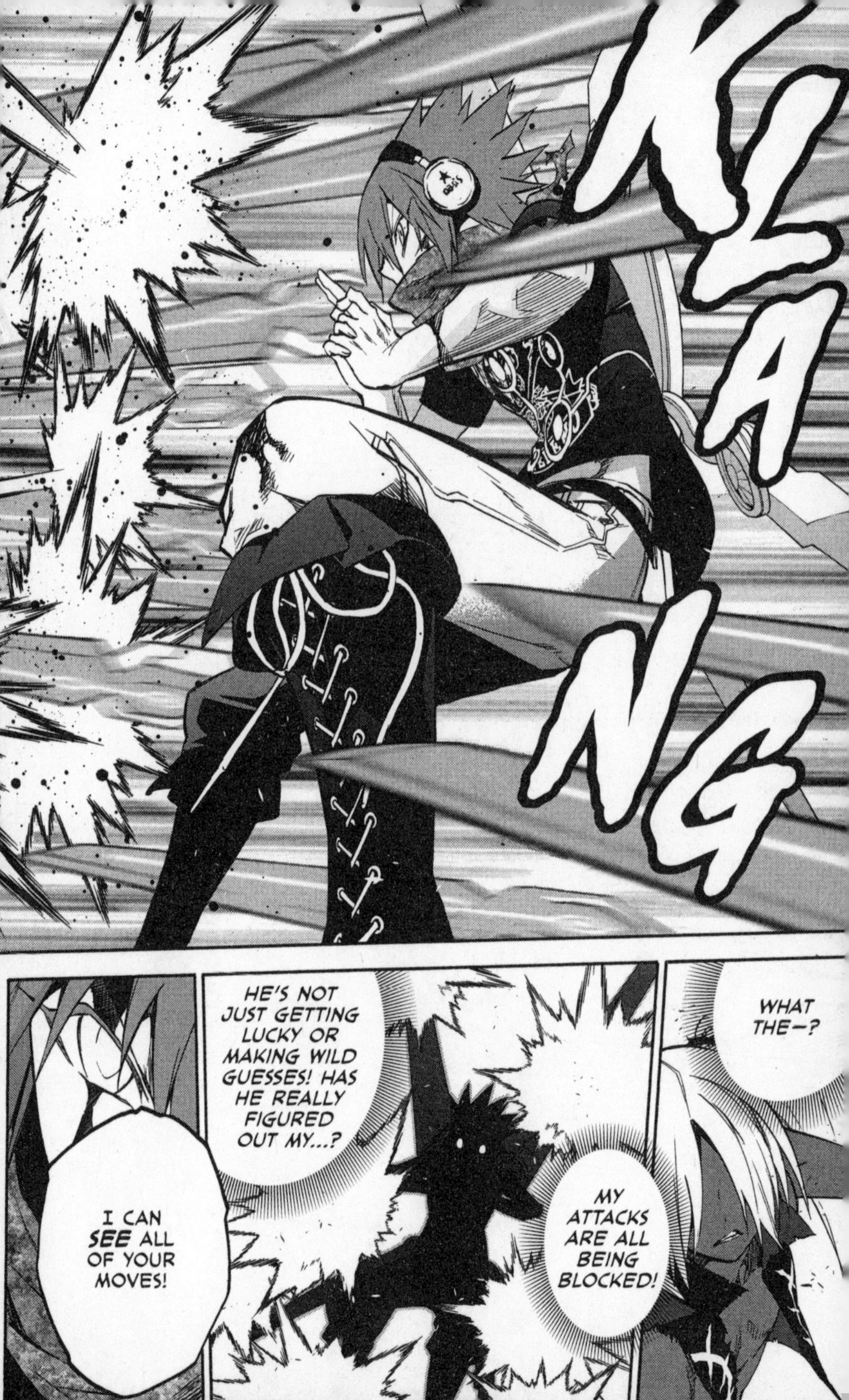
KLANG
WHAT THE—?
HE'S NOT JUST GETTING LUCKY OR MAKING WILD GUESSES! HAS HE REALLY FIGURED OUT MY...?
MY ATTACKS ARE ALL BEING BLOCKED!
I CAN SEE ALL OF YOUR MOVES!

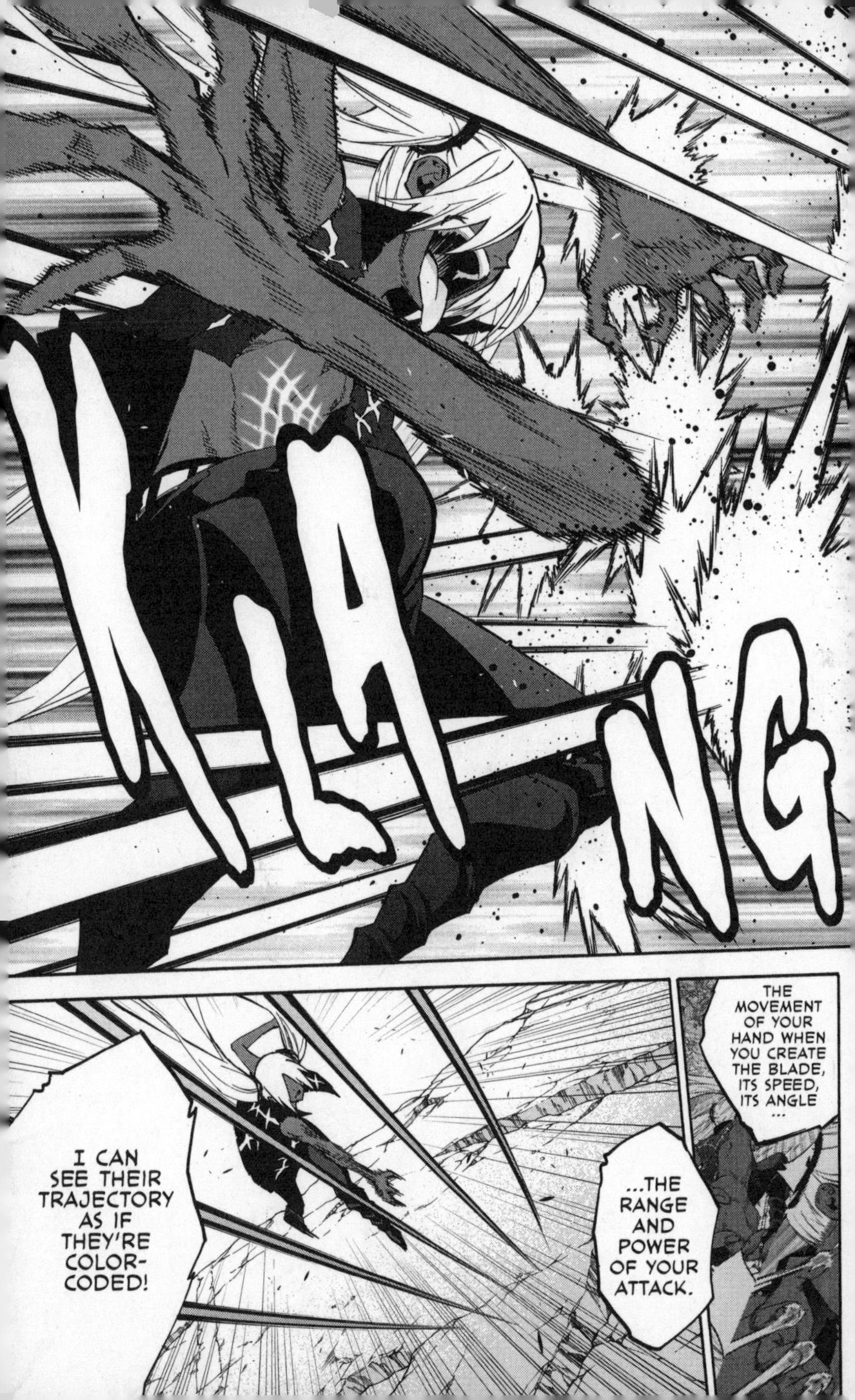
KLANG
THE MOVEMENT OF YOUR HAND WHEN YOU CREATE THE BLADE, ITS SPEED, ITS ANGLE...
...THE RANGE AND POWER OF YOUR ATTACK.
I CAN SEE THEIR TRAJECTORY AS IF THEY'RE COLOR-CODED!

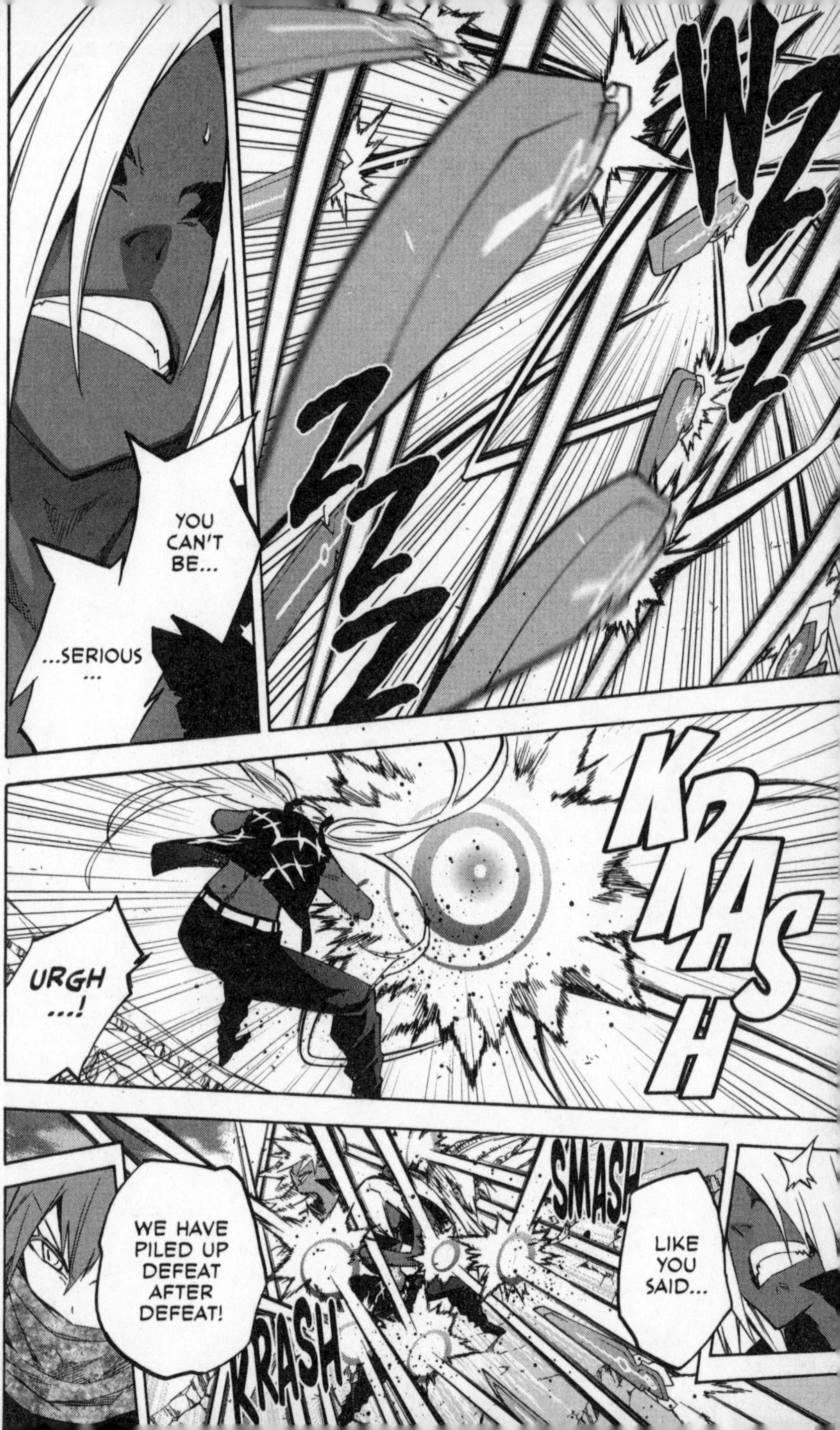
WZZ
ZZZ
YOU CAN'T BE...
...SERIOUS ...
KRASH
URGH ...!
SMASH
LIKE YOU SAID...
WE HAVE PILED UP DEFEAT AFTER DEFEAT!
KRASH

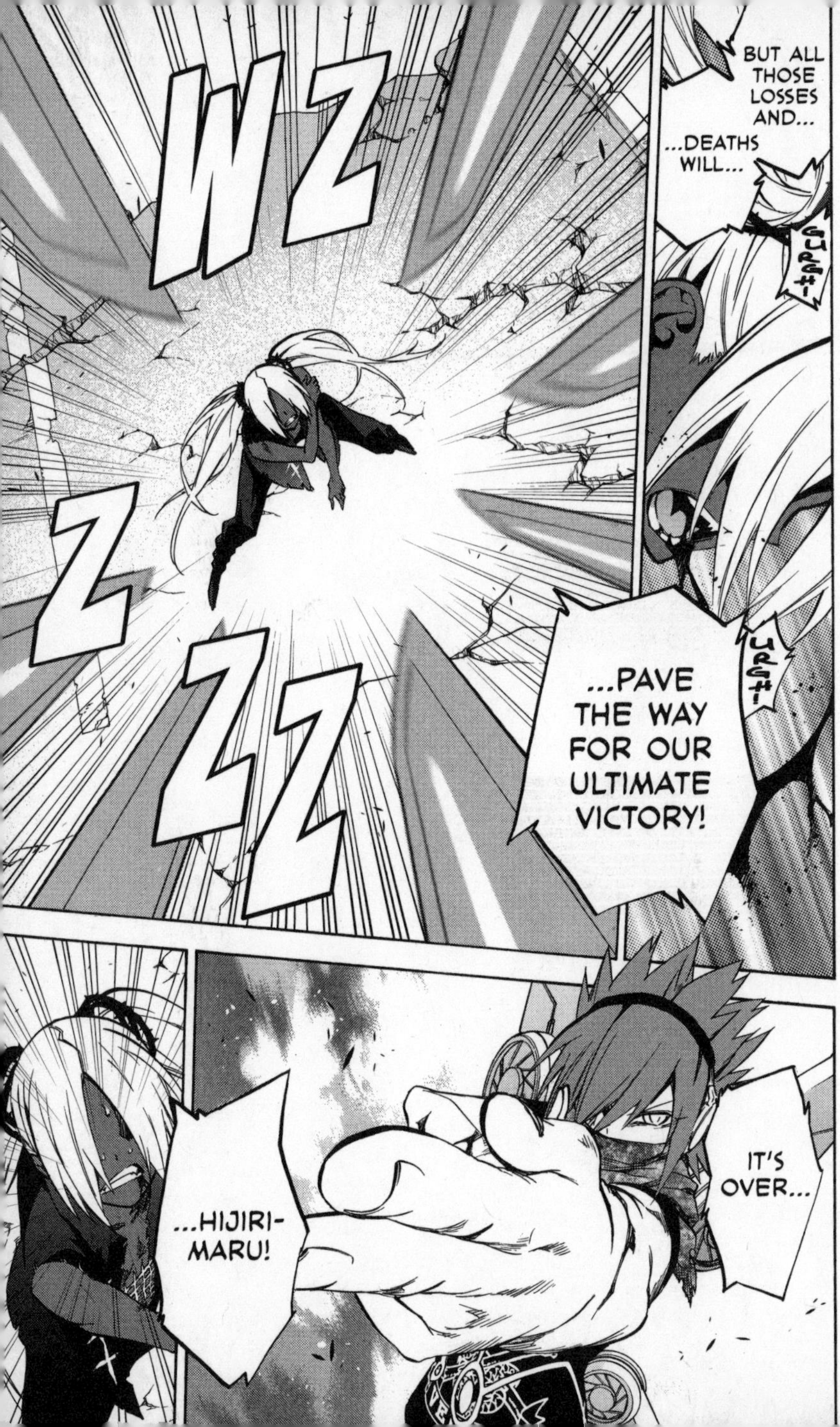

BUT ALL THOSE LOSSES AND...
...DEATHS WILL...
GURGH!
URGH!
...PAVE THE WAY FOR OUR ULTIMATE VICTORY!
WZZZZ
IT'S OVER...
...HIJIRI-MARU!

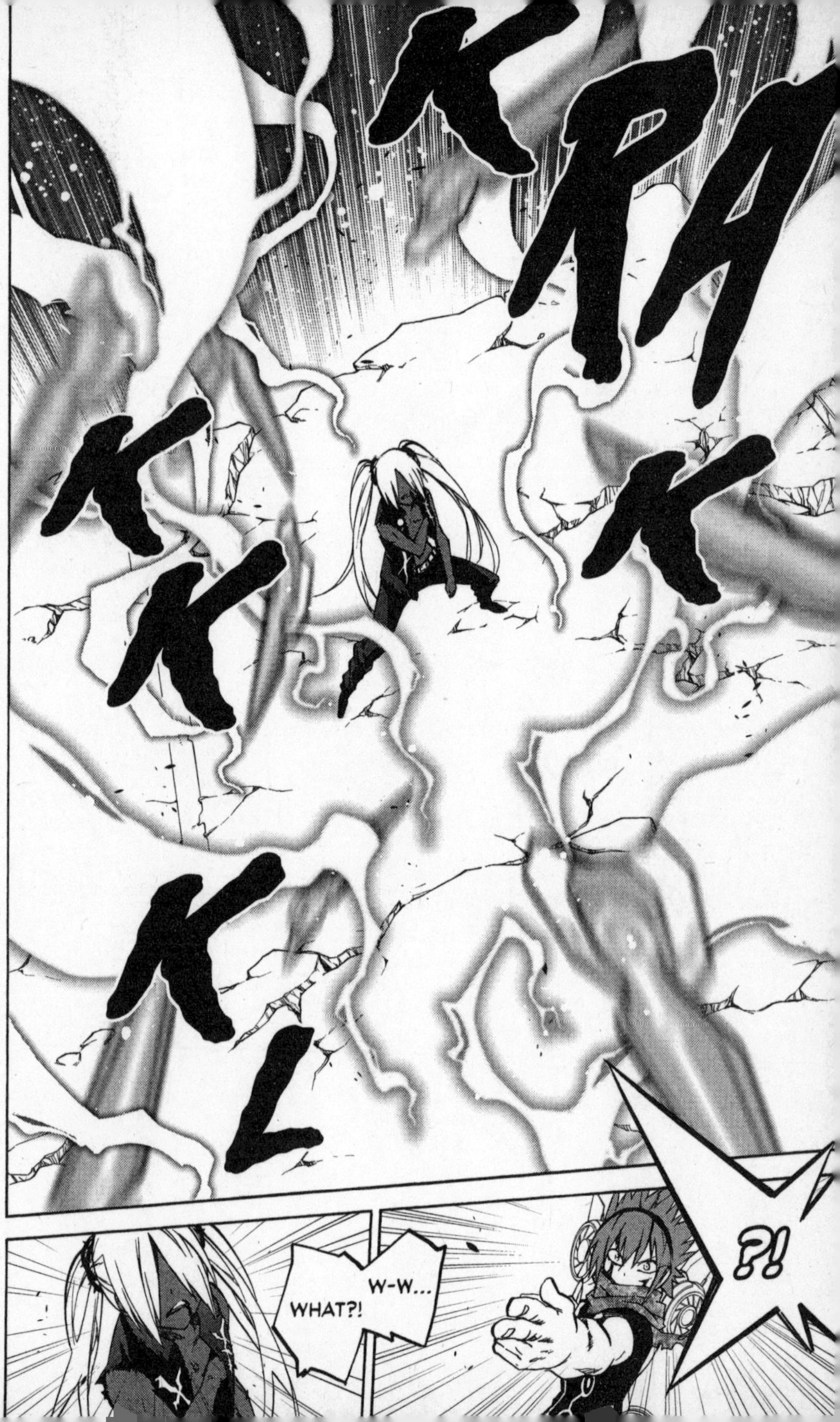
KRAK
KKKL
?!
W-W...
WHAT?!

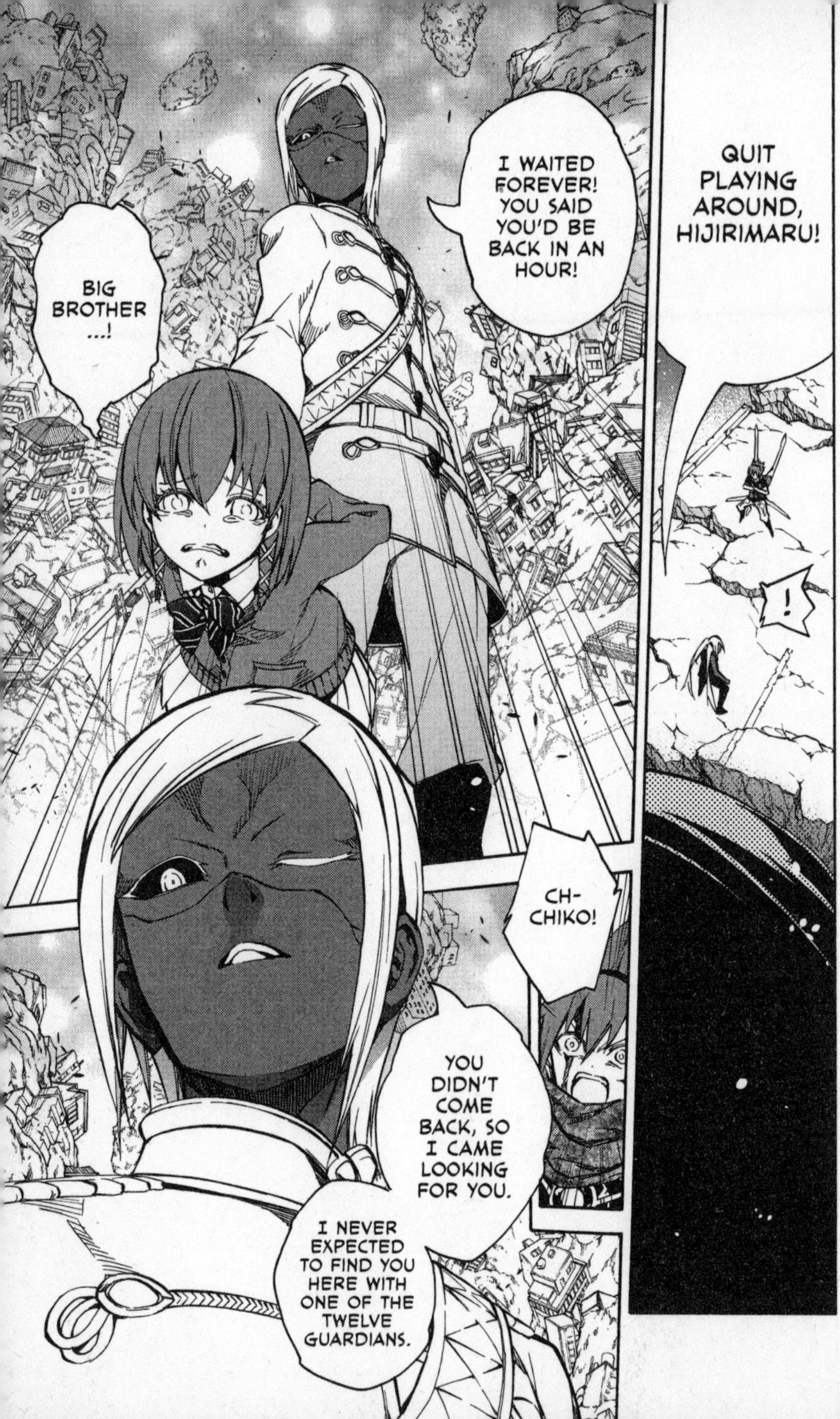
QUIT PLAYING AROUND, HIJIRIMARU!
!
I WAITED FOREVER! YOU SAID YOU'D BE BACK IN AN HOUR!
BIG BROTHER ...!
CH-CHIKO!
YOU DIDN'T COME BACK, SO I CAME LOOKING FOR YOU.
I NEVER EXPECTED TO FIND YOU HERE WITH ONE OF THE TWELVE GUARDIANS.

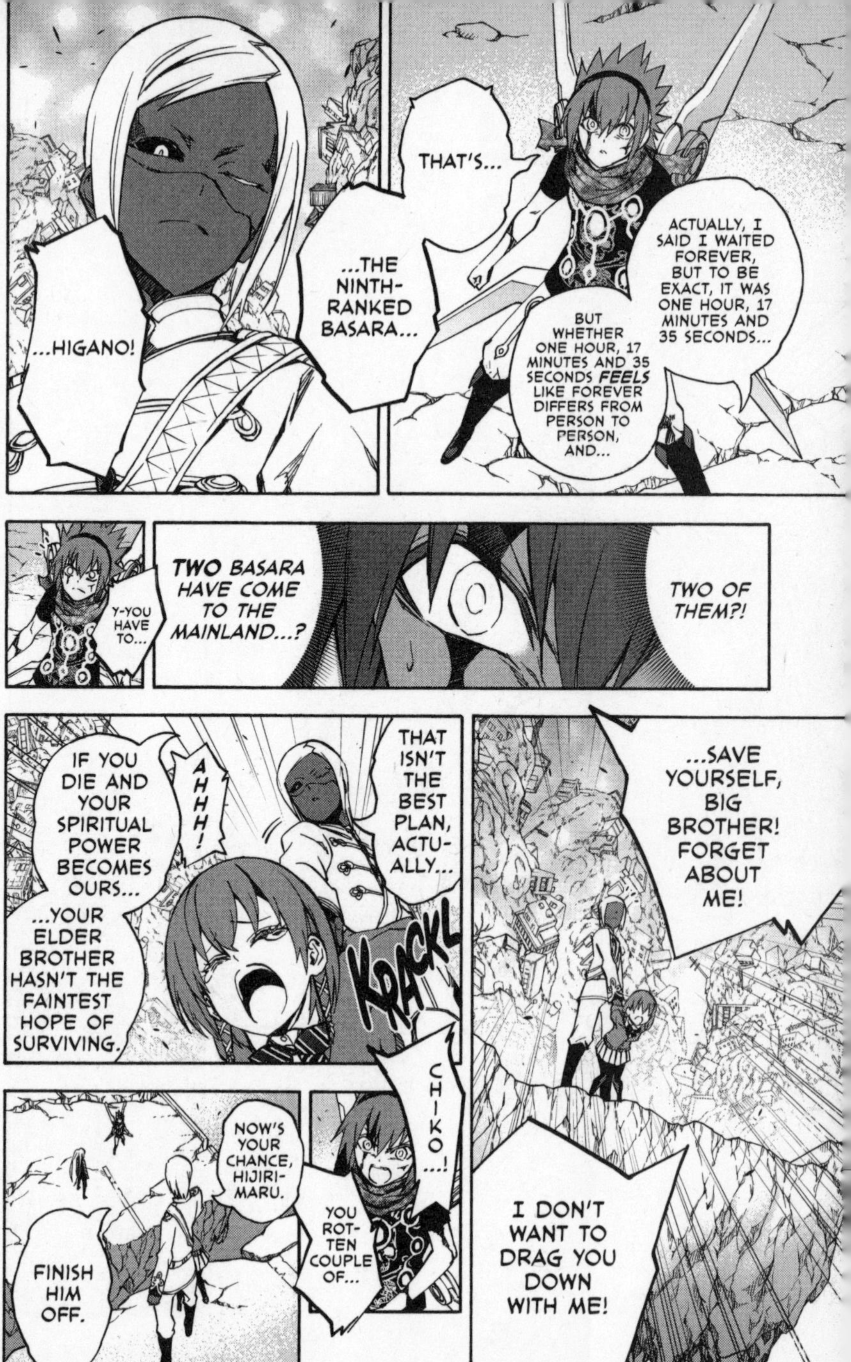
THAT'S...
...THE NINTH-RANKED BASARA...
...HIGANO!
ACTUALLY, I SAID I WAITED FOREVER, BUT TO BE EXACT, IT WAS ONE HOUR, 17 MINUTES AND 35 SECONDS...
BUT WHETHER ONE HOUR, 17 MINUTES AND 35 SECONDS FEELS LIKE FOREVER DIFFERS FROM PERSON TO PERSON, AND...
TWO OF THEM?!
TWO BASARA HAVE COME TO THE MAINLAND...?
Y-YOU HAVE TO...
...SAVE YOURSELF, BIG BROTHER! FORGET ABOUT ME!
I DON'T WANT TO DRAG YOU DOWN WITH ME!
THAT ISN'T THE BEST PLAN, ACTUALLY...
AHHHH!
IF YOU DIE AND YOUR SPIRITUAL POWER BECOMES OURS...
...YOUR ELDER BROTHER HASN'T THE FAINTEST HOPE OF SURVIVING.
KRACKL
CHIKO...!
NOW'S YOUR CHANCE, HIJIRI-MARU.
YOU ROTTEN COUPLE OF...
FINISH HIM OFF.

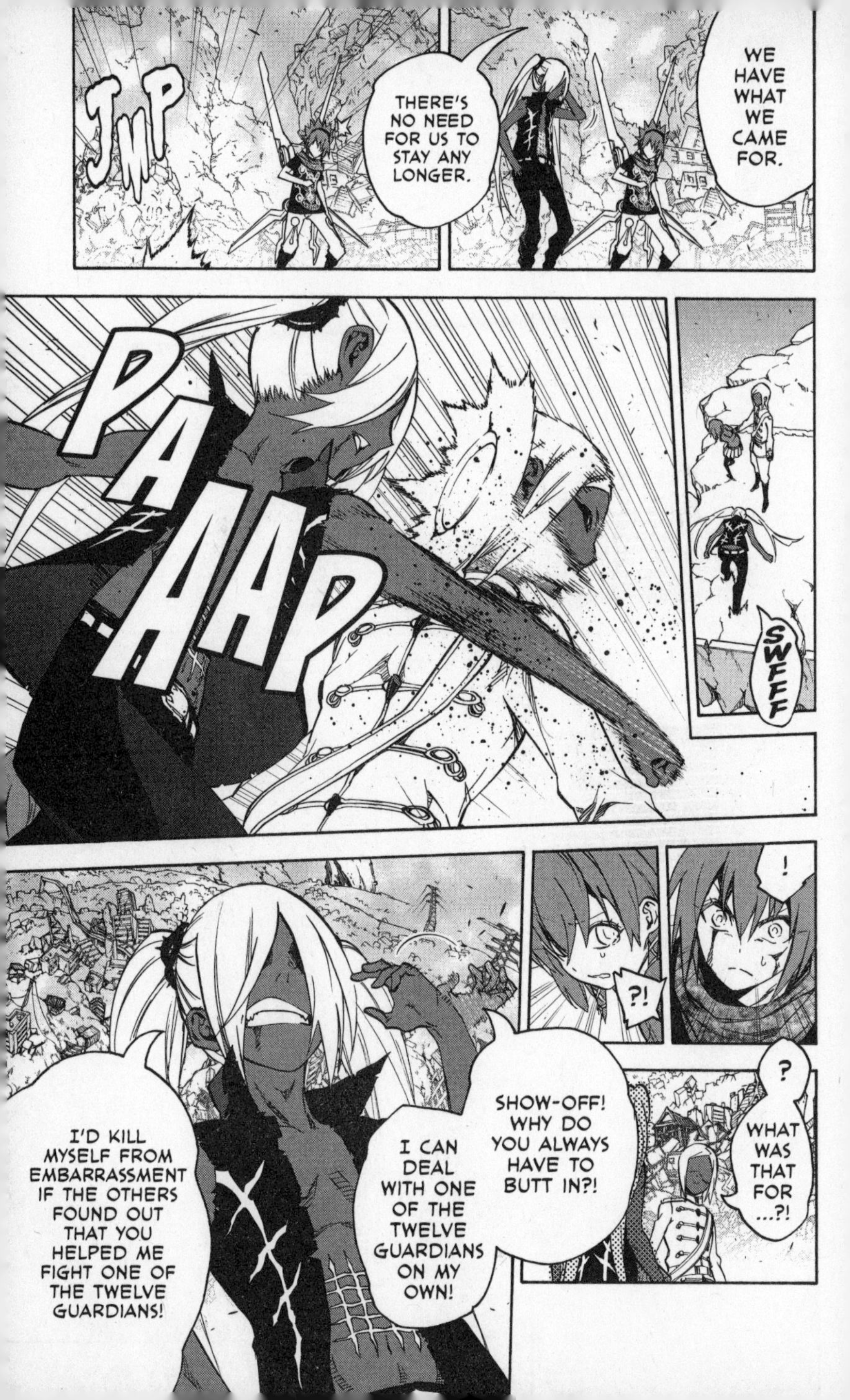
WE HAVE WHAT WE CAME FOR.
THERE'S NO NEED FOR US TO STAY ANY LONGER.
JMP
SWFFF
PAAAP
!
?!
?
WHAT WAS THAT FOR ...?!
SHOW-OFF! WHY DO YOU ALWAYS HAVE TO BUTT IN?!
I CAN DEAL WITH ONE OF THE TWELVE GUARDIANS ON MY OWN!
I'D KILL MYSELF FROM EMBARRASSMENT IF THE OTHERS FOUND OUT THAT YOU HELPED ME FIGHT ONE OF THE TWELVE GUARDIANS!

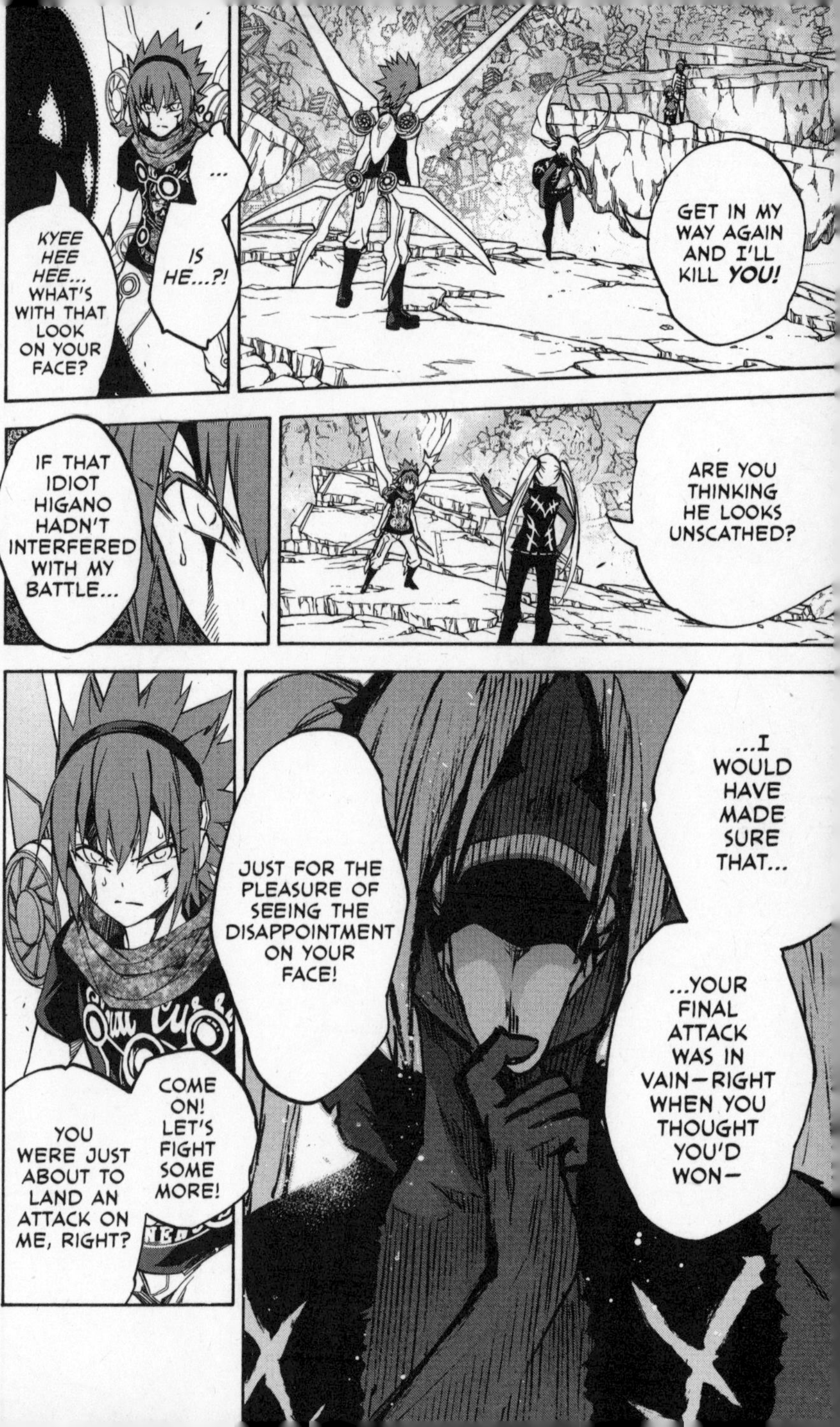
GET IN MY WAY AGAIN AND I'LL KILL *YOU!*
...
IS HE...?!
KYEE HEE HEE... WHAT'S WITH THAT LOOK ON YOUR FACE?
ARE YOU THINKING HE LOOKS UNSCATHED?
IF THAT IDIOT HIGANO HADN'T INTERFERED WITH MY BATTLE...
...I WOULD HAVE MADE SURE THAT...
...YOUR FINAL ATTACK WAS IN VAIN—RIGHT WHEN YOU THOUGHT YOU'D WON—
JUST FOR THE PLEASURE OF SEEING THE DISAPPOINTMENT ON YOUR FACE!
COME ON! LET'S FIGHT SOME MORE!
YOU WERE JUST ABOUT TO LAND AN ATTACK ON ME, RIGHT?

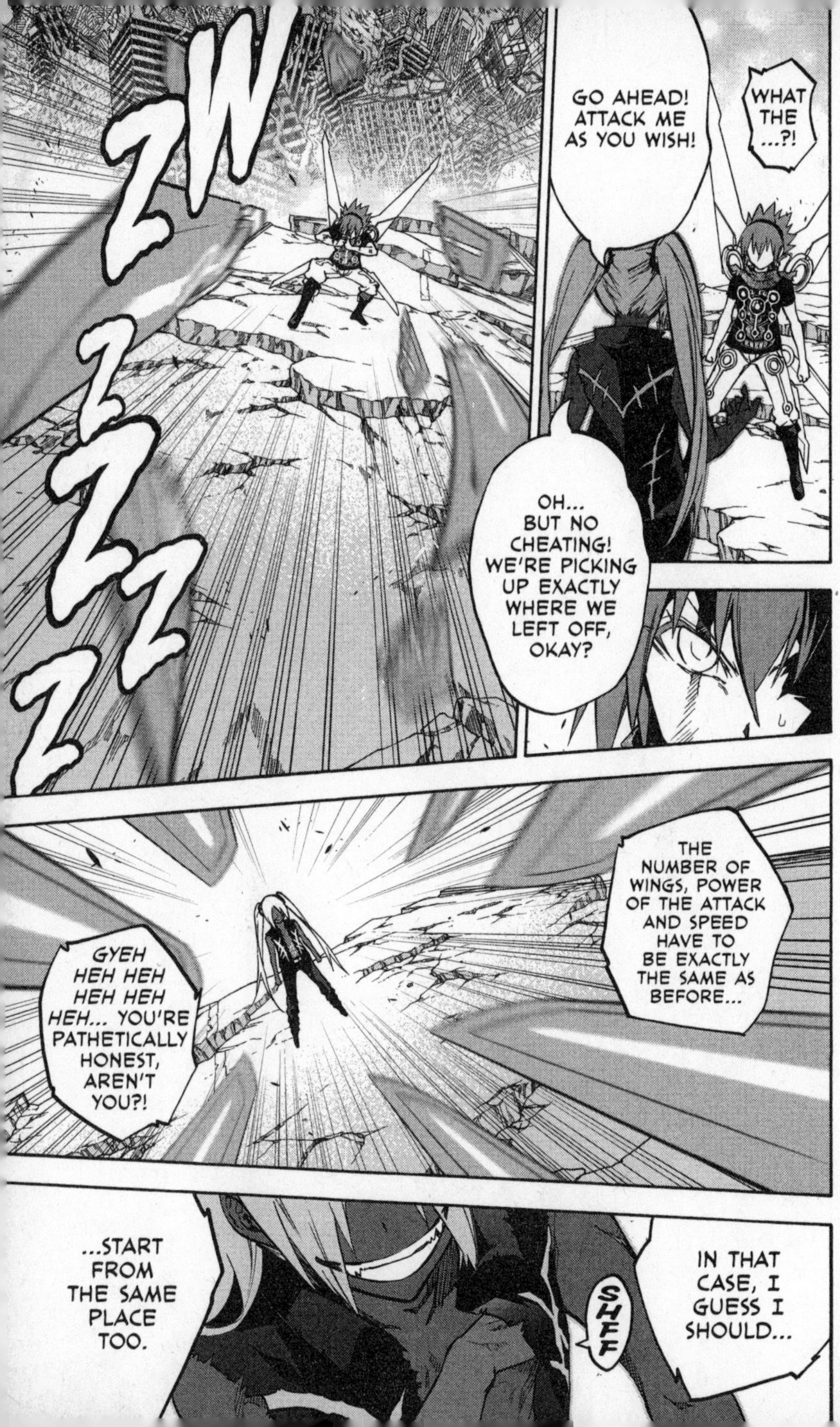
GO AHEAD! ATTACK ME AS YOU WISH!
WHAT THE ...?!
OH... BUT NO CHEATING! WE'RE PICKING UP EXACTLY WHERE WE LEFT OFF, OKAY?
ZWZZZZZ
THE NUMBER OF WINGS, POWER OF THE ATTACK AND SPEED HAVE TO BE EXACTLY THE SAME AS BEFORE...
GYEH HEH HEH HEH HEH HEH... YOU'RE PATHETICALLY HONEST, AREN'T YOU?!
IN THAT CASE, I GUESS I SHOULD...
SHFF
...START FROM THE SAME PLACE TOO.

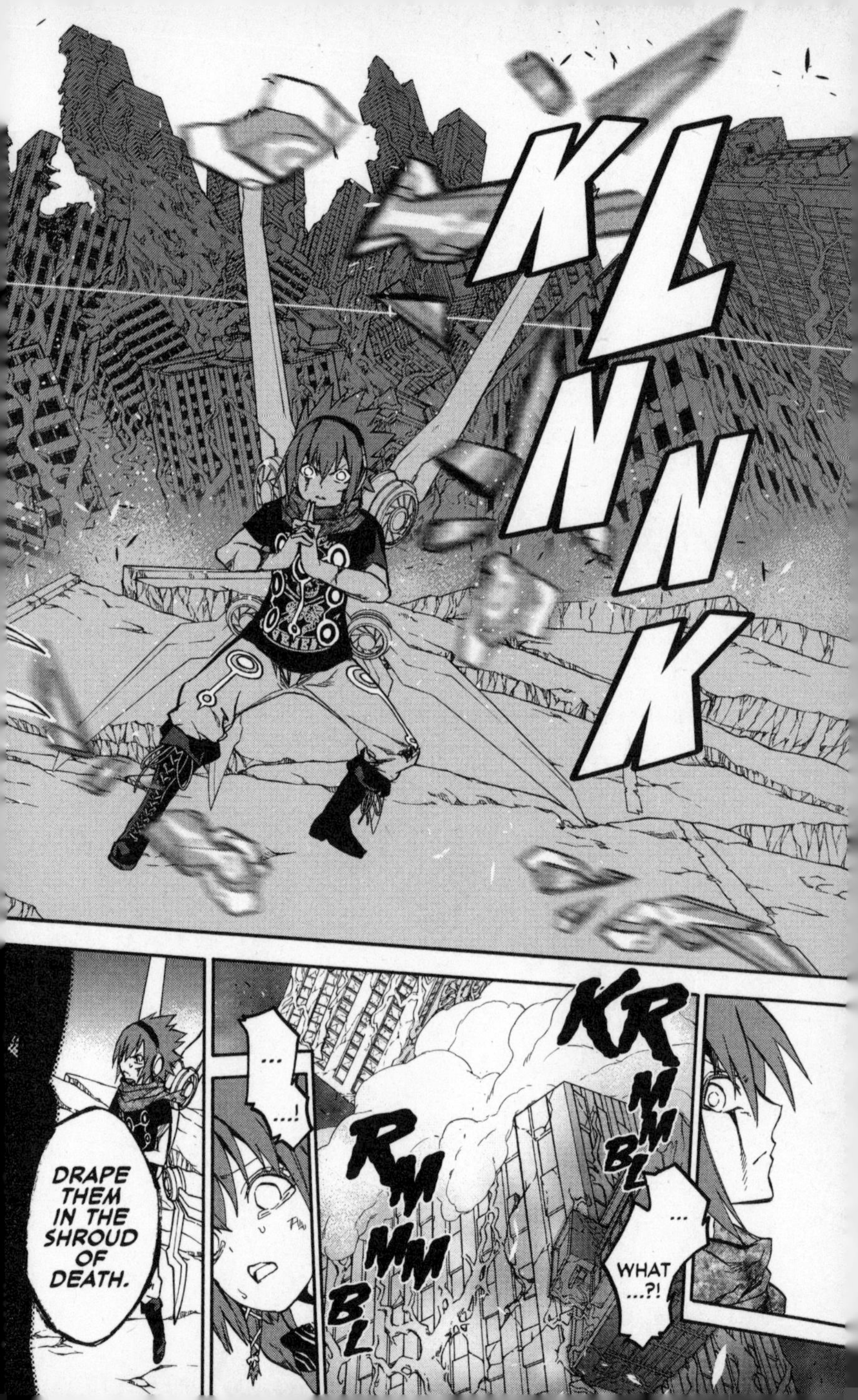
KLNNK
...
WHAT ...?!
KRMMBL
...
...!
RMMMBL
DRAPE THEM IN THE SHROUD OF DEATH.

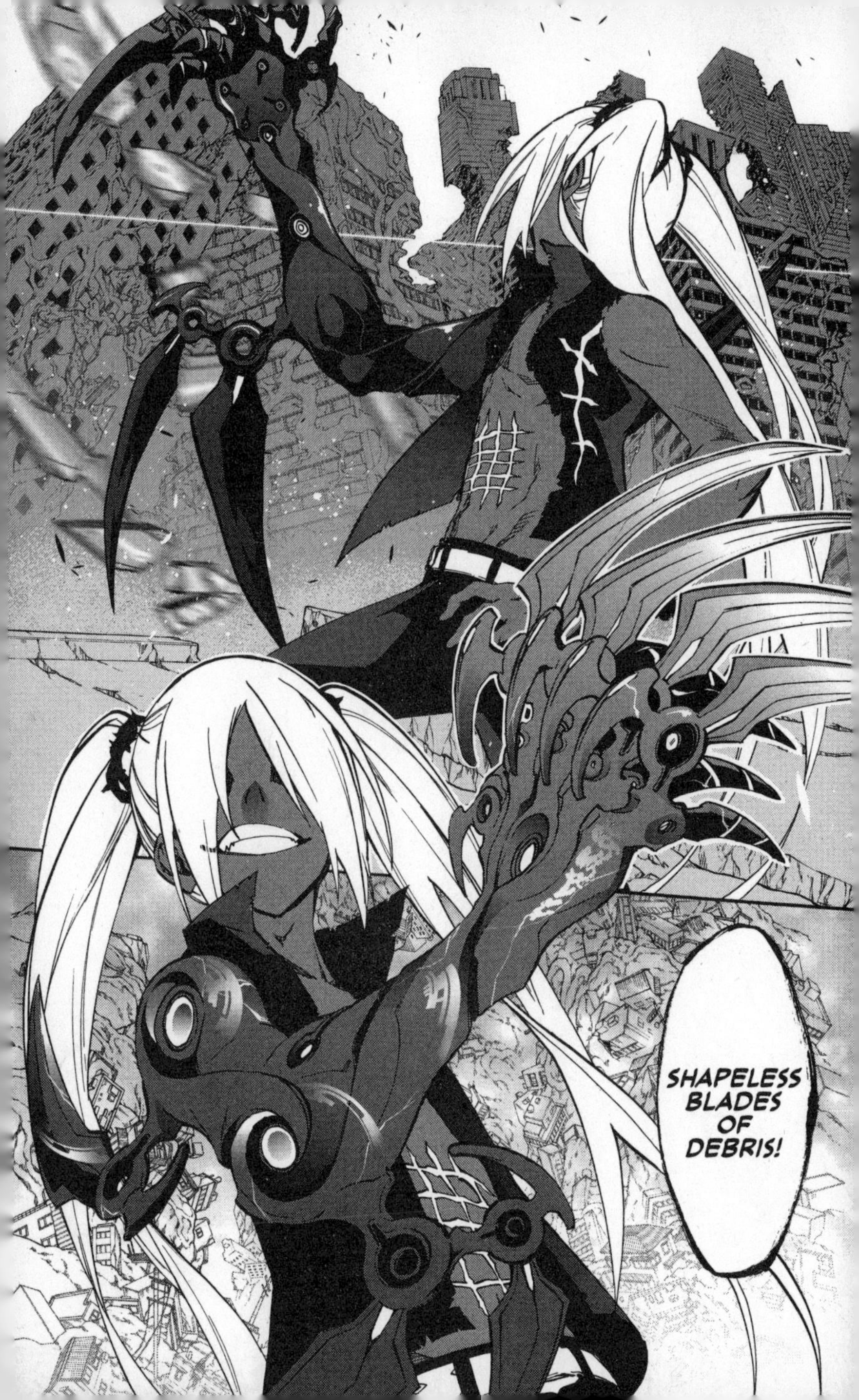
SHAPELESS BLADES OF DEBRIS!

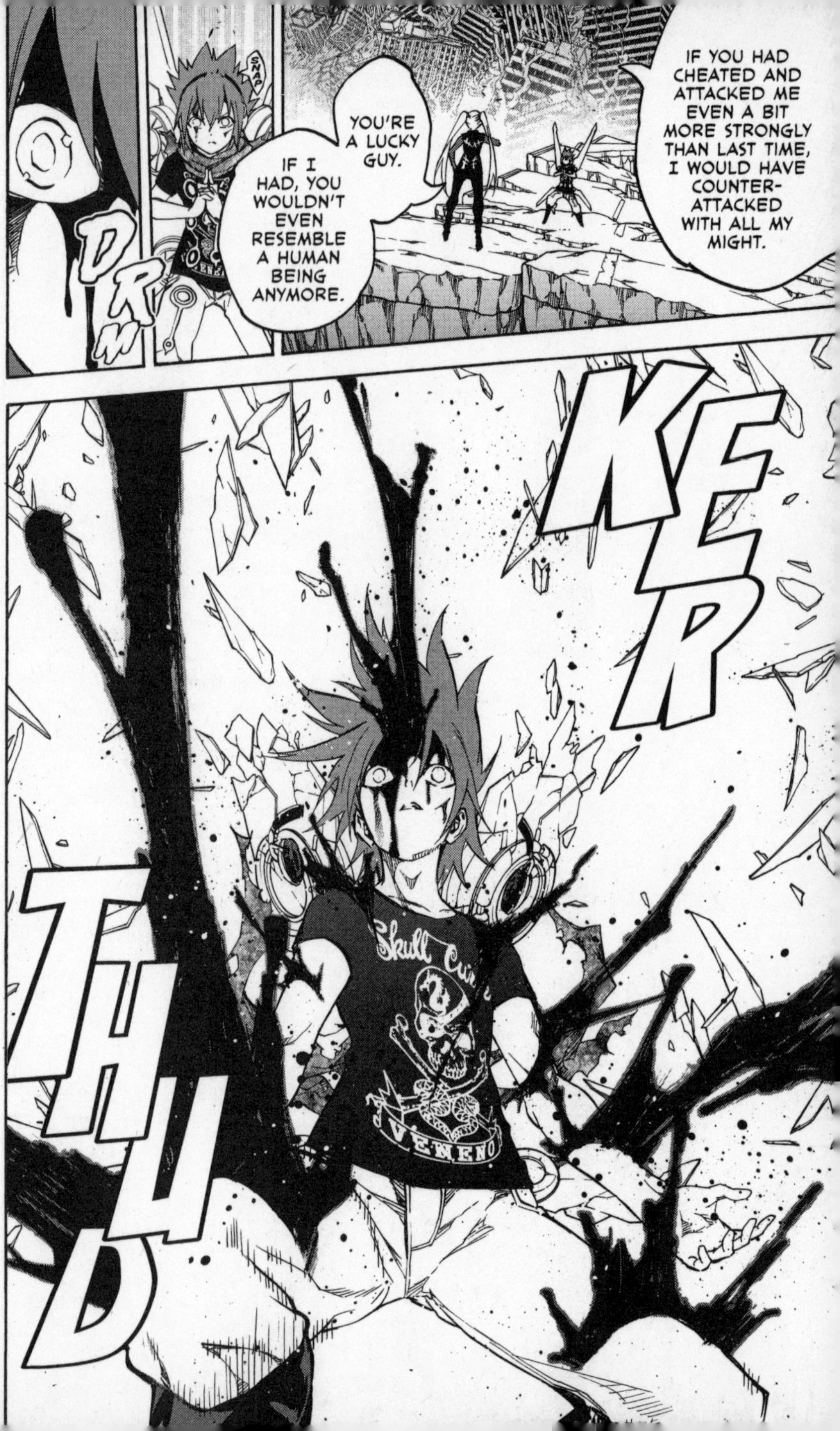
IF YOU HAD CHEATED AND ATTACKED ME EVEN A BIT MORE STRONGLY THAN LAST TIME, I WOULD HAVE COUNTER-ATTACKED WITH ALL MY MIGHT.
YOU'RE A LUCKY GUY.
IF I HAD, YOU WOULDN'T EVEN RESEMBLE A HUMAN BEING ANYMORE.
SNAP
DRM
KER
THUD

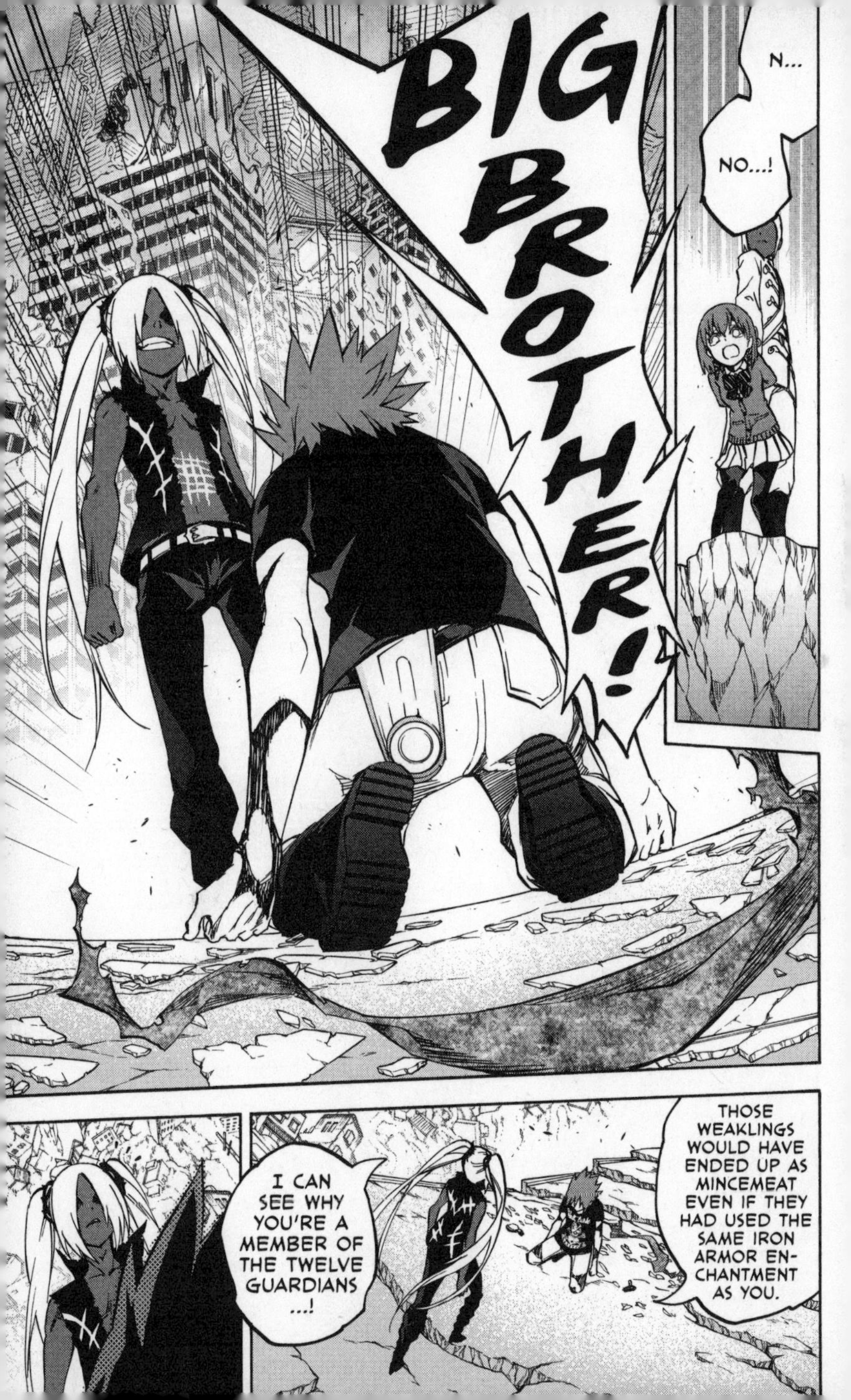
N...
NO...!
BIG BROTHER!!
THOSE WEAKLINGS WOULD HAVE ENDED UP AS MINCEMEAT EVEN IF THEY HAD USED THE SAME IRON ARMOR EN-CHANTMENT AS YOU.
I CAN SEE WHY YOU'RE A MEMBER OF THE TWELVE GUARDIANS ...!

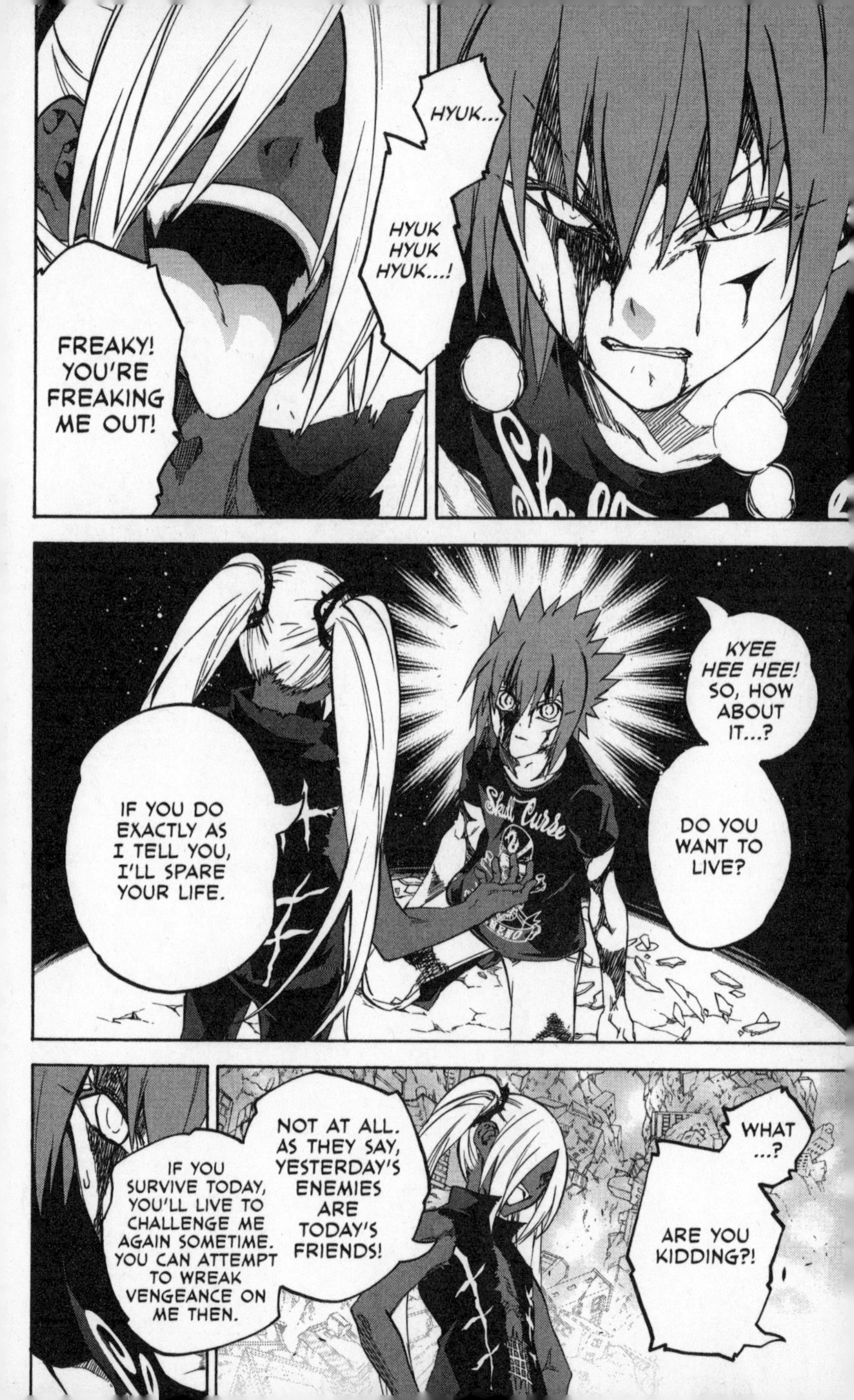
HYUK...
HYUK HYUK HYUK...!
FREAKY! YOU'RE FREAKING ME OUT!
KYEE HEE HEE! SO, HOW ABOUT IT...?
DO YOU WANT TO LIVE?
Skull Curse
IF YOU DO EXACTLY AS I TELL YOU, I'LL SPARE YOUR LIFE.
WHAT ...?
ARE YOU KIDDING?!
NOT AT ALL. AS THEY SAY, YESTERDAY'S ENEMIES ARE TODAY'S FRIENDS!
IF YOU SURVIVE TODAY, YOU'LL LIVE TO CHALLENGE ME AGAIN SOMETIME. YOU CAN ATTEMPT TO WREAK VENGEANCE ON ME THEN.

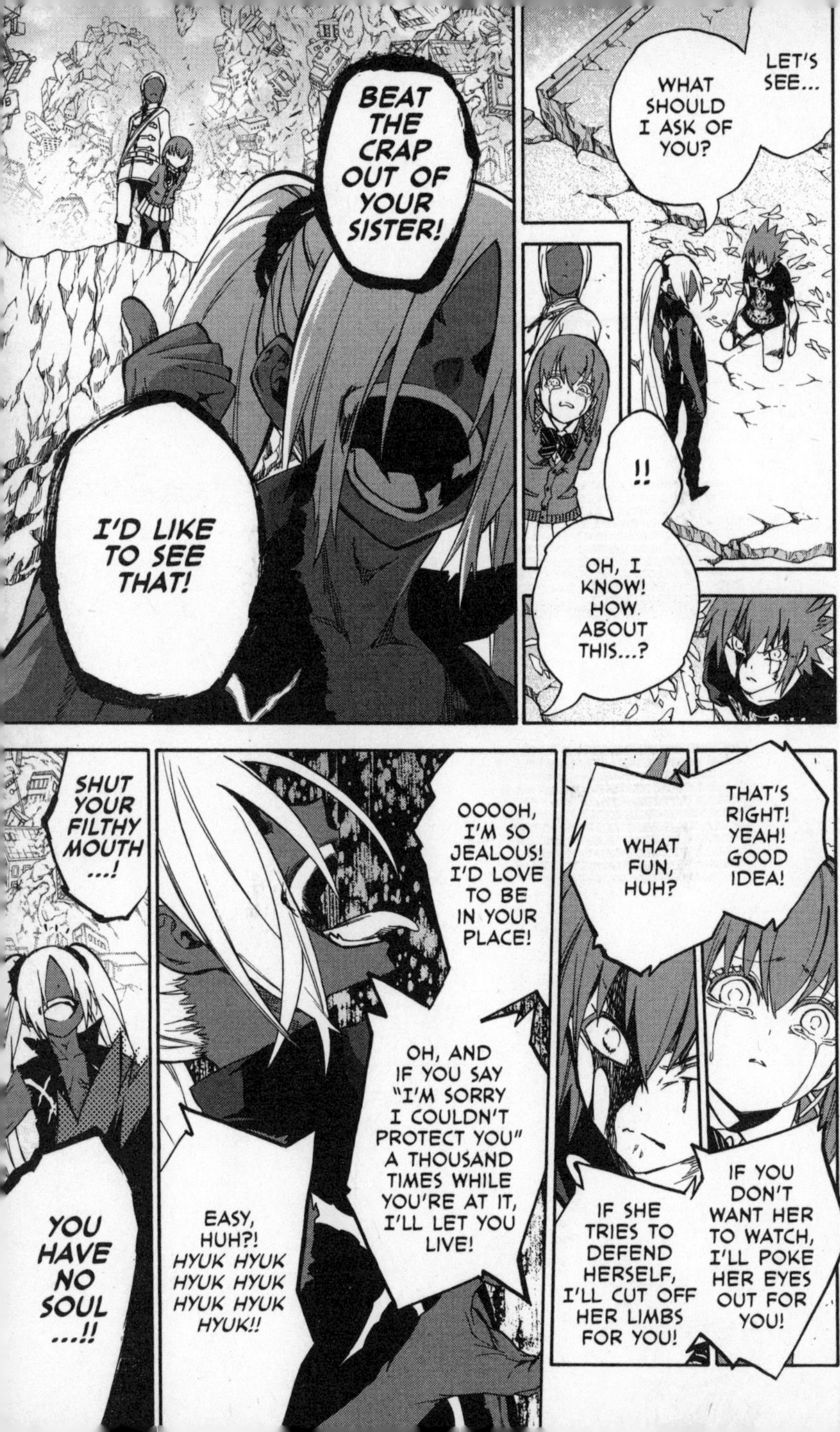
LET'S SEE...
WHAT SHOULD I ASK OF YOU?
!!
OH, I KNOW! HOW ABOUT THIS...?
BEAT THE CRAP OUT OF YOUR SISTER!
I'D LIKE TO SEE THAT!
THAT'S RIGHT! YEAH! GOOD IDEA!
IF YOU DON'T WANT HER TO WATCH, I'LL POKE HER EYES OUT FOR YOU!
WHAT FUN, HUH?
IF SHE TRIES TO DEFEND HERSELF, I'LL CUT OFF HER LIMBS FOR YOU!
OOOOH, I'M SO JEALOUS! I'D LOVE TO BE IN YOUR PLACE!
OH, AND IF YOU SAY "I'M SORRY I COULDN'T PROTECT YOU" A THOUSAND TIMES WHILE YOU'RE AT IT, I'LL LET YOU LIVE!
EASY, HUH?! HYUK HYUK HYUK HYUK HYUK HYUK HYUK!!
SHUT YOUR FILTHY MOUTH...!
YOU HAVE NO SOUL...!!

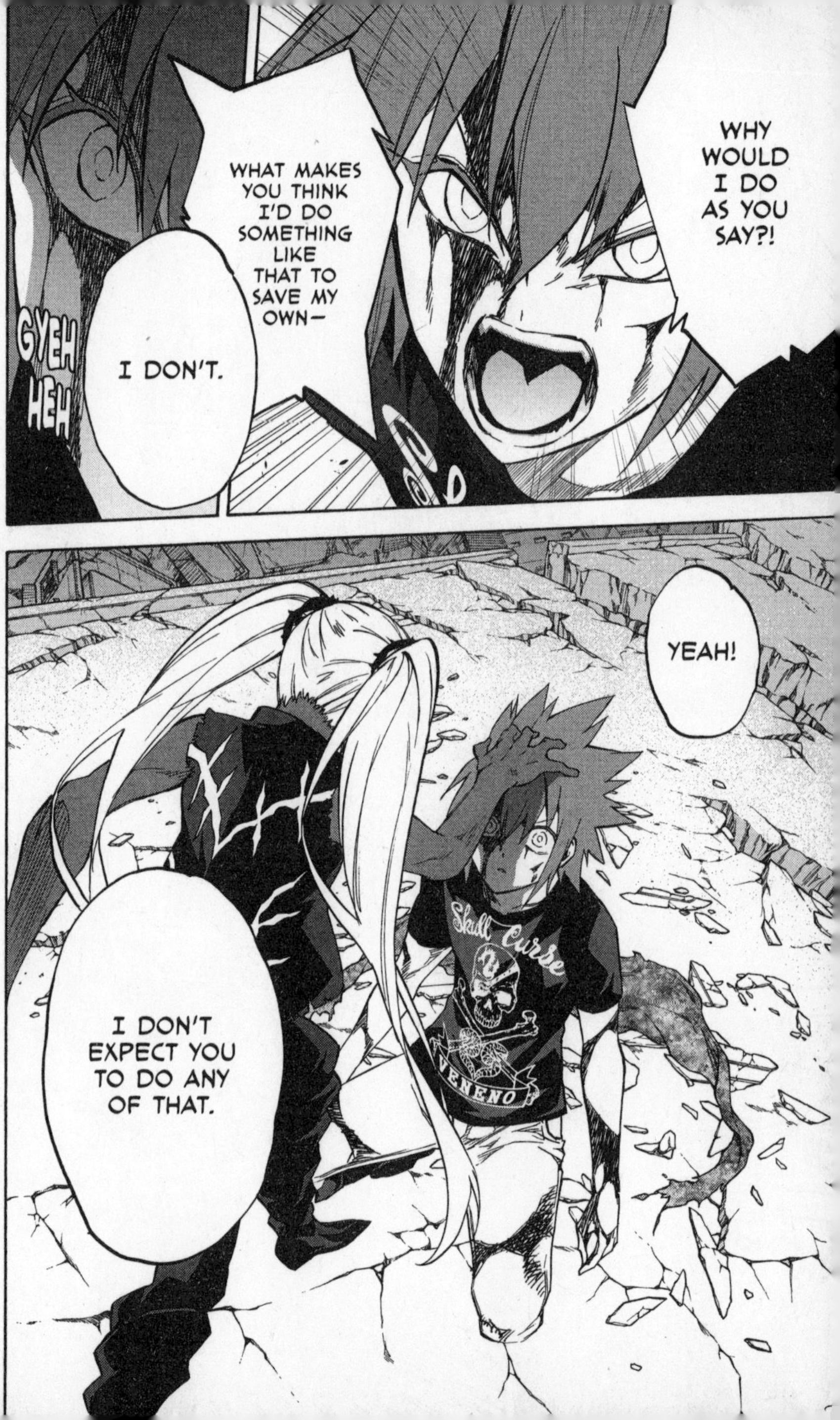
WHY WOULD I DO AS YOU SAY?!
WHAT MAKES YOU THINK I'D DO SOMETHING LIKE THAT TO SAVE MY OWN—
I DON'T.
GYEH HEH
YEAH!
Skull Curse
VENENO
I DON'T EXPECT YOU TO DO ANY OF THAT.

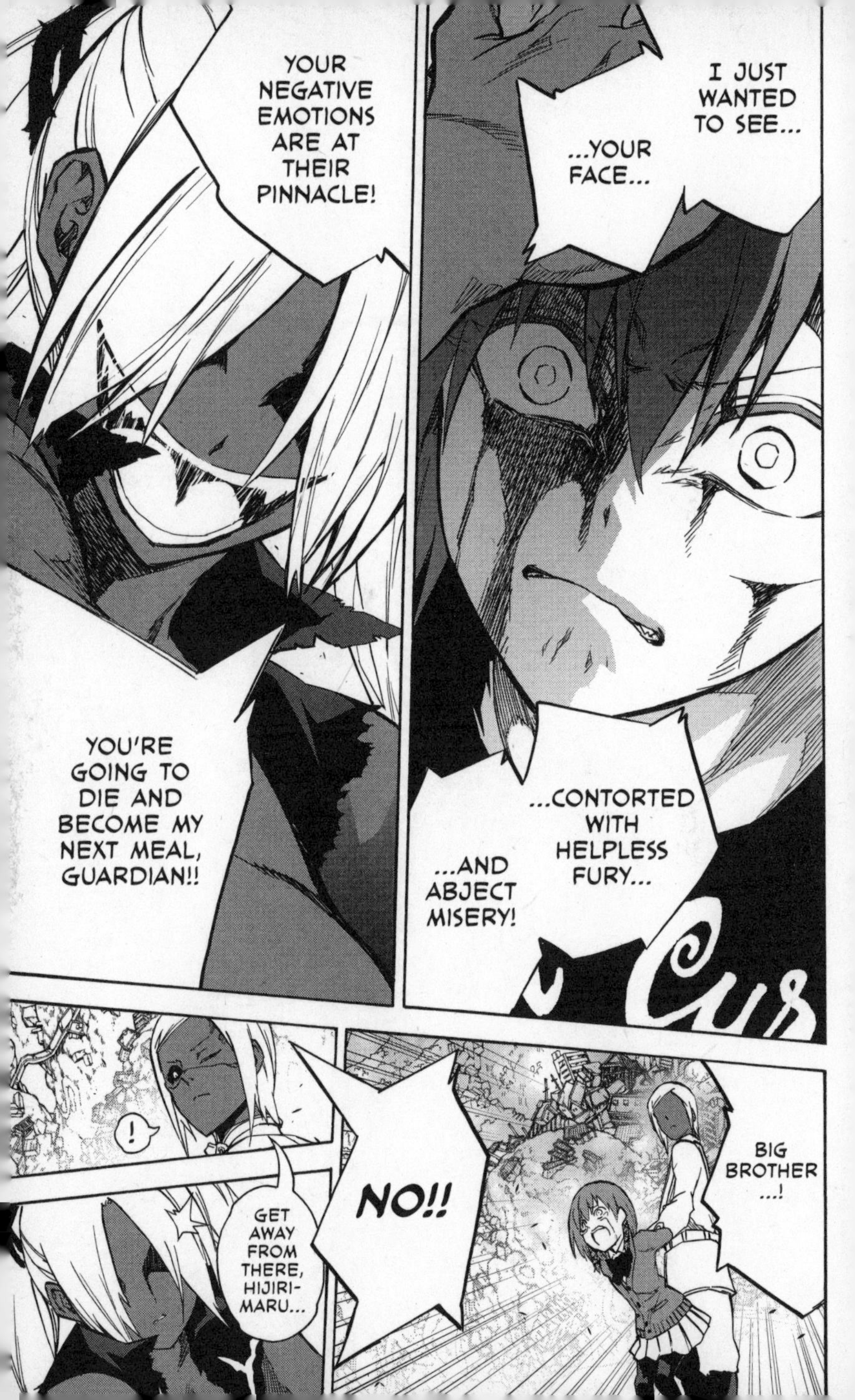

I JUST WANTED TO SEE...
...YOUR FACE...
...CONTORTED WITH HELPLESS FURY...
...AND ABJECT MISERY!
YOUR NEGATIVE EMOTIONS ARE AT THEIR PINNACLE!
YOU'RE GOING TO DIE AND BECOME MY NEXT MEAL, GUARDIAN!!
BIG BROTHER ...!
NO!!
!
GET AWAY FROM THERE, HIJIRI-MARU...

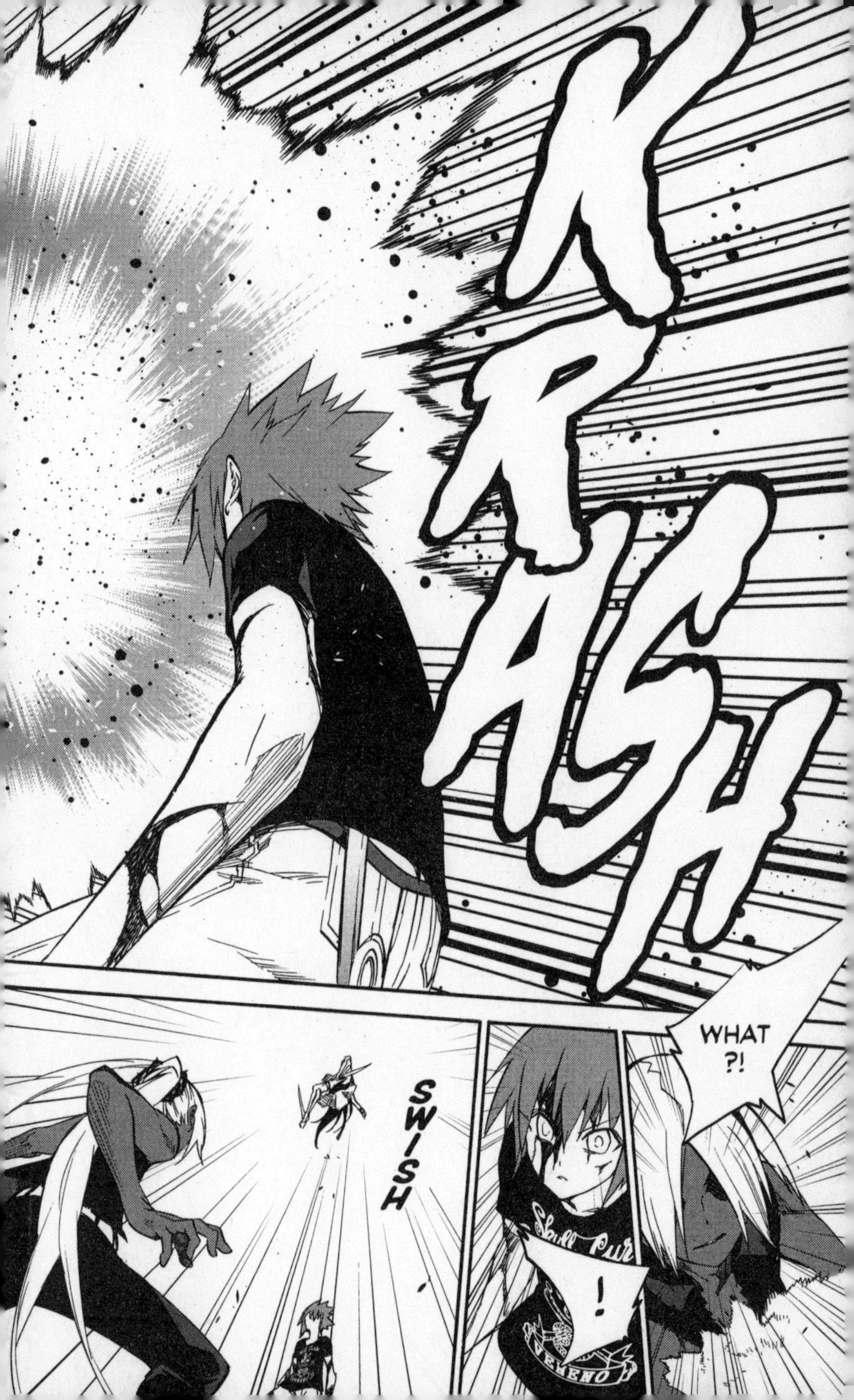
KRASH
WHAT ?!
!
SWISH

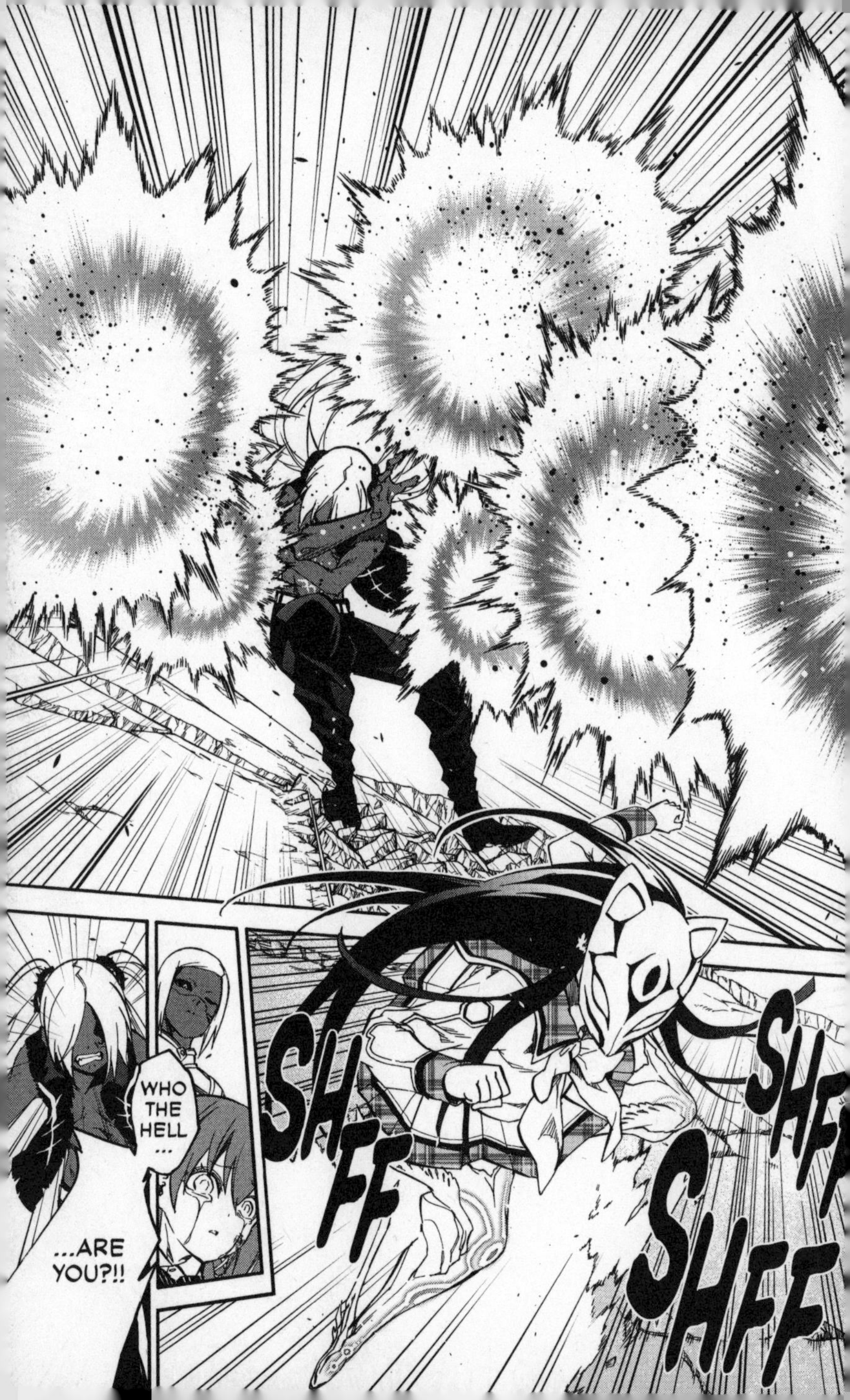
SHF
SHFF
SHFF
WHO THE HELL ...
...ARE YOU?!!

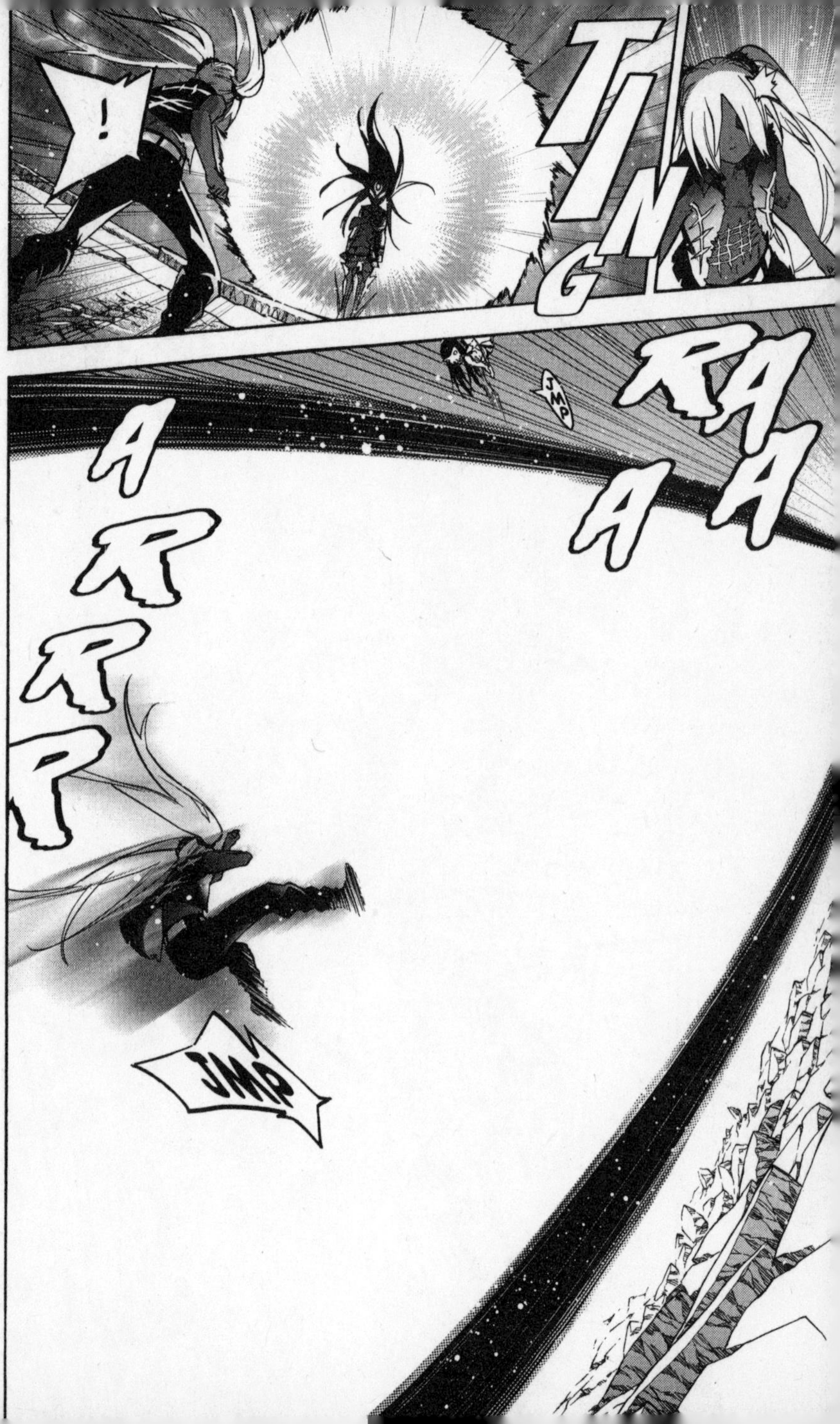
TING
!
RAAA
JMP
ARRRP
JMP

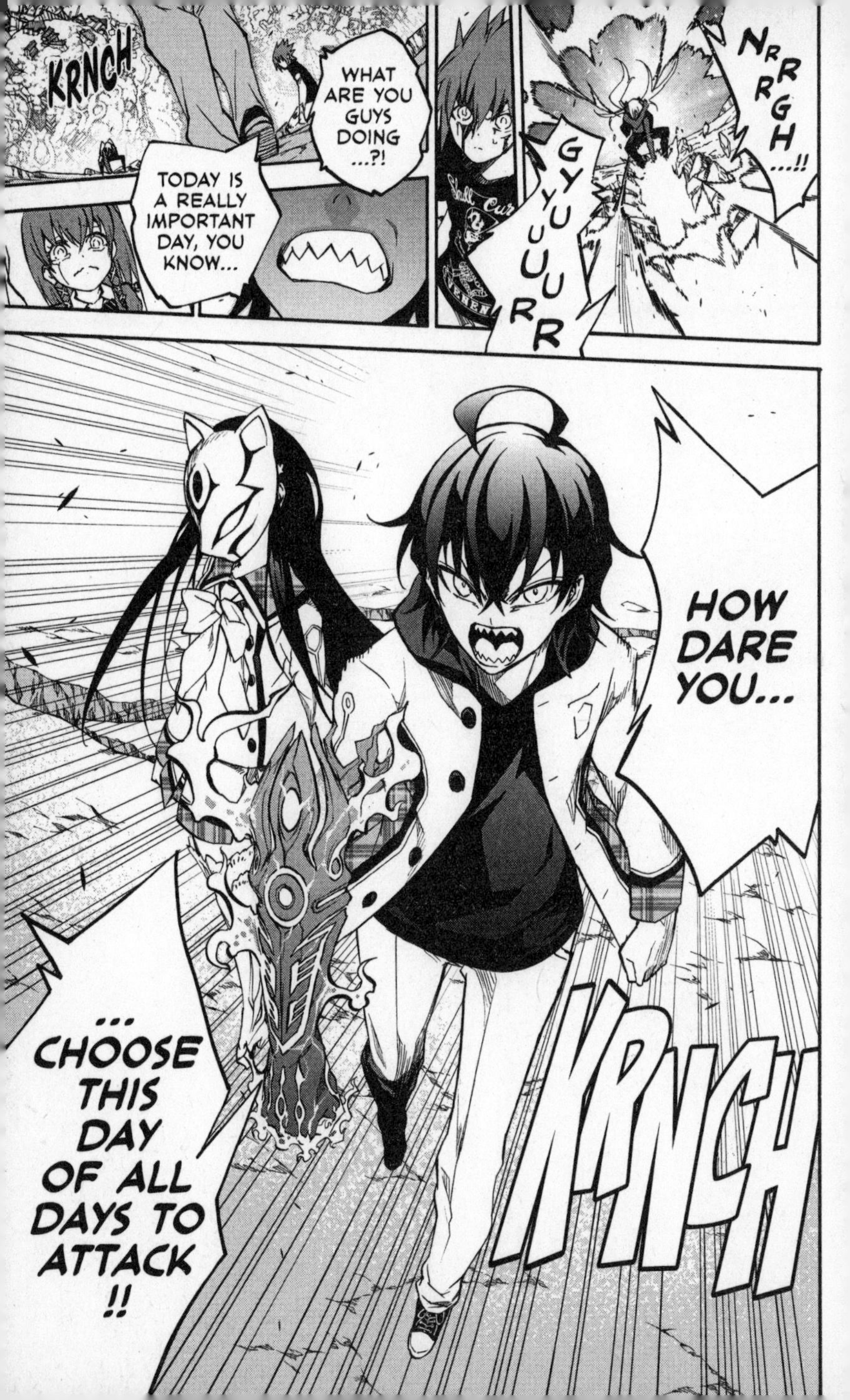

NRRRGH...!!
GYUUUURRR
WHAT ARE YOU GUYS DOING...?!
KRNCH
TODAY IS A REALLY IMPORTANT DAY, YOU KNOW...
HOW DARE YOU...
KRNCH
...CHOOSE THIS DAY OF ALL DAYS TO ATTACK!!

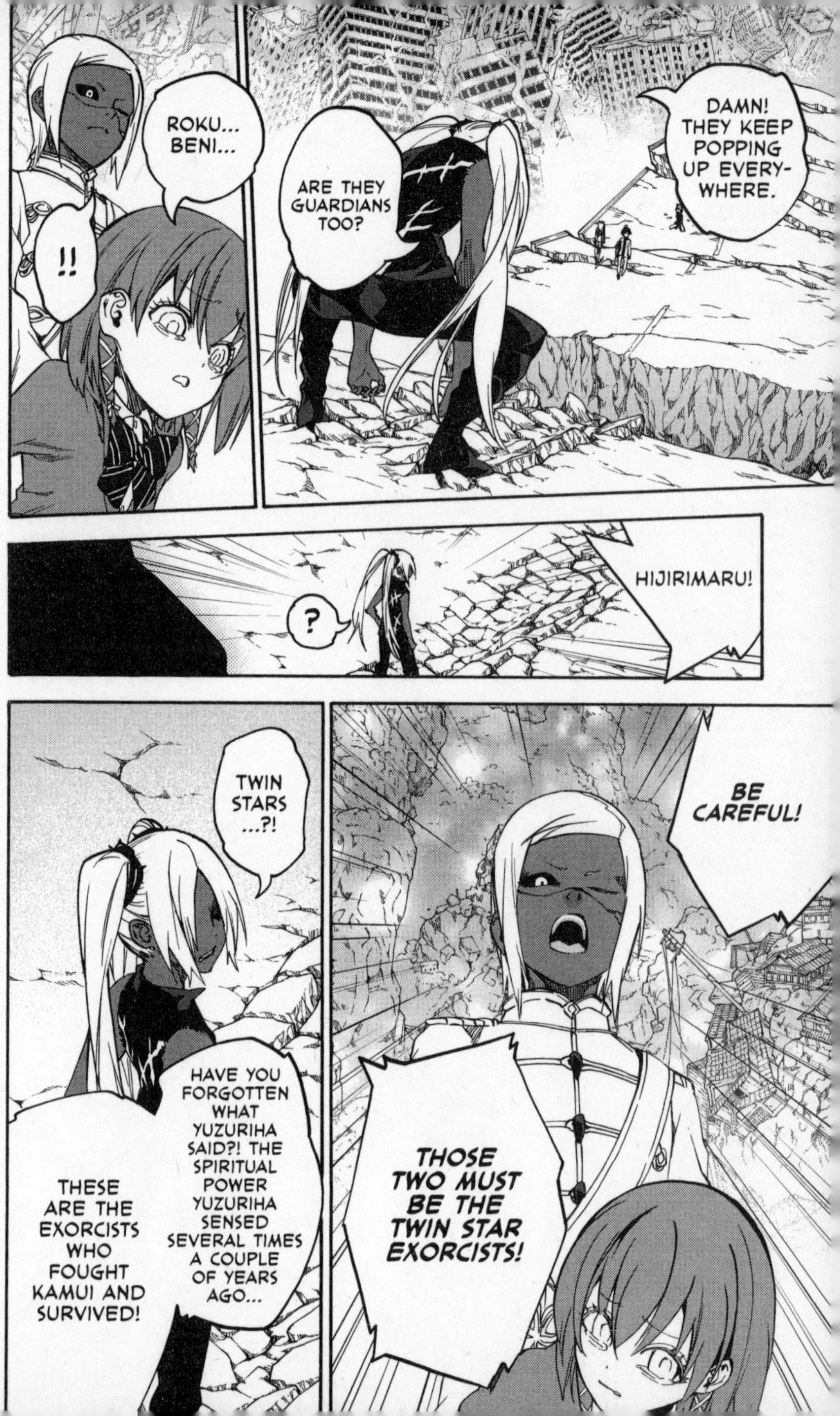
DAMN! THEY KEEP POPPING UP EVERY-WHERE.
ARE THEY GUARDIANS TOO?
ROKU... BENI...
!!
HIJIRIMARU!
?
BE CAREFUL!
THOSE TWO MUST BE THE TWIN STAR EXORCISTS!
TWIN STARS ...?!
HAVE YOU FORGOTTEN WHAT YUZURIHA SAID?! THE SPIRITUAL POWER YUZURIHA SENSED SEVERAL TIMES A COUPLE OF YEARS AGO...
THESE ARE THE EXORCISTS WHO FOUGHT KAMUI AND SURVIVED!

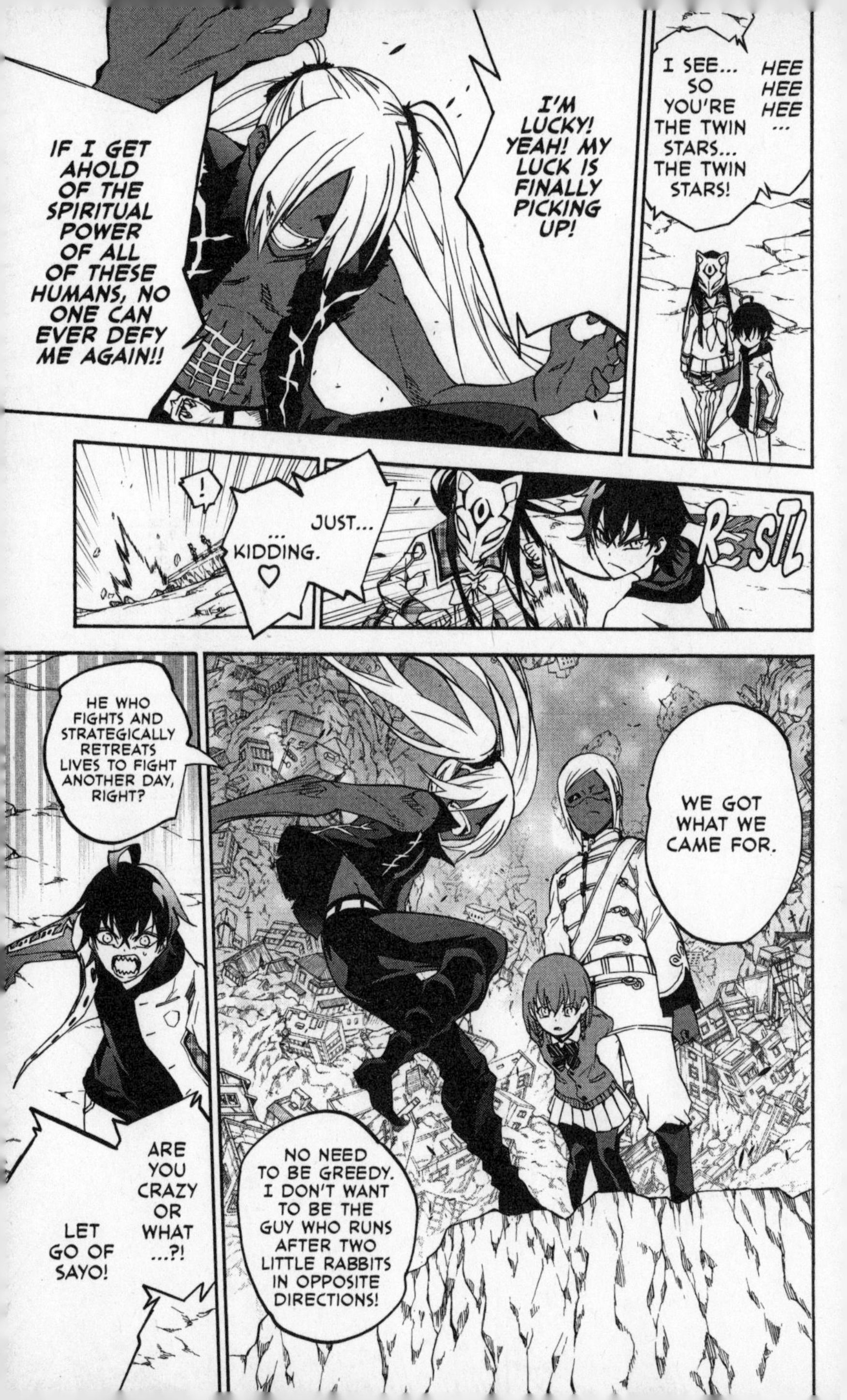
HEE HEE HEE...
I SEE... SO YOU'RE THE TWIN STARS... THE TWIN STARS!
I'M LUCKY! YEAH! MY LUCK IS FINALLY PICKING UP!
IF I GET AHOLD OF THE SPIRITUAL POWER OF ALL OF THESE HUMANS, NO ONE CAN EVER DEFY ME AGAIN!!
R-STL
JUST... ...KIDDING. ♡
!
WE GOT WHAT WE CAME FOR.
NO NEED TO BE GREEDY. I DON'T WANT TO BE THE GUY WHO RUNS AFTER TWO LITTLE RABBITS IN OPPOSITE DIRECTIONS!
HE WHO FIGHTS AND STRATEGICALLY RETREATS LIVES TO FIGHT ANOTHER DAY, RIGHT?
ARE YOU CRAZY OR WHAT...?!
LET GO OF SAYO!

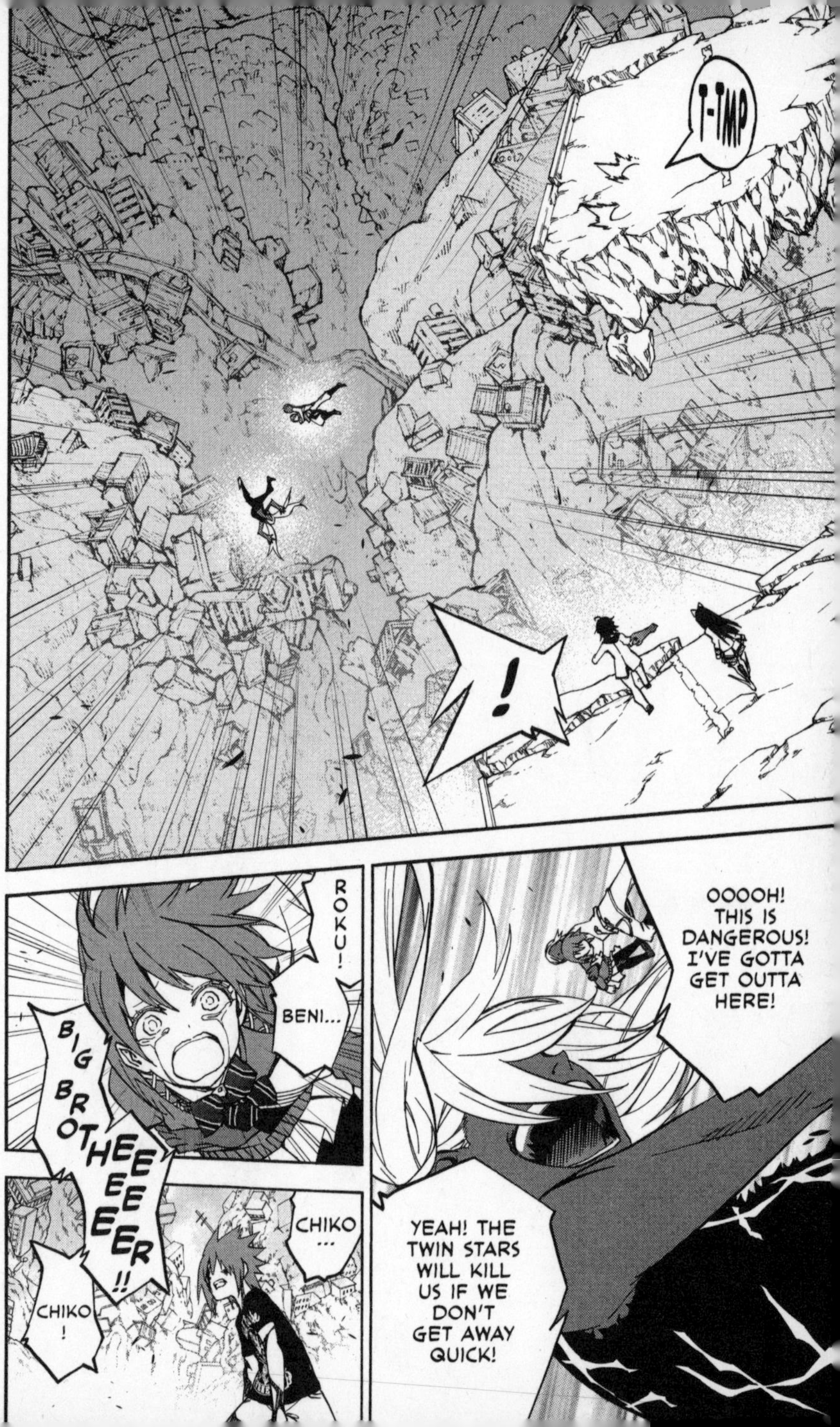
T-TMP
!
OOOOH! THIS IS DANGEROUS! I'VE GOTTA GET OUTTA HERE!
YEAH! THE TWIN STARS WILL KILL US IF WE DON'T GET AWAY QUICK!
ROKU!
BENI...
BIG BROTHEEEEEEEER!!
CHIKO...
CHIKO!

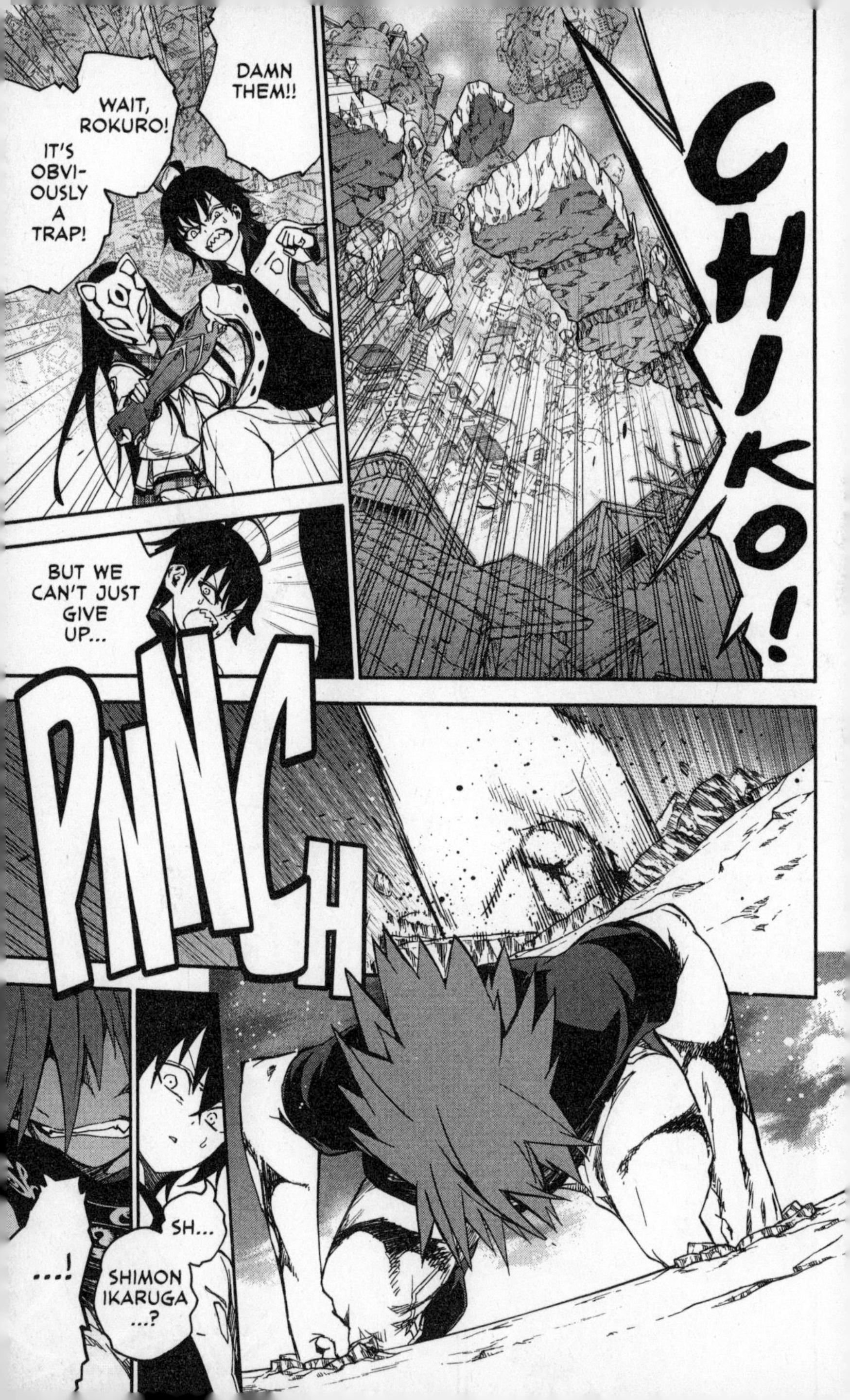
CHIKO!
DAMN THEM!!
WAIT, ROKURO!
IT'S OBVI-OUSLY A TRAP!
BUT WE CAN'T JUST GIVE UP...
PNNCH
SH...
SHIMON IKARUGA ...?
...!

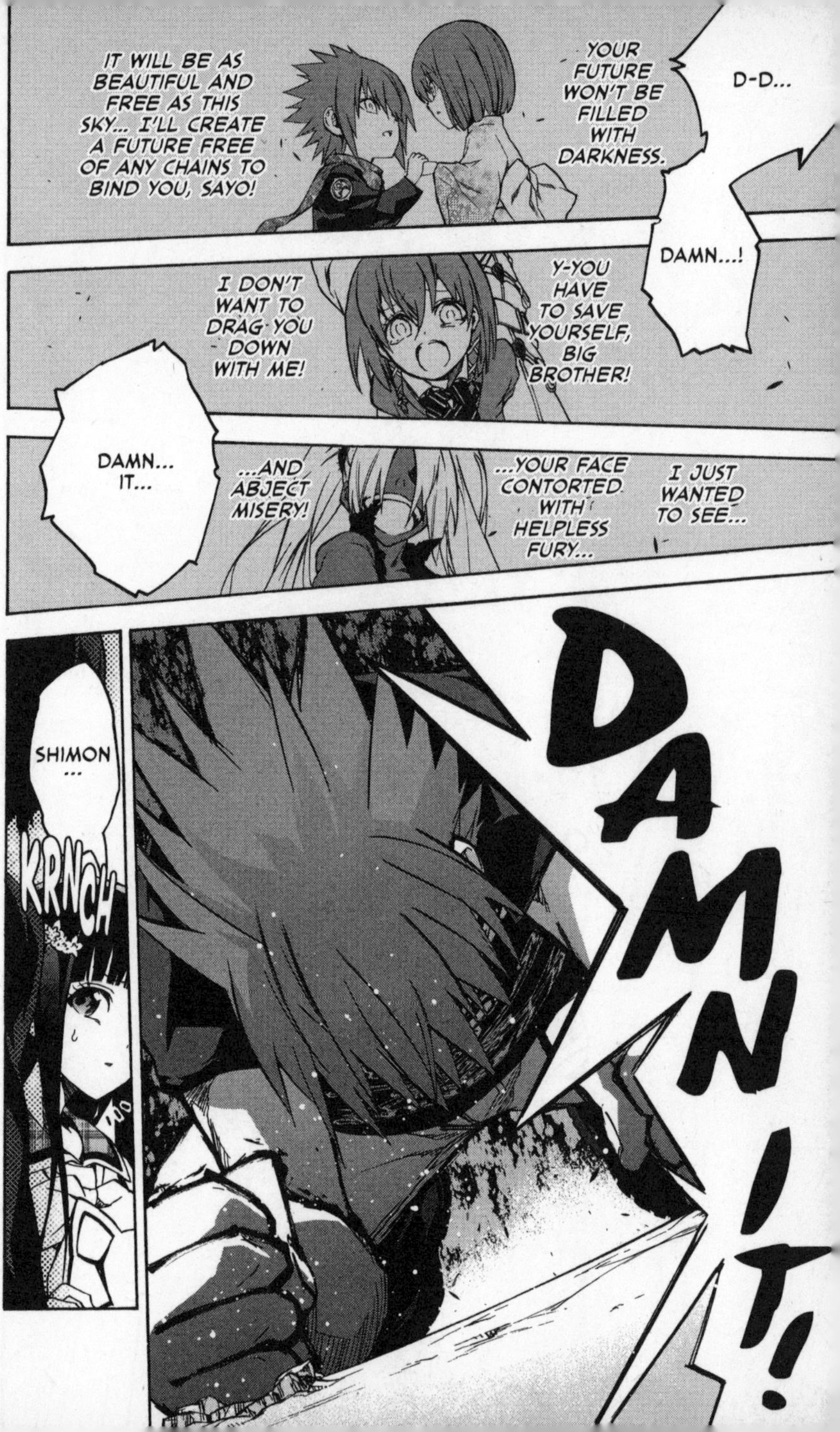
D-D...
YOUR FUTURE WON'T BE FILLED WITH DARKNESS.
IT WILL BE AS BEAUTIFUL AND FREE AS THIS SKY... I'LL CREATE A FUTURE FREE OF ANY CHAINS TO BIND YOU, SAYO!
DAMN...!
Y-YOU HAVE TO SAVE YOURSELF, BIG BROTHER!
I DON'T WANT TO DRAG YOU DOWN WITH ME!
I JUST WANTED TO SEE...
...YOUR FACE CONTORTED WITH HELPLESS FURY...
...AND ABJECT MISERY!
DAMN... IT...
DAMNIT!!
SHIMON...
KRNCH

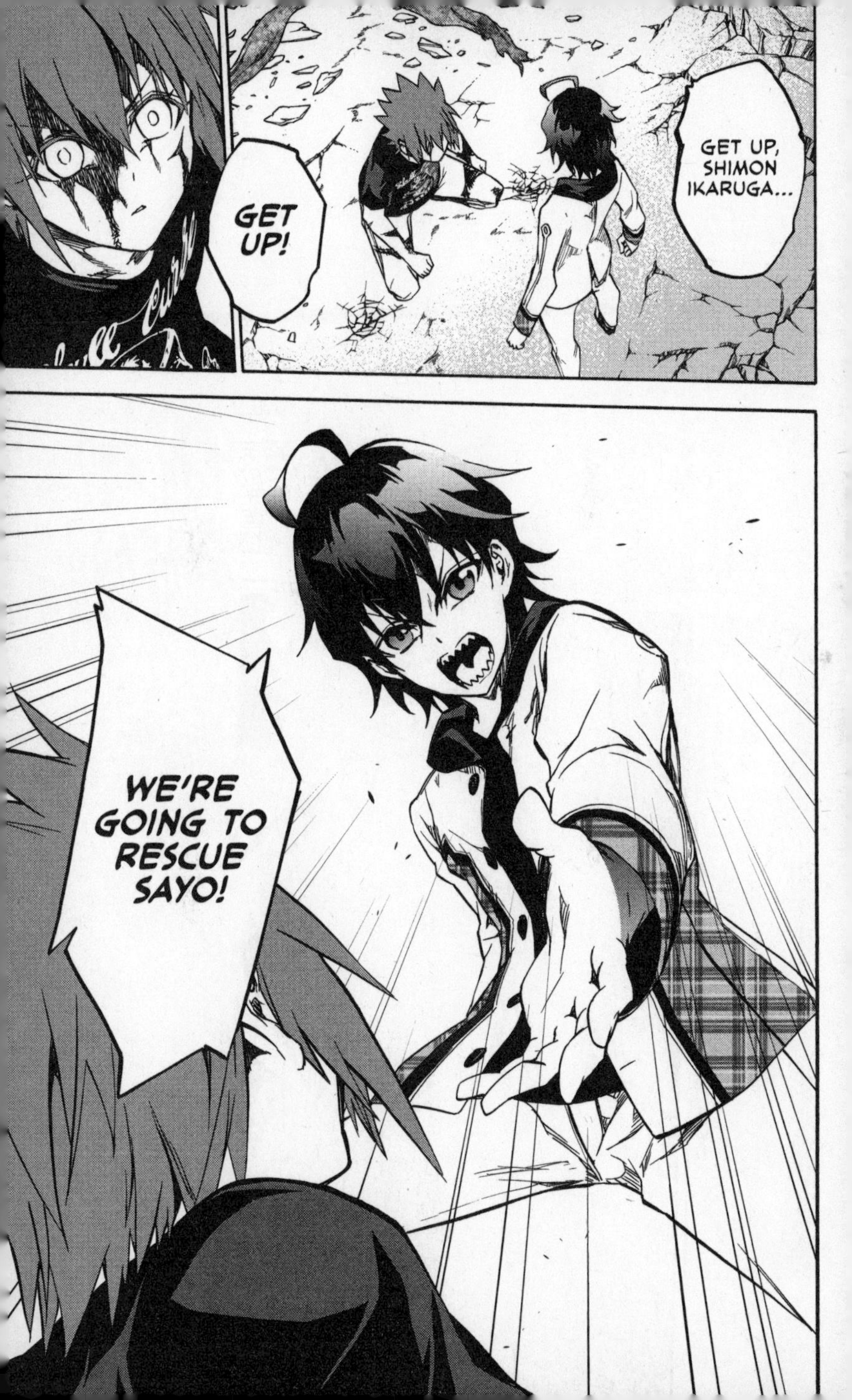
GET UP, SHIMON IKARUGA...
GET UP!
WE'RE GOING TO RESCUE SAYO!

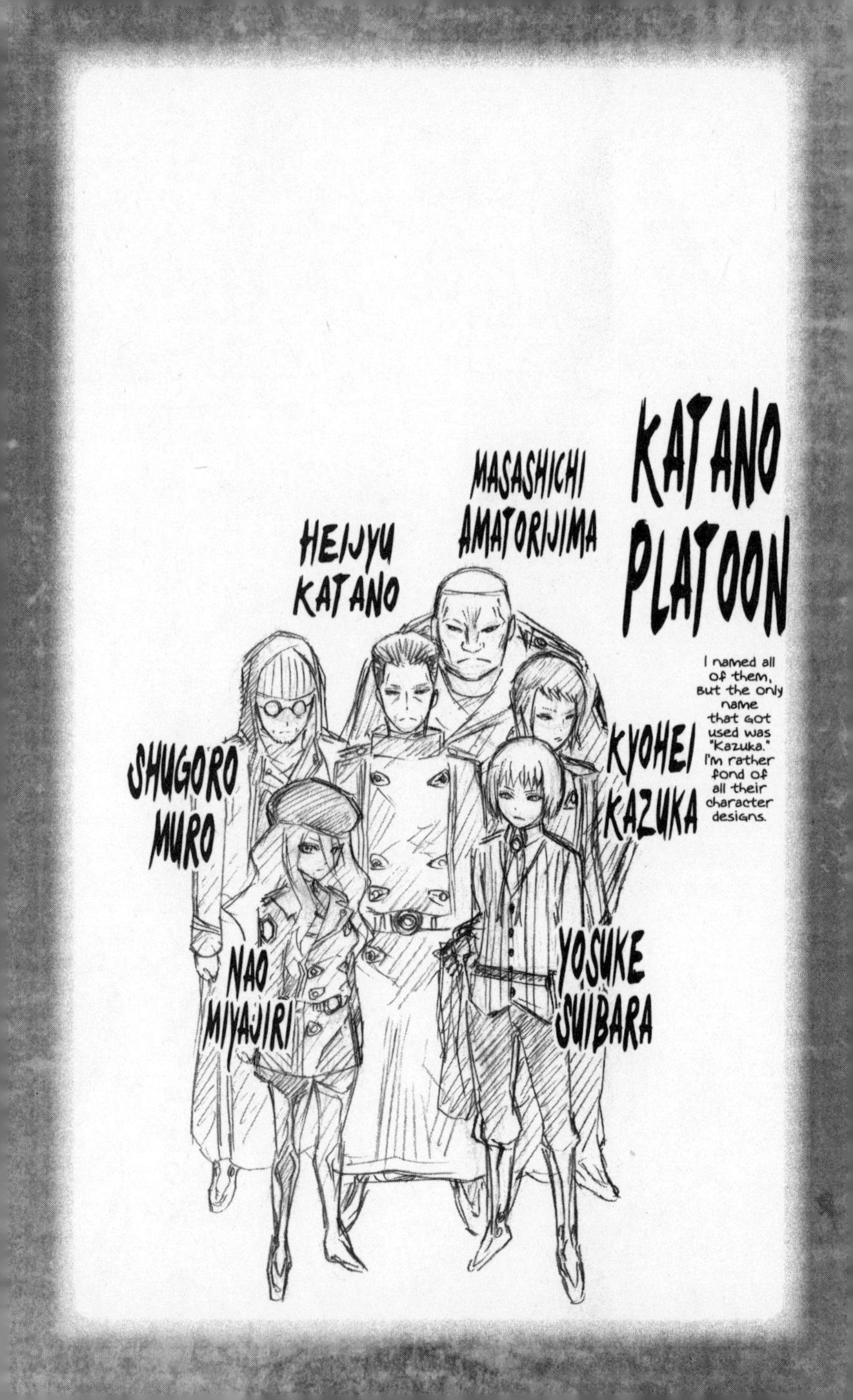
KATANO PLATOON
I named all of them, but the only name that got used was "Kazuka." I'm rather fond of all their character designs.
MASASHICHI AMATORIJIMA
HEIJYU KATANO
KYOHEI KAZUKA
SHUGORO MURO
YOSUKE SUIBARA
NAO MIYAJIRI

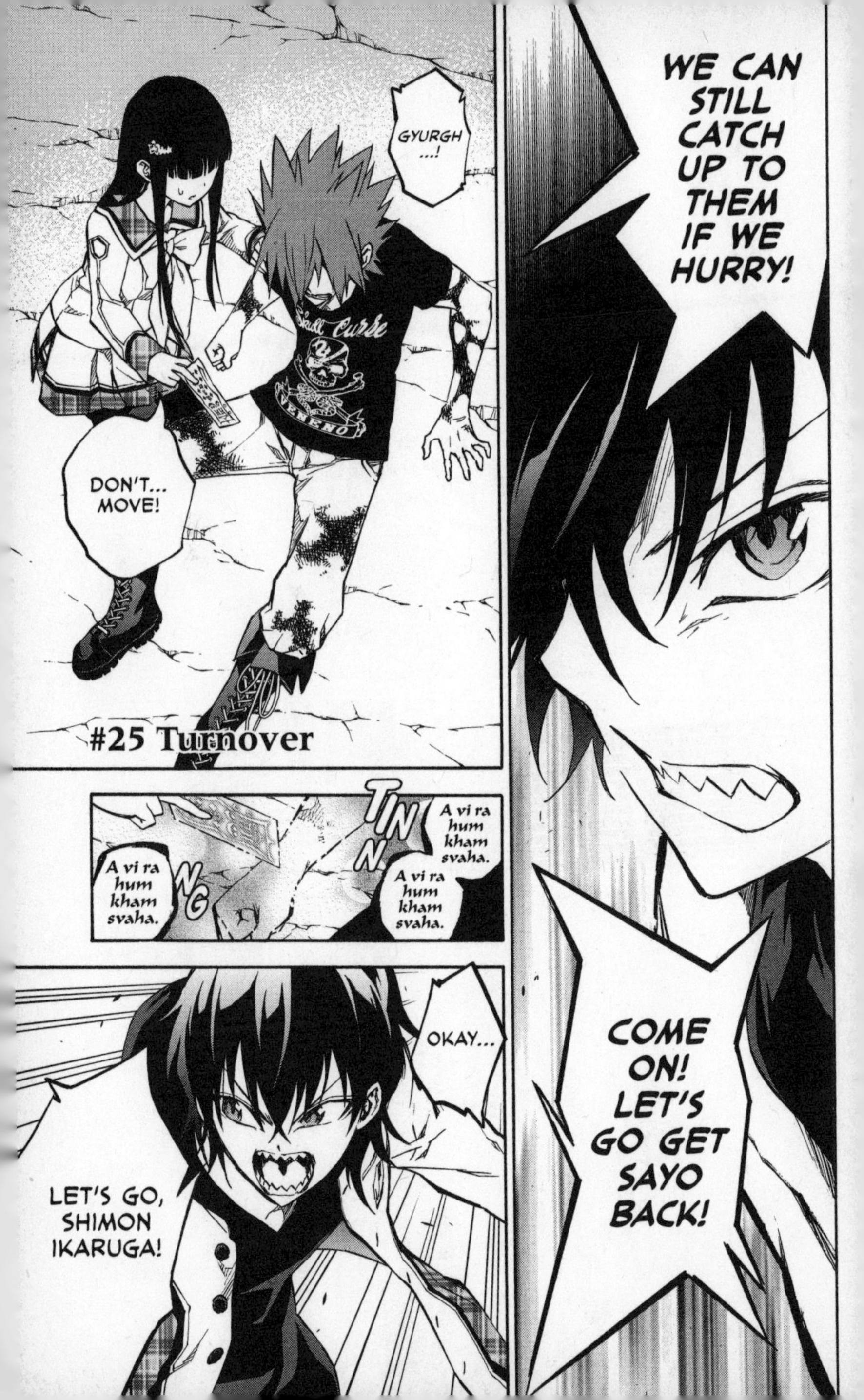
WE CAN STILL CATCH UP TO THEM IF WE HURRY!
COME ON! LET'S GO GET SAYO BACK!
GYURGH ...!
DON'T... MOVE!
#25 Turnover
TINNNG
A vi ra hum kham svaha.
A vi ra hum kham svaha.
A vi ra hum kham svaha.
OKAY...
LET'S GO, SHIMON IKARUGA!

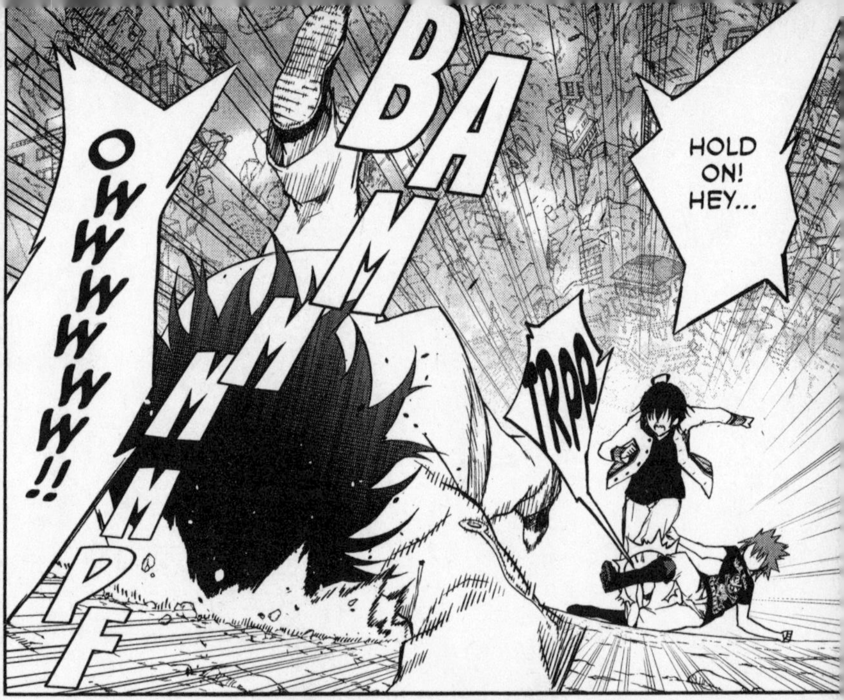
HOLD ON! HEY...
TRPP
BAMMMMMPF
OWWWWWWW!!
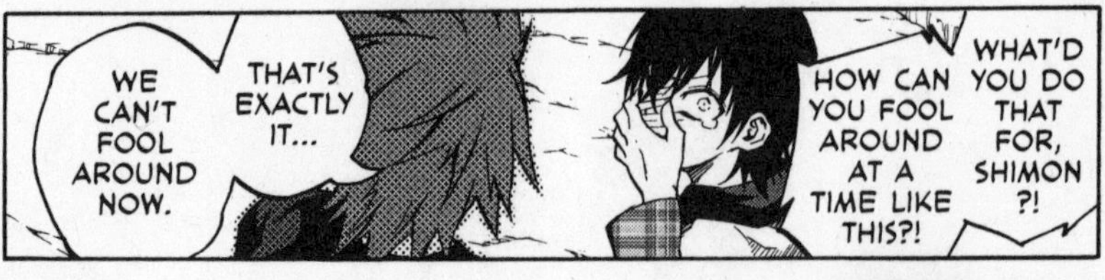
WHAT'D YOU DO THAT FOR, SHIMON?!
HOW CAN YOU FOOL AROUND AT A TIME LIKE THIS?!
THAT'S EXACTLY IT...
WE CAN'T FOOL AROUND NOW.
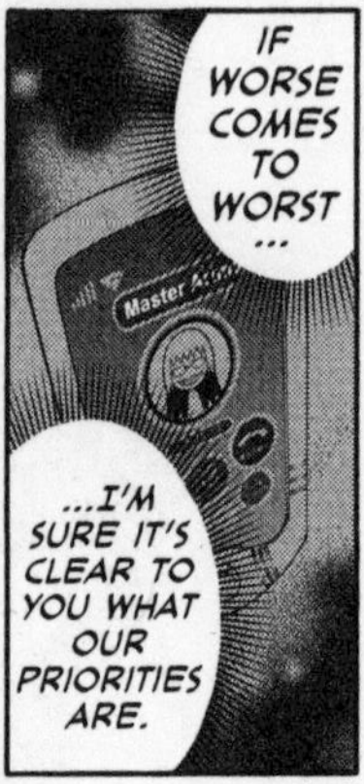
IF WORSE COMES TO WORST...
...I'M SURE IT'S CLEAR TO YOU WHAT OUR PRIORITIES ARE.
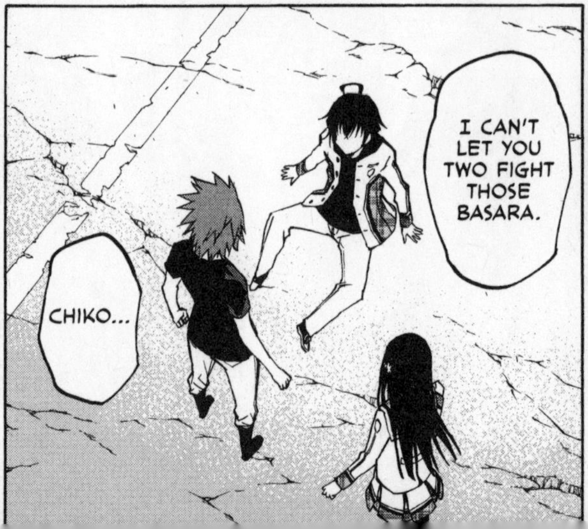
I CAN'T LET YOU TWO FIGHT THOSE BASARA.
CHIKO...

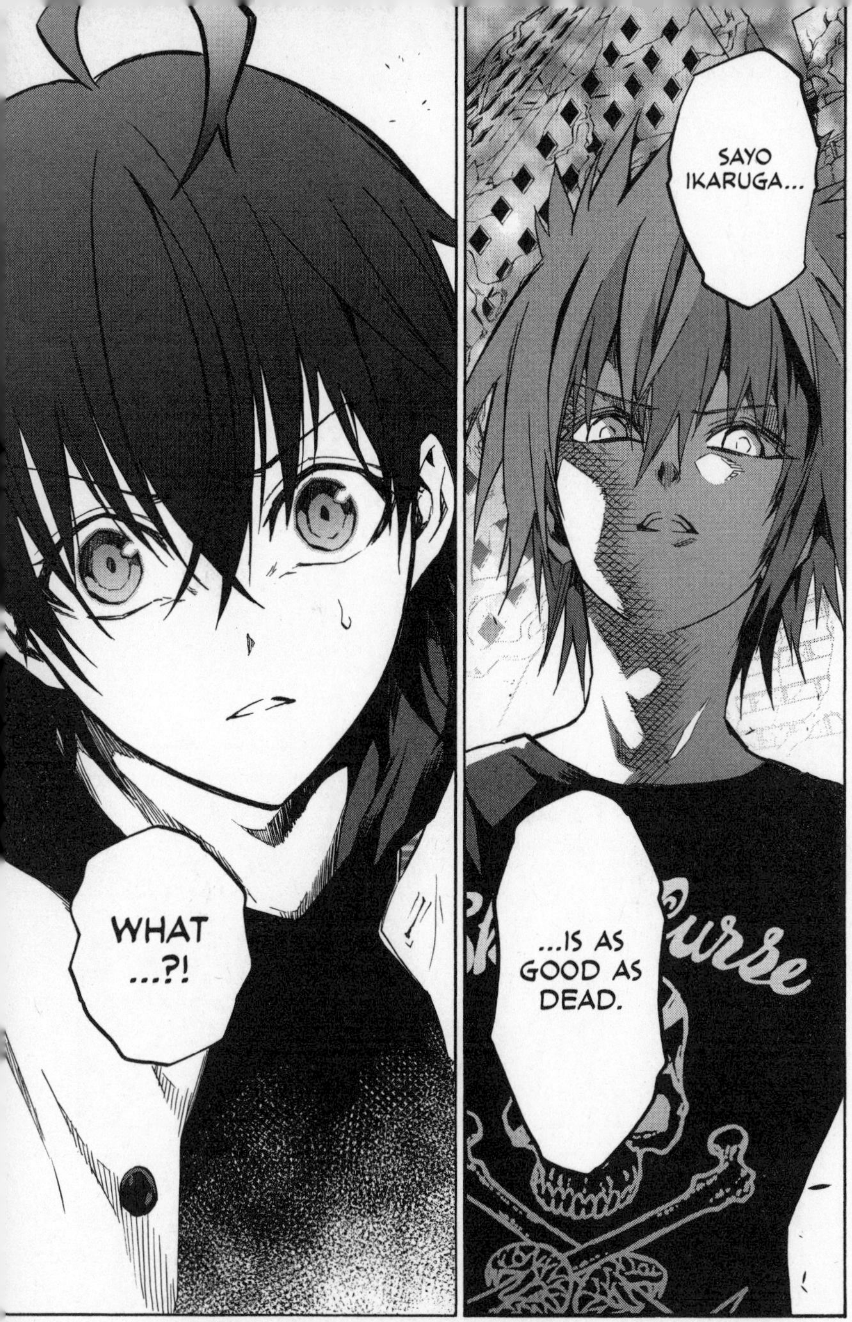
SAYO IKARUGA...
...IS AS GOOD AS DEAD.
WHAT ...?!

#25 Turnover

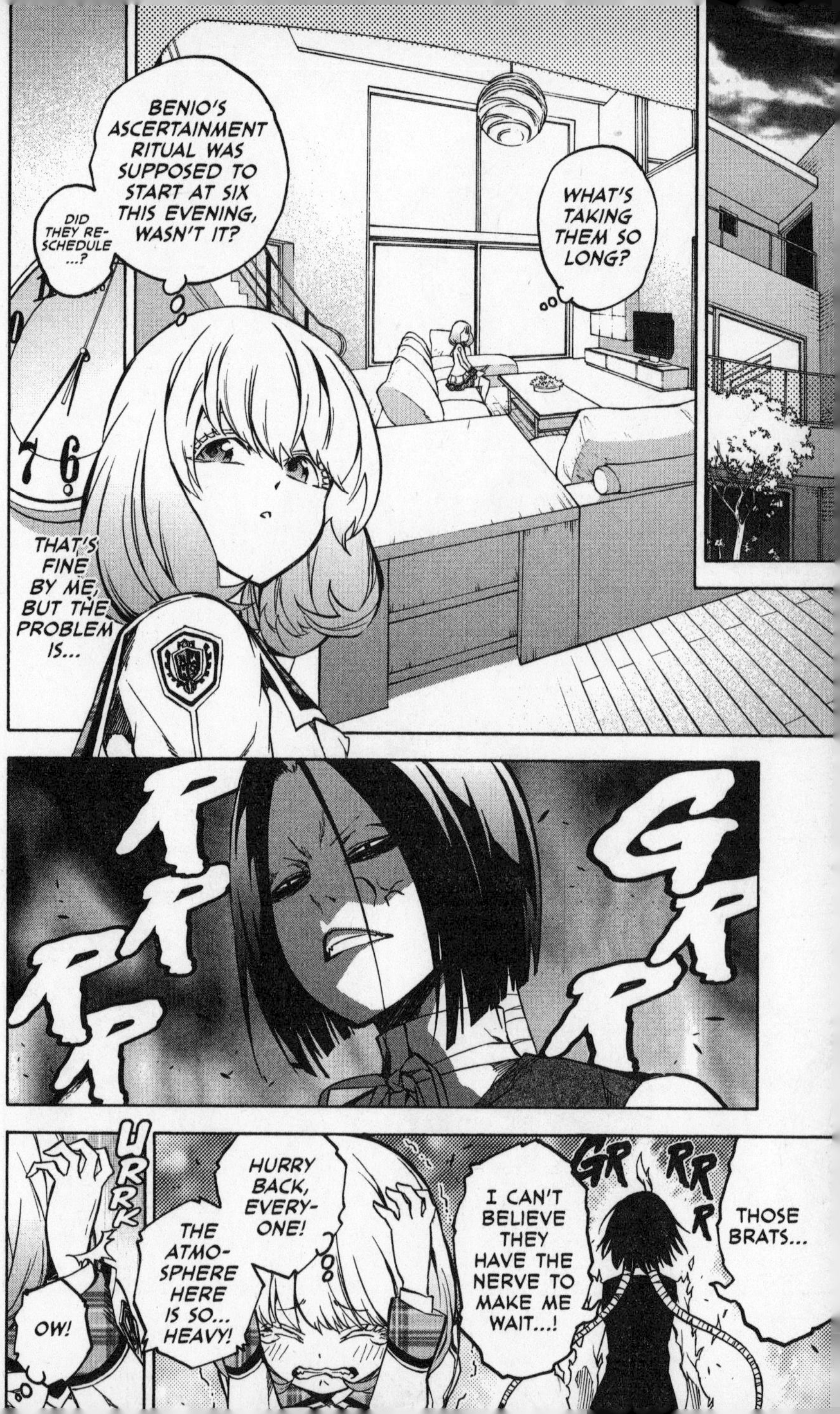
WHAT'S TAKING THEM SO LONG?
BENIO'S ASCERTAINMENT RITUAL WAS SUPPOSED TO START AT SIX THIS EVENING, WASN'T IT?
DID THEY RE-SCHEDULE ...?
THAT'S FINE BY ME, BUT THE PROBLEM IS...
GRRR
RRRR
THOSE BRATS...
GRRRR
I CAN'T BELIEVE THEY HAVE THE NERVE TO MAKE ME WAIT...!
HURRY BACK, EVERYONE!
THE ATMOSPHERE HERE IS SO... HEAVY!
URRK
OW!

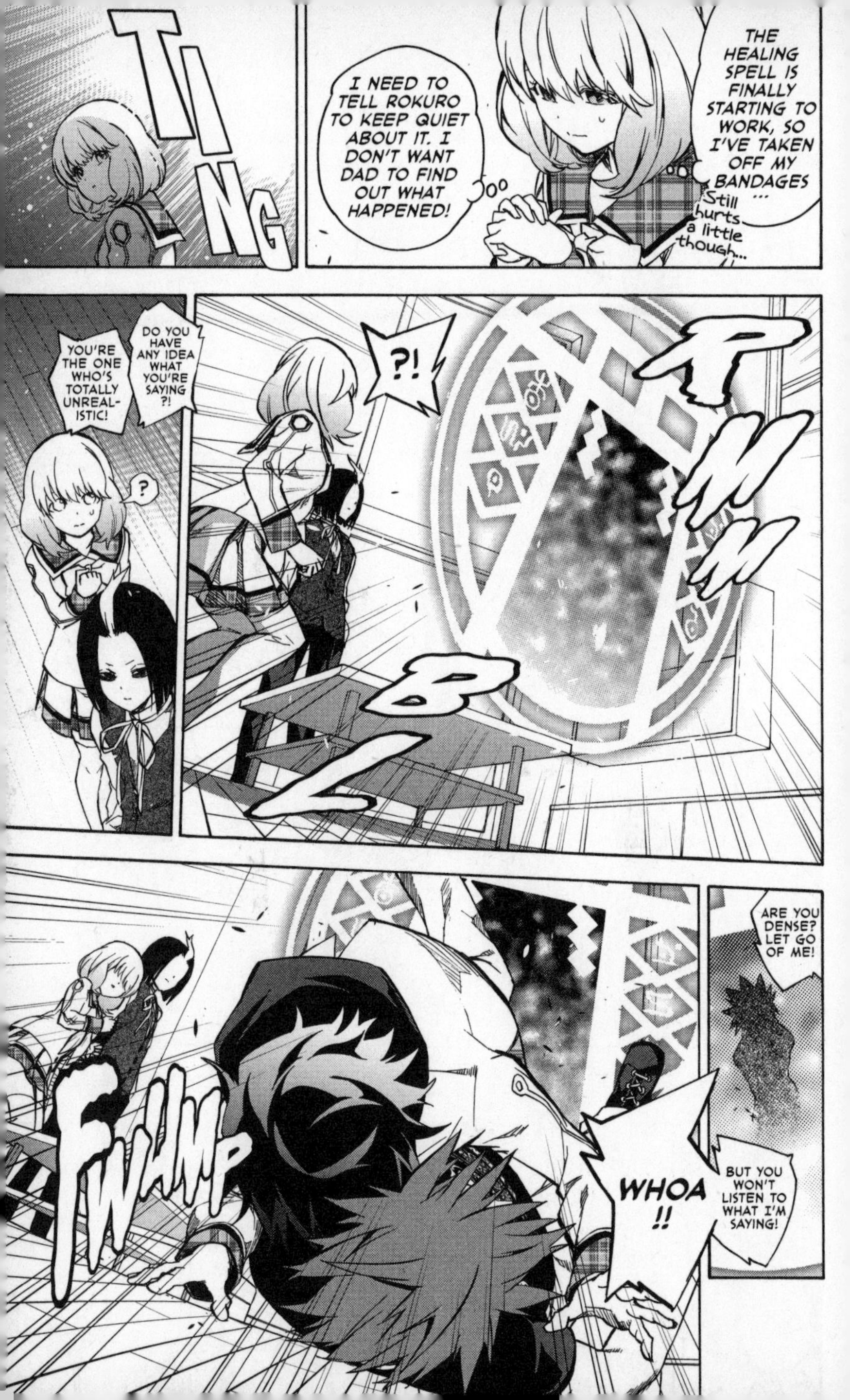
THE HEALING SPELL IS FINALLY STARTING TO WORK, SO I'VE TAKEN OFF MY BANDAGES...
Still hurts a little though...
I NEED TO TELL ROKURO TO KEEP QUIET ABOUT IT. I DON'T WANT DAD TO FIND OUT WHAT HAPPENED!
TING
?!
DO YOU HAVE ANY IDEA WHAT YOU'RE SAYING?!
YOU'RE THE ONE WHO'S TOTALLY UNREAL-ISTIC!
?
ARE YOU DENSE? LET GO OF ME!
BUT YOU WON'T LISTEN TO WHAT I'M SAYING!
WHOA!!
FWUMP

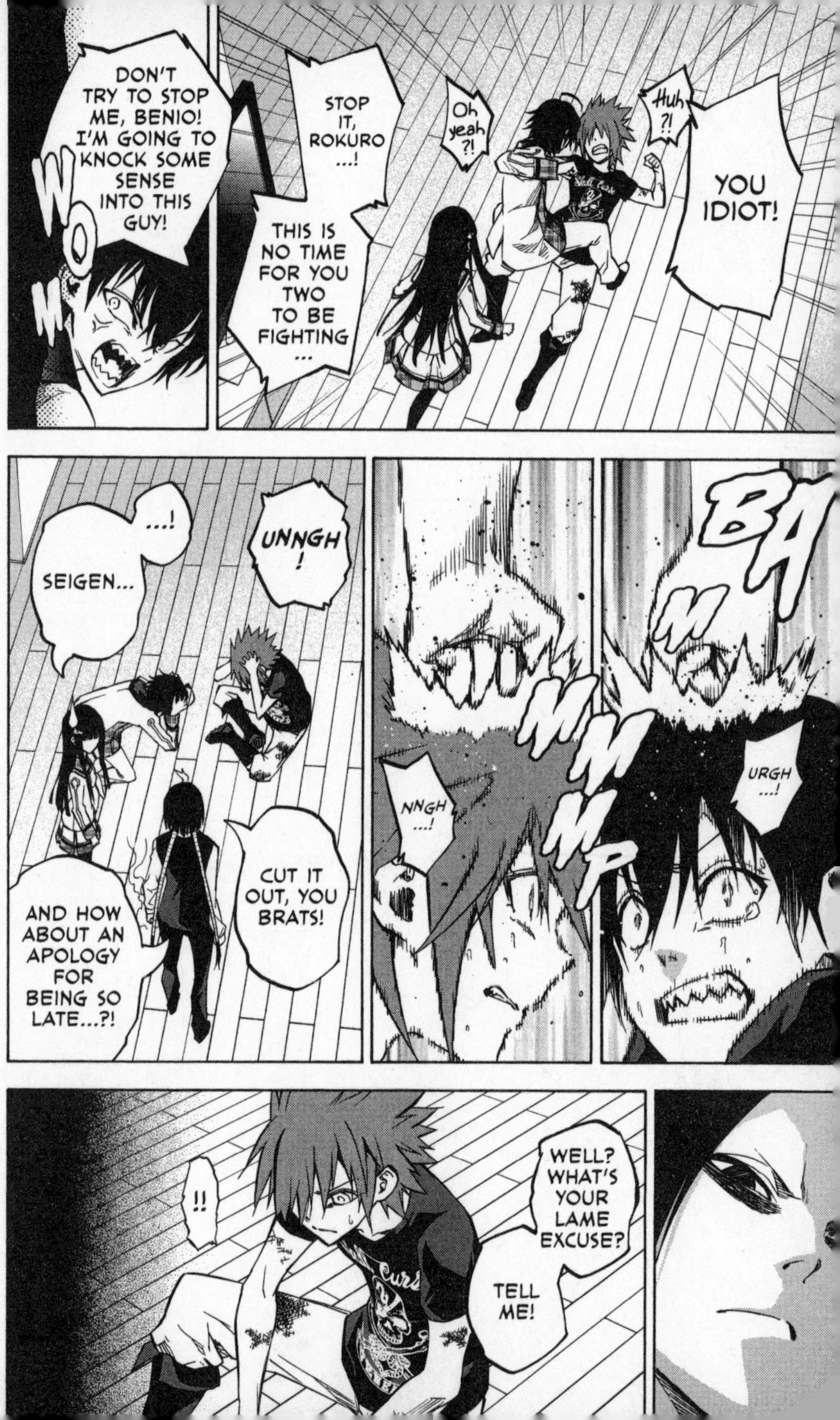
Huh ?!
YOU IDIOT!
Oh yeah ?!
STOP IT, ROKURO ...!
THIS IS NO TIME FOR YOU TWO TO BE FIGHTING...
DON'T TRY TO STOP ME, BENIO! I'M GOING TO KNOCK SOME SENSE INTO THIS GUY!
WOM
BAMMMMP
URGH ...!
NNGH ...!
...!
UNNGH !
SEIGEN...
CUT IT OUT, YOU BRATS!
AND HOW ABOUT AN APOLOGY FOR BEING SO LATE...?!
WELL? WHAT'S YOUR LAME EXCUSE?
!!
TELL ME!

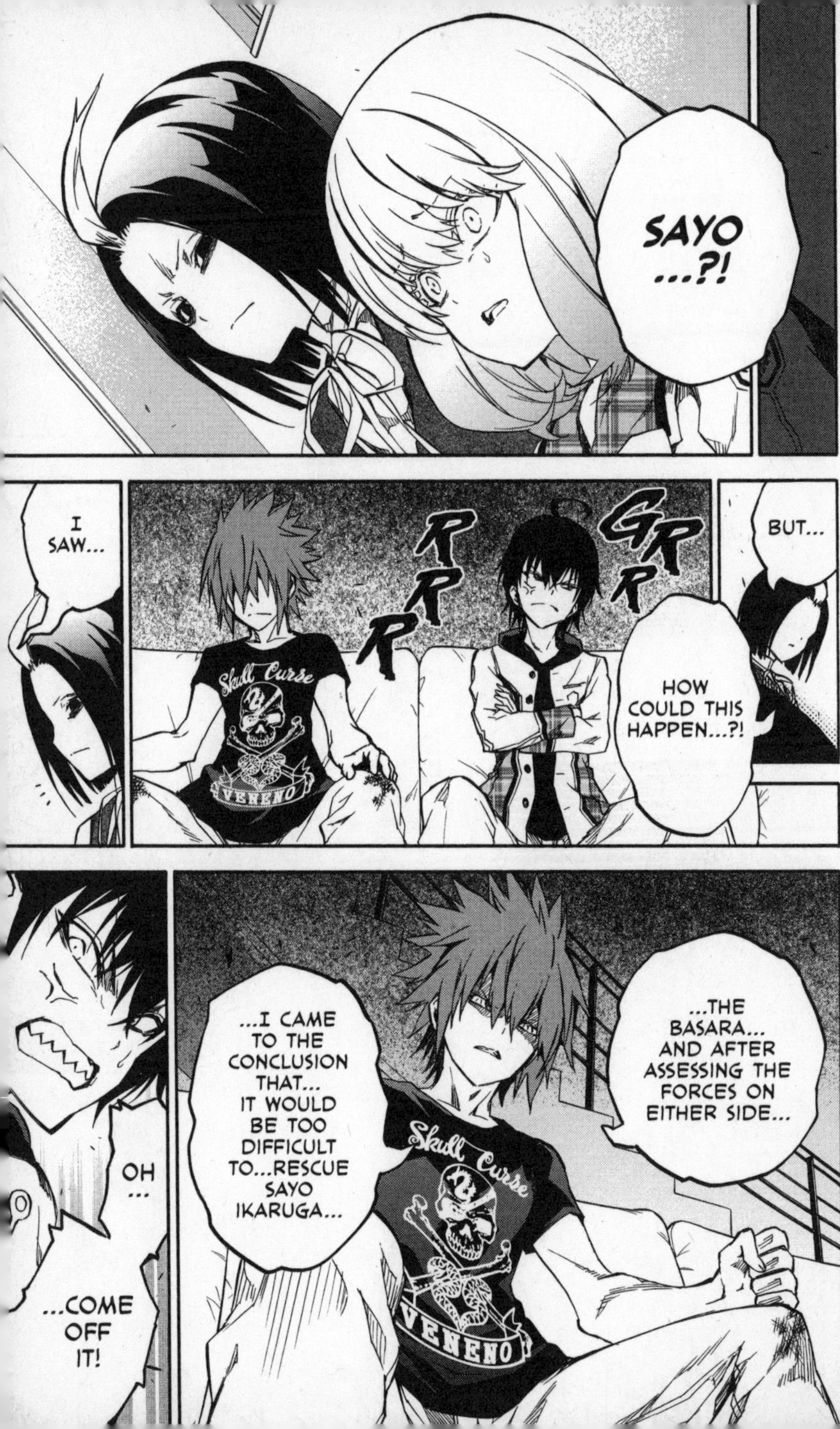
SAYO ...?!
BUT...
HOW COULD THIS HAPPEN...?!
GRRR
RRR
Skull Curse
VENENO
I SAW...
...THE BASARA... AND AFTER ASSESSING THE FORCES ON EITHER SIDE...
...I CAME TO THE CONCLUSION THAT... IT WOULD BE TOO DIFFICULT TO...RESCUE SAYO IKARUGA...
Skull Curse
VENENO
OH ...
...COME OFF IT!

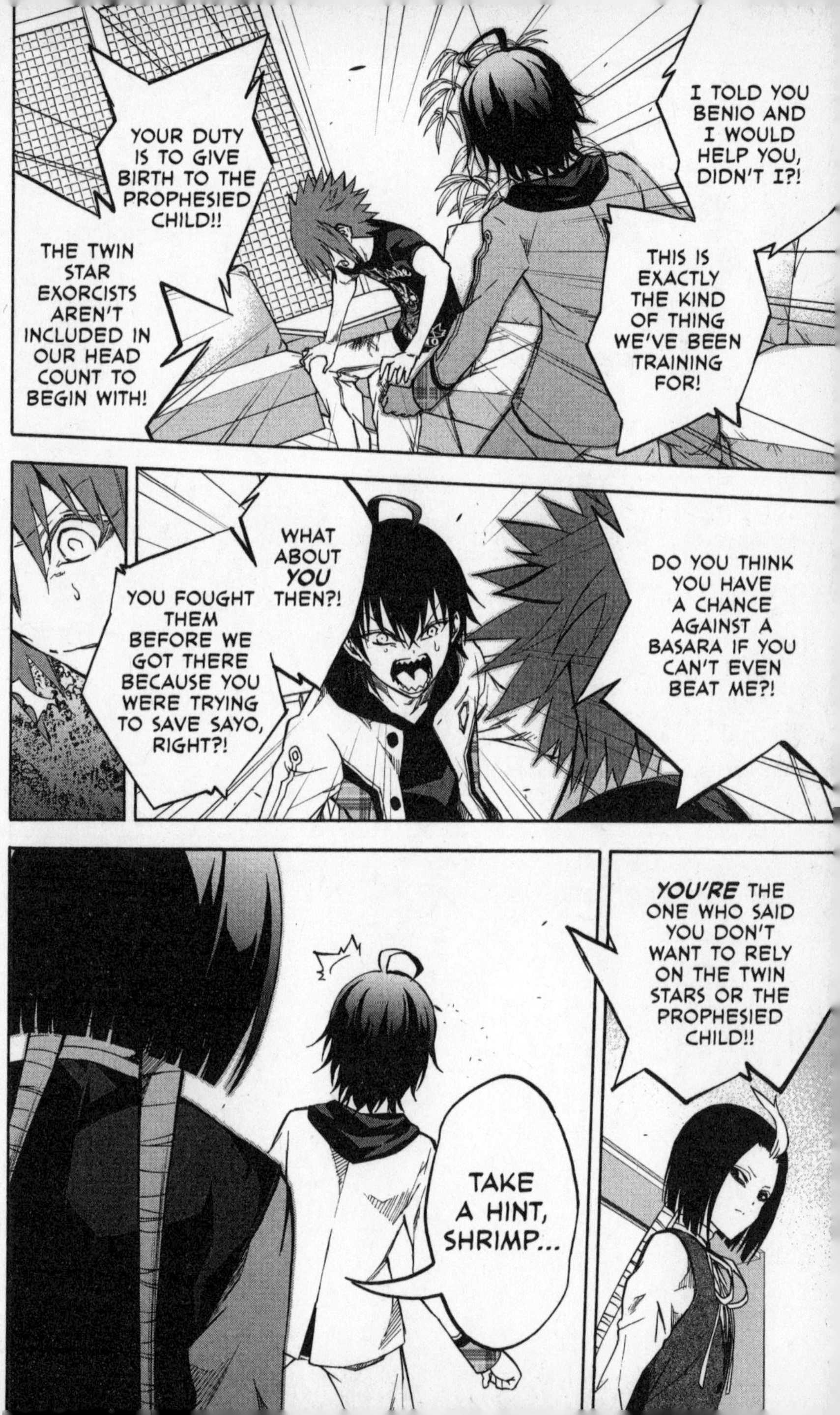
I TOLD YOU BENIO AND I WOULD HELP YOU, DIDN'T I?!
THIS IS EXACTLY THE KIND OF THING WE'VE BEEN TRAINING FOR!
YOUR DUTY IS TO GIVE BIRTH TO THE PROPHESIED CHILD!!
THE TWIN STAR EXORCISTS AREN'T INCLUDED IN OUR HEAD COUNT TO BEGIN WITH!
DO YOU THINK YOU HAVE A CHANCE AGAINST A BASARA IF YOU CAN'T EVEN BEAT ME?!
WHAT ABOUT *YOU* THEN?!
YOU FOUGHT THEM BEFORE WE GOT THERE BECAUSE YOU WERE TRYING TO SAVE SAYO, RIGHT?!
YOU'RE THE ONE WHO SAID YOU DON'T WANT TO RELY ON THE TWIN STARS OR THE PROPHESIED CHILD!!
TAKE A HINT, SHRIMP...

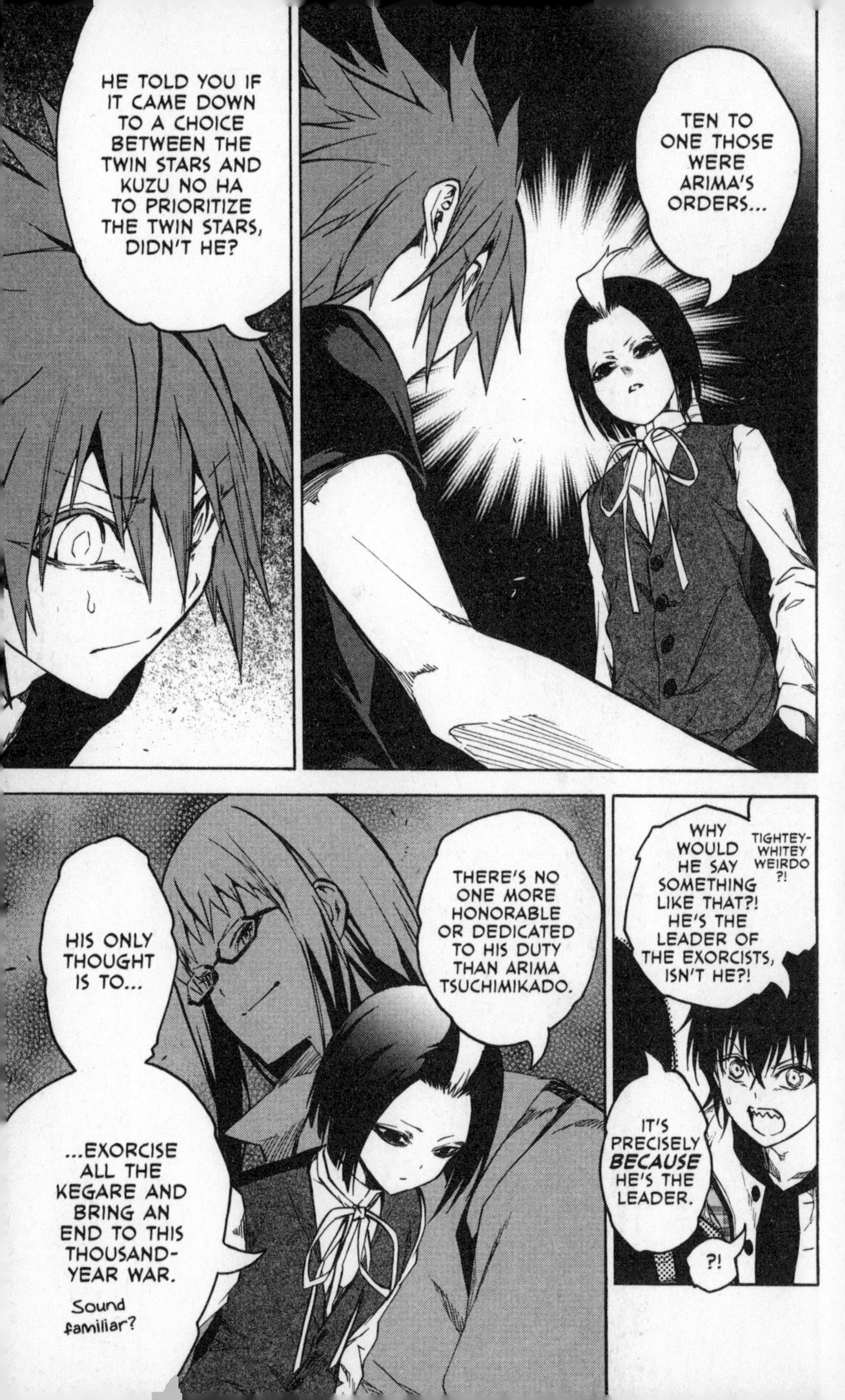
TEN TO ONE THOSE WERE ARIMA'S ORDERS...
HE TOLD YOU IF IT CAME DOWN TO A CHOICE BETWEEN THE TWIN STARS AND KUZU NO HA TO PRIORITIZE THE TWIN STARS, DIDN'T HE?
WHY WOULD HE SAY SOMETHING LIKE THAT?! HE'S THE LEADER OF THE EXORCISTS, ISN'T HE?!
TIGHTEY-WHITEY WEIRDO ?!
IT'S PRECISELY BECAUSE HE'S THE LEADER.
?!
THERE'S NO ONE MORE HONORABLE OR DEDICATED TO HIS DUTY THAN ARIMA TSUCHIMIKADO.
HIS ONLY THOUGHT IS TO...
...EXORCISE ALL THE KEGARE AND BRING AN END TO THIS THOUSAND-YEAR WAR.
Sound familiar?

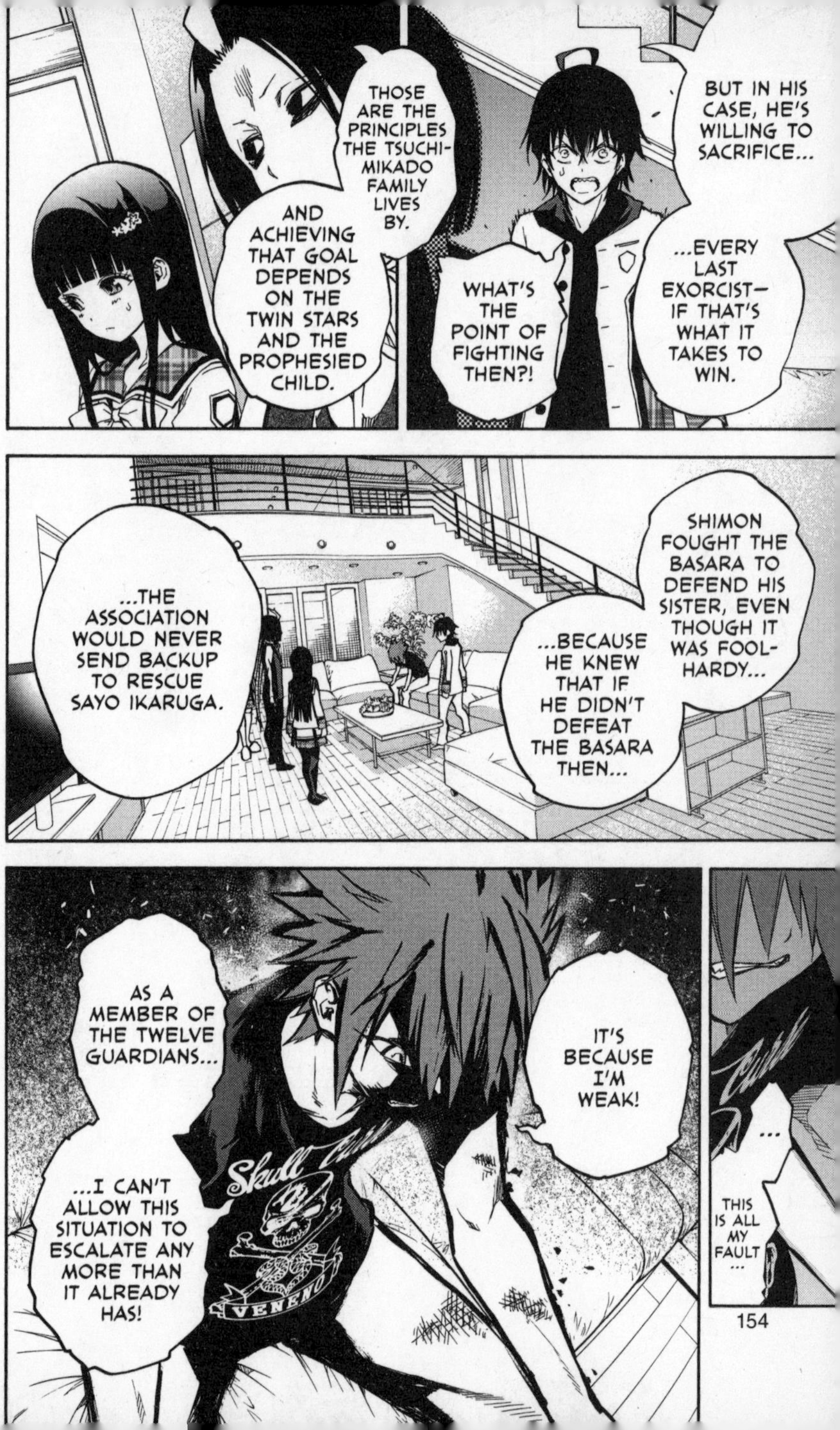
BUT IN HIS CASE, HE'S WILLING TO SACRIFICE...
...EVERY LAST EXORCIST—IF THAT'S WHAT IT TAKES TO WIN.
WHAT'S THE POINT OF FIGHTING THEN?!
THOSE ARE THE PRINCIPLES THE TSUCHIMIKADO FAMILY LIVES BY.
AND ACHIEVING THAT GOAL DEPENDS ON THE TWIN STARS AND THE PROPHESIED CHILD.
SHIMON FOUGHT THE BASARA TO DEFEND HIS SISTER, EVEN THOUGH IT WAS FOOLHARDY...
...BECAUSE HE KNEW THAT IF HE DIDN'T DEFEAT THE BASARA THEN...
...THE ASSOCIATION WOULD NEVER SEND BACKUP TO RESCUE SAYO IKARUGA.
...
THIS IS ALL MY FAULT...
IT'S BECAUSE I'M WEAK!
AS A MEMBER OF THE TWELVE GUARDIANS...
...I CAN'T ALLOW THIS SITUATION TO ESCALATE ANY MORE THAN IT ALREADY HAS!
VENENO

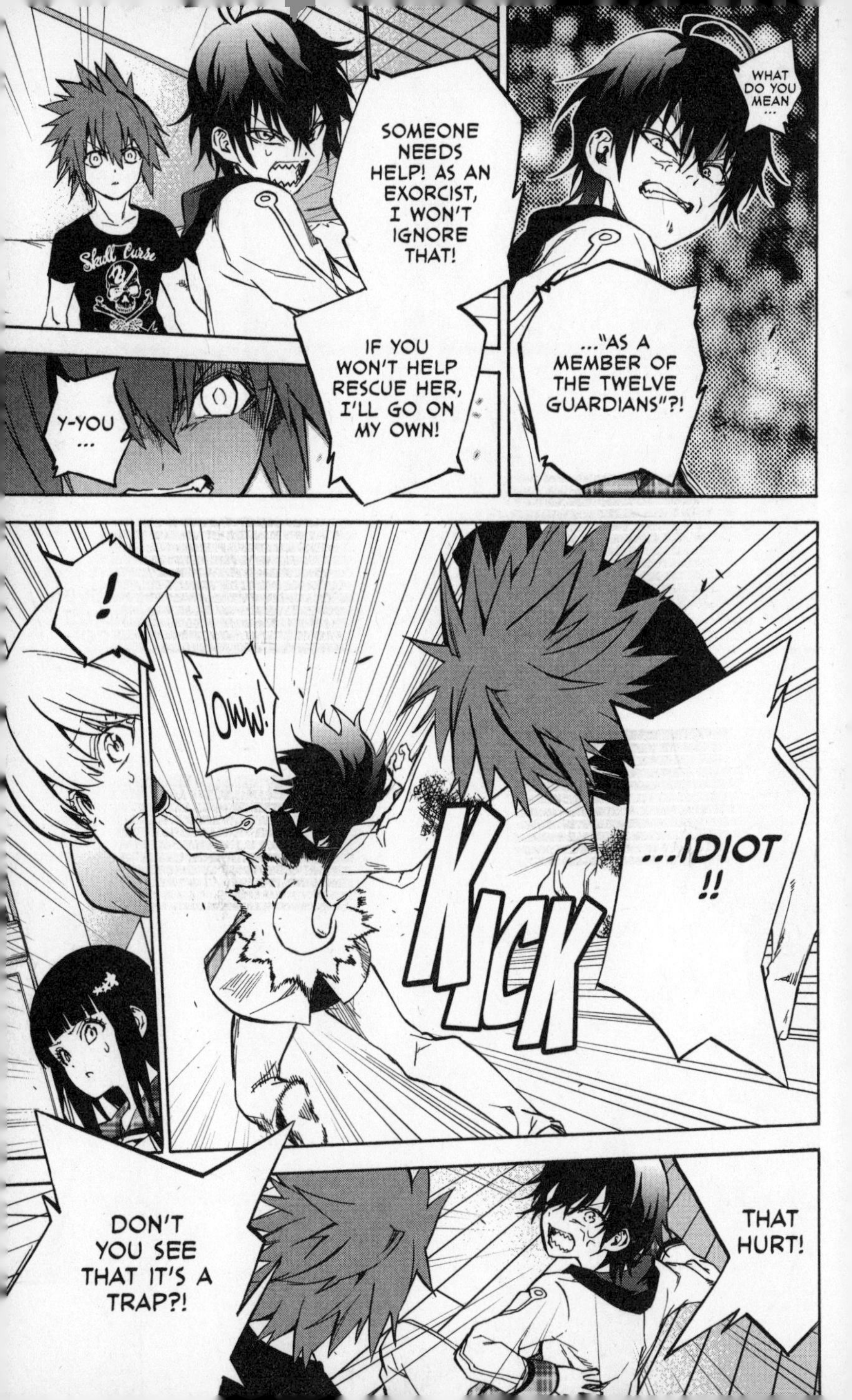
WHAT DO YOU MEAN ...
..."AS A MEMBER OF THE TWELVE GUARDIANS"?!
SOMEONE NEEDS HELP! AS AN EXORCIST, I WON'T IGNORE THAT!
IF YOU WON'T HELP RESCUE HER, I'LL GO ON MY OWN!
Y-YOU ...
...IDIOT !!
KICK
OWW!
!
THAT HURT!
DON'T YOU SEE THAT IT'S A TRAP?!

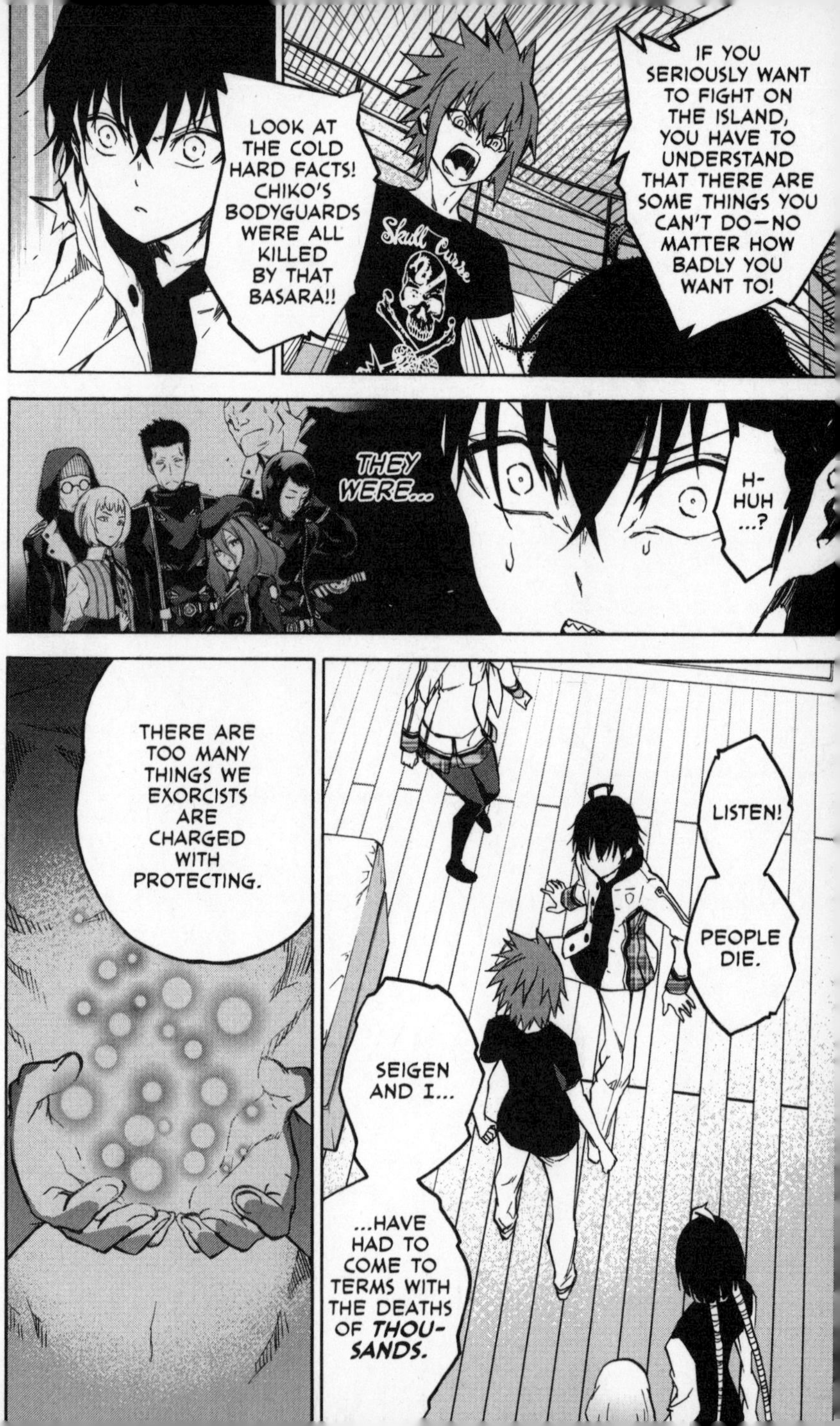
IF YOU SERIOUSLY WANT TO FIGHT ON THE ISLAND, YOU HAVE TO UNDERSTAND THAT THERE ARE SOME THINGS YOU CAN'T DO—NO MATTER HOW BADLY YOU WANT TO!
LOOK AT THE COLD HARD FACTS! CHIKO'S BODYGUARDS WERE ALL KILLED BY THAT BASARA!!
Skull Curse
H-HUH ...?
THEY WERE...
LISTEN!
PEOPLE DIE.
SEIGEN AND I...
...HAVE HAD TO COME TO TERMS WITH THE DEATHS OF *THOUSANDS.*
THERE ARE TOO MANY THINGS WE EXORCISTS ARE CHARGED WITH PROTECTING.

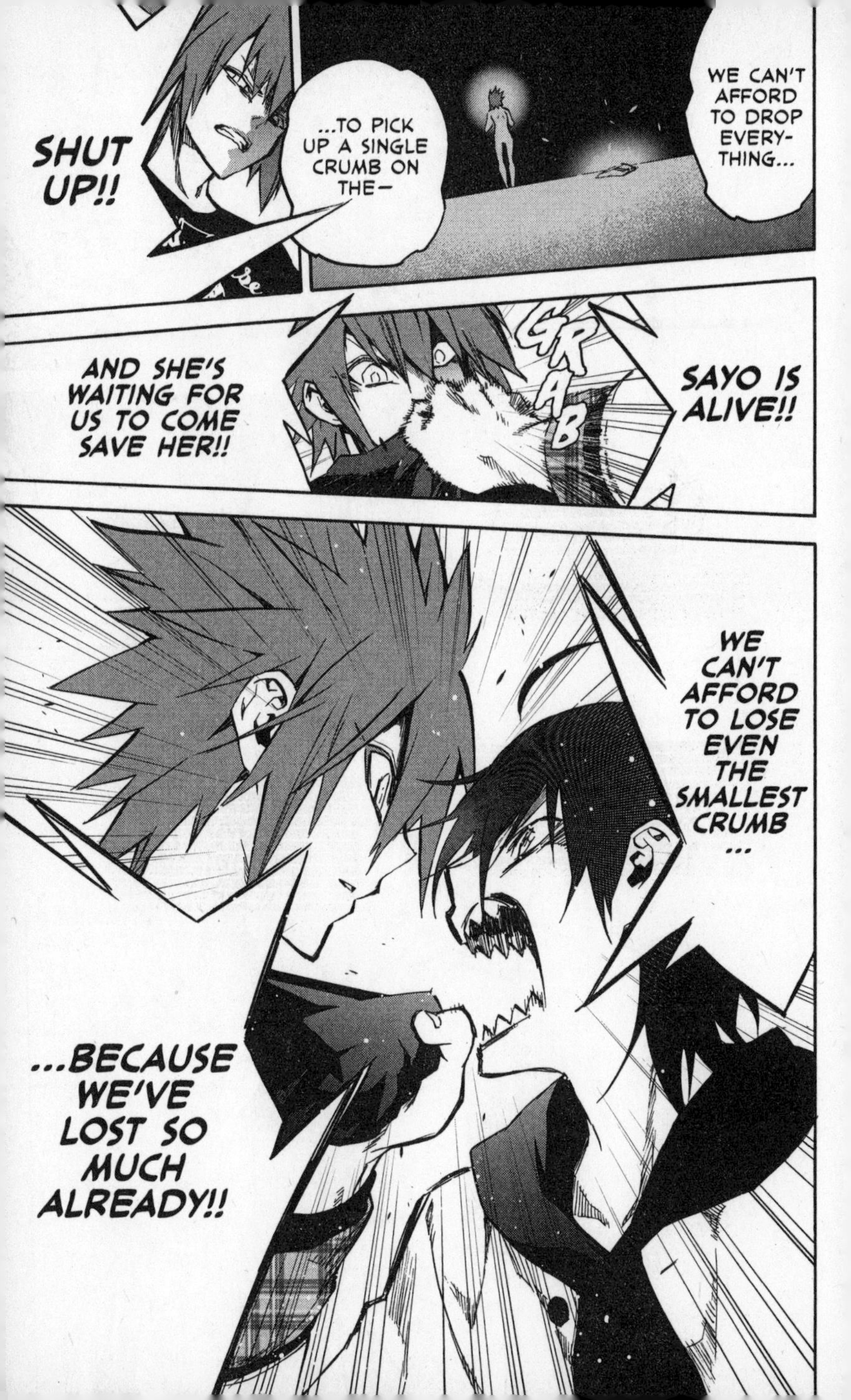
WE CAN'T AFFORD TO DROP EVERY-THING...
...TO PICK UP A SINGLE CRUMB ON THE—
SHUT UP!!
SAYO IS ALIVE!!
GRAB
AND SHE'S WAITING FOR US TO COME SAVE HER!!
WE CAN'T AFFORD TO LOSE EVEN THE SMALLEST CRUMB ...
...BECAUSE WE'VE LOST SO MUCH ALREADY!!

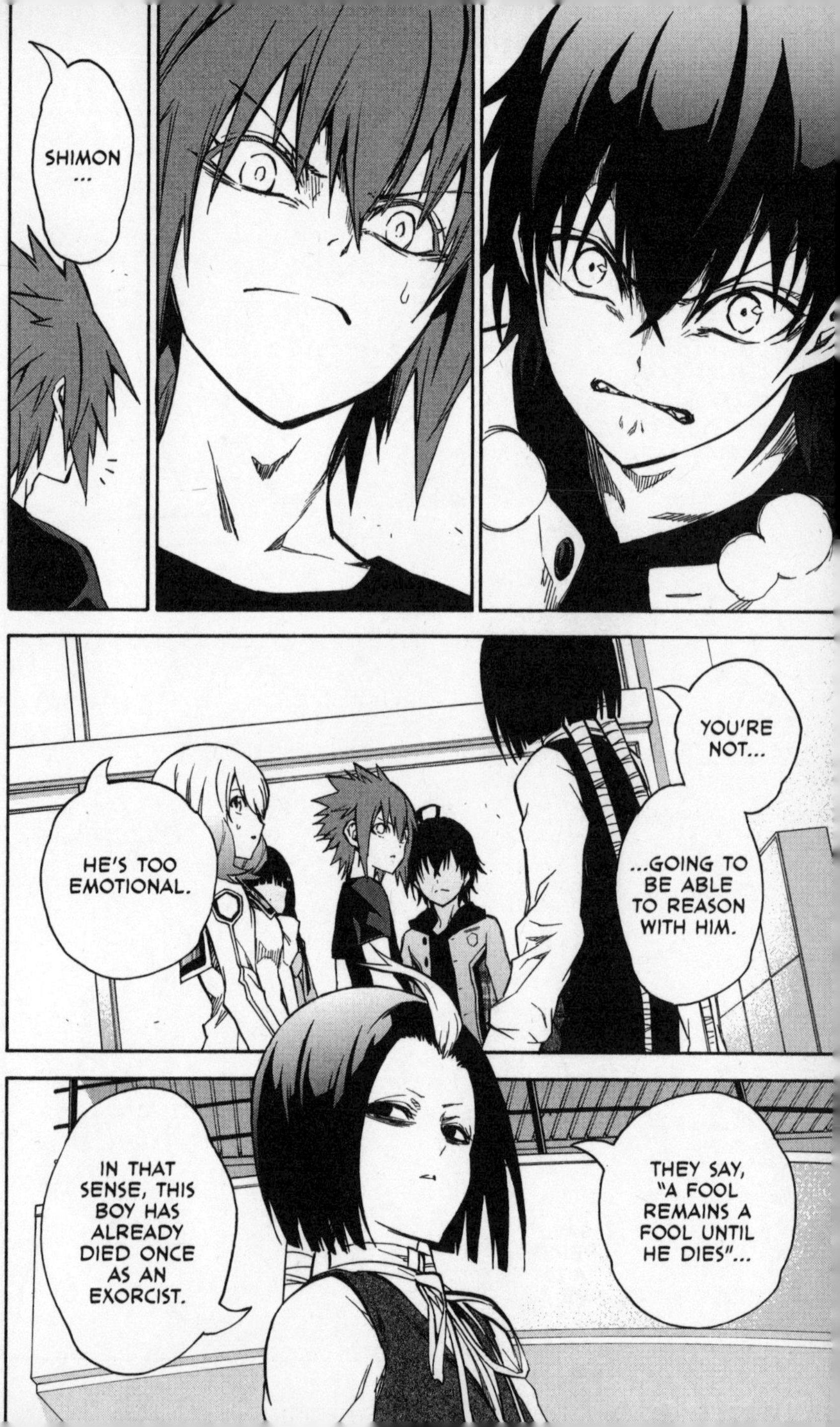
SHIMON ...
YOU'RE NOT...
...GOING TO BE ABLE TO REASON WITH HIM.
HE'S TOO EMOTIONAL.
THEY SAY, "A FOOL REMAINS A FOOL UNTIL HE DIES"...
IN THAT SENSE, THIS BOY HAS ALREADY DIED ONCE AS AN EXORCIST.

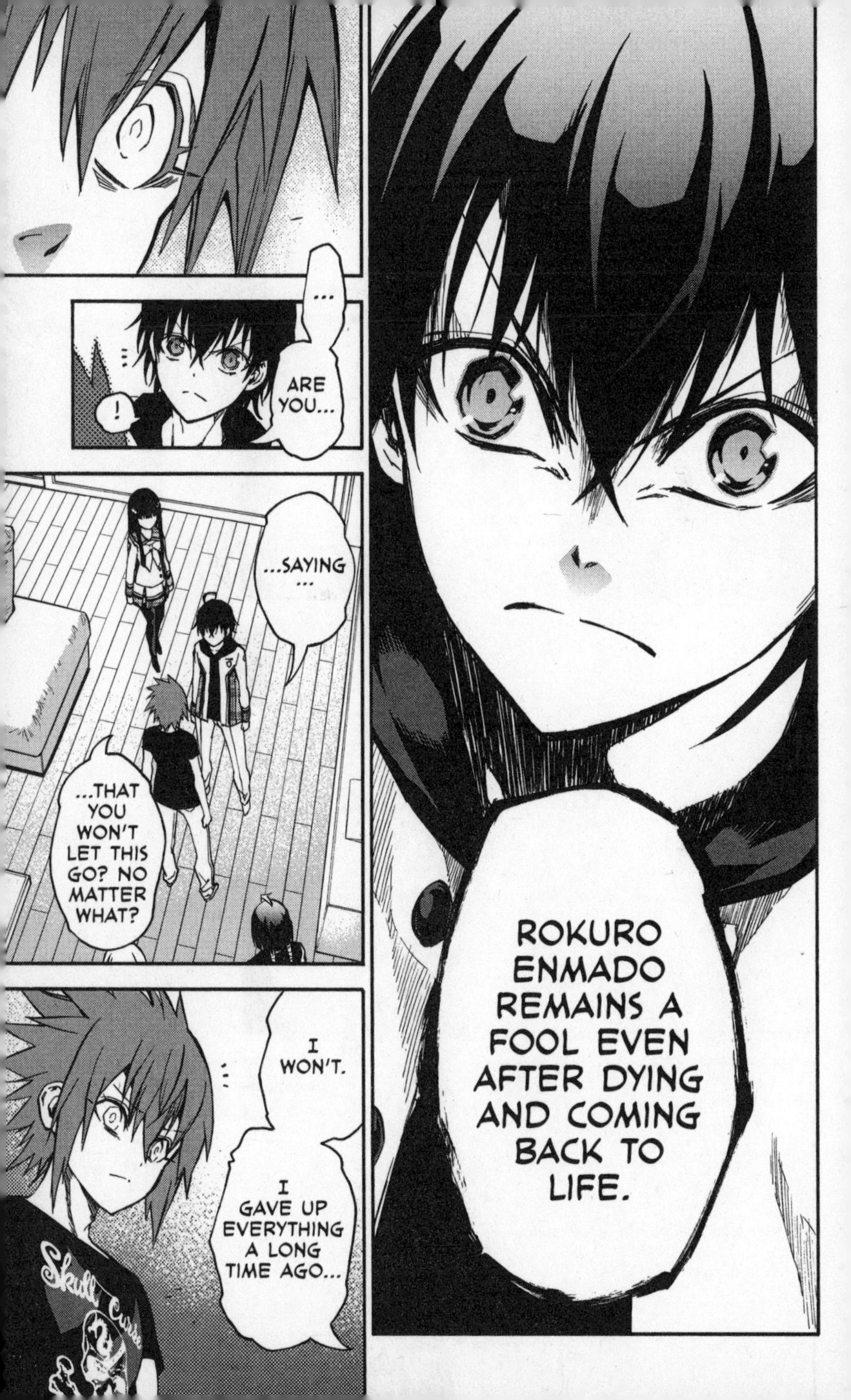
ROKURO ENMADO REMAINS A FOOL EVEN AFTER DYING AND COMING BACK TO LIFE.
...
ARE YOU...
!
...SAYING...
...THAT YOU WON'T LET THIS GO? NO MATTER WHAT?
I WON'T.
...
I GAVE UP EVERYTHING A LONG TIME AGO...

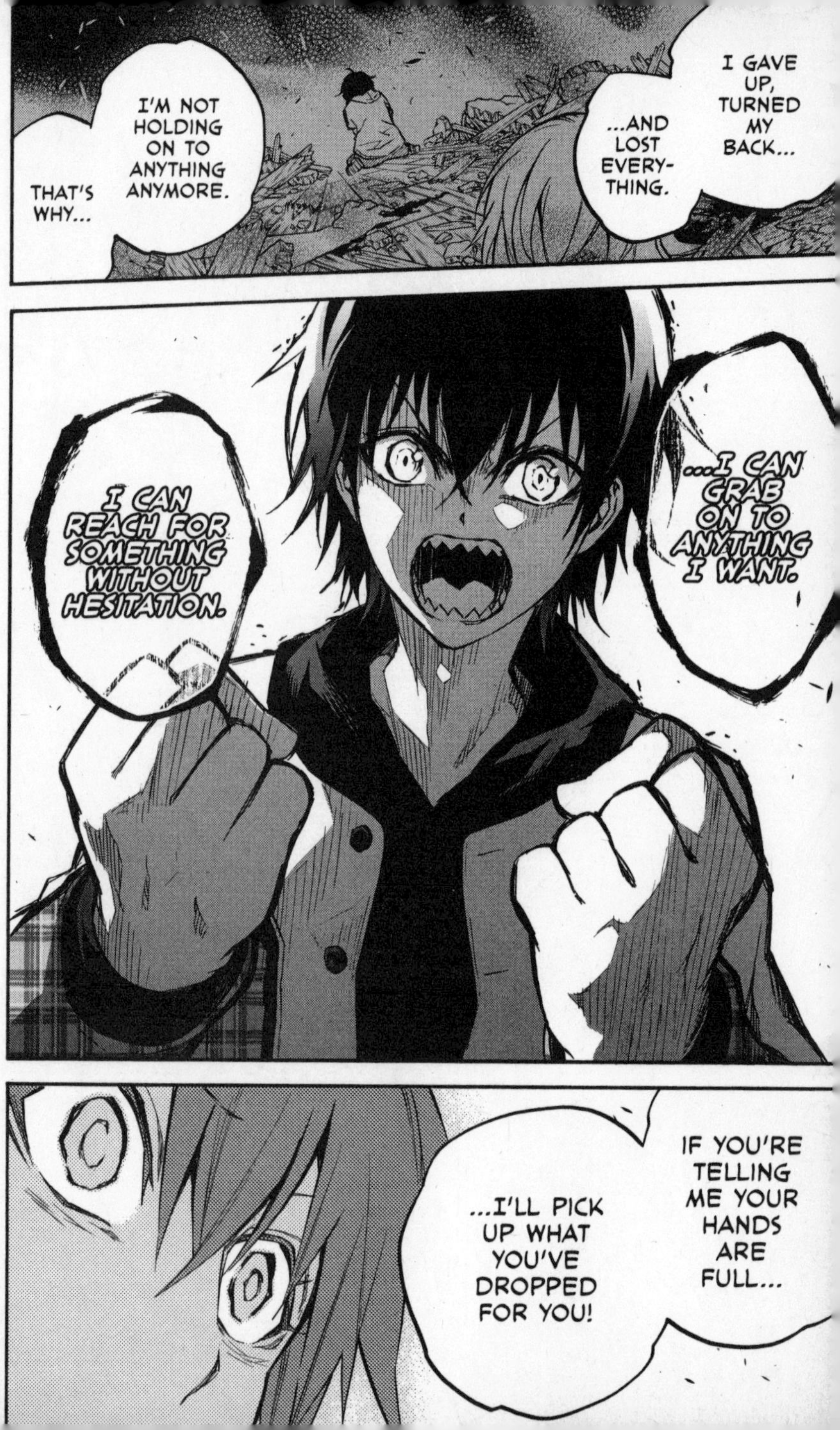
I GAVE UP, TURNED MY BACK...
...AND LOST EVERY-THING.
I'M NOT HOLDING ON TO ANYTHING ANYMORE.
THAT'S WHY...
...I CAN GRAB ON TO ANYTHING I WANT.
I CAN REACH FOR SOMETHING WITHOUT HESITATION.
IF YOU'RE TELLING ME YOUR HANDS ARE FULL...
...I'LL PICK UP WHAT YOU'VE DROPPED FOR YOU!

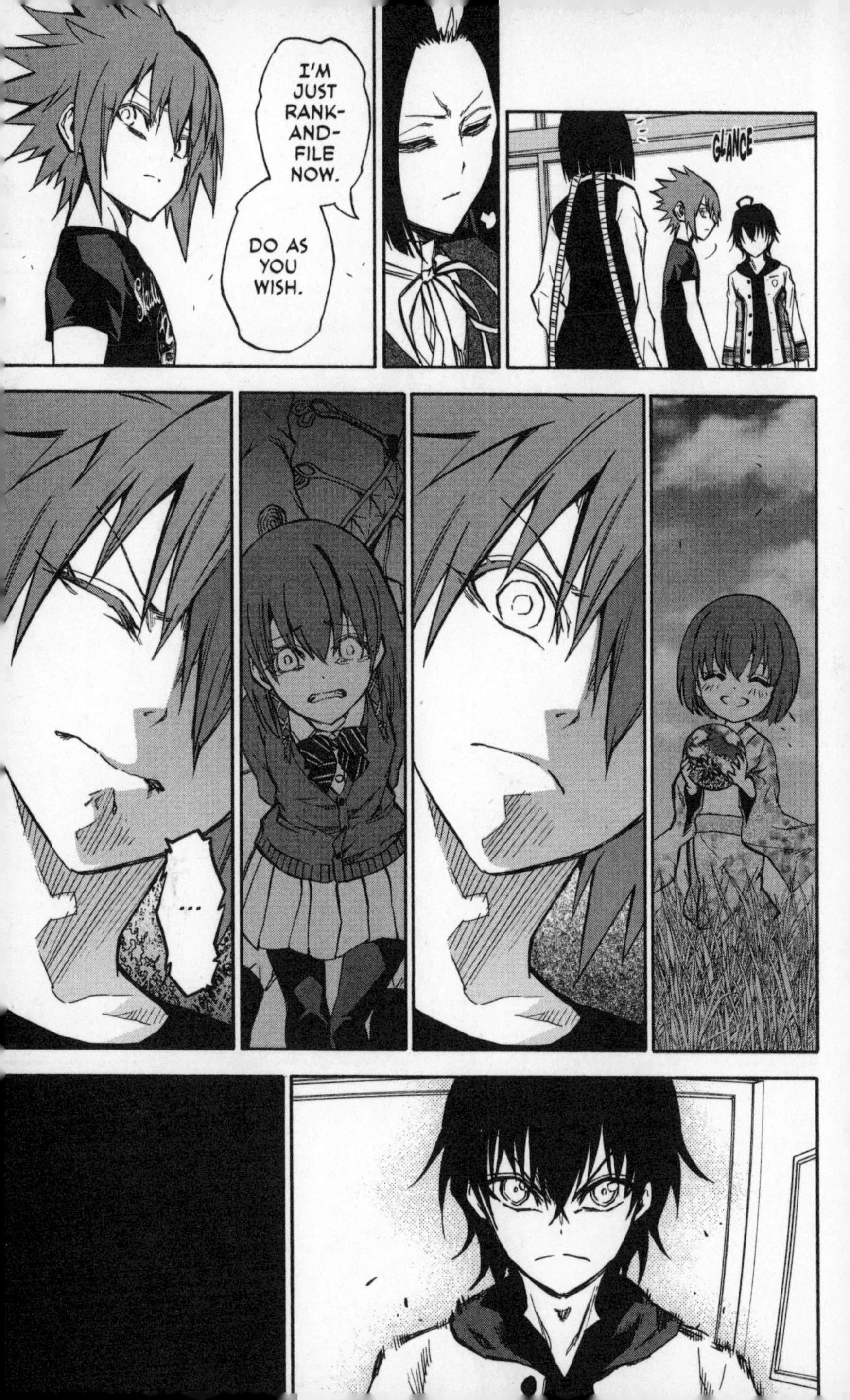
GLANCE
I'M JUST RANK-AND-FILE NOW.
DO AS YOU WISH.
...

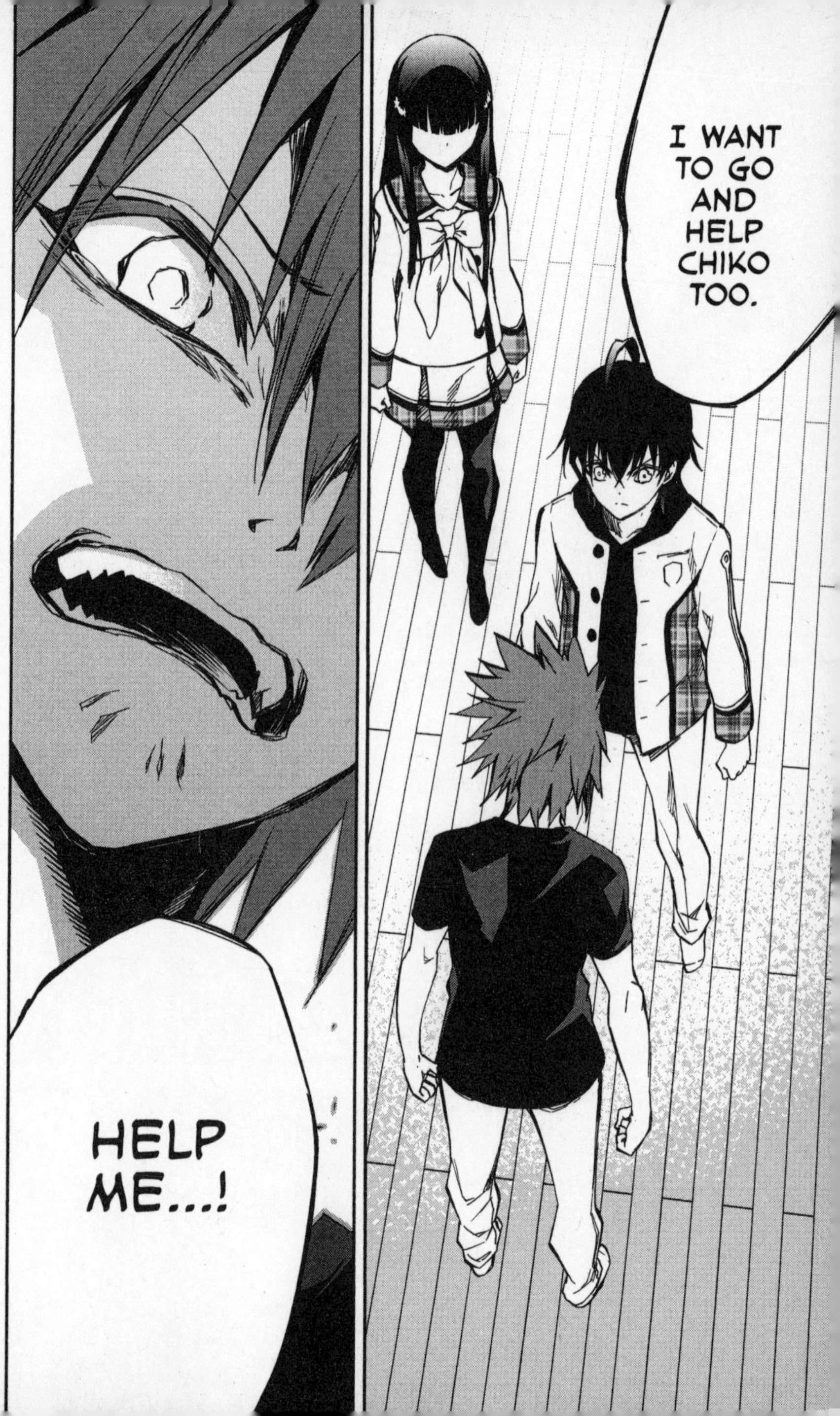
I WANT TO GO AND HELP CHIKO TOO.
HELP ME...!

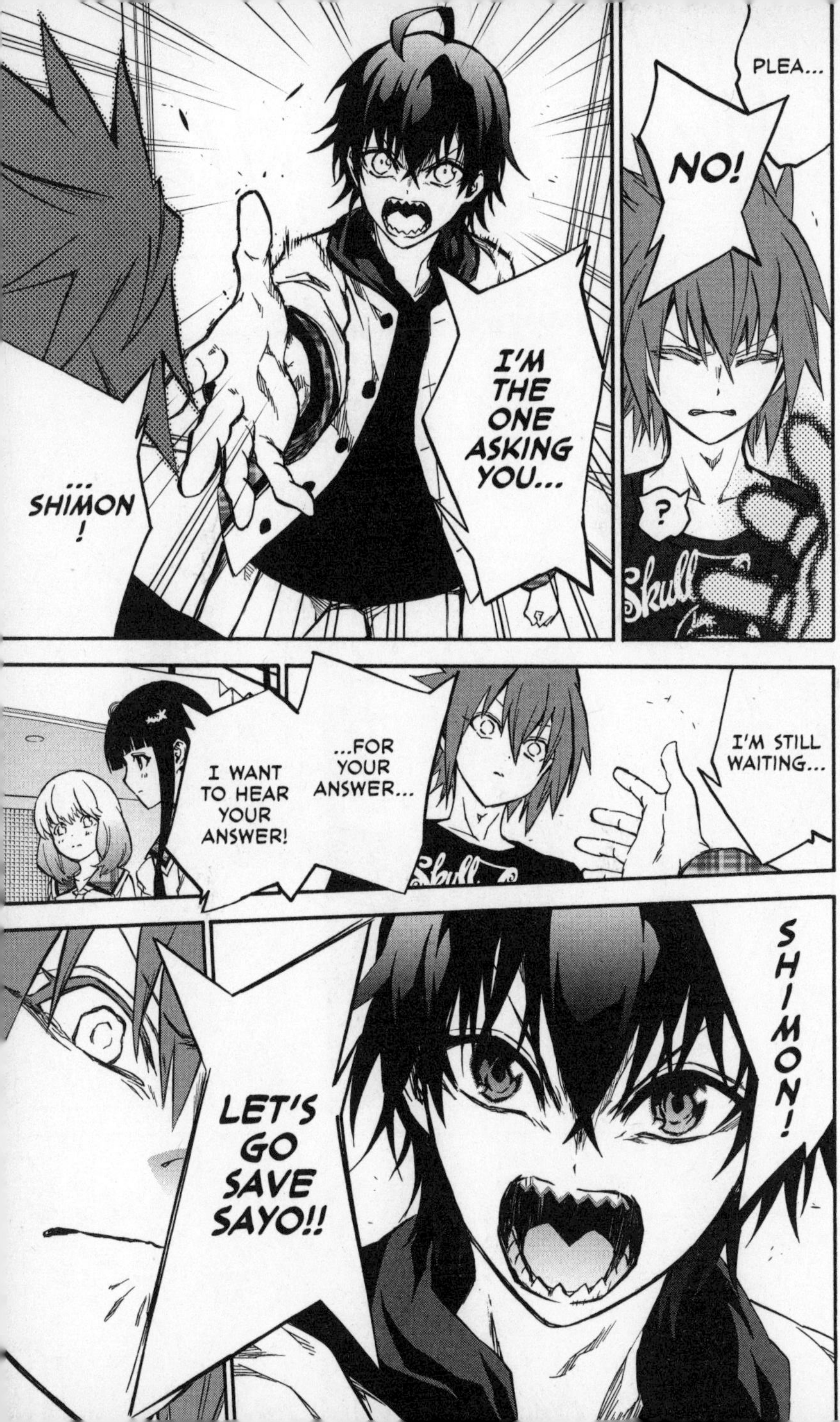
PLEA...
NO!
?
Skull
I'M THE ONE ASKING YOU...
...SHIMON!
I'M STILL WAITING...
...FOR YOUR ANSWER...
I WANT TO HEAR YOUR ANSWER!
SHIMON!
LET'S GO SAVE SAYO!!

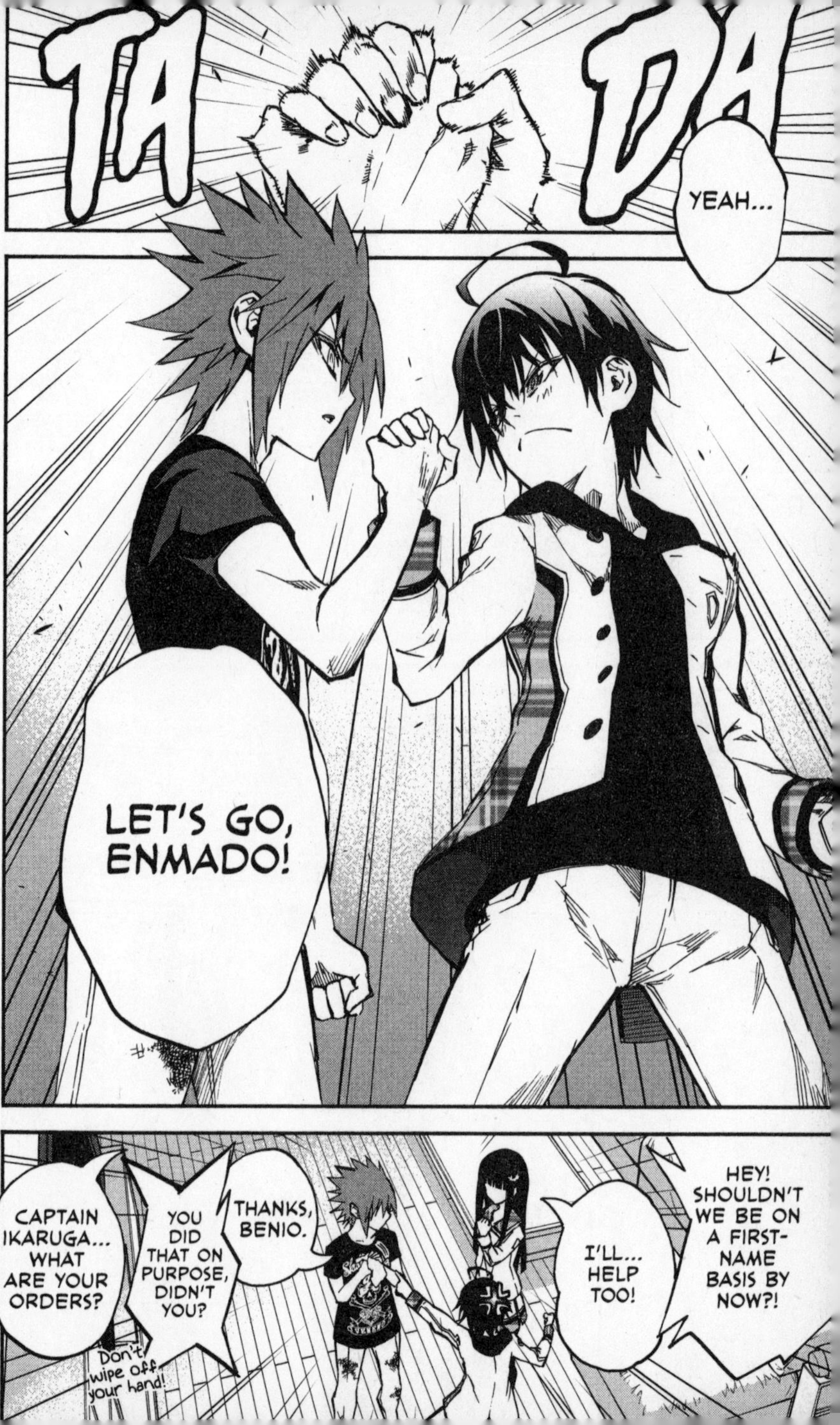

TA DA
YEAH...
LET'S GO, ENMADO!
HEY! SHOULDN'T WE BE ON A FIRST-NAME BASIS BY NOW?!
I'LL... HELP TOO!
THANKS, BENIO.
YOU DID THAT ON PURPOSE, DIDN'T YOU?
CAPTAIN IKARUGA... WHAT ARE YOUR ORDERS?
Don't wipe off your hand!

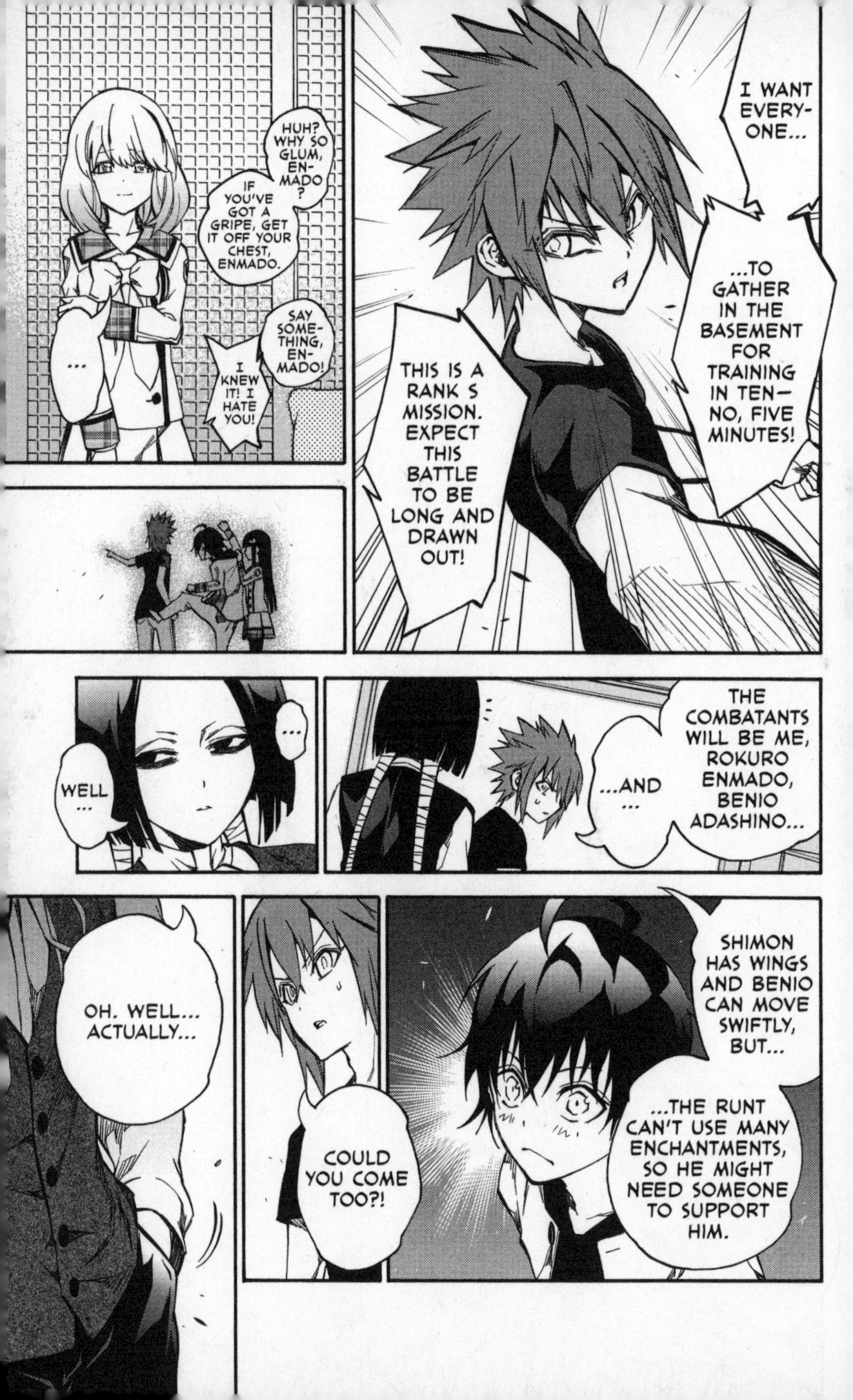
I WANT EVERYONE...
...TO GATHER IN THE BASEMENT FOR TRAINING IN TEN—NO, FIVE MINUTES!
THIS IS A RANK S MISSION. EXPECT THIS BATTLE TO BE LONG AND DRAWN OUT!
HUH? WHY SO GLUM, ENMADO?
IF YOU'VE GOT A GRIPE, GET IT OFF YOUR CHEST, ENMADO.
SAY SOMETHING, ENMADO!
I KNEW IT! I HATE YOU!
...
THE COMBATANTS WILL BE ME, ROKURO ENMADO, BENIO ADASHINO...
...AND ...
...
WELL ...
SHIMON HAS WINGS AND BENIO CAN MOVE SWIFTLY, BUT...
...THE RUNT CAN'T USE MANY ENCHANTMENTS, SO HE MIGHT NEED SOMEONE TO SUPPORT HIM.
COULD YOU COME TOO?!
OH. WELL... ACTUALLY...

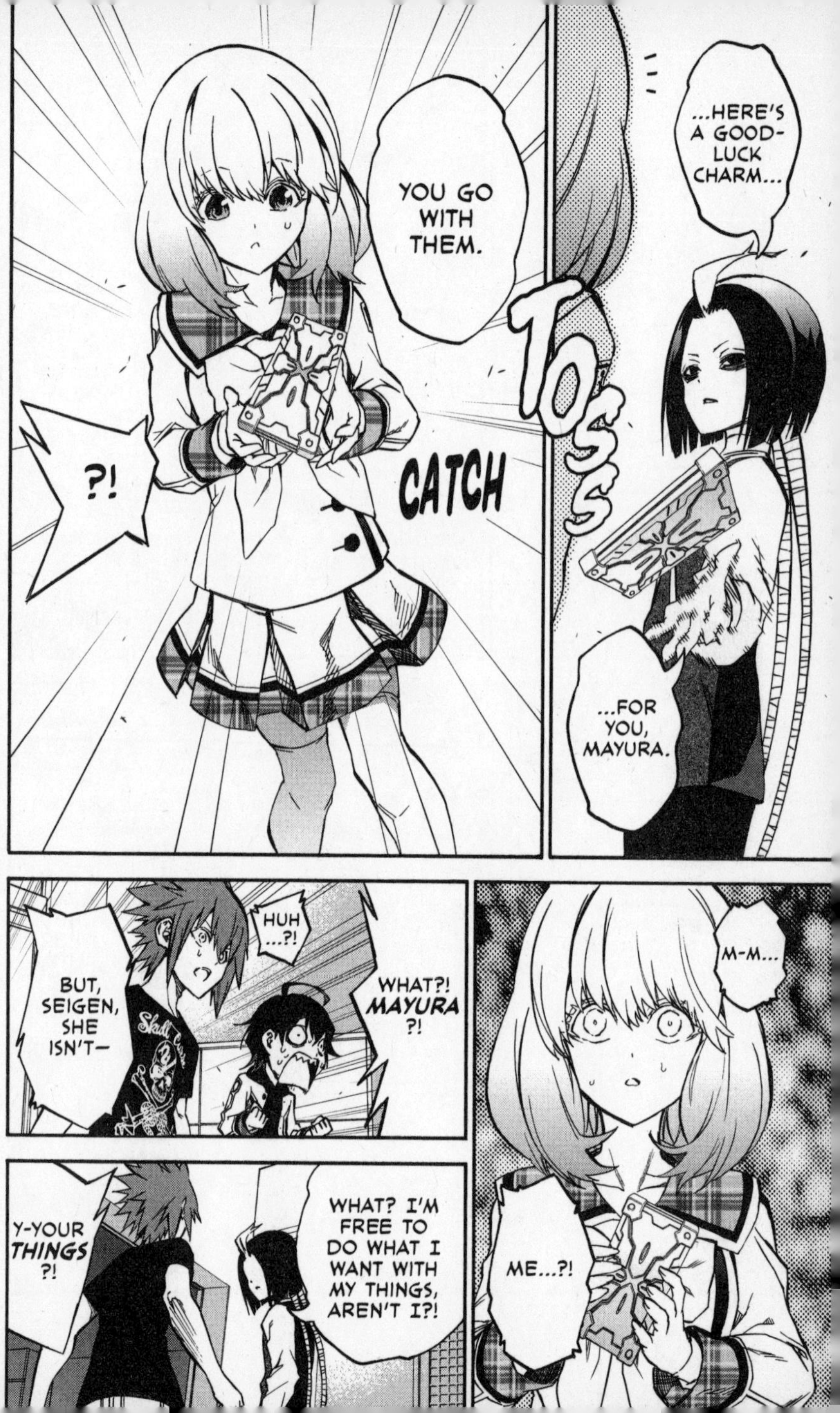
...HERE'S A GOOD-LUCK CHARM...
TOSS
...FOR YOU, MAYURA.
YOU GO WITH THEM.
CATCH
?!
M-M...
ME...?!
WHAT?! MAYURA ?!
HUH ...?!
BUT, SEIGEN, SHE ISN'T—
WHAT? I'M FREE TO DO WHAT I WANT WITH MY THINGS, AREN'T I?!
Y-YOUR THINGS ?!

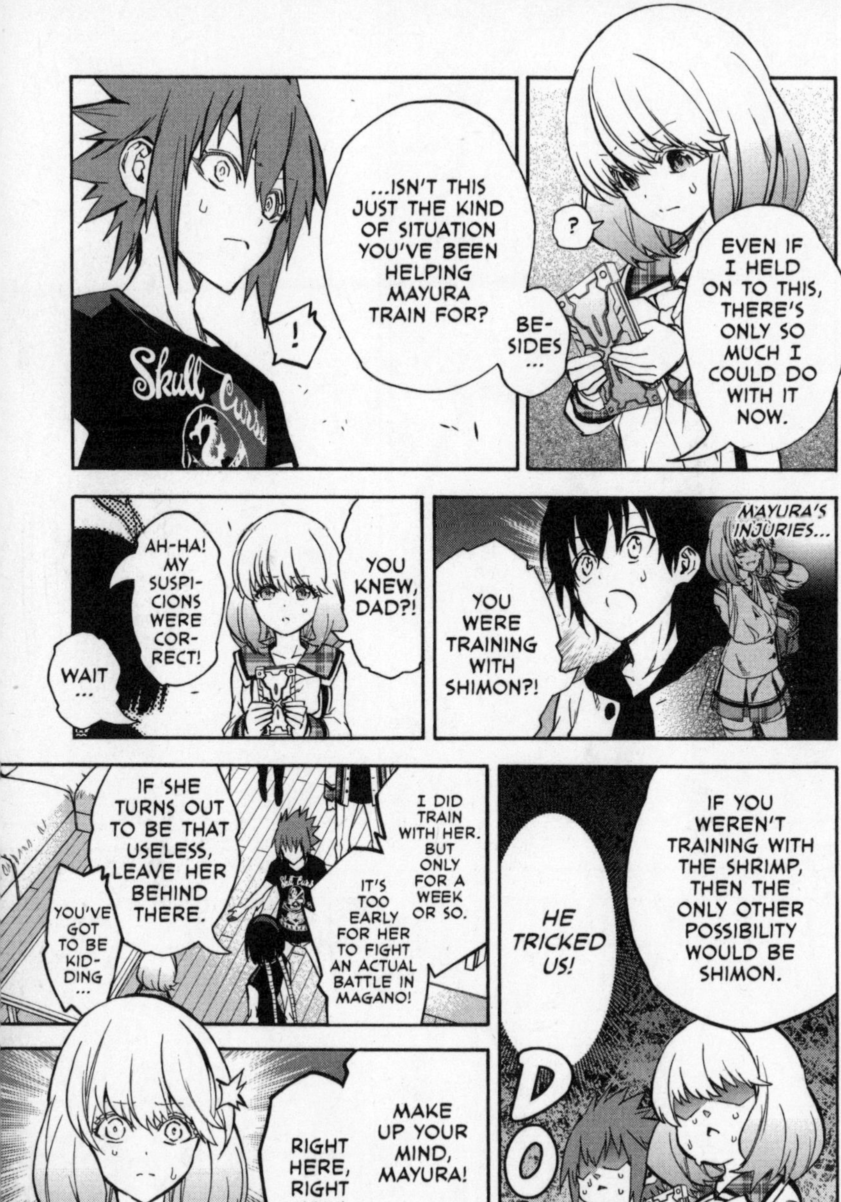
?
EVEN IF I HELD ON TO THIS, THERE'S ONLY SO MUCH I COULD DO WITH IT NOW.
BE-SIDES...
...ISN'T THIS JUST THE KIND OF SITUATION YOU'VE BEEN HELPING MAYURA TRAIN FOR?
!
MAYURA'S INJURIES...
YOU WERE TRAINING WITH SHIMON?!
YOU KNEW, DAD?!
AH-HA! MY SUSPICIONS WERE CORRECT!
WAIT...
IF YOU WEREN'T TRAINING WITH THE SHRIMP, THEN THE ONLY OTHER POSSIBILITY WOULD BE SHIMON.
HE TRICKED US!
DOH
I DID TRAIN WITH HER. BUT ONLY FOR A WEEK OR SO.
IT'S TOO EARLY FOR HER TO FIGHT AN ACTUAL BATTLE IN MAGANO!
IF SHE TURNS OUT TO BE THAT USELESS, LEAVE HER BEHIND THERE.
YOU'VE GOT TO BE KID-DING...
MAKE UP YOUR MIND, MAYURA!
RIGHT HERE, RIGHT NOW!

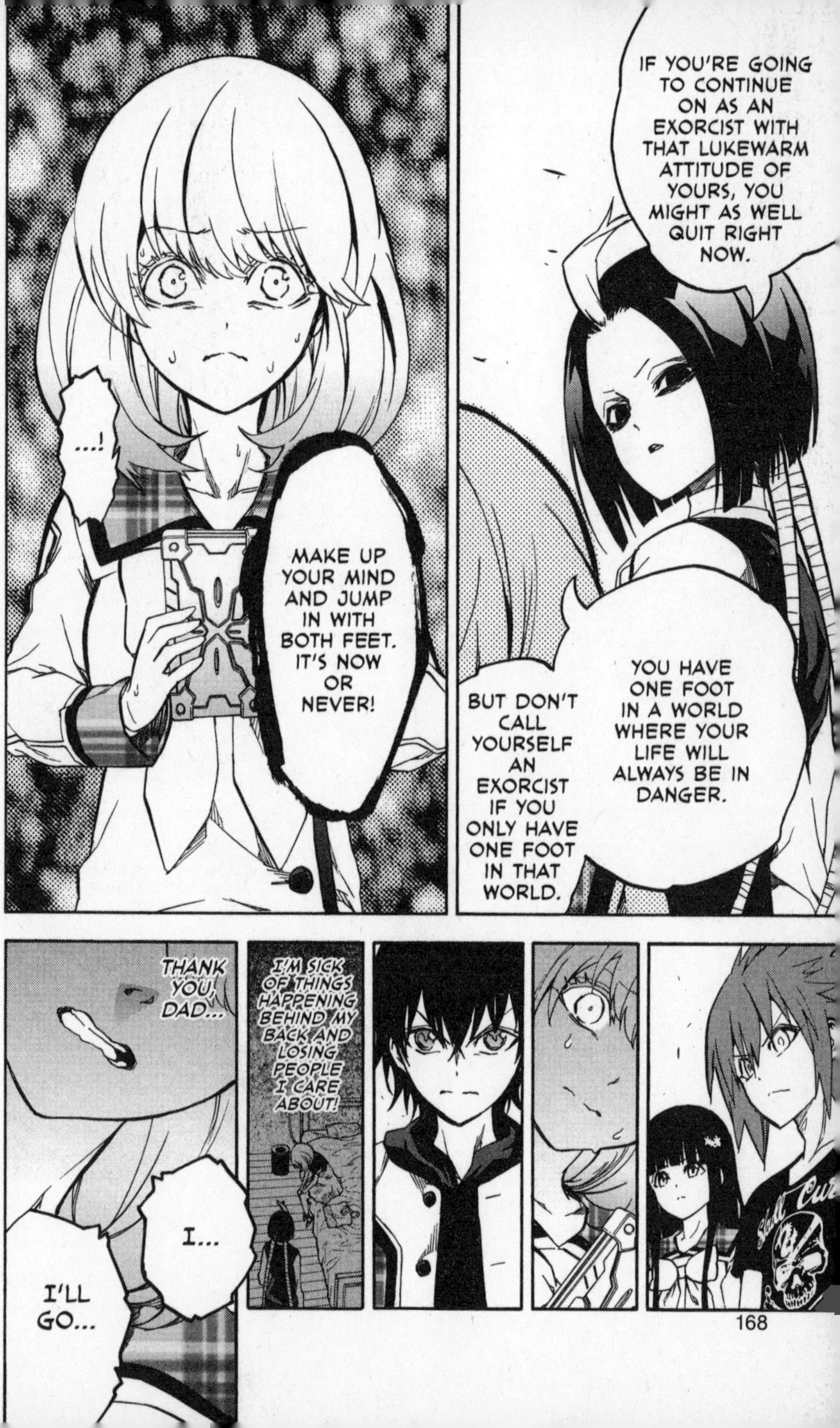
IF YOU'RE GOING TO CONTINUE ON AS AN EXORCIST WITH THAT LUKEWARM ATTITUDE OF YOURS, YOU MIGHT AS WELL QUIT RIGHT NOW.
YOU HAVE ONE FOOT IN A WORLD WHERE YOUR LIFE WILL ALWAYS BE IN DANGER.
BUT DON'T CALL YOURSELF AN EXORCIST IF YOU ONLY HAVE ONE FOOT IN THAT WORLD.
...!
MAKE UP YOUR MIND AND JUMP IN WITH BOTH FEET. IT'S NOW OR NEVER!
I'M SICK OF THINGS HAPPENING BEHIND MY BACK AND LOSING PEOPLE I CARE ABOUT!
THANK YOU, DAD...
I...
I'LL GO...

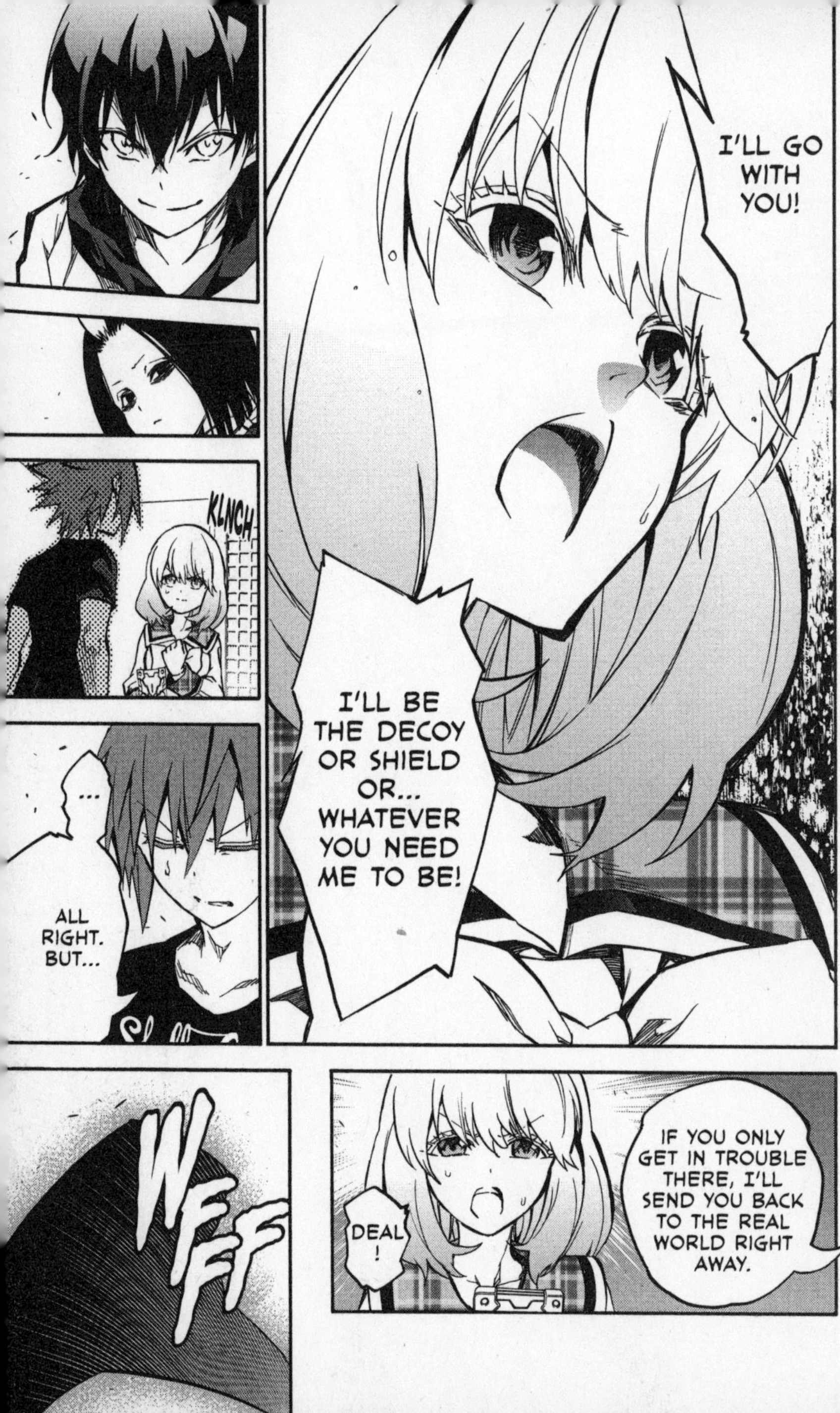
I'LL GO WITH YOU!
I'LL BE THE DECOY OR SHIELD OR... WHATEVER YOU NEED ME TO BE!
KLNCH
...
ALL RIGHT. BUT...
IF YOU ONLY GET IN TROUBLE THERE, I'LL SEND YOU BACK TO THE REAL WORLD RIGHT AWAY.
DEAL!
WFFF

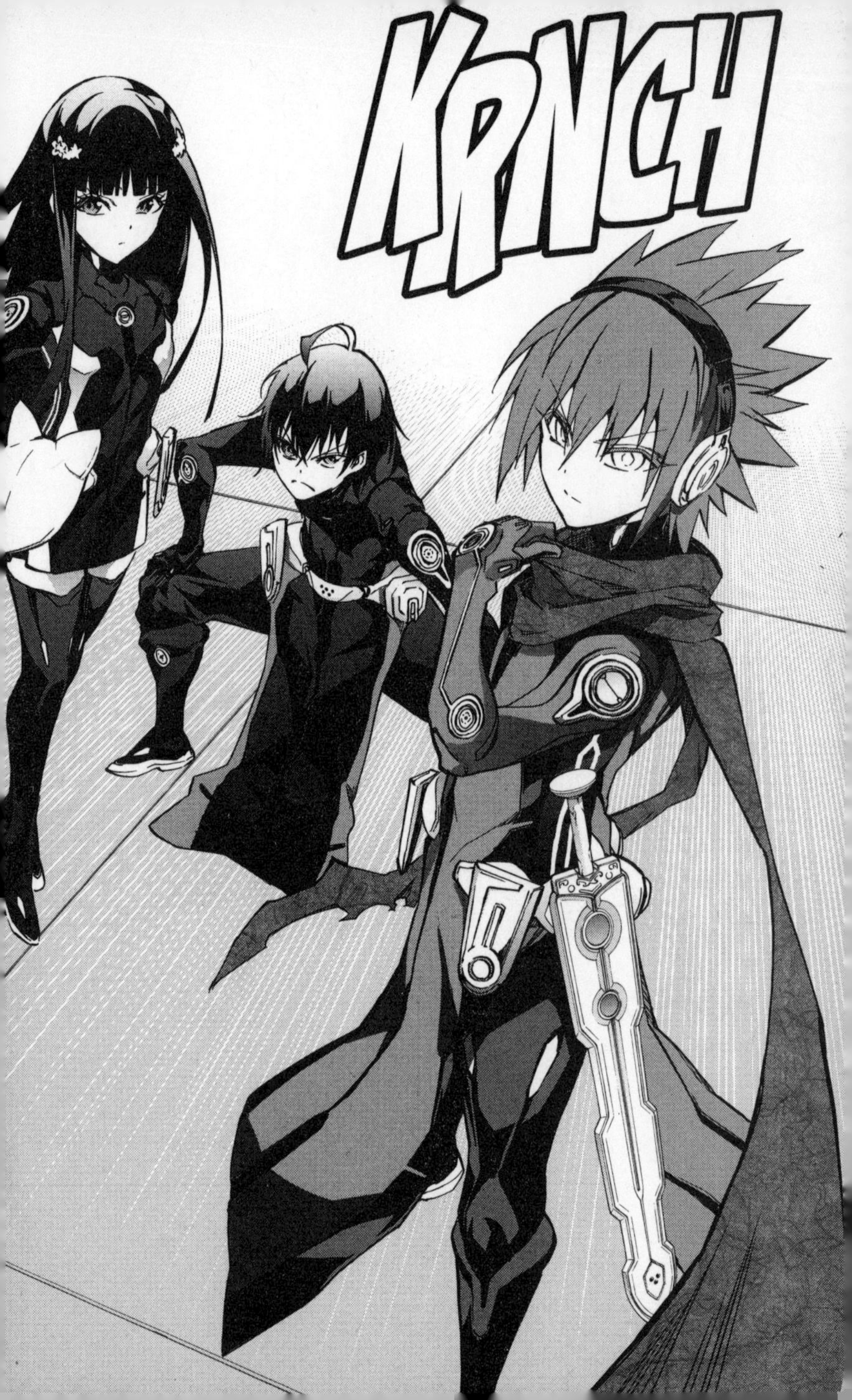
KRNCH

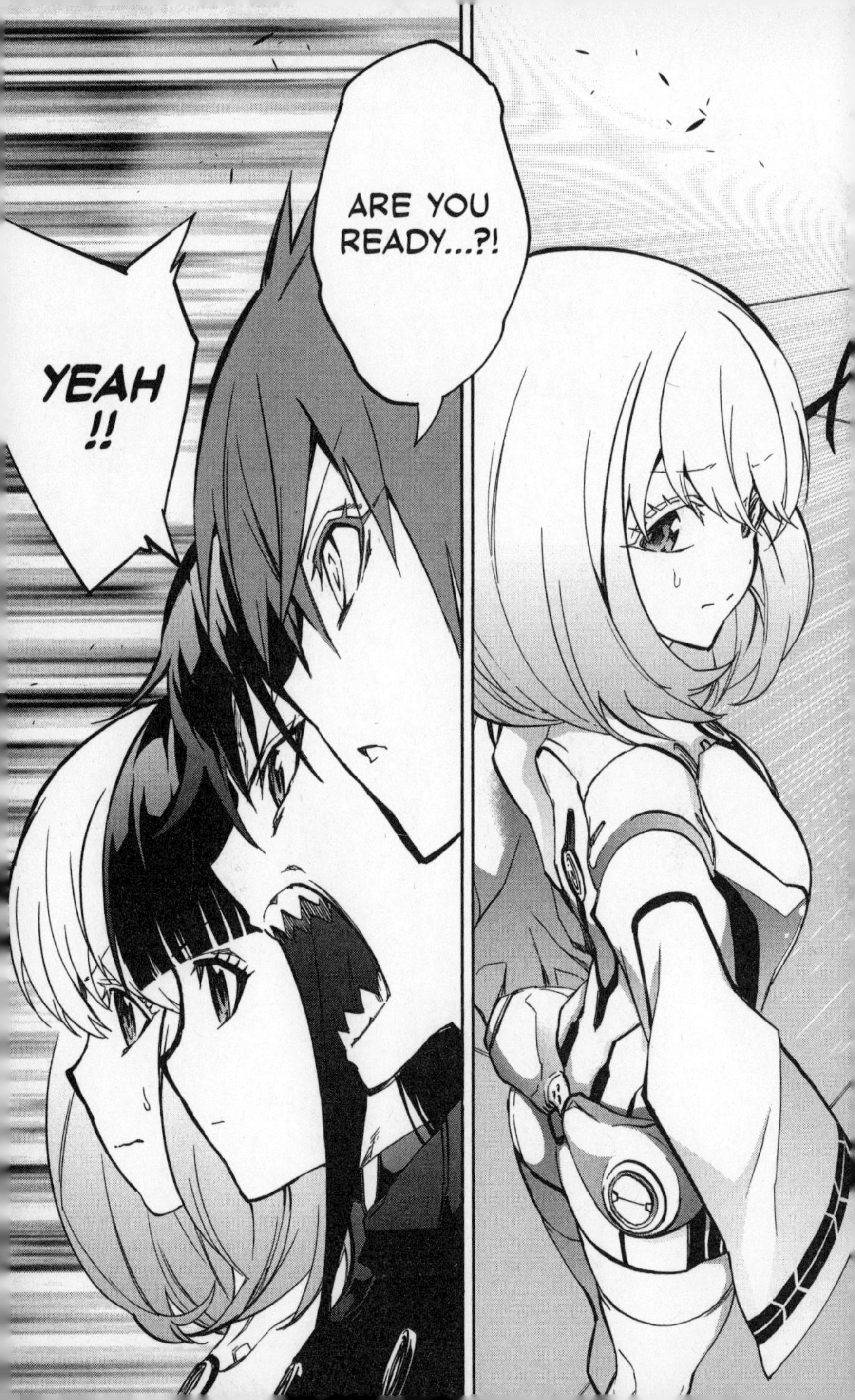
ARE YOU READY...?!
YEAH !!

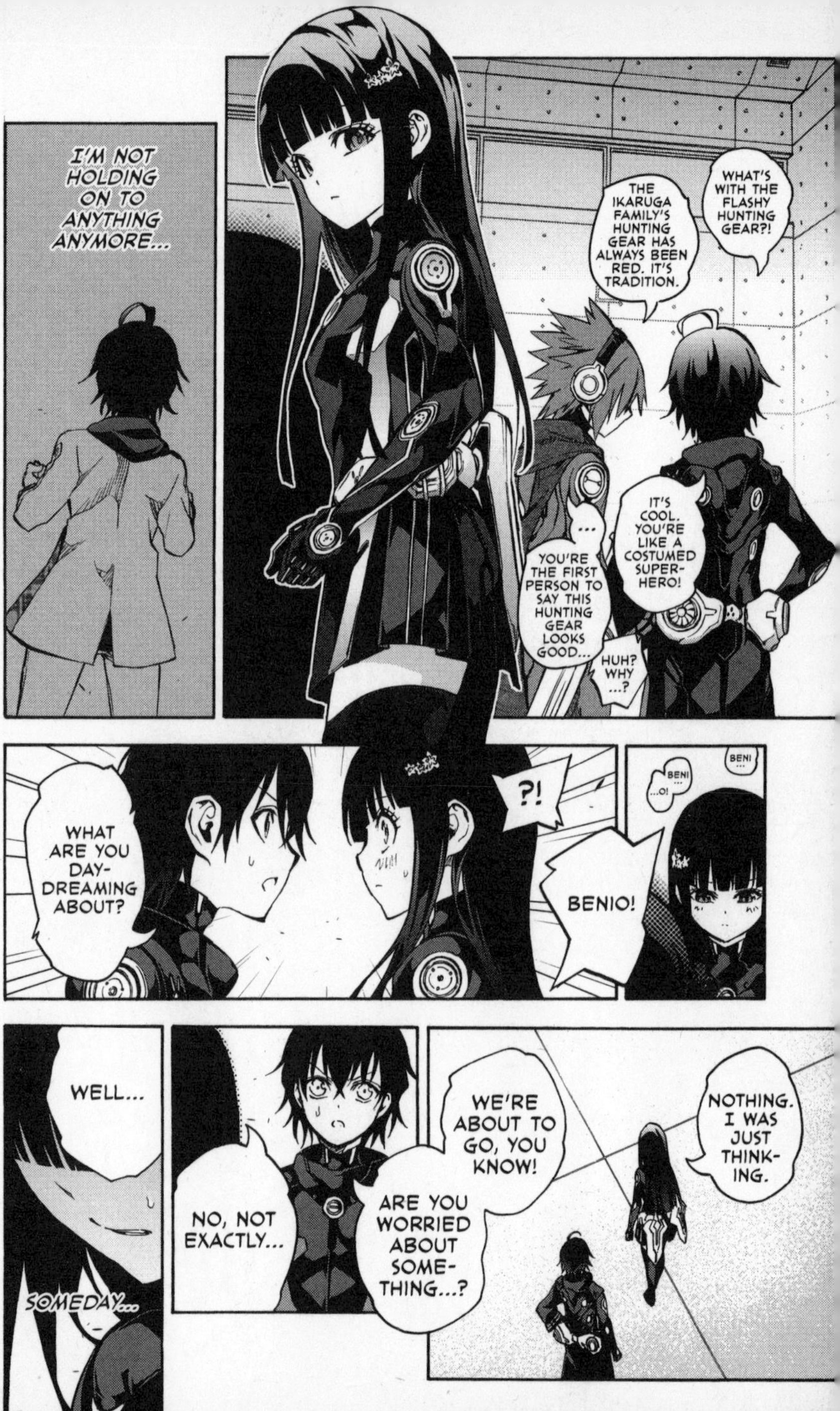
WHAT'S WITH THE FLASHY HUNTING GEAR?!
THE IKARUGA FAMILY'S HUNTING GEAR HAS ALWAYS BEEN RED. IT'S TRADITION.
IT'S COOL. YOU'RE LIKE A COSTUMED SUPER-HERO!
...
YOU'RE THE FIRST PERSON TO SAY THIS HUNTING GEAR LOOKS GOOD...
HUH? WHY ...?
I'M NOT HOLDING ON TO ANYTHING ANYMORE...
BENI ...
BENI ...
...O!
BENIO!
?!
WHAT ARE YOU DAY-DREAMING ABOUT?
NOTHING. I WAS JUST THINK-ING.
WE'RE ABOUT TO GO, YOU KNOW!
ARE YOU WORRIED ABOUT SOME-THING...?
NO, NOT EXACTLY...
WELL...
SOMEDAY...

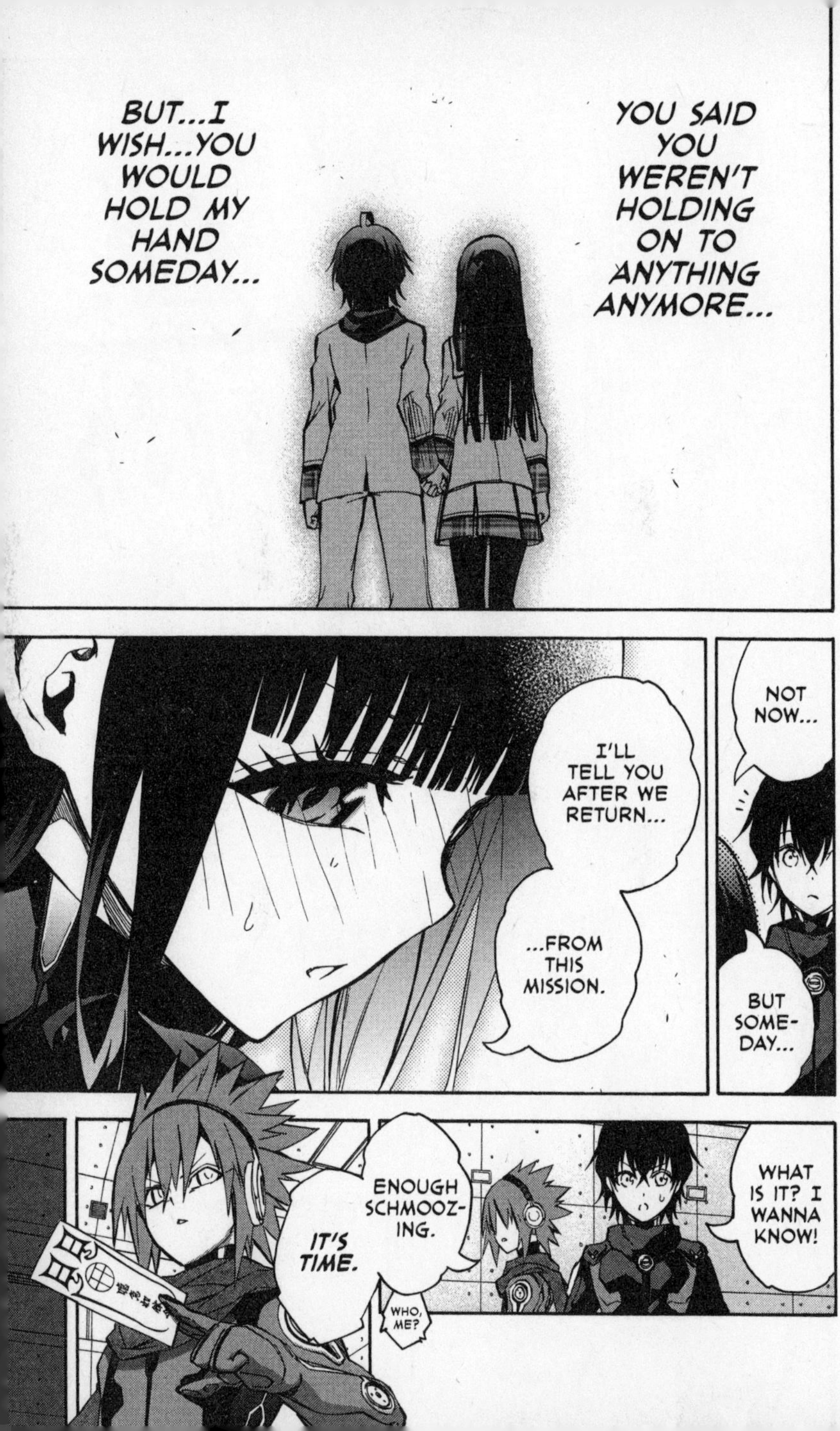
YOU SAID YOU WEREN'T HOLDING ON TO ANYTHING ANYMORE...
BUT...I WISH...YOU WOULD HOLD MY HAND SOMEDAY...
NOT NOW...
BUT SOME-DAY...
I'LL TELL YOU AFTER WE RETURN...
...FROM THIS MISSION.
WHAT IS IT? I WANNA KNOW!
ENOUGH SCHMOOZ-ING.
IT'S TIME.
WHO, ME?

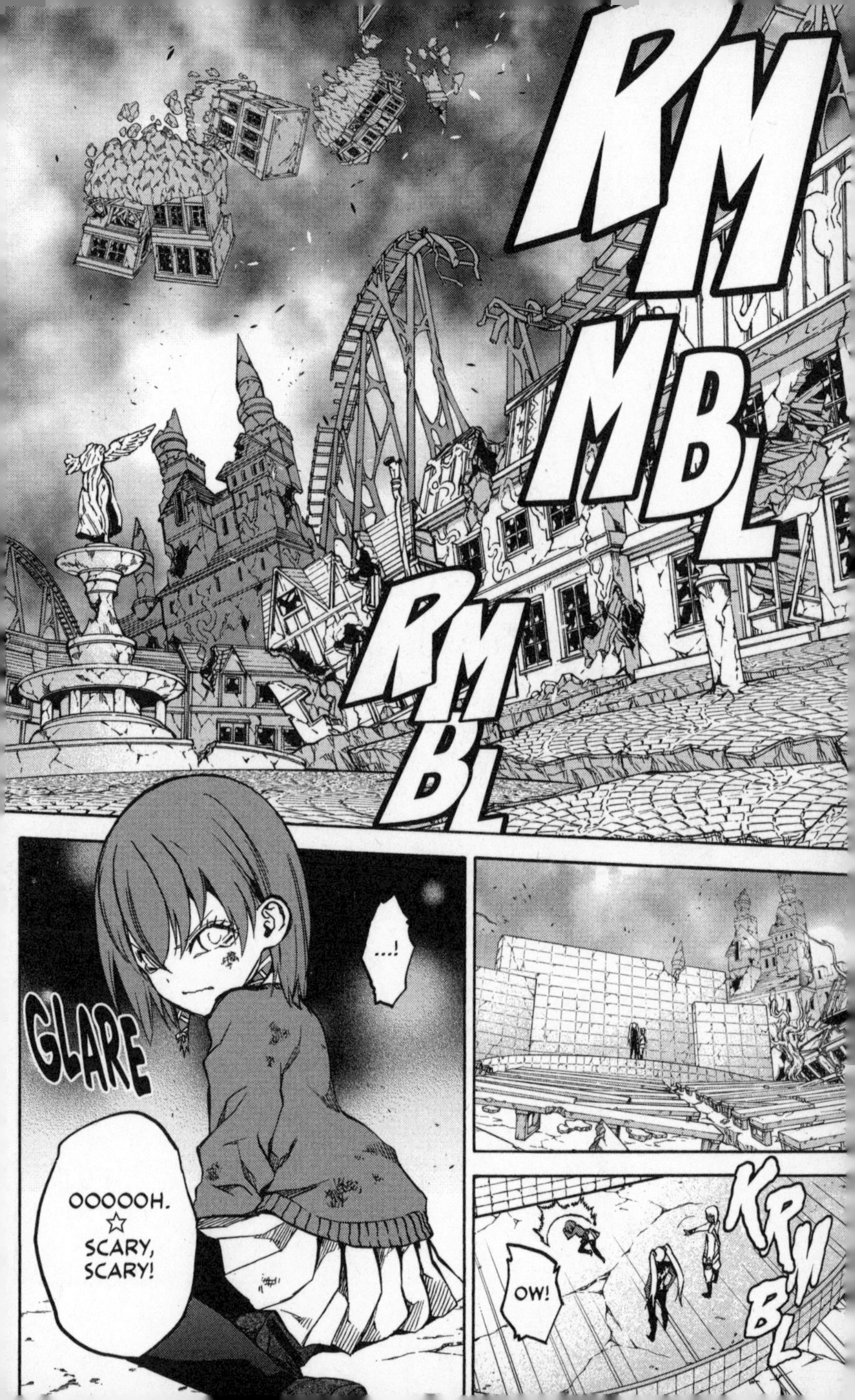
RMMBL
RMBL
KRMBL
OW!
...!
GLARE
OOOOOH. ☆
SCARY, SCARY!

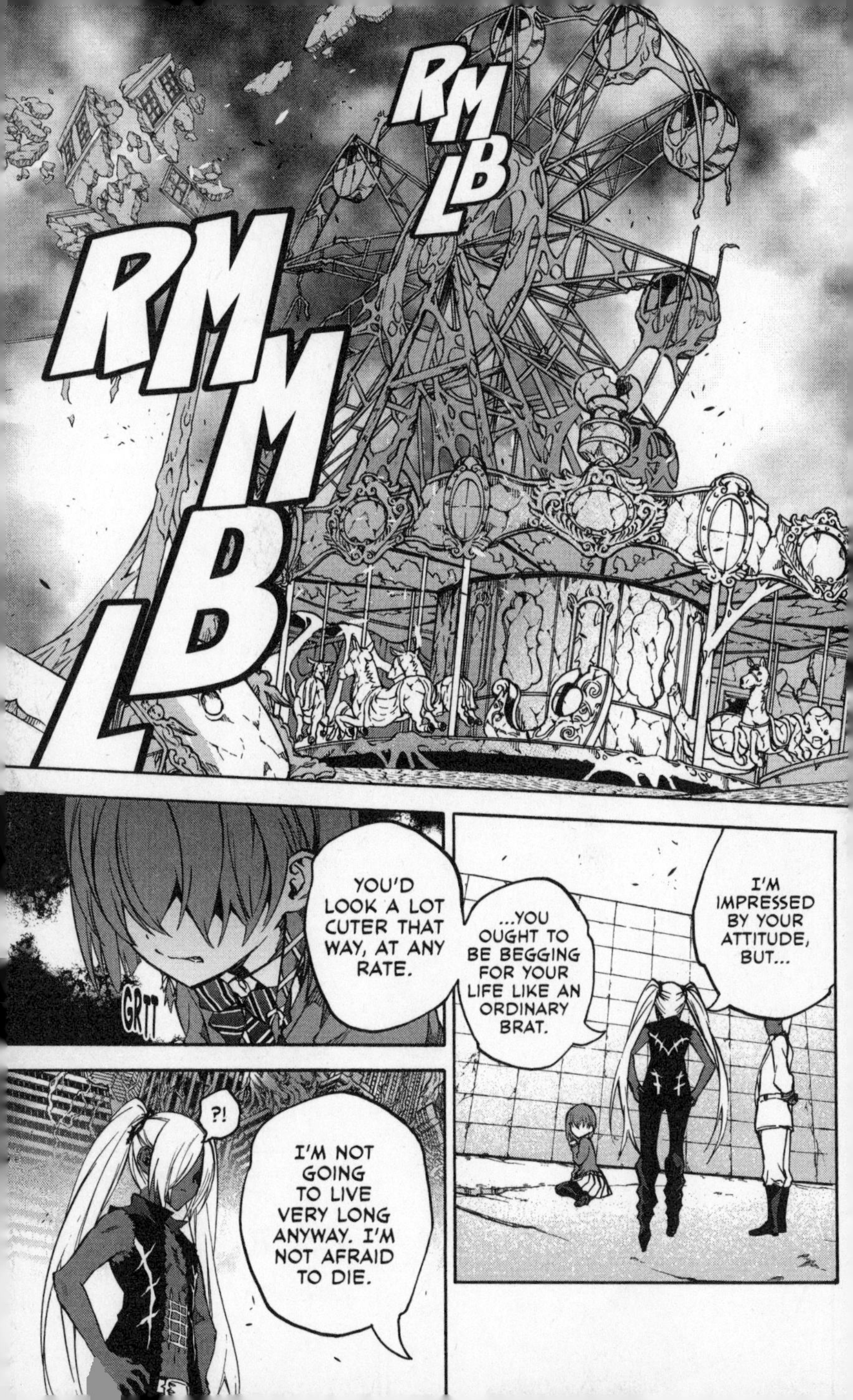
RMBL
RMMBL
I'M IMPRESSED BY YOUR ATTITUDE, BUT...
...YOU OUGHT TO BE BEGGING FOR YOUR LIFE LIKE AN ORDINARY BRAT.
YOU'D LOOK A LOT CUTER THAT WAY, AT ANY RATE.
GRTT
?!
I'M NOT GOING TO LIVE VERY LONG ANYWAY. I'M NOT AFRAID TO DIE.

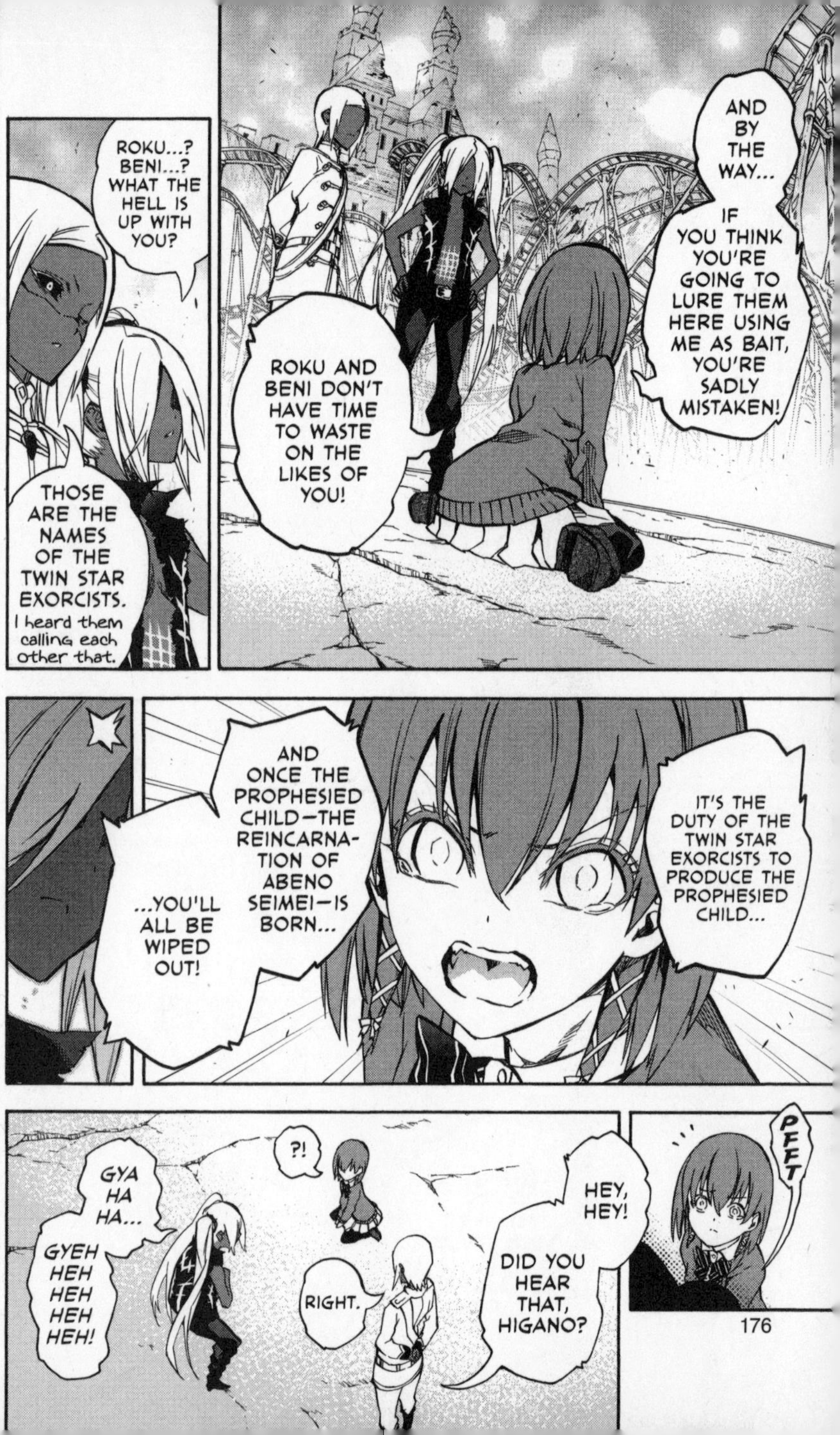
AND BY THE WAY...
IF YOU THINK YOU'RE GOING TO LURE THEM HERE USING ME AS BAIT, YOU'RE SADLY MISTAKEN!
ROKU AND BENI DON'T HAVE TIME TO WASTE ON THE LIKES OF YOU!
ROKU...? BENI...? WHAT THE HELL IS UP WITH YOU?
THOSE ARE THE NAMES OF THE TWIN STAR EXORCISTS.
I heard them calling each other that.
IT'S THE DUTY OF THE TWIN STAR EXORCISTS TO PRODUCE THE PROPHESIED CHILD...
AND ONCE THE PROPHESIED CHILD—THE REINCARNATION OF ABENO SEIMEI—IS BORN...
...YOU'LL ALL BE WIPED OUT!
PFFT
HEY, HEY!
DID YOU HEAR THAT, HIGANO?
RIGHT.
?!
GYA HA HA...
GYEH HEH HEH HEH HEH!

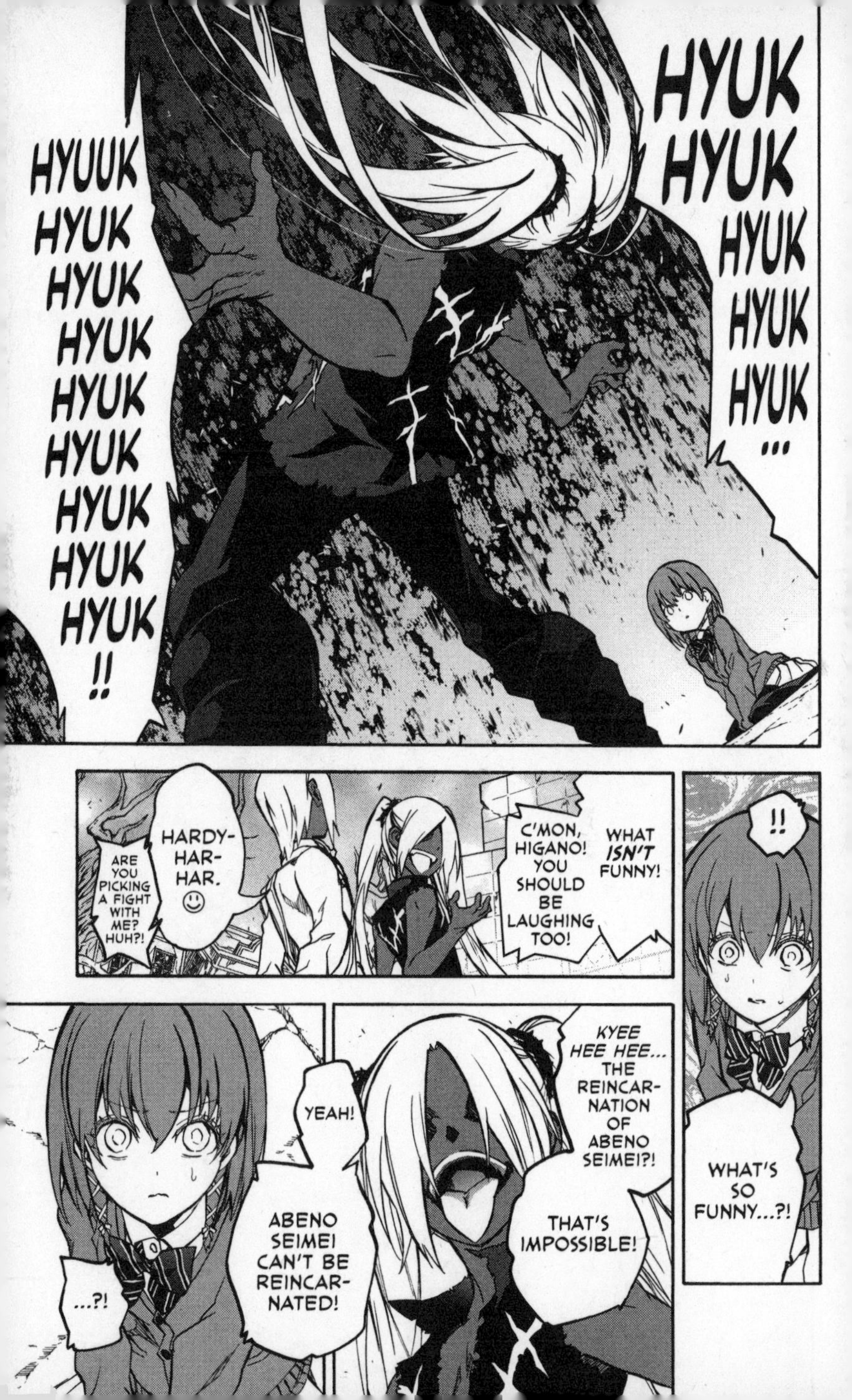
HYUK HYUK HYUK HYUK HYUK ...
HYUUK HYUK HYUK HYUK HYUK HYUK HYUK HYUK HYUK !!
!!
WHAT'S SO FUNNY...?!
WHAT *ISN'T* FUNNY!
C'MON, HIGANO! YOU SHOULD BE LAUGHING TOO!
HARDY-HAR-HAR. ☺
ARE YOU PICKING A FIGHT WITH ME? HUH?!
KYEE HEE HEE... THE REINCARNATION OF ABENO SEIMEI?!
THAT'S IMPOSSIBLE!
ABENO SEIMEI CAN'T BE REINCARNATED!
YEAH!
...?!

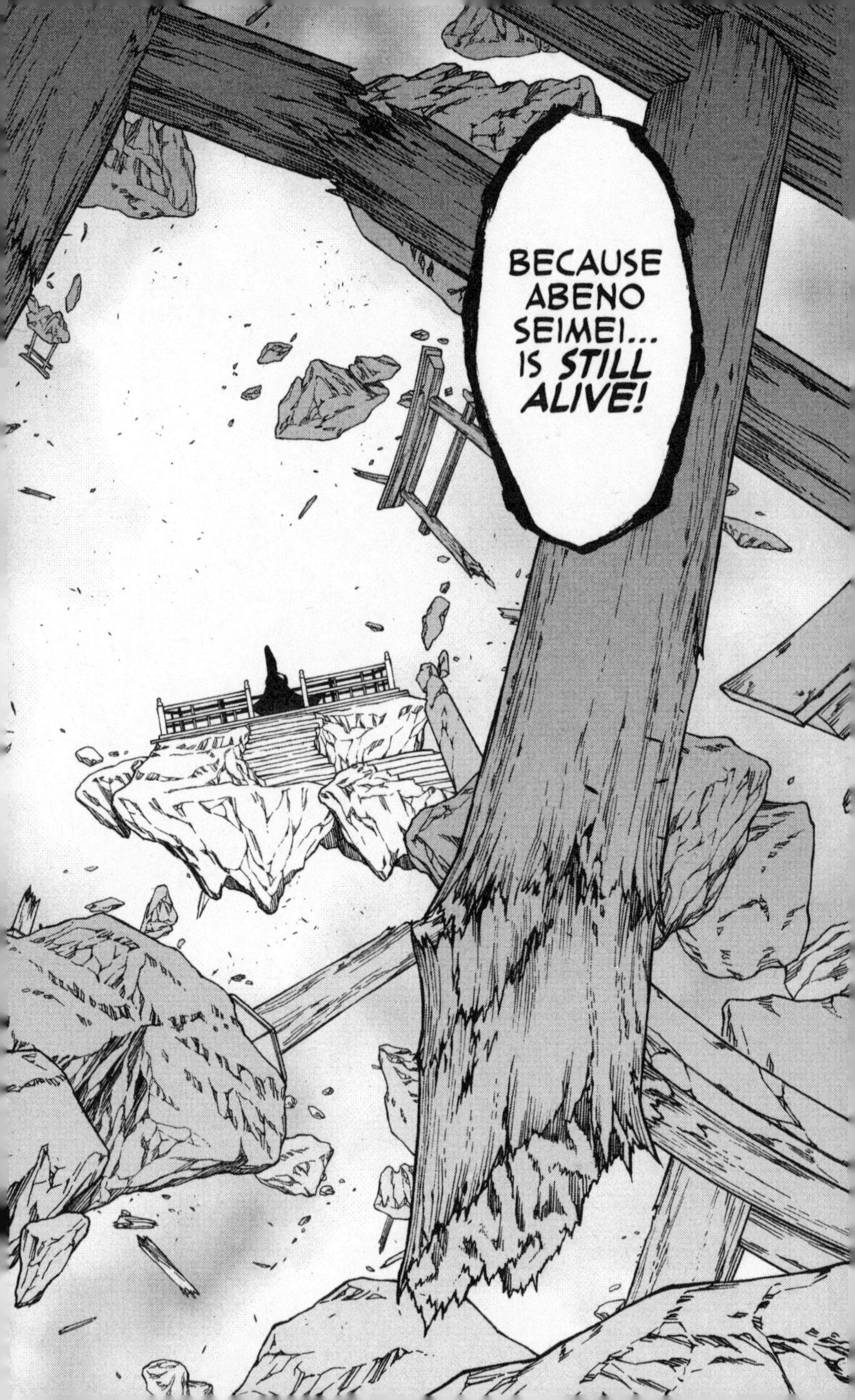
BECAUSE ABENO SEIMEI... IS STILL ALIVE!

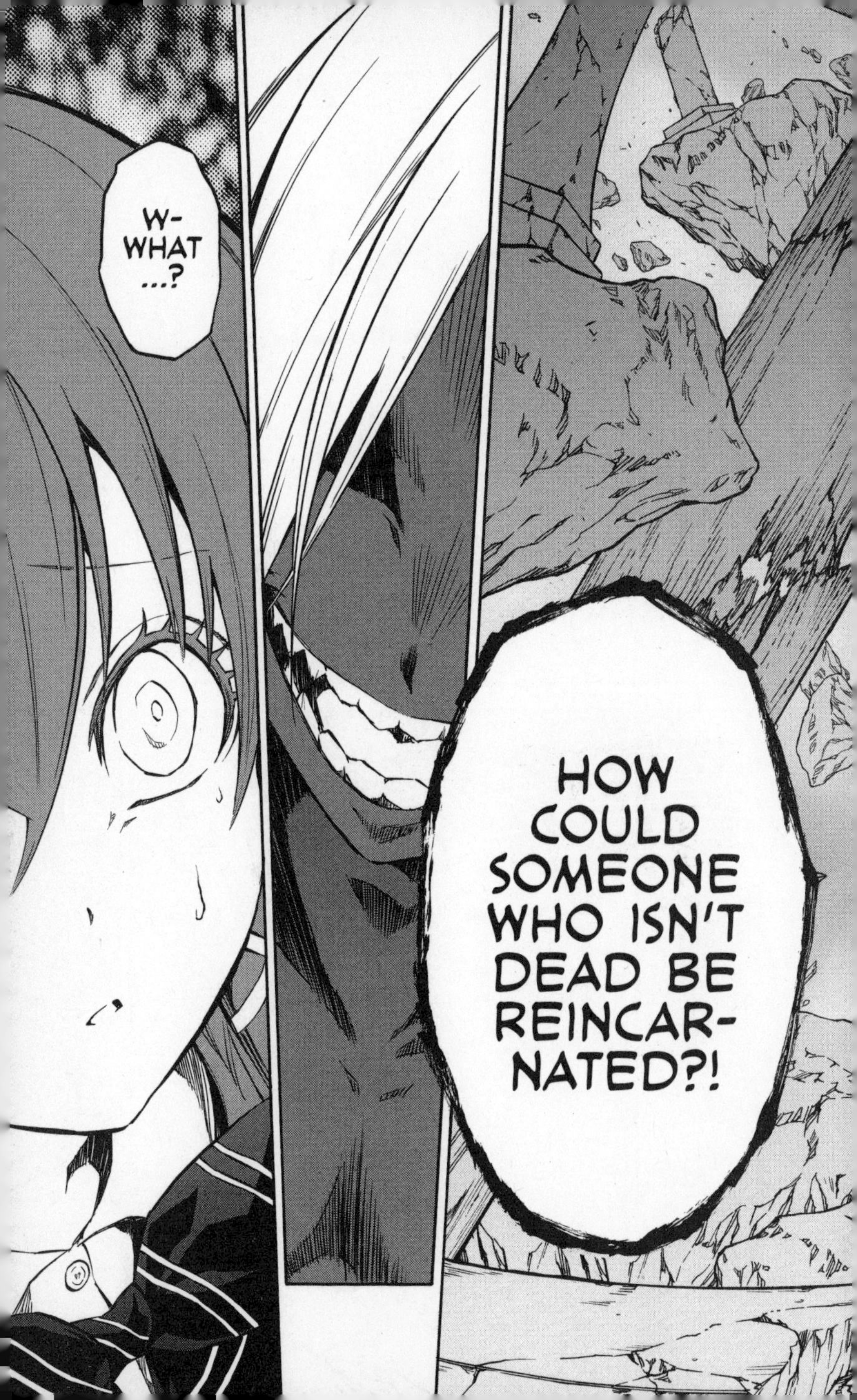
HOW COULD SOMEONE WHO ISN'T DEAD BE REINCAR-NATED?!
W-WHAT ...?

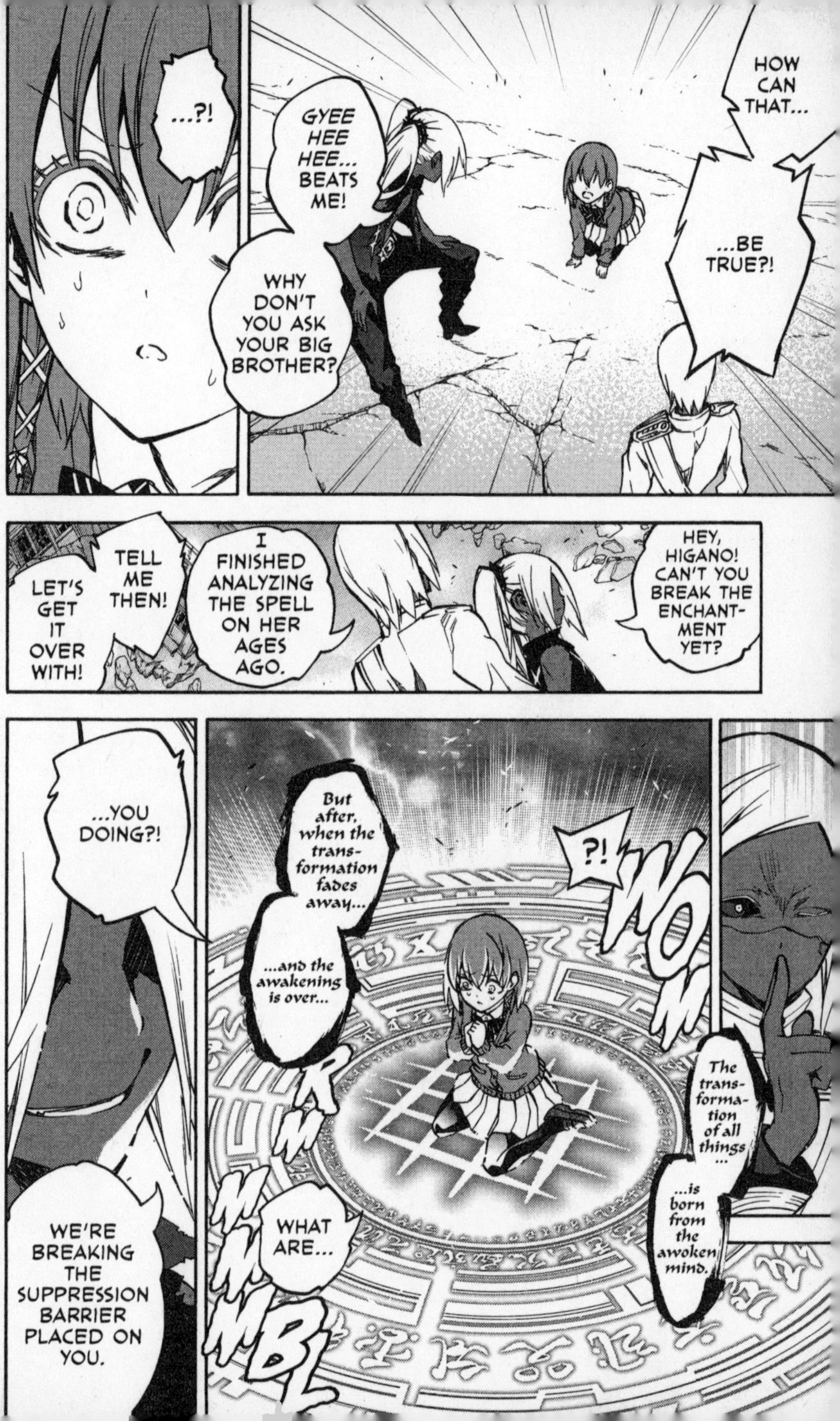
HOW CAN THAT...
...BE TRUE?!
GYEE HEE HEE... BEATS ME!
WHY DON'T YOU ASK YOUR BIG BROTHER?
...?!
HEY, HIGANO! CAN'T YOU BREAK THE ENCHANT-MENT YET?
I FINISHED ANALYZING THE SPELL ON HER AGES AGO.
TELL ME THEN!
LET'S GET IT OVER WITH!
The trans-forma-tion of all things...
...is born from the awoken mind.
?!
But after, when the trans-formation fades away...
...and the awakening is over...
WHAT ARE...
...YOU DOING?!
WE'RE BREAKING THE SUPPRESSION BARRIER PLACED ON YOU.

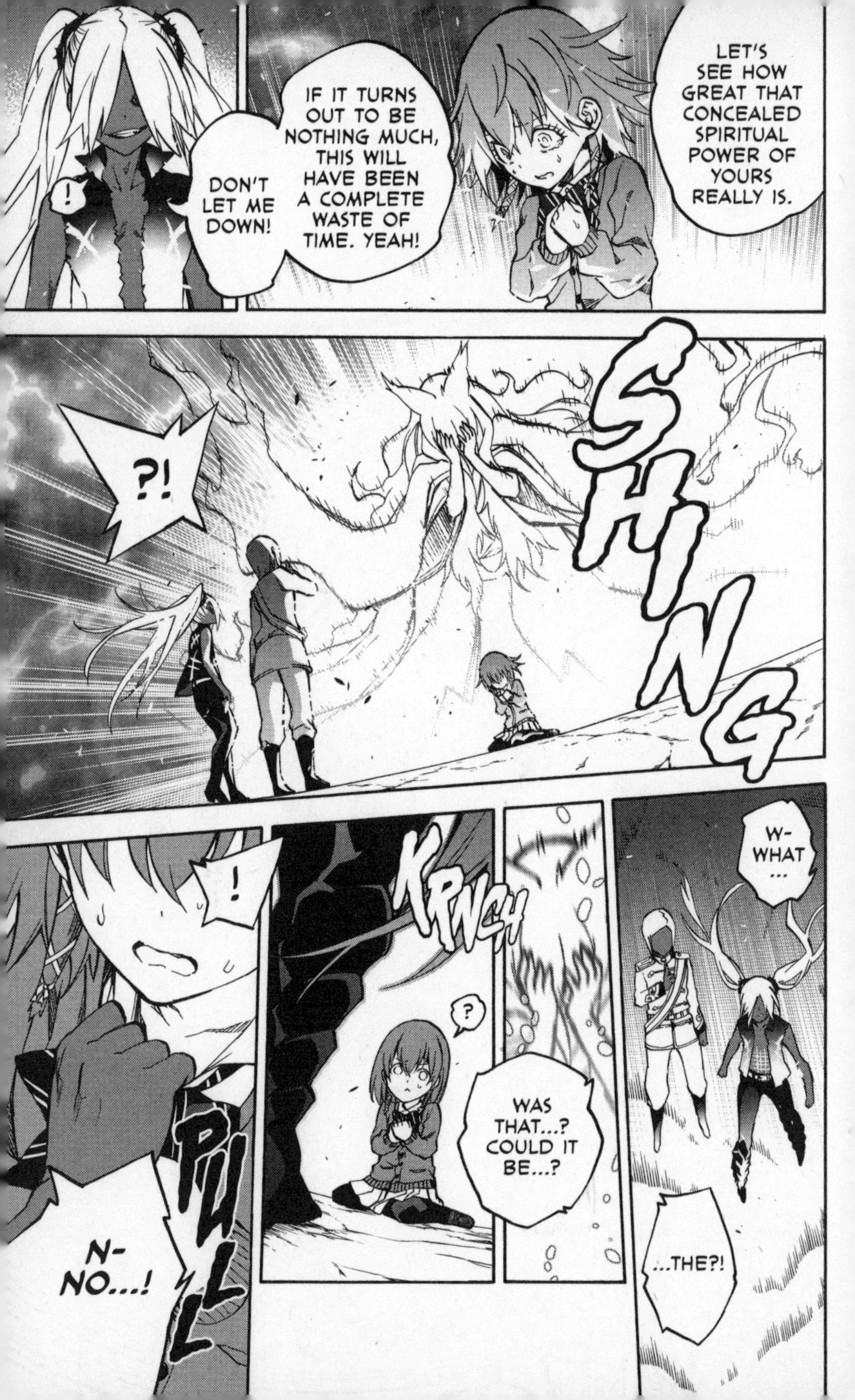
LET'S SEE HOW GREAT THAT CONCEALED SPIRITUAL POWER OF YOURS REALLY IS.
IF IT TURNS OUT TO BE NOTHING MUCH, THIS WILL HAVE BEEN A COMPLETE WASTE OF TIME. YEAH!
DON'T LET ME DOWN!
!
SHING
?!
W-WHAT...
...THE?!
KPNCH
?
WAS THAT...? COULD IT BE...?
!
PULL
N-NO...!

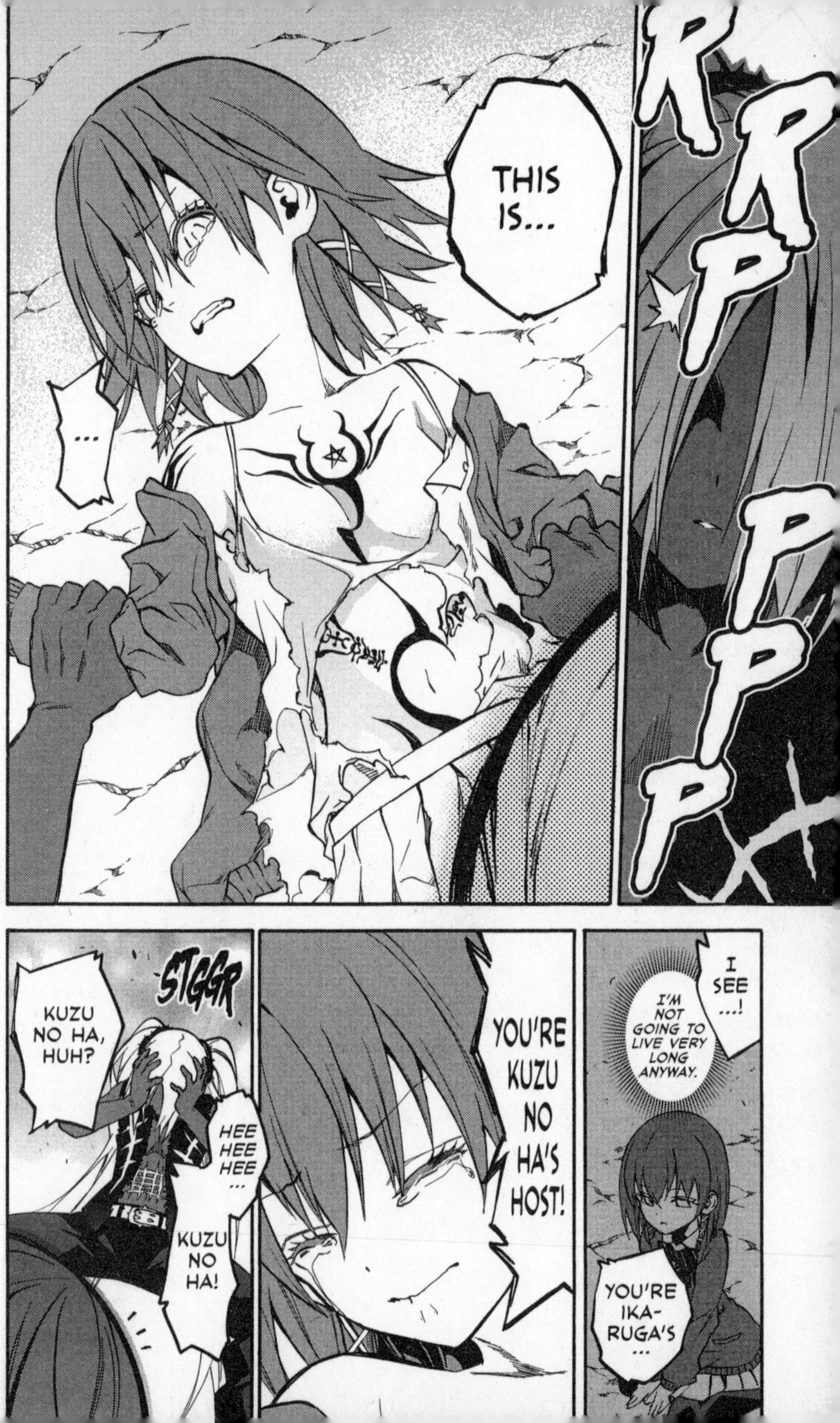
RRPPPP
THIS IS...
...
I SEE ...!
I'M NOT GOING TO LIVE VERY LONG ANYWAY.
YOU'RE IKA-RUGA'S ...
YOU'RE KUZU NO HA'S HOST!
STGGR
KUZU NO HA, HUH?
HEE HEE HEE ...
KUZU NO HA!
!!!

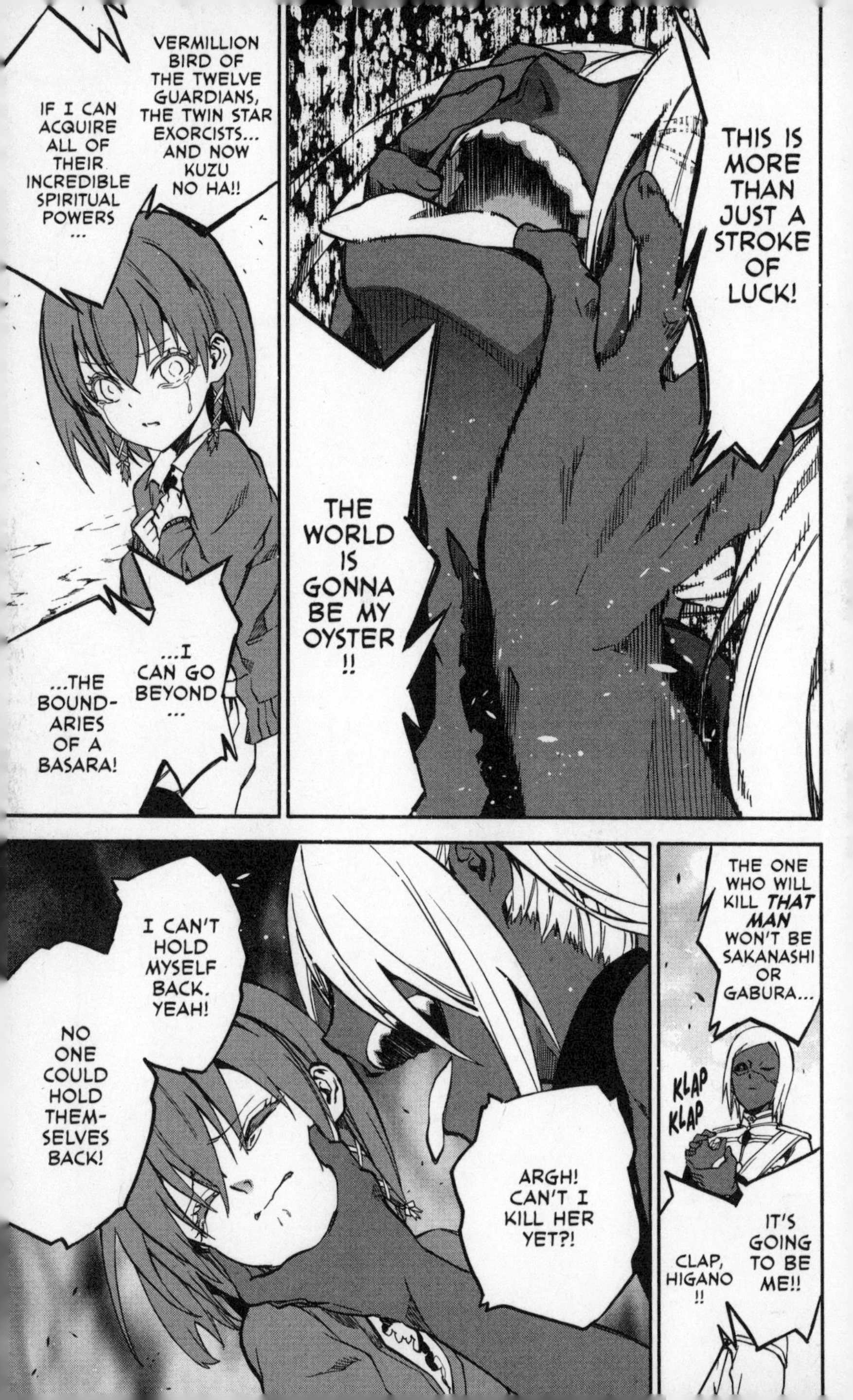
THIS IS MORE THAN JUST A STROKE OF LUCK!
THE WORLD IS GONNA BE MY OYSTER!!
VERMILLION BIRD OF THE TWELVE GUARDIANS, THE TWIN STAR EXORCISTS... AND NOW KUZU NO HA!!
IF I CAN ACQUIRE ALL OF THEIR INCREDIBLE SPIRITUAL POWERS...
...I CAN GO BEYOND...
...THE BOUNDARIES OF A BASARA!
THE ONE WHO WILL KILL *THAT MAN* WON'T BE SAKANASHI OR GABURA...
KLAP KLAP
IT'S GOING TO BE ME!!
CLAP, HIGANO!!
I CAN'T HOLD MYSELF BACK. YEAH!
NO ONE COULD HOLD THEMSELVES BACK!
ARGH! CAN'T I KILL HER YET?!

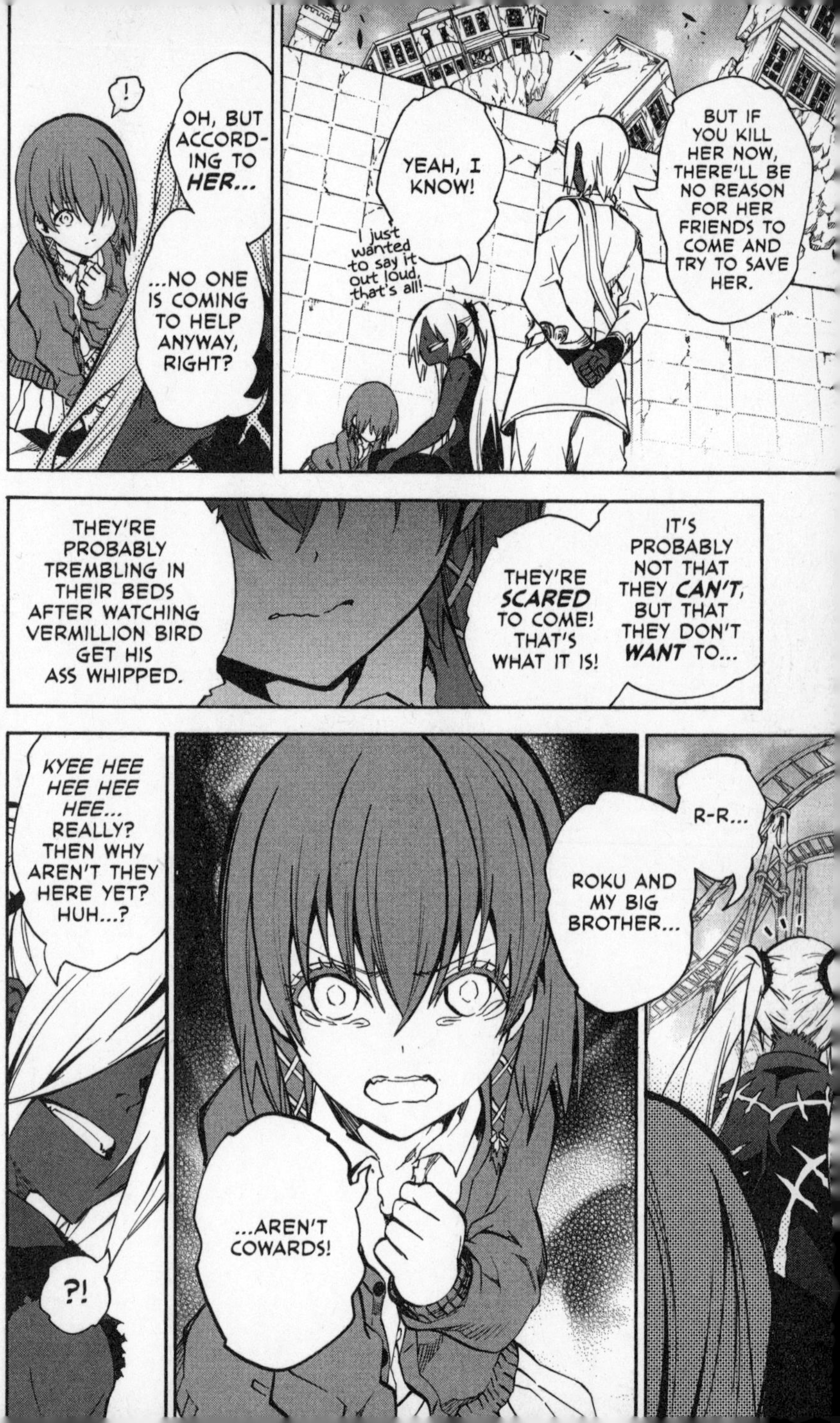
BUT IF YOU KILL HER NOW, THERE'LL BE NO REASON FOR HER FRIENDS TO COME AND TRY TO SAVE HER.
YEAH, I KNOW!
I just wanted to say it out loud, that's all!
!
OH, BUT ACCORDING TO *HER*...
...NO ONE IS COMING TO HELP ANYWAY, RIGHT?
IT'S PROBABLY NOT THAT THEY *CAN'T*, BUT THAT THEY DON'T *WANT* TO...
THEY'RE *SCARED* TO COME! THAT'S WHAT IT IS!
THEY'RE PROBABLY TREMBLING IN THEIR BEDS AFTER WATCHING VERMILLION BIRD GET HIS ASS WHIPPED.
R-R...
ROKU AND MY BIG BROTHER...
...AREN'T COWARDS!
KYEE HEE HEE HEE HEE... REALLY? THEN WHY AREN'T THEY HERE YET? HUH...?
?!

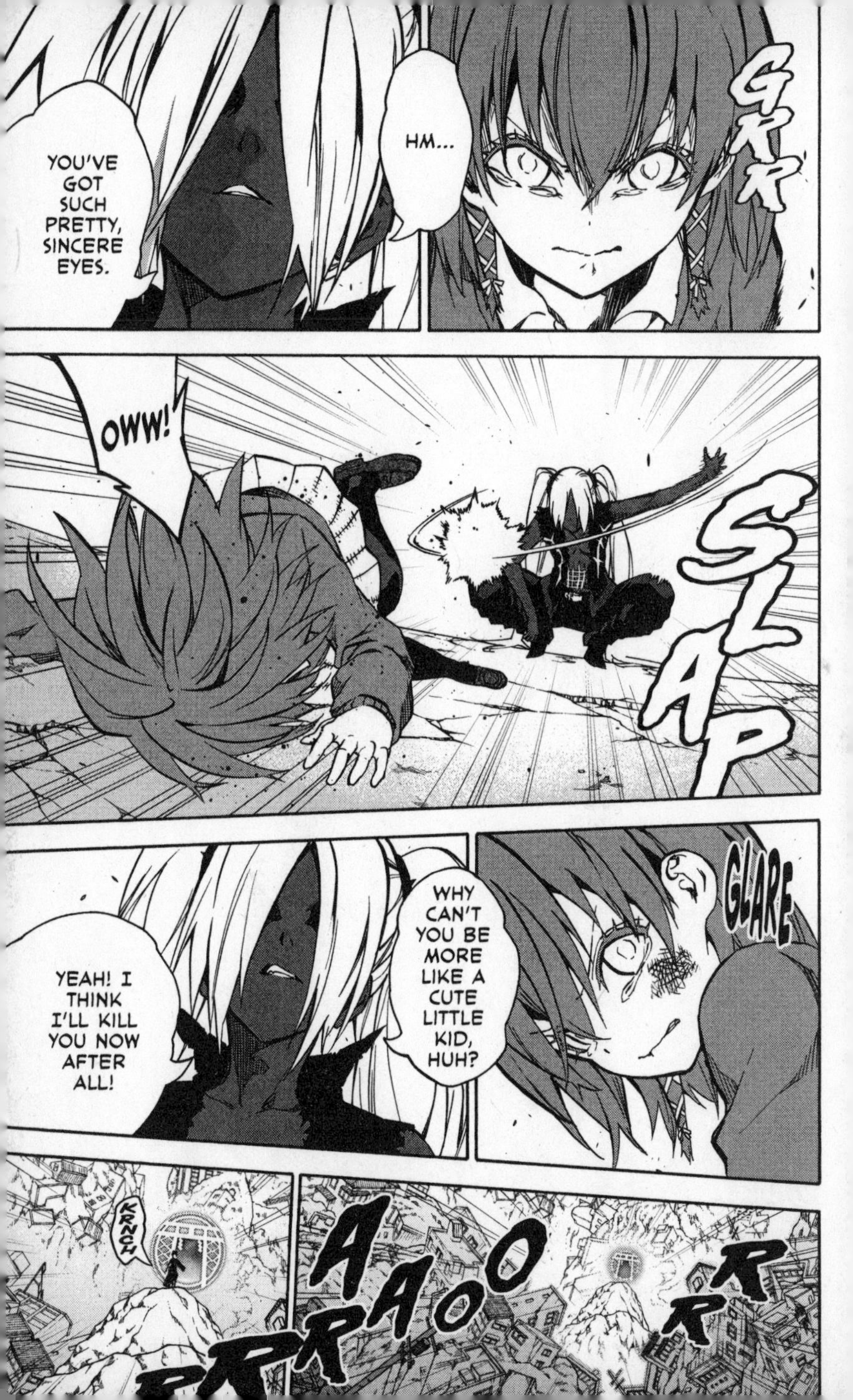
GRR
HM...
YOU'VE GOT SUCH PRETTY, SINCERE EYES.
SLAP
OWW!
GLARE
WHY CAN'T YOU BE MORE LIKE A CUTE LITTLE KID, HUH?
YEAH! I THINK I'LL KILL YOU NOW AFTER ALL!
RRRAAOO RR
KRNCH

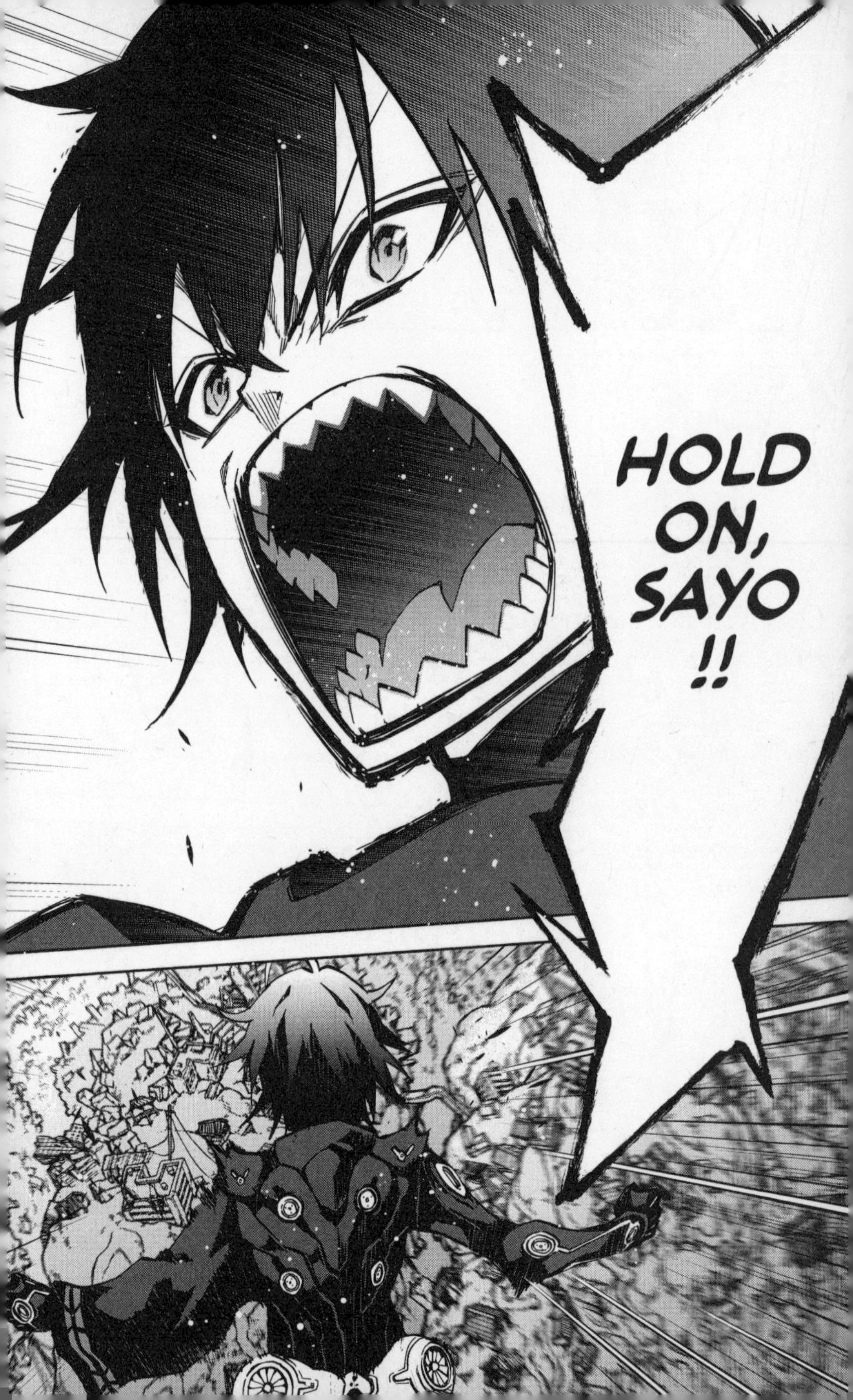
HOLD ON, SAYO !!

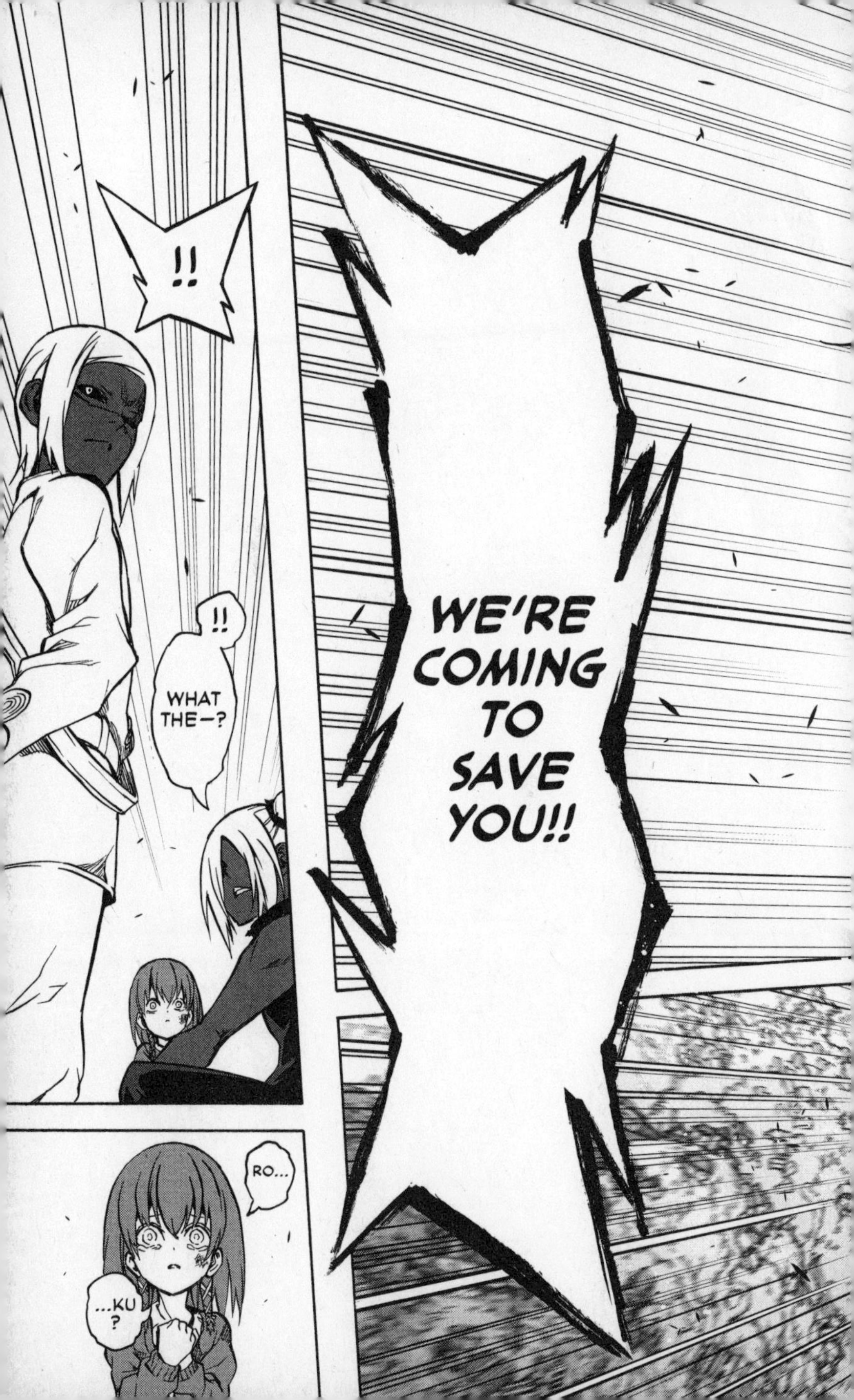
WE'RE COMING TO SAVE YOU!!
!!
!! WHAT THE—?
RO...
...KU ?

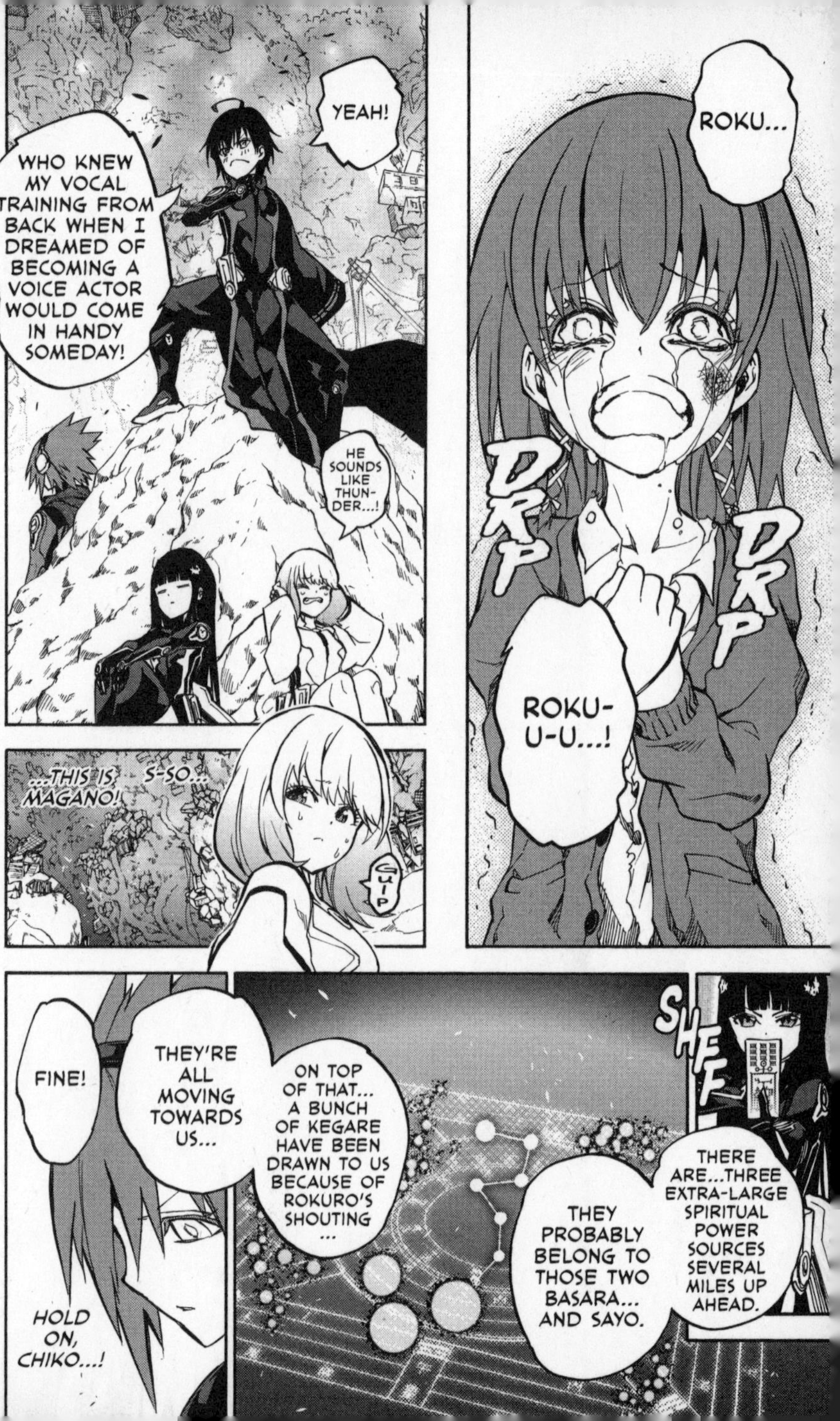
ROKU...
DRP
DRP
ROKU-U-U...!
YEAH!
WHO KNEW MY VOCAL TRAINING FROM BACK WHEN I DREAMED OF BECOMING A VOICE ACTOR WOULD COME IN HANDY SOMEDAY!
HE SOUNDS LIKE THUN-DER...!
S-SO...
...THIS IS MAGANO!
GULP
SHFF
THERE ARE... THREE EXTRA-LARGE SPIRITUAL POWER SOURCES SEVERAL MILES UP AHEAD.
THEY PROBABLY BELONG TO THOSE TWO BASARA... AND SAYO.
ON TOP OF THAT... A BUNCH OF KEGARE HAVE BEEN DRAWN TO US BECAUSE OF ROKURO'S SHOUTING ...
THEY'RE ALL MOVING TOWARDS US...
FINE!
HOLD ON, CHIKO...!

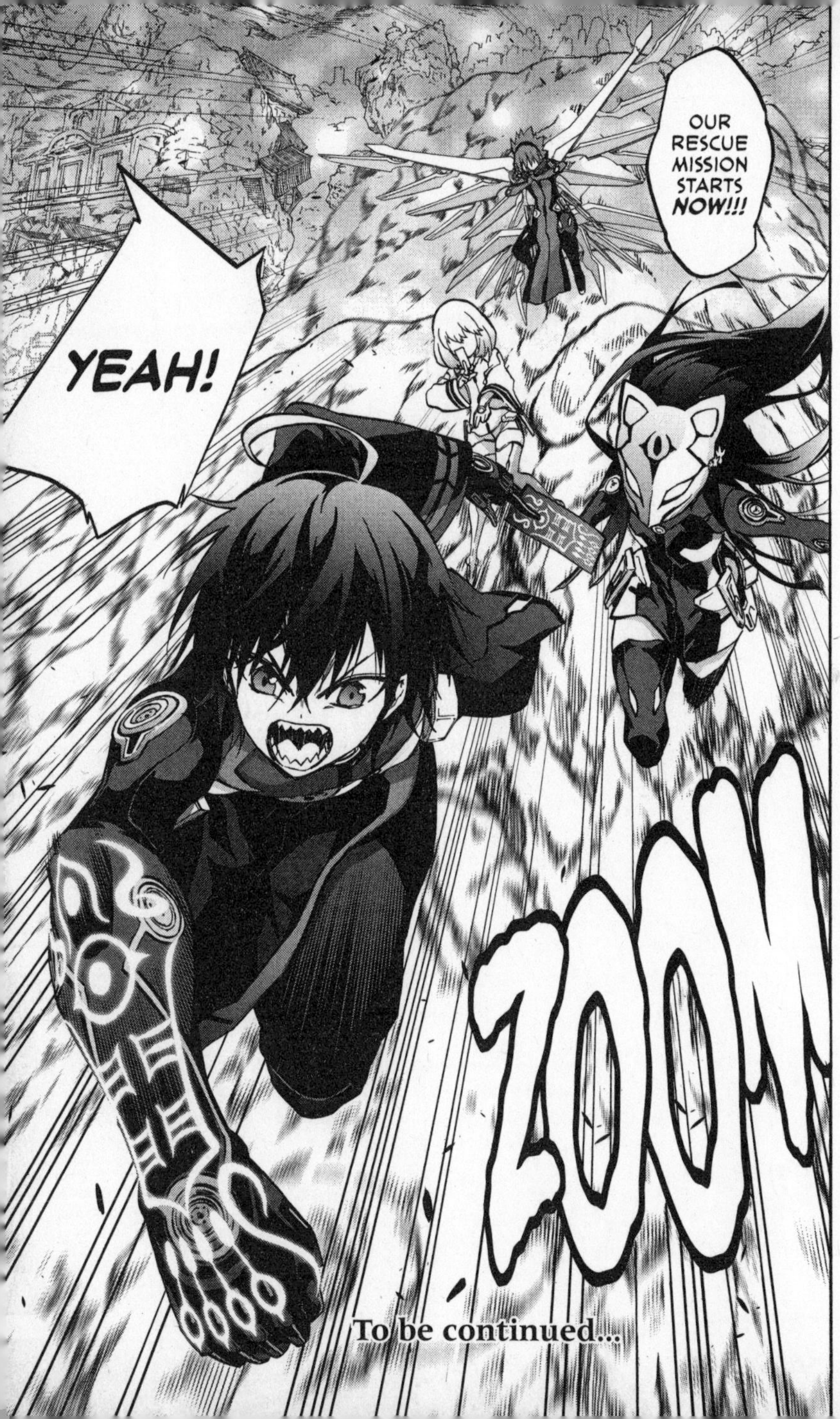

OUR RESCUE MISSION STARTS NOW!!!
YEAH!
ZOOM
To be continued...

TSUCHIMIKADO ISLAND TRAVELOGUE 2

TSUCHIMIKADO HOT SPRINGS ♨

A large area of Tsuchimikado Island consists of Tsuchimikado Fuji, a volcano. Natural hot springs burst forth from it everywhere. The hot springs that heal both mind and body are essential to the exorcists of the island.☆

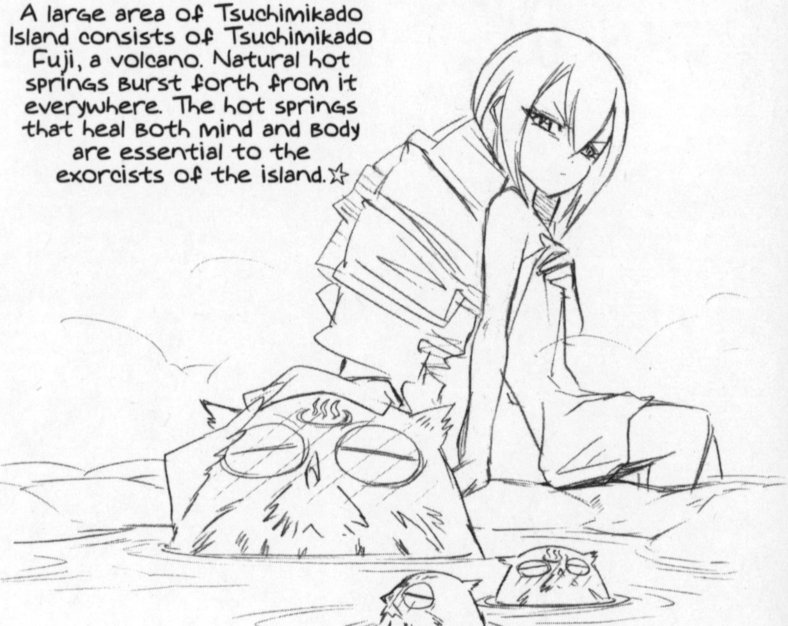

Bath Owl

A bath-loving species of owl indigenous to Tsuchimikado Island. They hop into the baths without permission and use as much shampoo as they want—consequently, the bathhouse owners are extremely annoyed with them. Every now and then, you find the owls floating in the tub because they got faint from staying in the hot water too long.

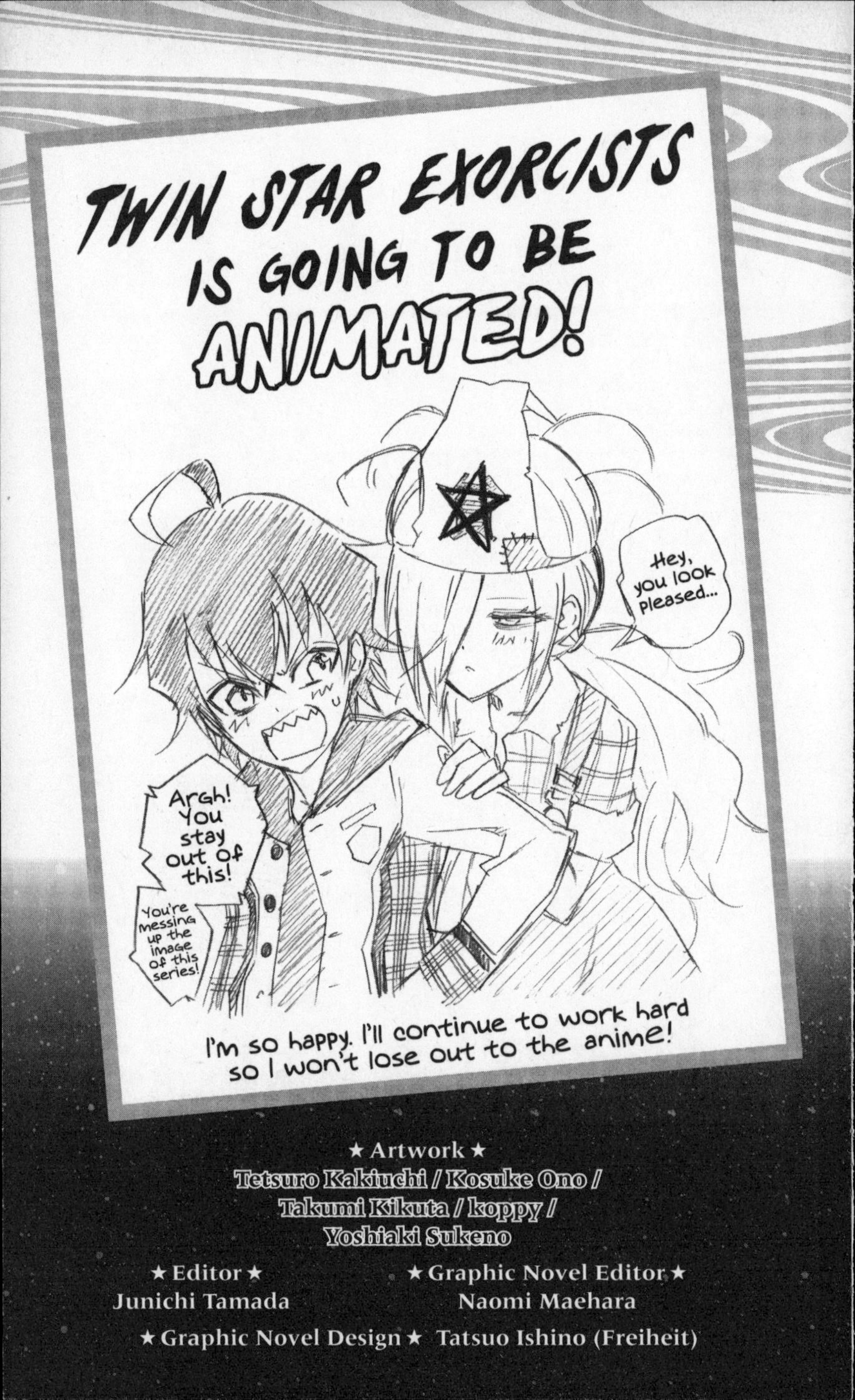
TWIN STAR EXORCISTS IS GOING TO BE ANIMATED!
Hey, you look pleased...
Argh! You stay out of this!
You're messing up the image of this series!
I'm so happy. I'll continue to work hard so I won't lose out to the anime!

★Artwork★
Tetsuro Kakiuchi / Kosuke Ono /
Takumi Kikuta / koppy /
Yoshiaki Sukeno

★Editor★
Junichi Tamada

★Graphic Novel Editor★
Naomi Maehara

★Graphic Novel Design★ Tatsuo Ishino (Freiheit)

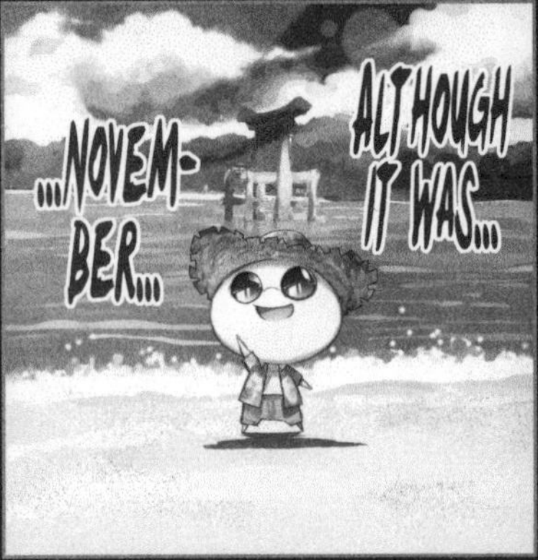
ALTHOUGH IT WAS...
...NOVEM-BER...

...I went on my very first research trip!

I flew an hour south from Haneda Airport to Hachijojima in Tokyo Prefecture. The island provided me with a lot of helpful inspiration for Tsuchimikado Island, which is scheduled to appear later in the story.

By the way, the background in the illustration above is Miyajima, which I visited on an ordinary family trip.

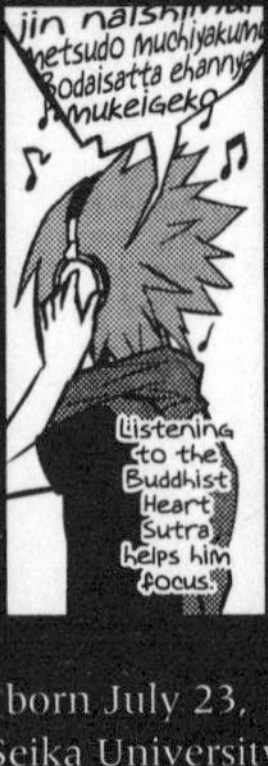
Listening to the Buddhist Heart Sutra helps him focus.

YOSHIAKI SUKENO was born July 23, 1981, in Wakayama, Japan. He graduated from Kyoto Seika University, where he studied manga. In 2006, he won the Tezuka Award for Best Newcomer Shonen Manga Artist. In 2008, he began his previous work, the supernatural comedy *Binbougami ga!*, which was adapted into the anime *Good Luck Girl!* in 2012.

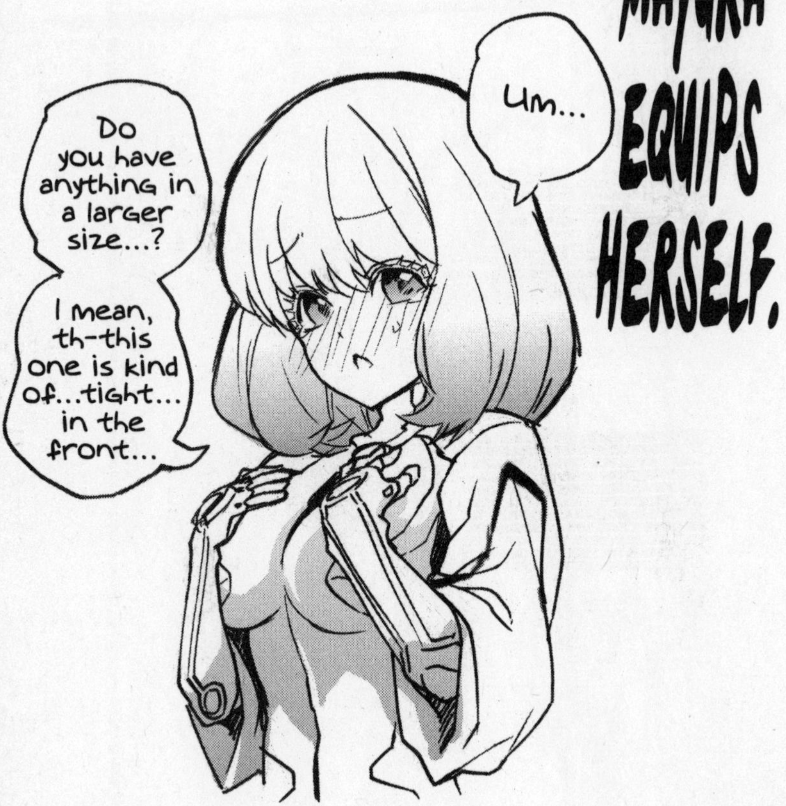
MAYURA EQUIPS HERSELF.
Um...
Do you have anything in a larger size...?
I mean, th-this one is kind of...tight... in the front...

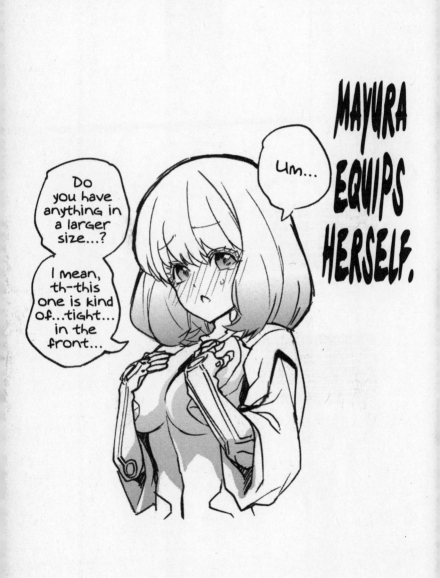

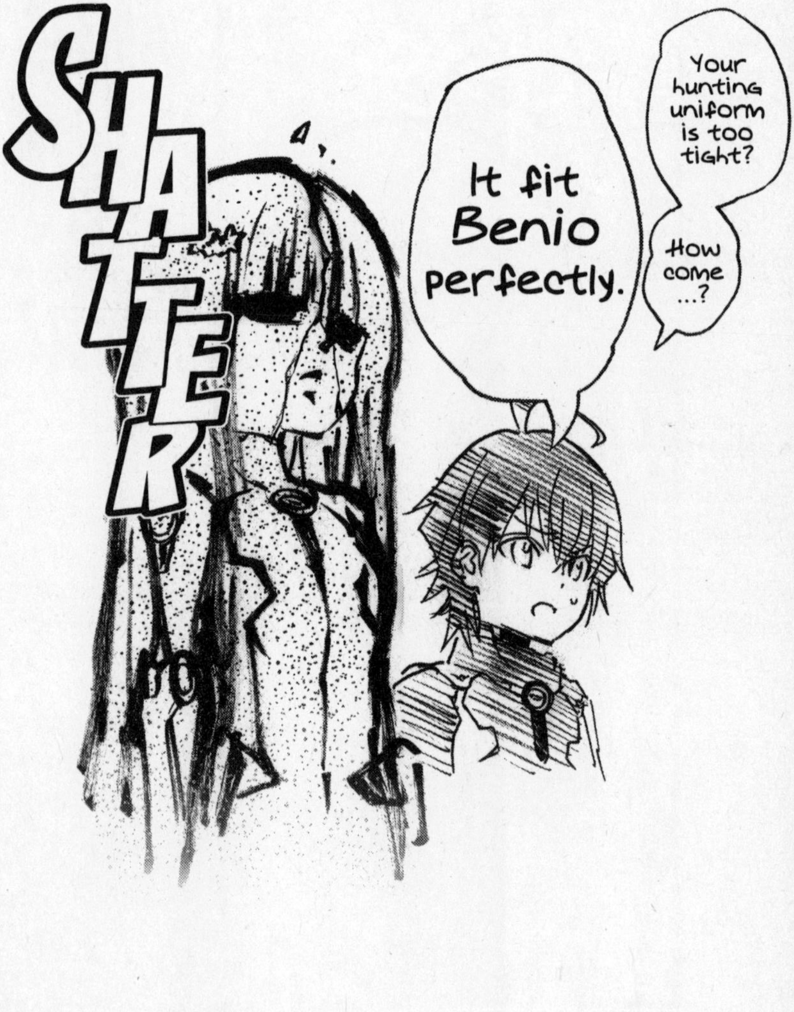
Your hunting uniform is too tight?
How come ...?
It fit Benio perfectly.
SHATTER

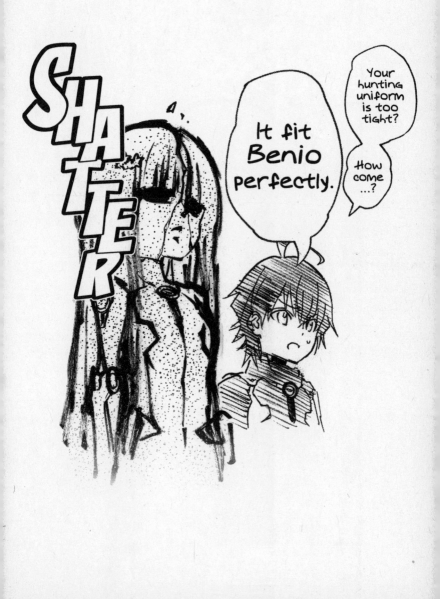

—SHONEN JUMP Manga Edition—

STORY & ART Yoshiaki Sukeno

TRANSLATION **Tetsuichiro Miyaki**
ENGLISH ADAPTATION **Bryant Turnage**
TOUCH-UP ART & LETTERING **Stephen Dutro**
DESIGN **Shawn Carrico**
EDITOR **Annette Roman**

SOUSEI NO ONMYOJI © 2013 by Yoshiaki Sukeno
All rights reserved.
First published in Japan in 2013 by SHUEISHA Inc., Tokyo.
English translation rights arranged by SHUEISHA Inc.

The stories, characters and incidents mentioned in this publication are entirely fictional.

Printed in the U.S.A.

Published by VIZ Media, LLC
P.O. Box 77010
San Francisco, CA 94107

10 9 8 7 6 5 4 3 2 1
First printing, January 2017

www.viz.com

PARENTAL ADVISORY
TWIN STAR EXORCISTS is rated T for Teen and is recommended for ages 13 and up. This volume contains fantasy violence.
ratings.viz.com

www.shonenjump.com

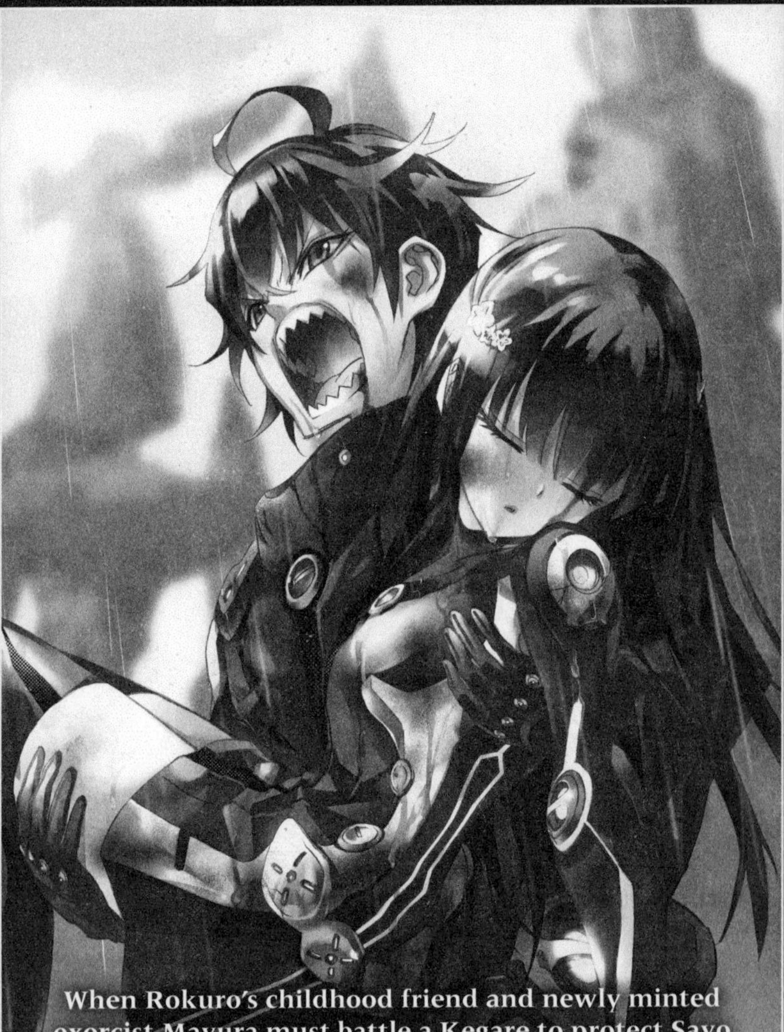
When Rokuro's childhood friend and newly minted exorcist Mayura must battle a Kegare to protect Sayo and Benio, she discovers mysterious hidden resources within—and outside!—herself. Then, a disconcerting truth about Benio's spiritual guardian is revealed...
Volume 8 available April 2017!

Twin Star Exorcists

Seraph of the End

VAMPIRE REIGN

STORY BY **Takaya Kagami**   ART BY **Yamato Yamamoto**

STORYBOARDS BY **Daisuke Furuya**

Vampires reign— humans revolt!

Yuichiro's dream of killing every vampire is near-impossible, given that vampires are seven times stronger than humans, and the only way to kill them is by mastering Cursed Gear, advanced demon-possessed weaponry. Not to mention that humanity's most elite Vampire Extermination Unit, the Moon Demon Company, wants nothing to do with Yuichiro unless he can prove he's willing to work in a team—which is the last thing he wants!

THE LATEST CHAPTERS SERIALIZED IN WEEKLY SHONEN JUMP

www.shonenjump.com   www.viz.com